Essay Writing

for Canadian Students

with readings

fourth edition

Kay L. Stewart
University of Alberta

Chris J. Bullock
University of Alberta

Marian E. Allen
Grant MacEwan Community College

Prentice Hall Allyn and Bacon Canada
Scarborough, Ontario

Canadian Cataloguing in Publication Data

Stewart, Kay L. (Kay Lanette), 1942-
       Essay Writing for Canadian students: with readings
4th ed.
Includes index
ISBN 0-13-758459-8

1. Exposition (Rhetoric). 2. English language - Rhetoric.   I. Bullock,
Chris, 1945-   .   II. Allen, Marian, 1945-   .   III. Title.

LB2369.S87 1998   808'.042   C97-931672-3

Pearson Education

Prentice-Hall, Inc., Upper Saddle River, New Jersey
Prentice-Hall International (UK) Limited, London
Prentice-Hall of Australia, Pty. Limited, Sydney
Prentice-Hall Hispanoamericana, S.A., Mexico City
Prentice-Hall of India Private Limited, New Delhi
Prentice-Hall of Japan, Inc., Tokyo
Simon & Schuster Asia Private Limited, Singapore
Editora Prentice-Hall do Brasil, Ltda., Rio de Janeiro

ISBN 0-13-758459-8

Vice President, Editorial Director: Laura Pearson
Acquisitions Editor: Rebecca Bersagel
Developmental Editor: Lisa Berland
Marketing Manager: Kathleen McGill
Marketing Coordinator: Dayna Vogel
Production Editor: Susan James
Copy Editor: Kelli Howey Robinson
Production Coordinator: Jane Schell
Permissions/Photo Research: Susan Wallace-Cox
Interior Design: Julia Hall
Cover Design: Julia Hall
Cover Image: Photonica/Ann Cutting
Page Layout: Hermia Chung

         5   01

Printed and bound in the United States of America..

Visit the Prentice Hall Canada Web site! Send us your comments, browse our
catalogues, and more. **www.phcanada.com** Or reach us through e-mail at
phabinfo_pubcanada@prenhall.com

Dedication

To my parents, with thanks — K.S.

To Aunt Margaret and the memory of Aunt Pat — C.B.

To Laurie, with thanks — M.A.

Contents

4 Using Sentence Structure and Length to Clarify Ideas   198

5 Using Transitions to Connect Ideas   203

Sample Essays   444

Preface to the Fourth Edition

To the Student

If you are trying to figure out how to cope with essay assignments in your college or university courses, you are the student we had in mind when we wrote this book.

We present a systematic approach to writing essays which we believe works for most writers. Feel free to adapt it to suit your needs. As you develop your own strategies for writing better essays more efficiently, you will probably discover that writing is a skill that you can learn, not a talent you either have or don't have. Great writers may have a special talent, but most writers are made, not born. And these days, everyone is a writer.

To the Instructor

If you are new to *Essay Writing for Canadian Students*, you will notice that we present the writing process as a systematic set of procedures. Like most teachers, we have found that many weaknesses in student writing stem from confused thinking about the subject of the essay, the topic, or both. For this reason, we set out a method that helps students to explore the subjects they write about more completely. We recognize that one disadvantage of this approach is that it may seem to limit creativity. The deductively organized analysis is, after all, only one kind of academic essay. Nevertheless, we believe there is value in an approach that encourages students to think through their ideas as they systematically gather material, draft an essay, and revise it.

These are the changes we have made to this edition:

Part 1, Rhetoric

- Chapter 3, Gathering Material: Analyzing Content has a new section called Analyzing the Content of Nonfiction Writing, designed to give students skills for doing the reading expected of them in college and university courses. For classroom convenience, our examples are drawn from the essays reprinted in Part 3, Readings. You may want to take up or return to this section as preparation for writing research papers.

- Chapters 10 and 11, on gathering material for and writing evaluation essays, have been revised to show more clearly how to evaluate the logic of an argumentative essay, with a new example.

- Chapter 11, Gathering Material for Research Papers, contains new and updated information on using electronic sources, such as the Internet. Chapter 12 has been streamlined to focus on the most troublesome aspects of writing research papers—integrating research material and documenting sources.

Part 2, Handbook for Final Editing

- A new chart giving examples of each problem discussed in the Handbook will help students identify and locate appropriate sections.

- The Handbook has been reorganized to make some sections easier to find.

- Documentation provides new information on citing electronic sources and easy-to-follow guidelines based on the most recent editions of the *MLA Handbook* and the *Publication Manual* of the American Psychological Association.

Part 3, Readings

- In the Published Writings, three long essays have been omitted to make room for nine shorter ones, along with a cluster of newspaper responses to the film version of *The English Patient*. The nineteenth century is now represented by selections from Poe and Thoreau; among contemporary authors, there are pieces by aboriginal writers Lenore Keeshig-Tobias and Linda Hogan as well as a personal essay by Scott Russell Sanders. We have also added that perennial favourite, George Orwell's "Shooting an Elephant."

- In the Sample Essays section, we've added Karin Swanson's comparison of poems by Robert Frost and Edward Thomas to demonstrate how to discuss the relation between form and content in poetry.

Part 4, Resources for Writing

- Making Effective Use of Your Computer, Strategies for Research, and the Annotated Survey of Reference Sources have been updated.
- Websites of interest to students and teachers of writing are identified in Resource 3.
- Resource 4, now called Common Perspectives for Content Analysis, presents the relation between types of analysis and the perspectives of four academic disciplines in easy-to-use chart form.

Throughout, we've added, deleted, and changed material to make explanations clearer, exercises more useful, and examples more interesting. You will find helpful suggestions for using this text and answer keys for the Handbook exercises in the Instructor's Manual prepared by Stephen Scott. We hope you find *Essay Writing for Canadian Students* stimulating and productive.

Acknowledgements

Revising this text has been a collaborative activity, one involving not only the three of us as authors, but also many others.

First and foremost we would like to thank our students at the University of Alberta and Grant MacEwan Community College who helped us to see what did and didn't work in the previous edition. We are especially indebted to Karin Swanson for allowing us to use her essay.

Several assistants have made our work much easier. Len Falkenstein updated material and provided us with the sample topic on censorship and the Internet in Chapter 3. Carolyn Lee compiled biographical notes and explanatory notes to accompany the new essays and proofread the old. Elizabeth Entrup compiled the index, and Stephen Scott put together the Instructor's Manual. We appreciate the careful attention to detail they brought to these tasks.

We would also like to thank colleagues Mary Chapman, Sandra Mallett, Jon Stott, and others who have made suggestions for improvements.

We have also benefited from the institutional support we received. Marian would like to express her appreciation for the time provided to work on this fourth edition and for the encouragement given by Barbara North, Chair of the English Department, and Allen Watson, Dean of Arts and Science at Grant MacEwan Community College. A special thanks as well to Marilyn Nikish, also at GMCC, for her patience and creative assistance with the charts. At the University of Alberta, Astrid Blodgett provided speedy and cheerful assistance with the manuscript.

Our thanks to Rebecca Bersagel, Acquisitions Editor; Lisa Berland, Developmental Editor; Susan James, Production Editor; and Kelli Howey Robinson, Copy Editor, for their help and timely nudges along the way.

Finally, Marian would like to thank Laurie Allen for his continued support and encouragement.

Rhetoric

part one

chapter 1

Writing Essays: An Overview

This book is about essay writing. We focus on essay writing for two reasons. The first is that the thinking skills you practise in the process of writing essays are central to the work you do in college or university. The second is that the procedures you learn for writing and revising essays will help you with many other kinds of writing assignments.

Essay Writing: Purposes

Writing to Learn

How will writing essays help you to develop thinking skills? One way is by encouraging you to explore your ideas. This purpose is reflected in the French word from which the term *essay* comes: *essai*, meaning "attempt." The term was first used to refer to a particular kind of writing by the French author Michel de Montaigne, who published a book of short prose pieces entitled *Essais* in 1580. This title suggests the personal, exploratory nature of Montaigne's attempts to understand the world around him by writing on everyday subjects such as "Liars" and "The Art of Conversation." You may study informal essays of this type in composition and literature courses, and create them as well.

Since Montaigne's day, the term essay has come to include formal writing on a wide range of subjects, from the nature of love in Shakespeare's *King Lear* to theories about the origins of the universe. Writing academic essays of this kind will help you to develop systematic analytic thinking. It is this more formal type of essay writing that you will most often be asked to do in your university and college courses, and that we will focus on in this text.

Writing essays gives you the opportunity to learn what you think about a particular subject. In writing about friendship, for example, you may discover which qualities you most value in your friends. Similarly, you may not know what you really think about issues such as Canada's role as a peacekeeper or the desirability of genetic engineering until you write about them, because you have not had to define your opinion or to defend it.

Writing essays also transforms passive learning into active learning. If you were taking a painting course, you would recognize that no matter how good the instructor's lessons might be, you would learn to paint only by painting. The same holds true for writing. Through writing essays, whether formal or informal, you develop greater awareness of the language you and others use to make meaning. What may be less obvious is that you learn the theories, concepts, and procedures of academic disciplines more thoroughly by actively employing them in writing essays.

Writing to Communicate

Some of the writing you do—such as class notes, responses to reading, drafts that go nowhere—may have no other reader but yourself. Writing essays, however, is a means of sharing your understanding of a particular issue with others.

The style and organization of essays differs from discipline to discipline; so does what counts as evidence and proof. But central to most academic essays is an opinion substantiated by reasons and evidence; by setting out these reasons and evidence, you open up the possibility of dialogue with those who hold other views.

Consider, for example, an argument in which you claim that genetic research should be stopped while a friend claims it shouldn't. At this level, each statement is "just an opinion" and your discussion isn't likely to go very far. But suppose that you were to say genetic research should be stopped because lethal organisms could be released into the environment, endangering millions of lives. Given this reason, your friend might concede the possible danger. If you give reasons, your argument will be more persuasive.

In an academic essay, this combination of an opinion and the reason(s) supporting it is called a *thesis*. A thesis is like a hypothesis in a scientific experiment: it is the statement or assertion that is to be proved. Proof in an academic essay consists of the logical, orderly development of your thesis through explaining your reasons and giving evidence (such as factual information, examples, and quotations from authorities) to support them. By explaining your thesis carefully and giving evidence to support it, you are likely to persuade readers to take your opinion seriously, whether or not they agree with it.

Essay Writing: Product

Both informal essays and formal academic essays present the writer's opinion on a particular subject. But the way the writer chooses to present that opinion will depend upon the audience for whom the piece is written.

Audience

Most of the informal essays you study in composition and literature courses were originally published in magazines or newspapers where they had to compete for readers' attention with photographs, advertising, and a host of other articles. In these circumstances, essay writers may attempt to catch the reader's eye by starting with a controversial claim they will eventually reverse, or by describing an incident from their lives. Having caught the reader's attention, popular essayists may try to maintain suspense by narrating a series of events with an unexpected outcome or by revealing their thesis at the end. You will find several essays of this type in Part 3, Readings.

Formal essays on academic subjects, in contrast, are written for specialized audiences already familiar with the subject. Readers of these essays want to know the writer's thesis from the beginning and to have the evidence supporting the thesis laid out in a logical, orderly fashion. They also appreciate essays that are well written according to the conventions of the discipline. Most of the essays you write in college and university courses will be of this second type. You will be writing for instructors and classmates who know something about the subject and want to hear your opinion about it.

Structure

You can meet your reader's needs and demonstrate your understanding of your subject most effectively by writing essays that have these main structural elements:

INTRODUCTION
The introduction establishes the context for the discussion (for example, by defining necessary terms or giving historical background) and presents the thesis of the essay.

MIDDLE PARAGRAPHS
Each middle paragraph discusses a single subpoint of the thesis. The purpose of the paragraph is defined by a topic sentence that links the paragraph to the thesis. Middle paragraphs usually contain both explanations of the point made in the topic sentence and specific details illustrating that point. Transitional words and phrases signal the movement from point to point and establish the relationship between points and the details that support them.

CONCLUSION
The conclusion ties together the points developed in the middle paragraphs and mentions the wider implications of the discussion, if any.

Sample Essay: Analysis of a Film

So that you can see what this kind of essay might look like in practice, here is an example. The topic asked students to choose their favourite film and explain its appeal. The main structural elements of the essay have been labelled.

SAMPLE WRITING

ROMANCE AND REALISM IN *CASABLANCA*

Introduction

Since its release in 1942, the movie *Casablanca*, directed by Michael Curtiz, has become a classic. Even people who have never seen the film recognize the theme song, "As Time Goes By," and the line "Play it again, Sam," even though this line never actually occurs in the film. Why has *Casablanca* remained so popular? The answer to this question undoubtedly lies partly in the appeal of its two stars, Humphrey Bogart and Ingrid Bergman, and talented supporting actors like Claude Rains, Sydney Greenstreet, and Peter Lorre. Its main appeal, however, is the mixture of romance and realism in its plot, setting, and characterization.

Thesis

Topic sentence

Middle paragraph 1

The obvious romanticism of the plot tends to obscure its realistic elements. Consider the details. After a few shots of a spinning globe and Casablanca street scenes, we are introduced to Rick Blaine (Humphrey Bogart), a mysterious American expatriate who owns the Café Américain, meeting place of Casablanca's smart set, and who appears to care for nothing and nobody. Into Rick's café walk Victor Laszlo (Paul Henreid), a famous Resistance leader, and Ilsa Lund (Ingrid Bergman), his wife, in search of stolen letters of transit that would guarantee them a safe exit from Casablanca to Lisbon and America. In a flashback we learn that just before the Nazis occupied Paris, Rick and Ilsa met there and fell in love. Because of their agreement not to speak of their pasts, however, Ilsa does not tell Rick of her marriage to Laszlo, whom she believes to have died in a concentration camp. On the day that the two are to leave Paris together, Ilsa discovers Victor is still alive and, without explanation, sends Rick a note saying she still loves him but can never see him again.

Transition
Topic sentence

Middle paragraph 2

Rick and Ilsa's past, then, is a romantic tale of love and self-sacrifice. When they meet and fall in love again in Casablanca, they must confront more realistic problems: Rick's cynicism, a product of his sense of betrayal; Ilsa's love, respect, and admiration for Victor; Victor's own sense of honour; and the very real threat posed to them all by the Nazis' determination to prevent Victor's escape.

Topic sentence

Middle paragraph 3

The reality of this threat is emphasized by the director's use of the setting. On the one hand, Casablanca is a romantic city. In its sun-baked streets, merchants in fezzes haggle with prospective buyers; inside Rick's Café Américain, the scene of much of the action, the wealthy gamble. On the other hand, Casablanca, governed by French authorities who are subservient to German "advisers," is the major point of escape for refugees from Nazi-occupied Europe. Consequently, we see the marketplace turn into a place of terror when a member of the Free French underground is shot by French police in front of the law courts bearing the motto "Liberty, Equality, Fraternity." Similarly, the glamour of Rick's café is offset by the plight of the refugees who frequent it and by the ease with which the Germans order the place closed. The setting thus emphasizes the film's mixture of romance and realism.

Transition

Topic sentence

Middle paragraph 4

What gives the film its appeal is not just the romantic hope that the good guys will eventually defeat the Nazis, however; it is the film's recognition of the struggle that goes on within characters who, while basically good, may make wrong choices. This issue arises for several of the minor characters, but is most fully explored in the relationship between Rick and Ilsa. Although Rick's past (running guns to Ethiopia, fighting in the Spanish Civil War) suggests that he is capable of idealism, his refusal to shield the man who stole the letters of credit raises the possibility that he will refuse to help Laszlo and Ilsa. Similarly, Ilsa's shift from threatening to shoot Rick for the letters of transit one minute, to planning to go away with him the next, makes us wonder whether she will again be capable of sacrificing her love for Rick to her duty to her husband. To emphasize these inner struggles, scenes between Rick and Ilsa are often shot in half-light, creating the juxtaposition between light and shadow that is one of the film's trademarks. Since most of us are faced with difficult moral choices, we identify more fully with characters who face similar struggles than we do with those who never question their own motives or behaviour.

Conclusion

In the end, it is the romantic ethic of love and self-sacrifice that triumphs, as Rick puts Ilsa and Victor on the plane for Lisbon and, with Captain Renaud, strides off into the fog to join the resistance fighters. But in its use of plot, setting, and characterization, the film reminds us that such triumphs arise out of our struggles against opposition, both without and within. It is this realistic recognition of the difficulty of living up to our best selves that gives the film its continuing appeal.

Discussion of the Sample Essay

"Romance and Realism in *Casablanca*" illustrates the effective use of the structural elements common to college and university essays. The introduction provides basic information about the film and introduces the issue of the film's popularity. It concludes with the **thesis**, signalled by the transitional phrase "Its main appeal, however,...." The placement of the thesis focuses attention on the main point: the relation between the film's popularity and the combination of romance and realism in its plot, setting, and characterization.

The thesis also serves as a guide to the structure of the essay as a whole. It sets out the order in which the three aspects of the film will be discussed. This order is one of **ascending interest**. That is, the writer puts the paragraph on the plot first because the point about the mixture of romance and realism in the plot is the most obvious and most easily explained. Next, the writer discusses details of the setting that illuminate the contrast between romance and realism. Then the point about characterization comes last to emphasize its importance.

In the middle paragraphs of the essay, each of these points is clearly made in a **topic sentence**. Each topic sentence identifies the aspect of the film to be discussed (such as plot) and connects that aspect to the thesis by stating how it contributes to the film's popularity. The topic sentences also provide **transitions** between one paragraph and the next.

The framework you create by establishing this kind of relationship between the thesis, topic sentences, and transitional devices will give your reader valuable assistance in following your line of thinking.

Important as this framework is, the essay would not be convincing if the middle paragraphs did not contain **details** to support the points made in the topic sentences and **explanations** to clarify what the details mean. In the first middle paragraph, for example, the point that the plot seems "romantic" would not seem very convincing without details of the plot. Details alone are not enough to define "romantic," however. And so the writer provides the explanation that the plot is romantic because it is a "tale of love and self-sacrifice."

The conclusion sums up the relationship the writer has established between the film's popularity and the mixture of romance and realism in its plot, setting, and characterization. Notice that the conclusion does not merely repeat what the writer has said in the thesis and topic sentences.

"Romance and Realism in *Casablanca*" thus illustrates how you can use the structure common to most college and university essays to present your opinion on a subject in a clear, straightforward way. You will find other ways of discussing *Casablanca* and a similar film, *The English Patient*, in Part 3, Readings.

Essay Writing: Process

Most people don't write an essay—or anything intended to be read by others, for that matter—by sitting down with paper and pen (or word processor) and rising an hour later with a finished product. The final draft is the last stage of a highly complex process of thinking and writing, rethinking and rewriting. If you want to produce an interesting, thoughtful essay, like the one on *Casablanca*, you have to be prepared to give time and serious attention to your subject. Without that willingness, you will not learn how to write from this book or from any other. But it is our belief that if you are willing, you can learn to write essays that have something to say and say it well.

To help you learn the skills you need, we have organized the first section of Part 1 according to the stages in writing basic analytic essays like the essay on *Casablanca*. The stages are as follows:

STAGE 1: CLARIFYING ESSAY TOPICS
Understanding essay assignments and exploring the possibilities of the topic you choose (Chapter 2)

STAGE 2: GATHERING MATERIAL
Using systems, process, and causal analysis to analyze your subject (Chapter 3); analyzing the content of nonfiction writing (Chapter 3); using analytic categories to analyze the aesthetic qualities of texts (Chapter 4)

STAGE 3: FORMULATING A THESIS
Forming and supporting an opinion about your subject (Chapter 5)

STAGE 4: DRAFTING
Selecting and organizing material in a first draft (Chapter 6)

STAGE 5: REVISING THESIS AND ESSAY STRUCTURE
Checking for possible problems with your thesis and essay structure and making necessary changes (Chapter 7)

STAGE 6: REVISING INDIVIDUAL PARAGRAPHS
Revising middle paragraphs, introductions, and conclusions (Chapter 8)

The second section of Part 1 focuses on writing and revising special types of essays: comparison essays (Chapter 9), evaluation (argumentative) essays (Chapters 10 and 11), and research papers (Chapters 12 and 13).

Part 2, Handbook for Final Editing, presents the current conventions regarding sentence structure, grammar, punctuation, mechanics, and format.

Part 3, Readings, contains essays and other pieces that we hope you find entertaining, enlightening, informative, and thought-provoking. The essays illustrate writing strategies discussed in Part 1, Rhetoric, and provide material for you to write about.

Part 4, Resources for Writing, provides a quick reference guide to some of the basic analytic and research procedures we describe in Part 1, a list of reference materials, and a glossary of terms used in this text.

Finally, a note on the stages model we use in this text. We are not claiming that the methods we propose are the only way to write or to write effectively; we don't even claim that they reflect exactly what writers—including ourselves—do when we write. For many of us, writing is far messier than our model would suggest (recursive, in the current jargon, rather than linear). This text is like a set of instructions for assembling a piece of furniture, not a videotape of one person's efforts to fashion bits of wood and glue into his or her own unique design. You may find that the order in which we present writing activities suits your method of composition perfectly; on the other hand, you may find yourself writing a draft to clarify your understanding of a topic or mentally revising the structure before a word hits the page. The stages of the writing process we describe cover what you will need to write effective analytic essays; as you work with the text, try out our suggestions, adjust them to suit your needs, and fit them into a writing process that works for you.

EXERCISE

Answer each of the following questions in a sentence or two.

1. What are the main differences between having an opinion on a subject and formulating a thesis on it?

2. What are the most important characteristics of an effective thesis? Where is the thesis usually located in an academic essay?

3. How are formal academic essays different from informal personal essays?

4. What are the main functions of topic sentences? Where are topic sentences usually located in an academic essay?

5. How do the thesis and the topic sentences create the skeleton of ideas in an essay?

chapter 2

Clarifying Essay Topics

Essay assignments are designed to allow you to come to terms with the concepts you have studied, the literature you have read, or the data you have collected. But in order to write an essay that demonstrates your understanding of your subject, you first need to know what the topic requires. If you were faced with the following topics, or similar ones, would you know exactly what to do?

What is the function of the graveyard scene in *Hamlet*?

Discuss the concept of the state in Plato's *Republic*.

Compare the use of the vampire myth in the films *Dracula* and *Interview with the Vampire*.

Explain the concept of narcissism as the term is used by Freud and his followers.

Is Alice Munro's "The Red Dress" a good story? Why or why not?

Compare Chomsky's and Skinner's theories of language acquisition.

Discuss the development of Canadian abstract painting.

Evaluate Canadian and U.S. policies on pollution in the Great Lakes.

Write a 1000-word essay on some aspect of computers.

These are typical assignments for college and university courses that require essays. Although in some disciplines multiple-choice exams have replaced essay assignments and essay exams (particularly in first-year courses), you are still likely to face a wide variety of writing assignments. The first stage in writing, then, is ensuring that you understand your assignment.

Step 1 Defining Unfamiliar Terms

Make sure that you understand all the terms used in the assignment. To write on the sample essay topics listed above, you would have to know the meaning of the terms *narcissism*, *abstract painting*, *myth*, and *language acquisition*.

Learning about a subject includes learning the vocabulary that specialists in the subject use. In psychology courses, you may learn the meaning of such terms as *conditioned response*, *narcissism*, and *depression*. In literature courses, you are likely to discuss the meaning of terms such as *myth*, *point of view*, and *tragedy*.

As these examples suggest, the specialized vocabulary of each discipline is likely to include terms seldom used outside the field as well as terms used in a more restricted way than you would use them in everyday speech. When you say, "I feel depressed," for example, you may be disappointed about an exam mark, sad about a friend's moving, or temporarily in low spirits for other reasons. But you are not using the word *depressed* in the way a psychologist or psychiatrist would. Similarly, the term *tragedy*, as used in literary criticism, is not simply a disastrous event, but a certain kind of play.

You can clarify the meaning of terms by consulting your course text(s) or specialized dictionaries. Many texts, including this one, contain *glossaries* that briefly define concepts and other specialized terms. If there is no glossary, or if you are still puzzled, check the index for discussions of the term elsewhere in your text.

If your text doesn't provide all the information you need, consult a *specialized dictionary* in the appropriate field. You will find selected titles in the Annotated Survey of Reference Sources in Part 4, Resources for Writing.

Step 2   Understanding Directions

If you were doing math, you would easily recognize the symbols that tell you whether to add, subtract, multiply, or divide; if you were cooking, you would know what to do if the recipe said to mix, bake, or fry. But you may be less familiar with the terms that give you directions for writing essays.

Although topics for academic essays are stated in a wide variety of ways, the basic procedure is the same: *analysis*. For some topics, you may need to combine analysis with *comparison* or *evaluation*.

Analysis

The main purpose of analysis is to illuminate something, such as a concept, a text, an event, or a set of data, by examining its parts in detail. When you analyze something, you answer questions like these:

What parts can this X be divided into?

What do these parts indicate about the nature of X as a whole?

Why does X have this particular nature?

If you were analyzing the artifacts from an archaeological site, for example, you would divide them into parts according to their type (flints, trade goods, animal remains, and so forth) and according to where they were found. From your analysis of this material, you would decide what kind of site this is: a winter camp used by Assinibones over a period of a hundred years, perhaps. To complete your analysis, you would explain why these artifacts indicate this kind of camp.

In this text we make a distinction between content analysis and textual analysis.

Content analysis is the examination of behaviour, data, written works, and other sources of information without regard to the form in which the information is communicated. "Explain the concept of the state in Plato's *Republic*" and "Discuss the causes of the English Civil War" are examples of topics that require content analysis. You will find step-by-step procedures for content analysis in Chapter 3, Gathering Material: Analyzing Content.

Textual analysis is the examination of written works or performances (such as plays, television programs, and films) with attention both to what is being said and to how the work or performance is presented. If you were writing on Joseph Conrad's *Heart of Darkness*, for example, you would discuss not only the events but also the techniques Conrad uses in presenting the story, such as imagery and symbolism. You will find a detailed examination of textual analysis in Chapter 4, Gathering Material: Analyzing Texts, with a sample analysis of a short story. This chapter will be especially useful when you are writing essays for literature or film courses.

Comparison

The main purpose of comparison is to examine the similarities and differences of two or more things in such a way as to understand both things better. The **basis of comparison** tells you which similarities and differences to focus on. You could compare apples and oranges, for example, as foods, as cash crops, or as objects to throw. Depending on which of these you chose, your comparison would illuminate not only the individual properties of apples and oranges, but also the general properties of foods, cash crops, or objects to throw.

Since comparison is based on analysis, your first step in comparing things is to divide them into parts and compare the parts. The questions you answer in making comparisons are therefore modifications of the questions for analysis:

What is the basis of comparison?

What matching parts can these things be divided into?

What is the central likeness or difference between these things?

Why are the things similar or different?

If you wanted to compare downhill and cross-country skiing, for example, you would first need to choose your basis of comparison. Would you compare them as competitive sports, forms of exercise, or recreational activities? Your basis of comparison would determine the parts you divide the two sports into, their central likeness or difference, and the reasons for that similarity or difference.

You might find comparison topics stated in these ways:

Choose two poems and show how they either attack or celebrate aspects of contemporary life.

How are the principles of solar heating systems similar to or different from the principles of geothermal systems?

Compare Chomsky's and Skinner's theories of language acquisition.

Discuss the symbolism of roses in three poems.

Compare two films.

Some of these topics state the basis of comparison ("attacks on or celebrations of contemporary life"; "principles of heating systems"; "symbolism of roses"). When the topic does not provide a basis of comparison (as in an assignment asking you to compare two theories or two films), you will have to find one. Chapter 9, Writing Comparison Essays, will show you how.

Evaluation

The main purpose of evaluation is to determine the strengths and weaknesses of something, such as government cost-cutting, a new novel by Margaret Atwood, or an argument favouring euthanasia. Like comparison, evaluation starts with analysis. To evaluate a hockey forward, for example, you would first analyze the player's skills as a skater, shooter, stick-handler, and play-maker. Your knowledge of the game and of other hockey forwards would give you a sense of what constitutes excellence in each of these categories. To evaluate a particular player, you would measure that person's strengths and weaknesses against this *standard of evaluation*.

In order to evaluate one or more things, you will need to answer questions like these:

What standard(s) of evaluation is(are) appropriate?

What parts can I divide my material into?

What are the strengths and weaknesses of each of these parts?

What is my evaluation of the overall weighting of strengths and weaknesses?

Why have I come to this evaluation?

The common *standards of evaluation* are practical, ethical, aesthetic, and logical. Since it is possible to evaluate things according to various standards, you have to define which one or ones you have chosen to use. If you chose to evaluate proposed federal policy on pollution in the Great Lakes on practical grounds, for example, you might consider the cost to participants, the technology used to control pollution, and the enforcement of government regulations. Your analysis of these areas might lead you to conclude that the proposed policy is good because it would provide cost-efficient, technologically sound, and easily enforced methods for reducing pollution. This evaluation would be based on a practical standard of evaluation. If you evaluated the proposal on ethical grounds, your conclusion might be quite different. You might decide, for example, that you found the proposal ethically unacceptable because it would infringe on Aboriginal fishing rights.

Because of the wide variety of possible viewpoints, essay topics seldom give the standard of evaluation you should use. For each of these topics, you would have to decide on an appropriate standard of evaluation:

Is Margaret Laurence's *The Diviners* a good novel?

Was the Riel Rebellion justified?

Are individual rights better protected under the Canadian Charter of Rights and Freedoms or under the U.S. Constitution?

So far we have discussed evaluation as a method of arriving at your own arguments about whether something is good or bad. Chapter 10, Gathering Material for Evaluation Essays, will help you to weigh the reasoning and evidence that authors present in support of their arguments.

Other Terms

Although most essay assignments require that you analyze, compare, or evaluate, these terms may not appear in the topics, as you will have noticed from the examples. You will therefore have to think about the meaning of the terms used. For instance, the word *discuss* may seem to mean "summarize the relevant information." *It doesn't.* "Discuss" may appear in topics that require analysis, comparison, or evaluation. *Explain, examine,* and *assess* are other words whose meaning may be ambiguous. *Explain* usually means *analyze; examine* may mean *analyze* or *evaluate; assess* means *evaluate.* Some topics may ask you to *compare* things when you are actually expected to both *compare and evaluate* them. If you are in doubt, ask your instructor.

Step 3   Exploring Your Subject

Most essay topics set limits as to what you should cover: the concept of the state in Plato's *Republic*; the use of the vampire myth in *Dracula* and *Interview with the Vampire*; Canadian and U.S. policies on pollution in the Great Lakes. Occasionally, however, you may be given an indefinite topic, such as "Write a 1000-word essay on some aspect of computers," or you may be invited to come up with a topic of your own.

Whether your topic is narrowly defined or open-ended, you can use various techniques such as freewriting, brainstorming, and tree diagramming to explore your topic and to define its limits. Limiting your topic allows you to examine your subject thoroughly enough to speak as an "expert" to less well-informed readers. If you try to write a five-page essay on a broad subject, such as computers or every aspect of the novel *Great Expectations*, your treatment is likely to be superficial. Narrowing your focus enables you to examine your subject in greater depth. It also helps you organize your information gathering and your writing.

Here are three quick ways of generating ideas about your topic.

Freewriting

Each time you come up with an idea, does another part of your brain say, "That's no good," or "You'll look silly if you say that"? Freewriting is one way of circumventing this mental editor. If you tend to agonize over a blank page, then freewriting may set your mind in motion.

Freewriting consists of writing continuously for ten minutes or longer, without stopping to organize, correct, or evaluate what you are doing. If your first freewriting does not give you a clear sense of what you might want to focus on in your essay, try variations on the freewriting process. You might, for example, look over your first freewriting material for the idea that seems most promising and then use this idea as a springboard for a second freewriting. Or, if you are trying to find an aspect of a text that interests you, you might freewrite a fantasy dialogue with the author, asking questions and recording the "replies." This dialogue may reveal possibilities that you would not have reached by more conventional means.

Brainstorming

Brainstorming is another way of circumventing your mental editor. Brainstorming consists of putting down, in point form, everything you can think of about your topic, however obvious or bizarre the ideas may seem. Begin by writing your subject in the middle of a page, and then jot down ideas as they come to you. When you finish, you will have a mixture of generalizations and details radiating from your central subject. You can then draw lines to connect related points. For example, if you wanted to explore the broad subject of fitness, you might come up with a brainstorming diagram such as the one shown in Figure 2.1 below.

Much of the material in the diagram relates to the physical effects of fitness, and so you might decide to focus your essay on that subject. Or you might be intrigued by the idea of fitness as big business.

FIGURE 2.1

Sample Brainstorming Diagram

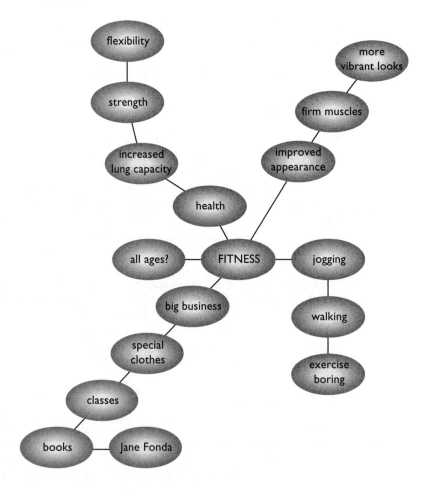

Tree Diagramming

Tree diagramming is a more systematic form of brainstorming. When you use this technique, you divide your broad subject into categories and subcategories in the form of an ever-expanding "tree." Because a tree diagram encourages you to develop equivalent categories, it is especially useful for narrowing comparison topics and developing arguments for and against something. For example, you might construct a tree diagram as a means of exploring arguments for and against Canada's role as a peacekeeper. Figure 2.2 on page 20 represents the type of diagram you will evolve by using this technique.

These discovery techniques are obviously useful for narrowing a broad subject such as "computers." Even when the topic is limited, you can use these techniques to prime your thinking or to discover an angle that interests you.

Step 4   Deciding What Sources to Use

Is your essay to be based solely on *primary sources*, or are you expected to consult *secondary sources* as well?

Primary Sources

Primary sources of information are first-hand experiences or first-hand accounts of experiences. Your own knowledge, experience, and observations would be considered primary sources of information. So would the novels you read, the plays you see, and the questionnaires you collect for your sociology class. Official documents (for example, the British North America Act, the Canadian Charter of Rights and Freedoms), eyewitness accounts of events, letters, diaries, and contemporary newspapers are also primary sources. When you analyze, compare, or evaluate texts, your primary source of information and ideas is the texts themselves.

Secondary Sources

You use secondary sources of information whenever you write a *research paper*. Secondary sources consist of second-hand (or third- or fourth-hand) accounts, such as critical discussions of a novel or books and articles about past events by modern historians. Such works are considered secondary sources because they select and present material to support a particular point of view. Only some facts are included and usually only one point of view is argued.

FIGURE 2.2

Sample Tree Diagram

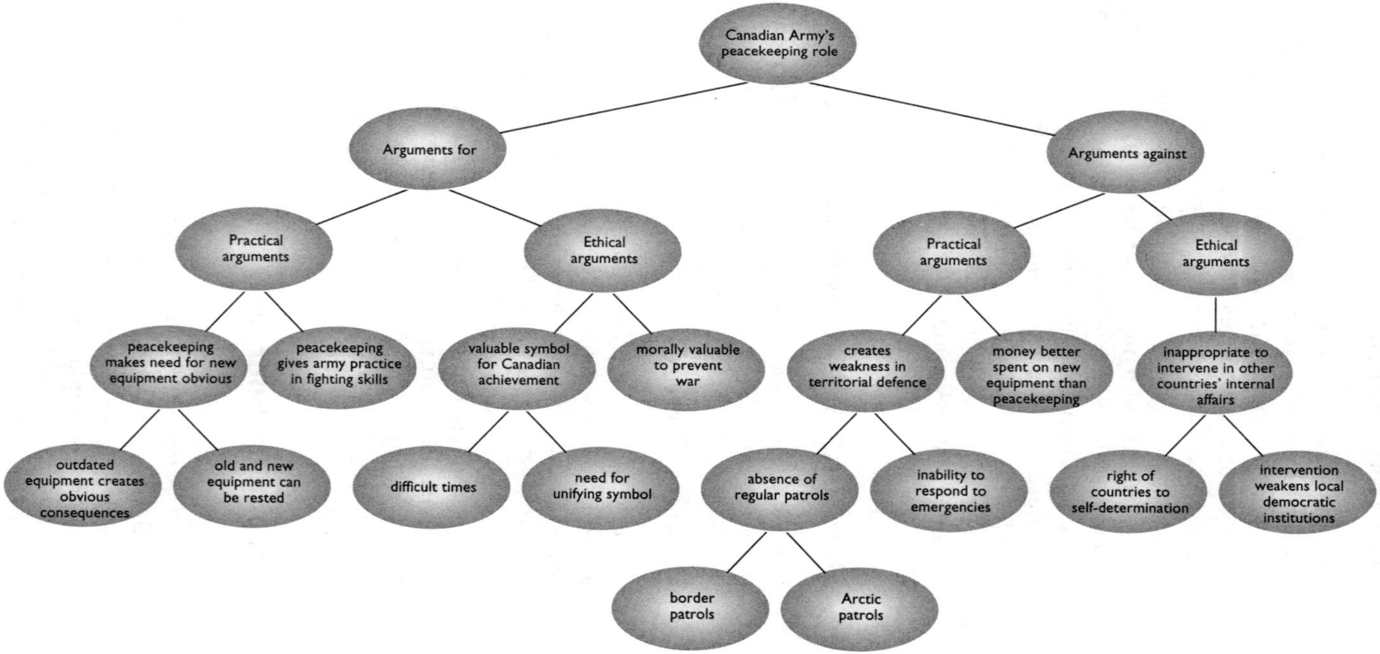

Canadian Army's peacekeeping role

- Arguments for
  - Practical arguments
    - peacekeeping makes need for new equipment obvious
      - outdated equipment creates obvious consequences
      - old and new equipment can be rested
    - peacekeeping gives army practice in fighting skills
  - Ethical arguments
    - valuable symbol for Canadian achievement
      - need for unifying symbol
      - difficult times
    - morally valuable to prevent war
- Arguments against
  - Practical arguments
    - creates weakness in territorial defence
      - inability to respond to emergencies
      - absence of regular patrols
        - border patrols
        - Arctic patrols
    - money better spent on new equipment than peacekeeping
  - Ethical arguments
    - inappropriate to intervene in other countries' internal affairs
      - right of countries to self-determination
      - intervention weakens local democratic institutions

Assignments based on secondary sources are designed to acquaint you with the important issues in your discipline and also with its methods of research and analysis. You can also use secondary sources to supplement your analysis of primary sources. Essays that require you to use both primary and secondary sources are often difficult to write. You will find a detailed discussion of how to do this kind of research paper in Chapter 13.

Working on Your Own Assignment

Clarifying the demands of your topic is a necessary first step towards writing a good essay.

- Identify terms that need to be defined.
- Decide whether you should analyze, compare, or evaluate (or compare *and* evaluate).
- Use freewriting, brainstorming, or tree diagramming to discover an aspect of your subject that interests you.
- Decide whether to use primary sources, secondary sources, or both.

EXERCISE

You are much more likely to write a successful essay, both outside of class and on an exam, if you understand exactly what the topic is asking you to do. Choose two to three of the topics below and practise clarifying essay topics. Define specialized terms, decide whether the topic calls for analysis, comparison, evaluation, or a combination of these procedures, and narrow down a topic that seems too general for the length of the essay required.

1. How does Swift use a persona to create irony in "A Modest Proposal"?
2. Write a 750-word essay on the concept of "sustainable growth" in the fishing industry.
3. Analyze Francis Ford Coppola's use of crosscutting in *Godfather I.*
4. Write a 1500-word essay comparing the kinship systems of the Cree and Chipewyan Aboriginal peoples.
5. What are the advantages of a trade economy over a gift economy? What are the disadvantages?
6. Write a 1500-word essay showing how Charlie Chaplin's rise to fame in the 1920s introduced a more complex kind of comedy into American films.
7. Write a 750-word essay discussing Freud's and Jung's concepts of dreams.

8. How useful is the Internet?

9. Explain how the weakening of the Ottoman Empire contributed to the conflicts that led to the First World War.

10. To what extent do the characters in any three novels we have studied achieve what most Existentialists would call an "authentic life"?

chapter 3

Gathering Material: Analyzing Content

Content analysis, as we defined it in Chapter 2, is the examination of behaviour, data, written works, and other sources of information and ideas without regard to the aesthetic qualities of the presentation. Researchers studying peer pressure, for instance, may observe how children of different ages respond to dares; an economist, after looking at current data on unemployment, inflation, the housing market, and retail sales, may predict higher interest rates; a columnist may argue against proposed changes to the Young Offenders Act. The researchers' study, the economist's report, and the columnist's article would be based on their examination of behaviour, data, written works, and other sources of information.

Most of the writing you do for courses other than those in literature and film studies is likely to be based on content analysis. Your basic task will be to analyze your material to arrive at your interpretation of what it means. Each academic discipline has a somewhat different way of handling this task, but it is possible to identify steps in content analysis that will work for many subjects and situations.

In this chapter we demonstrate two procedures for analyzing content. In the first section, Analyzing Your Subject, we suggest three ways of dividing topics for content analysis into parts. You will find these suggestions useful for planning and organizing essays on broad topics such as unemployment, Aboriginal land claims, or the media. In the second section, Analyzing the Content of Nonfiction Writing, we suggest ways of reading material on topics such as these so that you gather material more effectively.

Analyzing Your Subject

The basic procedure of analysis is that of dividing something into its parts. There are three main ways of making that division: systems analysis, process analysis, and causal analysis (see Figure 3.1). The first step in gathering material is to determine which of these types of analysis is most appropriate to your topic, or whether each has something to contribute. Use the following discovery questions.

Step 1 Using Systems, Process, and Causal Analysis

Systems Analysis

Is it possible to see my subject as a system that can be divided into parts? What are those parts? What is their function? How are they related?

You can think of a **system** as anything composed of parts that work together to create the whole. A car engine or a family can be analyzed as a system; so can a theory or an institution. For example, we commonly refer to different systems of government, such as parliamentary systems and presidential systems.

When you analyze a system, your purpose is not merely to describe its parts. You want to show how the parts work together to fulfill the function of the whole. If you were analyzing the criminal justice system within a democracy, for example, you might conclude that the parts (lawmakers, courts, lawyers, juries, prisons, and so forth) are designed to balance the rights of the person charged with a crime against the rights of society. In contrast, the criminal justice system in a dictatorship would likely have different parts and different relationships between the parts because the system would have a different purpose, such as maintaining the authority of those in power.

Process Analysis

Is it possible to see my subject as a process that can be divided into stages? What are those stages? What is their nature and function? How are they related?

Calling something a **process** suggests that it consists of either a sequence of actions directed to some end, such as the process of making a recording, or a series of identifiable changes over time, such as the process of aging. We think of processes as having a beginning and an end and stages in between. We divide the process into stages according to the points at which changes occur in the actions or states that make up the process.

There are many ways of describing processes. You are probably most familiar with instructions that set out a series of numbered steps for making or doing something, such as making cookies or assembling furniture. You have likely also read scientific descriptions of natural processes, such as the process of asexual reproduction in amoebas. The purpose of these types of process writing is to explain the process. When you write essays, you may examine more abstract processes, such as historical, psychological, or economic processes. These processes are appropriate subjects for essays because people have different opinions about them. Though they may agree about the facts, they will disagree about what the facts mean.

Understanding this point will help you recognize the similarities and differences between process analysis and other types of writing in which events are arranged in chronological sequence. This distinction is especially important when you are writing about history. We sometimes think of history as simply a record of events, a narrative of what happened. Historians, however, are concerned with explaining the processes of change in human societies. If you lose sight of this purpose, you may find yourself writing a narrative instead of analyzing the process of change.

Causal Analysis

Is it possible to analyze my subject according to its causes and/or effects? What are those causes/effects? How are those causes/effects related? What is their significance?

Causal analysis examines the **causes** that give rise to an event, a set of data, a concept, or a theory, or the **effects** that any of these produce.

It is often easy to identify causes and effects of events in our everyday lives. If you were in a car accident, for example, you might identify these causes: the road was icy, the tires were worn, and you panicked when a truck turned in front of you. It is sometimes harder to think of appropriate ways of describing the causes and effects of events less close at hand, such as the causes of traffic accidents in general. Here you would need to find more general terms for the causes you identify, terms such as "road conditions," "mechanical problems," and "driver error." (See Figure 3.1.) Causes and effects may also be interconnected ("for want of a shoe, a horse was lost, for want of a horse....").

Step 2   Categorizing Material

When you collect data on unfamiliar subjects, such as changes to the Criminal Code or Freud's theories of psychosocial development, you may initially feel that you have lots of little bits of information with no framework of general terms that would make sense of them. In this situation, it is helpful to recognize that each academic discipline focuses on particular kinds of systems, processes, and causes and effects. Part of what you learn in academic courses is the special analytic categories commonly used in particular disciplines.

If your subject or your discipline does not suggest appropriate categories, try these common perspectives: economic, social, political, psychological. For brief definitions of each of these perspectives, and suggestions for how to combine them with systems, process and causal analysis, see the chart entitled "Common Perspectives for Content Analysis" in Part 4, Resources for Writing.

FIGURE 3.1

**Discovery Questions for
Content Analysis**

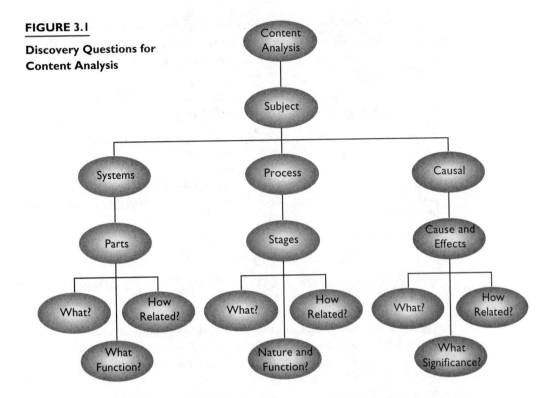

Sample Topic: Censorship and the Internet

To see how you might use Step 1 and Step 2 in dealing with a general interest topic, let's suppose that you are writing an essay for a media or cultural studies course, and that you have narrowed the broad subject of "The Internet" to a critical analysis of the ongoing debate over censoring or restricting access to certain materials on the Internet.

Categorizing the Parts of a System

Is it possible to see my subject as a system that can be divided into parts?

Think of the subject of censorship and the Internet as a complex system composed of many different parts: the media, governments, educational institutions, Internet providers, authors/publishers of potentially offensive or dangerous material, free speech advocates, parents and children, individual Internet users. You could group these parts into three categories: those who support censorship, those who oppose it, and those who have the power to regulate what appears on the Internet. You might discuss the different interests that each of these groups represents, and how the groups' various positions are likely to overlap and conflict.

Categorizing the Steps in a Process

Is it possible to see my subject as a process that can be divided into stages?

Another way to analyze the subject of censorship and the Internet is to examine the process of debate over individual censorship cases. If you were to draw up an outline of this process, it might look something like this:

STAGE 1: MEDIA COVERAGE OF COMPLAINTS ABOUT MATERIAL ON THE INTERNET

STAGE 2: PUBLIC DEBATE ON CENSORSHIP AS A SOLUTION
Those opposed to the allegedly offensive materials (parents, individuals, activist groups) are likely to lobby educational institutions, governments, and Internet providers to censor or restrict access to the materials; the authors of the materials and free speech advocates are likely to oppose any such actions.

STAGE 3: INSTITUTIONS AND INTERNET PROVIDERS DECIDE WHAT ACTION TO TAKE, IF ANY

STAGE 4: FALLOUT FROM THIS DECISION; PUBLIC DEBATE CONTINUES
If the lobbyists are successful, the authors of the allegedly offensive and dangerous materials are likely to try to challenge or circumvent the new restrictions through legal or technological means; if the lobbyists are not successful, they are likely to continue their battle.

Given this model, you might analyze the debate over censorship of the Internet as an ongoing struggle between pro- and anti-censorship advocates, an ethical and moral battle complicated by the continually changing and increasingly complex and sophisticated nature of Internet technology.

Categorizing Causes and Effects

Can I divide my subject into its causes and/or effects? If so, how can I categorize them?

As a further stage in analyzing the debate over censorship of the Internet, you might consider why the pressures for censorship have arisen, and the likely consequences of both censorship and a lack of censorship (a few of which have already been outlined above). You might find the four broad special categories we mentioned earlier particularly useful for this task. Here are a few possibilities:

Causes of the Debate

SOCIAL—Incidents in which the Internet has had a harmful effect on people (such as children exposed to pornography or pedophiles, or injured while constructing bombs built from Internet instructions) have been widely reported in the media.

PSYCHOLOGICAL—Pro-censorship forces are often led by older people who are not knowledgeable about the Internet and distrustful of the new liberties within our culture that the Internet embodies.

POLITICAL—Various advocates from across the political spectrum see the Internet as a forum for expressing their views even as they try to suppress views with which they do not agree.

Effects

1. Of Censorship

ECONOMIC—Internet providers that do censor or restrict access to materials may experience a consumer backlash from proponents of free speech.

SOCIAL—The censoring of any one type of material could create a precedent that would make the censoring of other materials easier and more justifiable. (This is the "slippery slope" argument used by anti-censorship advocates.)

POLITICAL—The repression of certain politically sensitive materials or viewpoints would make it impossible for individuals to form their own views on a subject on the basis of an informed knowledge of all positions, however extreme some may be. It also runs the risk of giving unwarranted publicity to those whose ideas are censored.

2. Of a Lack of Censorship

SOCIAL—Impressionable Internet users, especially children, may be exposed to materials that are sexually explicit or promote hatred or violence. The result could be an increase in crime, delinquency, and intolerance towards certain groups within society, which in turn could lead to widespread economic and psychological problems.

As you can see, systems, process, and causal analysis can stimulate your thinking about your subject and allow you to develop a fresh perspective. For a short essay you might decide to focus on one aspect of the subject, such as the social roots of pro-censorship feelings. For a longer essay, you might want to include a broad range of causes and effects or to examine censorship and the Internet as both a system and a process. Gathering material in this way is a necessary but preliminary step in thinking about your subject.

Analyzing the Content of Nonfiction Writing

Most of the material you need for writing essays in college and university courses will come from written sources. The reading you are expected to do will likely be much more difficult than your reading for high school. You may find that the concepts are new and the vocabulary is unfamiliar. Or you may grasp the details but miss the overall point. This section offers strategies that will help you gather material for content analysis essays. You can practise your analytical skills by following up the examples in Part 3, Readings.

Step 1 Figuring Out the Basic Ideas

What Is the Writer's *Subject?*

Check the title For most nonfiction, you will find the answer to this question in the title or first few paragraphs. The titles of scholarly books and articles, for example, customarily state their subject: "The Effects of Television Violence on Preschoolers"; "Masculine Roles in Pat Barker's War Trilogy"; *Ukrainian Settlements in Ontario, 1870–1900.*

Not all titles, however, will identify the writer's subject so precisely. Writing intended for a general audience may have a title designed to create interest or convey the writer's attitude rather than state a subject, as in Laura Robinson's "Starving for the Gold" (Readings). Other titles may be ironic or otherwise misleading, as in W. S. Merwin's "Unchopping a Tree" (Readings).

Check the introductory paragraph(s) Because titles can be misleading, it's always a good idea to check the first few paragraphs to confirm or correct your sense of the writer's subject. If, for example, you relied on the title of E. M. Forster's "My Wood" (Readings), you might say that Forster's subject is a piece of property he owns. From reading the introduction, however, you would find that Forster states his subject in three ways: "What is the effect of property on the character? . . . If you own things, what's their effect on you? What's the effect on me of my wood?" This introduction makes it clear that Forster is using his own experience to illustrate a broader moral question. You might say, then, that his subject is the effects of owning things on a person's character.

Check your sense of the whole   Sometimes identifying the subject won't be easy, either because the writer seems to discuss several subjects or because the details are so fascinating that you lose the big picture. Try to think about the work as a whole. How would you describe its particular focus, in ten words or less? Consider, for instance, Lenore Keeshig-Tobias' "He Was a Boxer When I Was Small" (Readings). On one level, of course, the subject is obvious—she is writing about her father. But lots of people write about their fathers. How would you describe her particular focus?

What Is the Writer's *Main Idea* About the Subject?

Check for an explicitly stated thesis   Reread the piece, focusing on the main point the author is making about the subject. You may find a one- or two-sentence **thesis** in the introduction (as in Suzuki's "It Always Costs"); in the conclusion (as in Forster's "My Wood"); or at another appropriate point (as in Orwell's "Shooting an Elephant").

To make sure you understand what you have read, restate the thesis in your own words. By the time you reach the end of "My Wood," for example, you may recognize that the phrases "enormously stout, endlessly avaricious, pseudo-creative, intensely selfish" summarize Forster's thesis about the effects of owning property. But can you explain what Forster means by those terms in your own words? If so, you can be confident you understand his main idea.

If you do not understand a key term, you may miss the overall point of the piece. In the Readings, we have defined many terms for you. When you encounter unfamiliar terms in your course materials, you can look them up in your textbook or in a specialized dictionary like those listed in the Annotated Survey of Reference Sources, Part 4.

Make an implied thesis explicit   In pieces that are ironic, humorous, or based on personal experience, the main idea is often strongly **implied** but not stated directly. In "Unchopping a Tree," for example, the absurdity of the process Merwin describes clearly suggests an opposite meaning. But you will not find a sentence or two that spells out Merwin's point.

What do you do if there is not an explicitly stated thesis? You may have a strong enough sense of the whole to sum up its main idea from an initial reading. You will often get a more accurate sense, however, if you examine the work more closely. Jot down your initial ideas, then reconsider them after you have completed your analysis.

How Does the Writer *Develop* This Main Idea?

Understanding how the writer organizes material to illustrate the main idea will help you to see the relation between main points and supporting details. Pay particular attention to key terms in topic sentences, transitions, and typographical devices such as headings. Focus on the ideas being presented, not the details. Write a sentence or two describing each of the main sections in your own words. There are five main methods writers use in developing ideas in nonfiction.

Listing a series of points What are the points? Writers often state in the introduction how they have divided their material: "I have four goals." "There are three basic reasons for opposing medically assisted suicide." "Early settlers built two types of shelters." Summarize each section in a sentence or two.

- Key transitions

    Number words, such as *first, second, third*; other words signalling addition, such as *also, furthermore, most important*

    Example: Forster, "My Wood"

Telling a story What are the main stages in the narrative? What point does the writer make (or what point can you make) about each stage?

In nonfiction, a narrative is a (true) story told to illustrate a point. It has a beginning and an end and several incidents in between. The incidents are usually grouped into stages, marked by significant external or internal changes. Summarize the *point* made by each of the main stages: not "The first section tells about their first week kayaking up the Mackenzie" but "In their first week kayaking [stage], they had to learn to work as a team [point]."

- Key transitions

    Time words, such as *before, after, one morning, the next day*

    Example: Orwell, "Shooting an Elephant"

Describing a process What are the main stages in the process? What point does the writer make (or what point can you make) about each stage?

A process, as we explained above, has a beginning and an end and can be divided into stages marked by significant changes. Summarize the point made by each of the main stages: not "The next stage is denial" but "The writer explains the next stage, denial, as the mind's attempt to protect the body from feeling pain."

- Key transitions

  First, next, third, final step/stage

  Example: Poe, "The Philosophy of Composition"

Showing how the parts of a whole work together   What are the main parts? What point does the writer make (or what point can you make) about each part?

As you have seen above, anything composed of parts that work together to create a whole can be considered a system. Writers often treat their subject as a system, dividing it into parts that correspond to the main sections of the work. Identify each main part and summarize the point the writer makes about it: not "Penal institutions are one aspect of the criminal justice system" but "Penal institutions, according to the writer, are the weakest link in the criminal justice system."

- Key terms and transitions

  The parts to be discussed may be identified in the introduction. Watch for the repetition of key terms and for terms such as these: *aspect, element, feature, part*

  Example: Sharon Doyle Driedger, "The Nurses" (analyzed later in this chapter)

Developing a chain of reasoning   What are the main points or stages in the argument?

A **chain of reasoning** is a series of interconnected points, each one necessary for establishing the point that follows. Here's an example: "I have to eat to live. I can't eat unless I have money. The only way to get money is to rob a bank. Therefore I am justified in robbing a bank." As you can see, to make the conclusion convincing—"I am justified in robbing a bank," the writer would have to persuade readers to accept each step in the argument. If there are weak links in the chain—as in this example—readers will reject the conclusion.

The need to establish each step often makes works based on a chain of reasoning difficult to follow. The writer may define terms, discuss alternative possibilities, or refute opposing arguments. These sections may distract you from the main line of the argument or explanation.

Use the writer's thesis as a guide to the points to watch for. Summarize each one. Pay careful attention to transitions that suggest the writer is indicating *disagreement* or *qualification*.

- Key transitions

    Words indicating cause and effect, such as *therefore, consequently, as a result*; words indicating disagreement or qualification, such as *although, while it is true that, despite*

    Example: Laura Robinson, "Starving for the Gold"

If the work you are reading does not seem to fit one of these five patterns, don't despair. Some pieces, especially long ones, may combine different types of development. Some may simply not be well organized. Do your best to identify and summarize the main points.

What Are the Main Types of Evidence/Detail the Writer Uses? For What Purpose(s)?

Each main point in a piece of nonfiction writing will be developed through **evidence** and **details** of the kinds listed below. The term *evidence* describes the specific information used to support an argument (think of the evidence offered in a murder trial). The term *details* refers specifically to particular actions in narratives and particular images in descriptions; more broadly, it refers to any material that explains or illustrates a general statement. Details may become evidence when used for a persuasive purpose (think of a prosecuting attorney reviewing the details of a murder case to decide which ones can be used as evidence of the defendant's guilt).

How much attention you pay to specific details will depend on your purpose in reading. If you are writing a research paper, specific information may be as useful to you as the writer's ideas on the subject. If you are studying for an exam, you may focus more on general principles, with a few selected facts or examples. If you are writing a summary of the piece as an assignment, you may be more interested in the *kinds* or *quality* of the evidence/details than in the specific information.

Note in a sentence or two which of these main types of evidence/detail the writer uses, and for what purpose.

- Examples

    Specific instances that illustrate a general point or principle. Taking a lost wallet to the police station could be used as an example of honesty.

- Facts and figures

  Specific information such as names of people, places, events; titles of publications and names of characters

  Precise numbers, as in measurements, statistics, dates

  Research studies and other "hard" evidence

- Quotations and other references to authorities

  Quotations from people interviewed or texts consulted

  References to recognized authorities on the subject or to authoritative texts (such as the Bible, the Koran), without direct quotation

- Narrative/descriptive details

  In telling a story or describing something, a writer may use few details (as in Caesar's "I came, I saw, I conquered") or many, as in an account of kayaking from Alaska to Tierra del Fuego. The details may seem fresh and vivid or flat and clichéd. The writer may use details for purposes such as creating suspense and conveying emotion.

- Other: definitions, analogies, allusions

  To make their explanations clearer, their arguments more persuasive, or their experiences more vivid, writers may define terms, provide analogies (the behaviour of gas molecules is like the behaviour of people in an elevator), or make passing references (allusions) to well-known historical figures and events ("My hopes sank like the *Titanic*"). For more on analogies, see Evaluating Evidence, Chapter 10; for more on allusions, see Style, Chapter 4.

For suggestions about how to evaluate a writer's arguments and evidence, see Chapter 10, Gathering Material for Evaluation Essays, and Chapter 11, Writing Evaluation Essays.

Step 2   Gaining a Broader Perspective

Once you've figured out the basic ideas in a piece of nonfiction, it's time to stand back and take another look at the work as a whole. As a result of considering the work's **purpose** and **tone**, you may modify your sense of the work's subject or thesis. Thinking about the work's **context** may lead you to a deeper understanding. After you've reread or thought about the whole piece, write a sentence or two answering these questions.

Purpose

Is the writer's main purpose to inform, to persuade, or to share personal experience? In "The Philosophy of Composition" (Part 3, Readings), for example, Poe's main purpose is to explain the principles by which he writes poems. In "It Always Costs" (Part 3, Readings), on the other hand, David Suzuki's main purpose is to persuade readers to accept his views. Lenore Keeshig-Tobias' purpose in "He Was a Boxer When I Was Small" (Part 3, Readings) is to share her experience of her father and her insights into his behaviour. Consider these possibilities carefully. You may discover that works seemingly designed to explain or to share personal experience are actually making a persuasive point.

In summarizing, choose words that show you understand the author's purpose. Use the author's name every few sentences to make clear you are stating another person's ideas, not your own.

PURPOSE	WORDS THAT CONVEY PURPOSE
To inform	explains, discusses, examines, analyzes
To persuade	argues, claims, makes the point, criticizes
To share experience	tells the story, reflects upon, describes

Tone

Does the tone of the piece suggest a different subject or purpose than you originally thought? A careful reading, for instance, may reveal that a humorous piece has a more serious subject than you thought, or that **irony** gives the piece a different meaning.

Context: Subject

What knowledge of the subject or the cultural/ historical circumstances can you bring to your understanding of the work?

Take a few minutes to consider how the piece fits with other things you know about the subject. Perhaps you've seen *Casablanca* or *The English Patient.* Do you agree or disagree with the opinions expressed by other viewers? (See *"The English Patient* Debate" in Readings). Or perhaps your knowledge of the ongoing "troubles" in Northern Ireland could enrich your understanding of Swift's "A Modest Proposal" (Readings).

Context: Writer

What do you know about the writer? Does the writer mention the source of his or her knowledge about the subject? Does the writer identify herself/himself with a specific political, religious, or intellectual position? What does the work itself suggest about the writer's perspective?

Writers often give some indication of the experience or training that qualifies them to speak about their subject, as you can see in the pieces by Henry Thoreau ("Economy") and David Suzuki ("It Always Costs," both in Readings). They may also identify the political, religious, or intellectual framework that guides their thinking, such as Judith Fetterley's feminist perspective on "A Rose for Emily" (Readings). The writer's perspective may be implied rather than stated. For example, Forster's biblical allusions in "My Wood" (Readings) suggest a particular religious framework. Considering these questions will help you to see the values that inform the piece of writing.

Step 3   Writing a Summary

When you finish your analysis, use your notes to write a brief summary of the piece. The summary will help you remember what you've read. You may also incorporate the summary, or parts of it, in your essay. For an example, see the sample topic below.

These guidelines will help you to analyze, and therefore to understand, the content of what you read. Since much of the writing you do will be based on your reading, reading more effectively will also help you to write better. Your ability to analyze content will aid you in explaining the relation between content and form (see Chapter 4, Gathering Material: Analyzing Texts). Analyzing the content of what you read is often the first step in writing essays based on comparison (see Chapter 9, Writing Comparison Essays) and evaluation (see Chapter 10, Gathering Material for Evaluation Essays and Chapter 11, Writing Evaluation Essays). It is an indispensable skill when you are writing research papers (see Chapter 12, Gathering Material for Research Papers).

Sample Topic: Analyzing the Content of Sharon Doyle Driedger's Article "The Nurses"

Sharon Doyle Driedger's article "The Nurses" (first published in *Maclean's*, April 28, 1997), is reprinted in Part 3, Readings. You will follow this example more easily if you read Driedger's article first.

Step 1 Figuring Out the Basic Ideas

What is the subject? The title is too general to be much help, but the lead-in says, "The front-line care-givers are burned out. Is it any wonder?" So we know the subject is burnout among nurses.

What is the main idea? Driedger does not explicitly state a thesis, but it's clear that the thesis will answer the question of why nurses are burned out. The first part of the article focuses on the pressures nurses are under: heavier workloads mean a decreased ability to meet the physical and emotional needs of patients. The second part examines different conceptions of the profession among nurses. At this stage of analysis, it may not be clear how these two concerns fit together.

How does the writer develop this main idea? The article begins by **telling a story** designed to arouse interest, but this is not the major method of development.

A more important method of development is **systems analysis**. Driedger shows how parts of the health-care system work together. Nurses are the front-line workers in a system that includes patients, doctors, technicians, cleaning staff, hospitals, clinics. Nurses have the initial contact with most hospital patients and attend most immediately to patient needs.

Driedger does not merely describe the system, however. To explain why nurses are burned out, she combines systems analysis with **causal analysis**. It is the effects of cutbacks in funding (the pressure to reduce costs by laying off nurses, releasing patients faster, replacing nurses with less qualified workers, increasing the educational requirements for nurses, replacing hospital care with cheaper community care, and so on), that are causing burnout among nurses. These health-care reforms, along with "medical technology, . . . research developments, the Internet, preventive and alternative medicine, a more informed public, feminism, increased education" are also "transforming the profession's traditional roles" (312).

Seeing this link allows us to state Driedger's thesis like this: "Cutbacks in funding for the health-care system are affecting nurses in two ways. The immediate effects are feelings of burnout because of increased workloads and a decreased ability to provide physical and emotional support for patients. A more far-reaching effect may be to hasten changes in the role of nurse as care-giver."

What are the main types of evidence/detail the writer uses? For what purpose(s)? Driedger uses lots of **narrative/descriptive details** at the beginning of the article to dramatize the pressures facing nurses. She gives a sense of the complexity of the problems by using many specific **examples. Quotations** from nurses show similar feelings about the current pressures but different opinions about changes in the profession. Some want to return to the "good old days" when nurses had more time to meet patients' physical and emotional needs; others welcome the opportunity to become more specialized health-care providers. The lack of job security upsets some nurses, while others are excited by the prospects of becoming nurse-entrepreneurs. All the nurses quoted are experts because of their experience in the field, and they are all identified by their position (for example, Rachel Bard, Moncton–based president of the Canadian Nurses Association).

Step 2   Gaining a Broader Perspective

Purpose   Driedger's main purpose is to explain how health-care cutbacks are affecting nurses. There is a slight persuasive edge to the piece because we as readers are likely to identify with patients who are not receiving adequate care.

Tone   Thoughtful, fairly objective. Most of the emotion comes from the comments of nurses: "We're running all the time. Nursing has gone to hell" (310). The overall impression is of a writer who is trying to be fair.

Context   The continuing debate in Canada over health care as a result of cutbacks in both federal and provincial funding.

Step 3   Writing a Summary

Now that you have gathered information for a content analysis, you can clarify the connections among your points by writing a summary. This summary should include the following:

1. Complete bibliographical information about the piece: author, title, and other details as appropriate for the type of publication (see Documentation in Part 2, Handbook for Final Editing).

2. The writer's thesis, in your own words, near the beginning of the summary.

3. An overview of the organization of the piece and the main points in each section. State these points in your own words but include brief quotations to capture the tone of the piece. Put quotation marks around any three or more consecutive words from the piece. If the piece is longer than a page, give page numbers in parentheses after each quotation and each paraphrase. Page numbers are handy in case you need to refer to specific material again. They are crucial when you are documenting research papers.

4. The main types of evidence and an explanation of their purpose.

5. Key terms and their definitions.

SAMPLE WRITING

SUMMARY OF "THE NURSES"

Sharon Doyle Driedger's article "The Nurses" (*Maclean's*, April 28, 1997) analyzes the effects of cutbacks in health-care spending on the "front-line care-givers," nurses. The first part of the article deals with the immediate consequences: the burnout nurses face as a result of increased workloads and decreased ability to meet patients' physical and emotional needs. The article begins with vivid accounts of nurses who must cope with bed closures, sicker patients, and staff shortages: conditions that have made some nurses feel that "We're running all the time—nursing has gone to hell" (310). The many examples and descriptive details help readers to understand why nurses are feeling burned out (overwhelmed, undervalued, insecure, locked into a dead-end job, and powerless to change these conditions). The second part of the article explores the far-reaching consequences of health-care reform, among other factors, on the traditional role of nurses as care-givers. While most nurses agree on the immediate problems, they have quite differing opinions about the solutions. Some want to return to "the good old days" when nurses had more time to meet patients' emotional and physical needs. Others welcome the opportunity to become more specialized health-care providers. While some are upset over the absence of job security, others like the opportunity to explore new opportunities that will take them out of the hospital and into the community. Driedger includes numerous comments from well-qualified nurses to explain both the pressures currently facing nurses and the changes in the definition of the role of the nurse within the health-care system.

Working on Your Own Assignment

The purpose of content analysis is to come to a better understanding of the nature and significance of your material by dividing it into relevant parts.

- Gain a better grasp of your subject by analyzing it as a system, a process, a series of causes and effects. Which type of analysis, or which combination, is most appropriate?

- Think about your subject from different perspectives, such as social, psychological, economic, political. Which perspective, or combination of perspectives, will give you the richest insights?
- Make more effective use of your material by analyzing its content: figure out the basic ideas; enrich your understanding by considering purpose, tone, and context; write a summary that will help you remember what you read.

EXERCISES

1. Choose two of the following subjects and decide whether you could gather material by using systems, process, or causal analysis, or a combination. Give brief examples of the parts of the system, stages of the process, or causes and effects you might look for. Decide which perspectives (economic, social, political, psychological) are relevant. Compare your responses with those of your classmates.
   - Video Lottery Terminal (VLT) addiction
   - homelessness
   - street gangs
   - fitness classes
   - vegetarian cooking
   - a subject of your own choice

2. Analyze the content of one of the essays from Part 3, Readings, or a chapter from a text you are studying. Use the steps demonstrated in the content analysis of "The Nurses" as your guide.

3. Use your notes from Exercise 2 to summarize the essay or chapter you have chosen. You can use the steps for writing a summary and the sample summary of "The Nurses" as a guide.

c h a p t e r 4

Gathering Material: Analyzing Texts

Every work of art is created from particular materials and techniques available to the artist. In creating written texts, writers use the "material" of language. Ways of using language to achieve certain effects would be the "techniques." Writers learn some techniques from studying other writers, but they may also develop new ways of using language. Thus when you analyze written texts as art, you focus not only on what is said but on how it is said, on the relationship between content and form of expression. Similarly, when you analyze performances as art, as in plays, films, and television programs, you pay attention not only to the message but also to the particular ways in which the director uses the materials and techniques available.

In doing textual analysis, then, you are treating a work (a poem, a movie, an essay) as a system of interrelated parts. Since one aim of textual analysis is understanding the content of the work, the parts you divide the work into overlap somewhat with the categories you use for analyzing the content of nonfiction (see Chapter 3). Another aim of textual analysis is appreciating the work's aesthetic qualities; the artistic choices about such matters as verse form, structure, and diction that help to shape its meaning.

There are other ways of writing about texts. Just as you can use process and causal analysis, as well as systems analysis, to analyze content, so you can use these three methods in analyzing texts. You could examine the process by which a text was composed, published, or performed, for instance (as Edgar Allan Poe does in "The Philosophy of Composition" in Part 3, Readings). You could also look at the social, economic, or psychological causes that may have shaped a particular text (as Chinua Achebe does in "An Image of Africa") or at its effects. We focus on analyzing a text as a system because this approach gives you practice in examining a text closely.

In this chapter we define and give examples of the general categories for analyzing a broad range of written texts and performances. If these terms are new to you, you may find it helpful to reread the definitions after you have gone through the sample topic. In Part 4, Resources for Writing, you will find a chart (General and Special Categories for Textual Analysis [Chart]) showing how these general categories can be adapted for specific genres of texts, as well as expanded lists of questions for each major genre (nonfiction, fiction, poetry, drama, films and television programs). You will also find an Annotated Survey of Reference Sources that will help you understand texts, such as handbooks of literary and film terms; biographical dictionaries; guides to symbolism, mythology, and religion; and specialized dictionaries on word usage.

Step 1   Using Analytic Categories

These are three basic questions for a systems analysis of a text: What are the parts of the text? What is their function within the work? How do the parts relate to each other? You can analyze a wide range of works by gathering material about these parts: subject, genre, context, methods of development, structure, style, tone, point of view. Here is a brief explanation of each of these terms.

Subject

Subject is the general issue(s) or concern(s) of the text, as you perceive it(them).

Sometimes your assignment will identify a subject for you, such as manhood in a Hemingway short story or the meaning of love in Emily Brontë's *Wuthering Heights*. But often you will have to decide what you think the subject is. Your statement about a text's subject(s) will be most useful to you if it is both tentative and precise: "This film seems to be about the meaning of heroism in war." If you keep your statement of subject tentative, you will find it easier to modify or change if necessary. And if you make it precise, you will have a better starting point from which to ask: how does the text treat this subject? Avoid both plot summary ("this film is about a soldier who...") and vague generalizations ("this film is about man against man" or "this film is about war").

Genre

The word *genre* means "kind." Genres are the types or kinds into which texts may be grouped because of similarities in form or subject.

There are "major" genres and "minor" genres (subgenres). The major genres you are likely to study are nonfiction, fiction, poetry, drama, and film. Each of these has many subgenres; for example, the genre of poetry includes the subgenres of the sonnet, the ballad, and the ode, among others. Some texts cross genre boundaries. The "new journalism," for instance, is nonfiction writing that uses many techniques of fiction.

Each major and minor genre has its own conventions, "rules" that authors either adhere to or break for their own purposes. The conventions that govern fantasy, for instance, are quite different from those that govern realistic fiction. Identifying the genre and subgenre of a text makes you more conscious of the "rules" the author is working with and/or against. This knowledge will not only improve your analysis, but also help you avoid serious mistakes. Some students, for example, confuse short stories with autobiographical essays and assume that short stories are accurate accounts of the writers' own experiences. A handbook of literary or film terms will explain the conventions of many kinds of works.

Context

Context means the historical and/or cultural situation in which the text was produced, including the specific audience (if any) for which it was intended.

Texts generally reflect the outlook and concerns both of the author/director and of the era in which they are created. You may therefore find that you understand a text better if you know something about the author or director and about such factors as the historical events, social conditions, and cultural issues that enter into the work, and about the audience for which a work might have been intended. You may find this kind of information in an introduction or notes to the text itself, or you may need to look it up in one of the guides listed in the Annotated Survey of Reference Sources, Part 4 . Be careful not to substitute information of this kind for a close analysis of the text. A poet may have had a drinking problem, for instance; that doesn't mean every poem he or she wrote is about alcoholism.

Methods of Development

Methods of development are the specific elements, such as points, events, and descriptions, by which the author/director unfolds or elaborates the central issue or concerns of the text.

A text consists of material that develops the overall point, the theme or thesis, of the work. You can analyze this material by examining the methods of development commonly used in specific genres or subgenres. In imaginative works that tell a story (whether in poetry, fiction, drama, or film), you would pay attention to details of events, setting, and characterization. In imaginative works that do not tell a story, you might find that the theme is developed through reflections, observations, or impressions. A love poem, for example, might be developed through a list of the beloved's virtues, or a nature poem through detailed observations of the landscape. For information on characteristic methods of development in various genres, consult handbooks of literary and rhetorical terms and handbooks that focus on specific literary forms (see Part 4, Annotated Survey of Reference Sources).

Structure

The term structure refers to the way that units of material are organized to convey a theme or thesis.

In thinking about structure, you need to be aware both of the general principles of structure within various genres and of the particular ordering of material within the text you are analyzing. Novels, drama, and film often organize events into a rising and falling action; short stories more often, though not always, focus on a single moment of revelation; essays often, though not always, arrange a series of points into an order of ascending interest. In addition to these broad structural principles, each work will have its particular way of organizing material.

Consider the following points when you analyze the structure of specific texts:

Generic principles of structure Among the conventions of various subgenres are conventions about structure. If you know that a poem is a sonnet, for instance, you can anticipate that its fourteen lines will be organized into one of two structures: an octave of eight lines setting out a problem and a sestet of six lines suggesting a solution; or three quatrains of four lines, each quatrain developing one idea, and a concluding couplet that sums up the previous lines or presents them in a new light. If you find variations on these forms, you can think about why the author violated the conventions. You can find information about the structural conventions of various genres in dictionaries of literary and rhetorical terms and in handbooks of specific literary forms.

Spatial and chronological principles of structure Space and time often function as principles in structuring material. Notice patterns of spatial structuring: contrasts between characters identified with different settings, such as city and country; events organized as a journey; changes in a character that occur as a result of moving from a familiar to an unfamiliar place.

Time is used as a structural principle in the following ways, among others: a chronological unfolding of events; movement between the present and the past; cycles of days, seasons, or years.

Typographical devices as indicators of structure Typographical devices often reinforce other kinds of structure. The most obvious are those that divide works into chapters or acts and scenes. Watch for the less obvious as well, such as the arrangement of lines on the page for some kinds of poetry.

Within the overall structure of the work, you may notice the way smaller blocks of material are organized. The overall structure of an essay, for example, might be chronological, but a paragraph of description within the essay might be organized according to a spatial arrangement of near to far. Making an outline of the text, or of its major divisions, will help you to identify its structural principles.

Style

Style is the characteristic or distinctive mode of expression within a text.

In analyzing style, you examine a text at its most detailed level, the level of lines, sentences, scenes (in plays), or shots (in films). While many elements enter into the style of a work, three are most important for written texts: **diction**; **figurative language and allusions**; and the rhythm created by **sentence structure** and other methods.

Diction refers to the kinds of words the author or characters use, both in level (colloquial, informal, formal) and in origin (for example, ethnic dialect, legal jargon). What is the effect of these choices? One essayist may use the informal language of everyday speech to seem like "one of us," for instance, while another writer may use the specialized vocabulary of economics to speak as a colleague to other experts.

Figurative language includes *images* (figures of speech like metaphor and simile, or visual, oral, tactile, and kinaesthetic images) and *symbols* (objects or actions that stand for a more abstract idea or value, such as a pair of scales that symbolizes justice).

Allusions are references to literary, historical, mythological, or religious events and figures, such as Adam and Eve. Repeated images, symbols, or allusions that form a pattern are particularly important. For instance, the images of Emily Dickinson's poem "Because I could not stop for Death" form a pattern in which life is conceived of as a journey with death as a kindly companion.

Sentence structure determines the rhythms of prose and, with other devices, of poetry and drama. Is there a high proportion or distinctive use of basic sentences, long or short sentences, sentence fragments, parallelism or inversion? How do line length and sound patterns contribute to the rhythms of poetry? How does the pacing of dialogue and action contribute to the effects of drama?

In analyzing the style of film and television productions, you focus on the way the camera is used, with less attention to the language. Shooting techniques, visual images and symbols, and editing techniques together create the style.

To analyze style, you may need the help of resources such as dictionaries of slang, symbols, or film terms; or a handbook of poetics.

Tone

Tone refers to the attitude of the author/narrator towards the self, the subject of the text, and the reader, as conveyed by style. In plays and films, this quality is referred to as the *mood* or *atmosphere* of the work.

When you read silently, you likely hear the words inside your head as though they were being spoken by the author or character. The voice may seem like that of a modest gentleman or a frightened child, a witty woman of the world or a dreamy adolescent. It is this sense of a voice speaking that we mean by the attitude towards the self created by a written work.

The tone (created through stylistic choices) establishes a particular relationship among the author or narrator, the subject of the text, and the audience. The author of an essay might, for example, adopt a playful attitude towards the subject of addiction to coffee, and treat the reader either as playmate or disapproving parent. Or the essayist might deliver a serious lecture about the dangers of caffeine and treat the reader as a peer to share ideas or as a pupil to be instructed. In plays and films, the tone or mood may be established through music, lighting, costuming, and other devices.

Terms commonly used to describe tone or mood include sentimental, businesslike, authoritative, comic, nostalgic, menacing, reflective, playful, serious. The piece is **ironic** when we understand its meaning to be different from, or the opposite of, what is expressed.

Point of View

The perspective from which the text is presented is called point of view.

Here are the distinctions commonly made in analyzing point of view.

Fiction: Who is the narrator (storyteller)?

First-Person Narration

MAJOR PARTICIPANT: The story is told in the first person by an "I" who has a major role in the events (Naomi telling the story of her life in Joy Kogawa's novel *Obasan*).

MINOR PARTICIPANT: The story is told in the first person by an "I" who recounts events but does not have a major role in them (the unnamed narrator of William Faulkner's short story "A Rose for Emily").

Omniscient Narration The story is told in the third person by an anonymous narrator who has access to the thoughts and feelings of more than one character (as in D. H. Lawrence's short story "The Horse-Dealer's Daughter").

Limited Omniscient Narration The story is told in the third person by an anonymous narrator who has access to the thoughts and feelings of only one character (as in Nathaniel Hawthorne's short story "Young Goodman Brown").

Objective Narration The story is told in the third person as though recorded by a camera, with no access to the thoughts or feelings of any character (as in Ernest Hemingway's short story "Hills Like White Elephants").

You will see how to analyze point of view in a short story in the sample topic below.

Poetry: Who is the speaker? Like fiction, poems can be expressed in the first person or the third person. The most important distinction is between the first-person speaker who is a character completely separate from the poet (as in dramatic monologues such as Robert Browning's "My Last Duchess") and the first-person speaker who seems hard to distinguish from the person who wrote the poem (as in lyric poems such as Robert Frost's "Stopping by Woods on a Snowy Evening"). Although it's tempting to treat the second type as wholly autobiographical ("Frost was driving a wagon one night and . . ."), this "I" too is a literary creation, one that allows poets to transform purely individual insights and experiences into ones their readers can more easily share. That's why you ordinarily refer to the "speaker" of the poem rather than to the poet. For an example of how to use this term, see Karin Swanson's "Spontaneity and Enjoyment of the Natural World," Part 3, Readings.

Nonfiction: Who is speaking—writer or persona? As you will remember from Chapter 3, nonfiction writers generally speak for themselves, in either the first or third person, or they create a **persona** to speak for them, usually for purposes of humour or irony. A persona is like a character an actor might play. The writer adopts a role, usually for purposes of humour or irony. In "A Modest Proposal" (Readings), for example, Jonathan Swift creates a persona quite different from himself to comment on conditions in Ireland.

Step 2   Connecting Textual Features to Figure Out the Work's Theme/Thesis

In most texts, the features that we have just described work together to convey an overall point about the subject. The term *thesis* is generally used to refer to the more explicit point made in essays, while *theme* refers to the more indirect points made by imaginative literature.

At first glance it may seem difficult to distinguish theme/thesis from *subject*. To some extent the difference is between the general and the specific. The *subject* is the general topic of discussion in the work; the *theme* or *thesis* is the specific point the work makes about the subject. Chinua Achebe's *subject* in "An Image of Africa" is the writer Joseph Conrad's vision of Africa and Africans; his *thesis* seems to be that Conrad's vision is racist. You might describe the *subject* of Alice Munro's short story "Thanks for the Ride" as the dating rituals of adolescence, and her *theme* as the necessity of recognizing the class barriers that obstruct some relationships.

A word of caution is in order here. To analyze texts effectively you will need to formulate a clear statement of thesis or theme. But remember that it is impossible to capture everything that could be said about any complex and interesting work in a brief phrase, and that this statement reflects only your current interpretation, which may change with time or reflection. There may also be discordancies, gaps, or contradictions in the text that you will need to take into account. As you write your essay, keep your mind open to other possible interpretations. Remember, too, that the thesis or theme of the text is not the same as the thesis of your essay; finding your own thesis belongs to the next stage of the writing process.

Sample Topic: Analyzing a Short Story: Frederic Raphael's "Special English"

When you work through a textual analysis topic yourself, you will often find that you do not collect material in all the categories outlined. Your assignment may ask you to focus on an element such as structure or setting, or you may decide some categories are not relevant, or you may not be able to find certain material. You may use all the categories when you do not know how to approach the essay assignment, and so need a wide range of material. In this chapter we will treat the sample topic as an assignment of this kind. In the next, we will show how you would use this material to work out a thesis for a specific topic.

Step 1   Using Analytic Categories

To demonstrate how to use the categories for textual analysis, we have chosen "Special English," a one-paragraph short story by Frederic Raphael. First read the story, which is reprinted in Part 3, Readings. As you go through the process of analysis with us, think about what material you would include in each of these categories.

Subject The story seems to focus on the subject of male–female relationships.

Genre The *genre* of the work is short story, but "Special English" is a short story of a rather unusual kind. Whereas short stories often focus on a specific incident, a moment of revelation and then its aftermath, "Special English" describes no particular incident but a developing process with a "twist" at the end.

Context According to the *Dictionary of Literary Biography*, Raphael is a contemporary writer, born in America but making England his home. His focus is usually on the middle class and issues of religious and racial allegiance.

Methods of development The most striking thing about this story is the absence of specific details. The story focuses on no specific **event**, but rather presents a repeated happening: the couple's listening to the radio and the woman's learning more English. The **setting** is equally unspecific: the couple met on a "winter steamer"; they are now on a "remote island," possibly one of the Greek islands ("wine-dark sea" is a favourite formula of the classical Greek poet Homer), at a time when a colonial war is going on. Most unspecific of all is the **characterization**. All we learn of the woman is that she does not know English when the two meet, and that learning it makes her proud and hopeful of increased love. All we learn of the man is that he is probably well-off (since he can rent a cottage), probably a writer (from the reference to the typewriter) and that the woman's progress in learning English leads him to hate her. The details of the story seem to focus on the news broadcasts and on the woman's reactions to them; the man's reaction comes only in the story's last clause.

Structure "Special English" seems to use a straightforward chronological structure involving the summary of a repeated daily event: "Every night...the lovers listened...As day succeeded day, evening evening." A causal sequence is implied in this structure; the learning produces one kind of reaction in the woman, another kind in the man. Only the woman's reaction is explained; the man's reaction comes as the climax of the story. It is a climax of surprise; nothing prepares us for his reaction, and the story does not go on to explain it.

Style The **diction** is that of formal educated speech; words and phrases like "saline rail," "tempo," "distinct variations," "kindled" and "eloquent" seem typical in the story, as does the vocabulary of teaching and learning: "instructively simple," the "vocabulary of their understanding," her "newly educated vanity" and "special English." The

sentence structure of the story echoes its diction. All but three or four sentences are grammatically complex, and many involve the careful placement of multiple subordinate clauses and qualifying phrases. The last sentence, with its double parallelism, is the most formally elaborate of all: "Slowly...slowly...he read...he learned." The style of the story seems formal, careful, intellectual.

The **figurative language** is in keeping with other elements of the style. The most striking *image* of the story also seems controlled and intellectual: the metaphor of the broadcasts staining "the vocabulary of their understanding...with the world's blood." Other images reveal the man's sense of possession (the woman as "prize"), the woman's false sense of security (the "warming lamplight" is linked to her "dawning confidence") and a concern with a slow but inevitable process (as in "slow tempo," "slowly then," "unhurried stories," "unhurried...voice") that seems to pervade the story.

Tone The tone created by the summarizing structure of the story and by its style is one of careful detachment. The reader is kept at a distance from particular events, and the only real breath of passion in the story comes in its final phrase. But whose tone is this? It is not easy to answer this question because there is an ambiguity about *point of view* in the story.

Point of view On first impression, the story seems to shift from the objective to the omniscient point of view about halfway through, when we seem to gain access to the woman's pride in her accomplishments and then, startlingly, to the man's hatred. Yet the way that the woman's reflections are presented is curious; they are introduced with a reference to her "remote[ness]" and the fact that the man is "watch[ing]" her and they conclude with his "read[ing]" her smile and eyes. By these suggestions we are led to see that what seems to be objective and omniscient narration is actually third-person limited narration; what we are getting, presented with seeming objectivity, is the man's vision of the woman's feelings.

Step 2   Connecting Textual Features to Figure Out the Work's Theme/Thesis

Once we understand that the story reflects the point of view of the man, then we can see how several of its features are related. Both the summarizing structure and the unspecific nature of setting and characterization reflect the consciousness of someone who is not interested in a specific place and a specific person, except as they fit his concept of the remote and the exotic. When the woman threatens to escape this concept by learning his language, she threatens his way of dealing with the world, and thus incurs his hatred.

To figure out the theme of this story, we need to think about why Raphael depicts this man as a character who is interested in the remote and who wants both control and detachment. If we see in these qualities a traditionally masculine way of dealing with experience, Raphael's decision to narrate "Special English" from the man's point of view makes sense. This story shows us how masculine ideals of control and detachment can destroy a relationship between a man and a woman.

Working on Your Own Assignment

Your main purpose in textual analysis is to explain the relationship between *what* the work is about (its subject and theme) and *how* the ideas and emotions are conveyed.

- Make notes on the written text or performance in the appropriate categories: subject, genre, context, methods of development, structure, style, tone, and point of view. The "Questions for Analyzing" nonfiction, fiction, poetry, drama, film and television programs in Part 4, Resources for Writing, will give you specific guidelines.

- For nonfiction, look for an explicitly stated thesis. Does this thesis actually explain the most significant material you've gathered? If not, what do you find to be the work's thesis?

- For imaginative works, formulate a theme that connects and explains the most significant material you have gathered.

- For examples of textual analysis, see the following essays in Part 3, Readings:
  — Judith Fetterley, "A Rose for 'A Rose for Emily' "
  — A. Smith, "Colonialism and Masculinity in 'Special English' "
  — B. Smith, "Two Views of the Battle at Powder River"
  — D. Smith, "The Making of the Tragic Hero: The Graveyard Scene in *Hamlet*"

EXERCISES

A.   Respond to each of the following questions in a sentence or two.

1. What is the main purpose of textual analysis?
2. How would a textual analysis of Lewis Thomas' "Notes on Punctuation" (Readings) differ from a content analysis?
3. What does the term **analytic categories** mean?
4. What are the eight **general categories** of textual analysis?

B.   Analyze the figurative language in the following poem by answering the questions in the relevant section of Questions to Ask in Analyzing Poetry in Part 4, Resources for Writing. (For an exercise comparing "Love Lessons" and "Special English," see Chapter 9.)

PUBLISHED WRITING

LOVE LESSONS

When I said I would teach you English,
mi amante,*
I did not know
we would conjugate the verbs with our bodies.
When I promised you should write poetry again,
in another language,
mi corazon,*
I did not know
you would hold me in your arms, beating out the hexameters
absent-mindedly, on my back.
Your body, all Inca black and gold, smells of
dusky rivers, where blind white dolphins swim;
it tastes of sweet Andean woodsmoke,
blowing over the altiplano.
Your kisses glow and burn like snakes of lava
incinerating my carefully created image
as the bringer of knowledge.
When I said I would teach you English,
mi vida,*
I did not know
I would learn from you
the grammar of the heart.

Joan Seager, from *Vintage 91, Prize-Winning
Poems from the League of Canadian Poets*
(Sono Nis Press).

---

* "Mi amante," "mi corazon," and "mi vida" are terms of endearment in Spanish. Literally, they mean "my lover," "my heart," and "my life."

C.   Analyze either the structure or the tone of one of the following essays from Part 3, Readings, by answering the questions in the relevant section of Questions to Ask in Analyzing Nonfiction in Part 4, Resources for Writing.

• E. M. Forster's "My Wood"

• Linda Hogan's "The Voyagers"

• Maggie Helwig's "A Certain Hunger: The Body Language of Anorexia"

• George Orwell's "Shooting an Elephant"

D.   Write a paragraph developing one category of your analysis of "Love Lessons" or one of the essays above. Try to begin this paragraph with a topic sentence that states your main point about that aspect of the work (setting, for instance). Keep your work for possible use in the exercises for Chapter 8.

chapter 5

Formulating a Thesis

In Chapter 1 we defined the essay as a short piece of nonfiction writing that has an explicit overall point, or *thesis*, and said that a thesis usually consists of an *opinion* and the main *reason(s)* or *support* for that opinion. In this chapter we will focus on the process of formulating a tentative thesis for the analytic essays you write. We devote a whole chapter to this process because of the crucial function the thesis serves: it is the overall point that gives the essay shape and meaning.

What does it mean to say that the thesis consists of an opinion? First, an opinion is a belief or judgment; it is a statement about what is probable, not what is certain. If you were writing an essay on the First World War, for instance, you would not try to prove the point that such and such battles were fought on such and such days—that information is a matter of fact, not of opinion. But not everyone agrees about the main causes of the war. So you could write an analytic essay to support the thesis that the main causes of the war were economic rather than political.

Second, your thesis expresses *your own* belief or judgment. In a report, whether a book report or a business report, your aim may be to summarize another writer's main points. In an essay, however, you are expected to have a point of your own to make about the subject. David Suzuki argues in "It Always Costs" (Part 3, Readings) that the long-term costs of environmental damage always exceed the short-term economic benefits—that's his thesis. In writing an analysis of Suzuki's essay you would not merely use his thesis as your own; your thesis might, for instance, state your opinion about how successfully Suzuki argues his case. In a research essay, as in other kinds of essays, your thesis will express your opinion about your subject, not merely report the findings of other scholars or researchers.

Obviously there's more to writing a thesis than simply stating a personal opinion. "This film is disgusting" might be your opinion, but it would not be a satisfactory thesis if you have been asked to analyze shooting techniques. There are two important considerations about what you say in a thesis. The first is that your opinion has to be relevant to the assignment. Maybe your feelings of disgust *are* relevant. If so, you can make that relevance clear in your statement of opinion: "Shooting techniques in the film are designed to arouse disgust in the audience."

The second consideration is that you have to give one or more *reasons* for your opinion, some *support* for it. The quality of the reasons you give determines whether your reader will take your opinion seriously or simply dismiss it. You might support your opinion about the film, for example, by explaining how the shooting techniques arouse disgust. Your final thesis statement might then read something like this:

Shooting techniques in the film are designed to arouse disgust in the audience by magnifying bodily imperfections, by lingering over images of filth and decay, and by bathing key scenes in a sickly yellow light.

This thesis controls the content of the essay by stating each of the points to be developed in the middle paragraphs.

When you are writing on subjects about which you already have an opinion, such as censorship or date rape, you may have little difficulty in stating your opinion and giving reasons to support it. But when you are writing essays in academic disciplines, the material is likely to be new to you and your opinion about it harder to determine. We will therefore explain the process of finding a thesis from material you have gathered. We will then show how to find a thesis for the sample assignment on "Special English."

Step 1   Forming an Opinion

Let's suppose that you have been given the assignment "Choose a Canadian magazine or newspaper to determine whether its practices substantiate charges of bias in the news media." You have read several issues of the (hypothetical) weekly newsmagazine *Contemporary Views*, gathering material on the types of stories it prints and the way the stories are written. You are now ready to work out a tentative thesis for your essay.

A thesis opinion usually emerges from the connections you perceive among the details in the categories you used. Let us say that, in reviewing the material you have gathered about *Contemporary Views*, for instance, you notice that the writers slant the articles to favour increases in military spending, cuts in social programs, and tougher criminal penalties, and to oppose gun control legislation and the rights of minorities. This slanting might be evident in the writers' methods of development (quoting only certain authorities), style (diction that downplays white-collar crime and sensationalizes inner-city crime), and tone (such as a tone of moral superiority). What do these details have in common? You might conclude that these patterns suggest a conservative political bias. Your statement of opinion would thus be something like "*Contemporary Views* exhibits a conservative political bias."

Step 2   Checking Opinion Against Essay Topic

If the opinion you have formed is relevant to your assigned topic, you are ready to go on to Step 3. If the opinion does not seem to address your topic, you will need to re-examine your notes or your text, or both, to see whether you have missed something.

In the *Contemporary Views* example, the thesis fits the assigned topic.

Step 3   Supporting Your Opinion

In arriving at an opinion, as we have seen, you make connections among details to reach a generalization about them. The reasons you give to support your opinion will not be individual details, however. Your reasons will usually refer to the categories or subcategories you used in analyzing your material.

To support the opinion that *"Contemporary Views* exhibits a conservative political bias," for instance, you would not say "because one article describes those who favour government spending on social programs as 'do-gooders' and 'knee-jerk liberals.' " Instead you would refer either to the general categories in which you perceive bias (methods of development, style, and tone), or to your more particular points about these categories: the articles quote only experts who hold conservative views; downplay white-collar crime while sensationalizing inner-city crime; and adopt a tone of moral superiority towards minority groups.

At this stage of the writing process, you may not have worked through your material sufficiently to give precise reasons to support your thesis. Your general categories of analysis will give you a tentative thesis to guide you as you write your draft. You can make your supporting reasons more specific when you revise your thesis.

Sample Topic: Frederic Raphael's "Special English"

In this section we will explore the process of finding a thesis for an essay on Frederic Raphael's short story "Special English." You can review the process of gathering material on this story in Chapter 4, pages 50–53.

Step 1   Forming an Opinion

Some assignments that call for textual analysis ask you to show how a broad theme such as manhood is expressed through various elements of the work; other assignments ask you to focus on a specific element, such as the setting or the title. Even when you are asked to focus on a specific element, you are expected to show how that element relates to the theme or thesis of the whole. Thus your thesis statement for a textual analysis essay will always show the relationship between the work as a whole and one or more of its parts. The pattern you find in arriving at the theme or thesis of the work will therefore be your starting point in forming your own thesis.

If you examine the material gathered on "Special English," you will see that elements such as style and point of view share this common pattern: they convey the male character's desire for control, detachment, and the remote.

Step 2   Checking Opinion Against Essay Topic

Sometimes the pattern you find in your material is obviously relevant to your essay topic; other times there may be a gap between what you have figured out and what your essay topic asks you to focus on. Let's suppose that your essay topic on "Special English" reads like this:

> Discuss the treatment of colonialism in Frederic Raphael's
> "Special English."

Your thesis about how masculine ideals of control and detachment can destroy a relationship doesn't fit with this topic. To solve this problem, you need to take another look at your responses to the discovery questions and at the story itself to see whether you can find a link between your thesis and the essay topic.

Upon rereading "Special English," you might notice that Raphael raises the issue of colonialism through repeated references to broadcasts on the progress of the colonial war. If you take another look at your notes on style, you can see that Raphael connects masculine attitudes and colonialism through the word "prize." This term, used to describe the way the man regards the woman, is also commonly used to describe the way the builders of empires regarded the trading colonies they founded. This parallel suggests that the masculine attitude is also a colonial attitude. The detail of the cottage rented from the uneducated peasant provides further support for this interpretation. Most important, the progress of the relationship suggests that both women and colonized peoples are attractive to the man when they are remote and unknown but become much less attractive when they begin to assert human demands. You could close the gap between the essay topic and your original thesis by revising your thesis like this:

> In "Special English" Frederic Raphael shows that the mascu-
> line ideals of control and detachment that destroy a relation-
> ship between a man and a woman are, in fact, the same as
> the colonial attitudes responsible for the war in which this
> story is set.

Step 3   Supporting Your Opinion

You would draw your reasons to support this opinion from the categories of textual analysis you decide to use in your essay. Style and point of view, as we have seen, most clearly convey the male character's attitudes and thus support the thesis. Because "Special English" is less than a page long, you might not have enough material if you used only these two categories. In Chapter 6 we will carry this topic through the next stage in the writing process, drafting. There we will discuss other considerations in selecting material to support your thesis.

We have demonstrated a process by which you can work out a fairly complete thesis statement before you begin writing. Some writers prefer to let ideas and connections emerge as they write. If this is your preferred method, you might start with a more tentative thesis about male–female relationships and work out the connections with colonialism as you write. You would then need to revise your thesis to make sure that it addressed the issue of colonialism. For information on possible problems with thesis statements, see Chapter 7, Revising Thesis and Essay Structure.

Working on Your Own Assignment

When you try to formulate a thesis, you are looking for an overall point that expresses the connection(s) between some or all of the categories you have chosen and the details you have gathered in these categories. A full thesis will have both an opinion and support for that opinion.

- Read through all the material you have gathered: your notes on the essay topic, your prewriting, your answers to the questions for content or textual analysis, and any other notes and observations you have made. What opinion about your subject emerges?

- State this opinion as a tentative thesis. Make sure that it does not merely rephrase your essay topic or the theme or thesis of a work you are analyzing. Check that your thesis is a response to the assigned essay topic.

- Can you find tentative reasons for your opinion? You can work out your reasons more fully as you draft and revise.

EXERCISES

A.   Respond to the following questions in a sentence or two.

1. What is the difference between the **thesis** of your essay and the **subject** of your essay? Give a specific example to support your answer.

2. How does a thesis **control** the content of an essay?

3. What's wrong with the following thesis: This essay will show how Atwood uses setting, plot, and point of view to develop the theme of her story "The Man from Mars."

4. What is the best location for a thesis in an academic essay?

B.   When you write an essay as part of an examination, you need to figure out your thesis quickly. You can practise by formulating a thesis on one of the topics below. First gather some material on the topic you have chosen by using one or more of the techniques explained in Chapter 2: freewriting, brainstorming, tree diagramming. Then read over the material you have gathered to see what main idea about the essay topic emerges. Decide whether your main purpose is to explain, persuade, or share personal experience. State your thesis, including the most important support for your opinion, in a sentence or two. Be as clear and as specific as you can. Compare your responses with those of your classmates.

- body piercing
- medically assisted suicide
- balancing the demands of work and school
- political parties in Canada
- the influence of U.S. media

chapter 6

Drafting

You have chosen a topic for analysis, gathered material in appropriate categories, and found a thesis. What do you do next? Write a draft. It's tempting to wait until you feel inspired or until the night before the essay is due. Professional writers cannot afford to wait for inspiration, nor do they expect to produce a perfect piece of writing the first time. Their method is almost always to write out a rough draft, let it sit for a while, and then submit it to a process of revision and fine-tuning. Since it is virtually impossible to produce a good analytic essay in one draft, we recommend this method to you.

In writing a first draft you will need to make four major decisions:

- which categories of material to use
- what point to make about the material in each category
- how to organize your essay
- what to say in your introduction and conclusion.

Once you've made these decisions, you will be ready to write a draft. Think of your decisions as tentative, however, because you may discover in the process of writing the draft that parts of your plan will work and other parts won't.

First we will explain these four steps, with brief examples. Then we will go through the process of writing a draft, using the textual analysis assignment from the previous chapters. Some writers find an outline helpful at this stage. Others prefer to freewrite a draft and then use a *revision outline*, which we discuss in Chapter 7, to organize their material. If you don't usually write from an outline, try this method to see whether you find it useful.

Step 1   Selecting Material

When you review your material, you will need to decide which categories of your analysis are most relevant and will provide the best support for your thesis. All of your material will presumably be relevant to your subject, but it may not be equally relevant to your essay assignment. Let's assume you are writing on setting in Poe's "The Fall of the House of Usher." You might have made notes about the structure of the story, only to discover that structure had little relevance to your topic. You would therefore omit that category.

The rest of your material may be relevant but not provide equally strong support for your thesis. It is always better to explain a few points in depth than to skim over a great many. In a short essay (500–1000 words), you can usually develop three to five points. So if you had good material to show how style, tone, and point of view contributed to Poe's depiction of the setting, you might explore these categories in the body of your essay. You do not have to make just one point about each category, however. If you have analyzed the style in great detail, for instance, you might make separate points, in separate paragraphs, about Poe's use of diction, figurative language, and sentence structure. (By the way, don't discard material that you decide not to use in your middle paragraphs: you may be able to use it in your introduction and conclusion.)

If you were making a draft outline to record your decisions, the outline for the essay on setting in "The Fall of the House of Usher" might look like this:

TENTATIVE THESIS: In "The Fall of the House of Usher," Poe uses the setting as a symbol of Roderick Usher's physical and moral decay.

1. style

2. tone

3. point of view

Step 2   Making Points

If you write a draft before you have fully worked out your thesis, you might find yourself writing separate paragraphs on style, tone, and point of view in "The Fall of the House of Usher," without showing how these elements contribute to Poe's depiction of the setting. But if you have worked out a thesis, you can make points about these categories of material. Each point serves to organize one or more paragraphs in your draft and to show how this material relates to your thesis.

In your draft outline, then, you might show what point you want to make about each category of material:

THESIS: In "The Fall of the House of Usher," Poe uses the setting as a symbol of Roderick Usher's physical and moral decay.

1. style: diction emphasizes physical and moral decay of house and master

2. tone: sombre, puzzled tone suggests moral decay

3. point of view: narrator as outsider observes both physical and moral decay

These points will become your topic sentences.

Step 3   Organizing Material

Once you have determined which categories to use and what points to make, you will need to decide on the structure of your essay. There are two issues to consider:

- whether to organize your essay deductively or inductively
- in what order to present your points.

Choosing Deductive or Inductive Structure

When you argue *deductively*, you start with a principle and then support it with reasons and evidence. You use *deductive structure* when you start your essay with a thesis and then give reasons to support that thesis, usually developed through a series of points and evidence. When you reason *inductively*, you start from a specific case or cases and move towards the principles involved. Correspondingly, you organize your essay *inductively* when you present events, points, or details first and withhold the thesis to be derived from them until the end. Inductive structures are more often used for narrative and descriptive essays, and deductive structures for analytic essays. You would therefore most likely choose a deductive structure, with your thesis at the beginning.

Sequencing Points

Your next step would be to consider the order in which to make your points. The most common arrangement in academic essays is an **order of ascending interest**. In this method of sequencing material, you begin with your least important point and end with your most important. If you were writing on the three main causes of traffic accidents, for example, you would discuss the least important cause first and the most important cause last. That way, you would more easily keep your readers' attention and leave the strongest impression. You might also need to consider whether you needed to establish one point before readers could understand the next, as in a chain of reasoning.

Applying these principles to the three points about setting in "The Fall of the House of Usher," you might decide to begin with point of view, since your comments about tone and style depend upon your readers' understanding the role of the narrator. You might then discuss tone because it is readily apparent in the first few paragraphs, and end with style, since your most important point is about the symbolic meaning of the word "house." When you rearrange your points, you might need to reword them to make the reasons for your order more obvious, as in the following example:

1. Point of view—the setting is presented through a first-person narrator, whose outside perspective is reflected in tone and style.

2. Tone—narrator's troubled reflections upon the setting create a sense of moral as well as physical decay.

3. Style—setting as symbol is emphasized in the word "house," which refers both to the family and to the family mansion.

Step 4   Sketching Introduction and Conclusion

In writing a draft you may find that you get stuck trying to write an introduction. Many writers share this problem. It might help you to realize that writing an introduction and conclusion is the *least* important step of the drafting process, for often you simply cannot know how your essay should begin and end until you have written it out and started revising it.

You can sketch out an introduction by writing a sentence or two on the context of your topic, by stating your thesis (if you're giving your essay a deductive structure), or by asking the question your essay will answer (if you are using an inductive structure). You can then give your attention to the most important step in drafting, writing the middle paragraphs. Let your thinking carry you naturally into your conclusion. If you can't get started without a polished introduction, you will find explanations of the principles of writing introductions and conclusions in Chapter 8, Revising Individual Paragraphs.

Step 5   Writing the Draft

The basic point to remember as you write your draft is that you will eventually revise what you have written. This means, for one thing, that though you have an outline of the points you want to cover, either on paper or in your head, you should also follow where your writing leads. As you write, you may find that some of your points are not working well, or that you have too many points or too few, or that you are discovering new ideas. Let the writing flow; you can check thesis, structure, and development as part of the revision process (see Chapters 7 and 8).

The fact that you will revise also means that you can resist the temptation to polish sentences as you write. Beginning writers often waste a good deal of time making changes in sentences that they eventually will discard. Trying to get a first draft perfect often results in having no draft at all. So concentrate on getting your ideas down on paper, and leave worrying about whether your ideas are valid and your grammar correct to the revision stage of the process.

Sample Topic: Colonialism in Frederic Raphael's "Special English"

In the previous two chapters you have seen how to gather material and find a thesis for the assignment: "Discuss the treatment of colonialism in Frederic Raphael's 'Special English.'" Here, you can follow the process of writing a first draft of this essay.

Step 1   Selecting Material

If you have answered all the discovery questions on the work you are analyzing, you will need to decide which material is most relevant to your topic. Here the material on setting, characterization, style, and point of view is more obviously relevant to an analysis of colonialism, so you could use these categories of your analysis for the draft.

Step 2   Making Points

If you consider how the material in each of these categories helps to convey the masculine attitudes and values that Raphael is examining in "Special English," you might come up with a draft outline something like this:

> THESIS: In "Special English" Frederic Raphael shows that the masculine ideals of control and detachment that destroy a relationship between a man and a woman are, in fact, the same as the colonial attitudes responsible for the war in which this story is set.
>
> 1. Methods of development—setting and characterization reflect the male character's detachment and desire for control
>
> 2. Style—formal, intellectual, carefully controlled
>
> 3. Point of view—reflects perspective of man interested in control

Step 3   Organizing Material

In preparing to write your first draft, you make preliminary decisions about how to sequence the material in the body of your essay. Is it a good idea to start with characterization and setting and end with point of view? Would a different sequence be more effective? The setting reveals the protagonist's interest in the remote and the characterization suggests his detachment and his desire to be in control. The style and tone of the story reinforce these characteristics. The significance of all of these aspects of the story becomes clearest when we examine the point of view.

When you are deciding how to sequence the middle paragraphs of your essay, the usual rule is to put them in an order of increasing importance so that you lead up to your most important material. For this reason, leading up to point of view makes sense.

Step 4 Sketching Introduction and Conclusion

Your draft introduction should do three things: identify your subject and the work(s) you are analyzing; set out the scope of your essay; state your thesis. Your draft conclusion should do two things: restate your thesis and sum up your main points.

Step 5 Writing the Draft

Here is the kind of draft you might write if you follow the procedures outlined above.

SAMPLE WRITING

COLONIALISM AND MASCULINITY IN "SPECIAL ENGLISH"

Colonialism and masculine attitudes are linked in Frederic Raphael's short story "Special English." The setting, characterization, style, and point of view reinforce this connection. Raphael shows that the masculine ideals of control and detachment that destroy a relationship between a man and a woman are, in fact, the same as the colonial attitudes responsible for the war in which this story is set.

"Special English" is set on a "remote island," possibly a Greek island as the allusion to Homer's "wine-dark sea" suggests. There is a brutal colonial war going on. The protagonist seems to be attracted to the remoteness of this island just as he is attracted to the woman who is also described as "remote." Perhaps he thinks of her as his colony. They are listening to radio stories about the atrocities in the colonial war, but they are in a colonial situation themselves.

The characterization lacks specific detail. The fact that the man brings his typewriter to a remote island might suggest that he is a writer. All we know about this woman is that she does not know English (one of the reasons he is attracted to her) and that she hopes he will love her more as her English improves. We are therefore surprised that as she understands more of the English in the broadcasts about the colonial war, he hates her more and more.

The language in "Special English" suggests someone who is well educated. The narrator uses formal words and phrases like "saline rail," "tempo," "distinct variations," "kindled," "enhanced," "eloquent." Most of the sentences are quite complex, with many subordinate clauses and qualifications, giving the impression of a thoughtful and controlled style. The most interesting metaphor in the story is that of the news broadcasts of the colonial war staining "the vocabulary of their understanding. . . with the world's blood" (386).

The characterization, setting, and style make more sense once you understand the point of view. The story seems to be told from an omniscient viewpoint that gives us access to the thoughts and feelings of both characters. We learn about the woman's pride in her accomplishments and then the man's surprising hatred. When we look more closely at the story, however, we can see that we are actually getting the man's point of view. He watches her and imagines what she is thinking and feeling. What we are getting is his version of her thoughts and feelings. His ideas about what she thinks and feels suggest that he liked her only when she was remote, when she belonged to him as a colony belongs to an imperial power. In that way he can be detached from her and in control. Raphael uses point of view to show the negative effects of traditionally masculine attitudes and values.

In "Special English" Frederic Raphael shows the similarities between the masculine attitudes that destroy a relationship between a man and a woman and the colonial attitudes reponsible for the war. The setting emphasizes the man's preference for what is remote and easily controlled. His actions reinforce these qualities as does the style. A close examination of the narrative perspective shows us that what seemed to be objective and neutral is actually the man's point of view. Initially he thinks of this woman as his "prize"; gradually she becomes hateful and threatening to him.

Working on Your Own Assignment

Your purpose when you write a first draft is to explore your ideas and to try out ways of working with your material.

- Make a draft outline of your essay. Start with your thesis and then list the most relevant categories of your analysis in the order that seems most appropriate.

- Use your outline as a guide for writing your first draft, but include new ideas as they occur to you.
- Focus on developing your middle paragraphs, rather than writing a polished introduction and conclusion.
- Try to write this draft in one sitting, without labouring over individual sentences.
- If you use a word processor, print out your draft before you begin revising.
- Keep all of your notes. You may need to add or check material as you revise.

EXERCISES

A.   Respond to each of the following questions in a sentence or two.

1. What decisions should you make before you write your first draft?
2. How can a draft outline help you to work out your thesis and your topic sentences?
3. What are the advantages of arranging the material in the body of your essay in an order of ascending interest?

B.   If outlining is new to you, then working out an outline for one of the essays listed below will help you to get a sense of how other writers organize their material. This is also excellent practice for summarizing. If you have trouble identifying the main points in a piece of writing, see Analyzing the Content of Nonfiction Writing in Chapter 3.

Put the writer's thesis first and include all the major points. Make sure you include all the important ideas in the essay. If possible, compare your outline with those of your classmates. Are there differences among your outlines? Are these differences mistakes? Or are there equally valid ways of outlining the same piece of writing?

- Laura Robinson's "Starving for the Gold"
- Robert S. Root-Bernstein's "Sensual Education"
- Scott Russell Sanders' "The Men We Carry in Our Minds"
- Charles Gordon's "Achieving Virtue Through Stinginess"

chapter 7

Revising Thesis and Essay Structure

Revision means literally re-vision, seeing again. The most important part of this "seeing again" is being able to look at your work as a reader. When you write a first draft, you are essentially writing it for yourself, to clarify your ideas and to try out your tentative plan for the essay. If you continue reading your work from this perspective, however, you may find it hard to see what changes are needed, because as the writer you know what you *mean* to say. The trick of revision is to maintain the writer's sense of intended meaning while adopting the reader's perspective to examine what you have actually said. In order to see your work from the reader's perspective, you will need to let your draft sit for a day or two before revising it.

Following a systematic method of revision will help you to look at your work objectively. Researchers into writing generally agree that the best method is to begin with the largest elements of the draft—its overall point and structure—and work down to the most detailed elements—the grammar and punctuation in individual sentences. Adopting this method means that you will not waste your time making small changes, only to find later that whole sections need to be revised. You are more likely to be willing to make substantial revisions if you can do so easily on a word processor rather than having to rewrite or retype. However, while writing on a word processor makes revision easy, it may also tempt you to make changes line by line. Print out a hard copy so that you have a better sense of the draft as a whole. You can also develop your revision skills by exchanging drafts with your classmates.

To illustrate this top-down process of revision, we show you in this chapter how to revise your thesis and essay structure. In Chapter 8 we will demonstrate how to revise middle paragraphs, introductions, and conclusions. You will find suggestions for final editing—checking word choice, sentence structure, grammar, and punctuation—in Part 2, Handbook for Final Editing.

Step 1   Making a Revision Outline

You can keep track of the changes you need to make by using a **revision outline**. A revision outline is an outline of the draft you have actually written, together with suggestions for changes. Using two columns, you note in the left column each point you make in your introduction, each of your middle paragraphs, and your conclusion. Record these points exactly as they stand in the draft, not as you intended them to be. As you go through the revision process, enter suggestions for changes in the right column. You will find an example of a revision outline in the sample topic below. Experiment with the revision outline to see if it is a useful tool for you.

Step 2 Revising the Thesis

If you have gone through the process of finding a thesis as set out in Chapter 5, you will likely have a good thesis. Some writers, however, prefer to write a draft as soon as they have gathered material, thinking through their material as they write. Other writers find that even though they have a fairly complete thesis statement when they begin a draft, their understanding of their subject develops in the process of writing. Whatever your preferred method, you will need to check your thesis.

Checking for Opinion and Support

A statement you think is a thesis can fail to be "an opinion with reasons." Or your tentative thesis may no longer fit what you have said in your draft. Check to be sure your thesis does not have any of the following problems.

Merely restating the assignment An essay assignment usually gives you a subject; your thesis is the opinion you develop about that subject. If your assignment is "Discuss Plato's concept of the state," then "This essay will discuss Plato's concept of the state" is a restatement of the assignment and not a valid thesis.

Merely stating facts Essays are written to support opinions, not to summarize information. "Chinua Achebe's *Things Fall Apart* has sold more than two million copies since it was published in 1958" cannot be a thesis; it is a statement of fact. On the other hand, the claim that "Chinua Achebe's *Things Fall Apart* is a male initiation novel because it emphasizes the process by which the young male protagonist works out his relation to clan values" is a valid thesis, since it presents an opinion and not a statement of fact.

Failing to give reasons A thesis without supporting reasons—such as "*Fanny and Alexander* is a depressing film," or "*Things Fall Apart* is a male initiation novel"—is likely to arouse readers' objections right at the beginning of your essay. Sometimes you may be able to include the reasons supporting your thesis in a simple one-sentence statement. For a complex subject, each reason may require a separate sentence in the introduction (or conclusion, for an inductive essay).

Failing to separate your thesis from theme/thesis of text or critics Occasionally you may have an essay assignment that asks you to determine the theme of a short story, or the main point of a particular psychological theory, since issues like these are matters of opinion, not fact. Usually, however, you will need to make a clear separation between your thesis and the overall point in any material you are examining. If you were analyzing the content of Maggie Helwig's essay "A Certain Hunger: The Body Language of Anorexia," for instance, you might decide that her thesis is something like "Eating disorders such as anorexia and bulimia are signs of spiritual emptiness in a materialistic society." But if you were evaluating her essay, you would not want to use Helwig's thesis as your thesis. Instead, you would say whether you agree or disagree with Helwig's opinion, and why.

Failing to signal essay structure   In deductively organized essays, the thesis often indicates the order of points. For instance, the thesis "The theme of failed initiation in 'Araby' is developed through symbols of earth, sexuality, and religion" sets up the expectation that the essay will make three main points, one about each symbol, in the order they are listed. An ordering of points such as this provides a useful guide to your reader. But in the process of drafting you may decide to add or drop points or to change their order. After you make a final decision about the order of middle paragraphs, you will need to check that your thesis matches.

Checking the Fit Between Thesis and Middle Paragraphs

You can, of course, have a good thesis, but one that does not accurately reflect what you have said in your draft. Check your revision outline to determine whether your thesis represents a valid generalization from the points you have made. If not, you may have wandered off topic (a problem you can adjust in the next stages of revision) or your points may suggest a better thesis. In the course of writing about symbolism in Joyce's "Araby," for instance, you might realize that the story has a political as well as a psychological and a religious dimension. This change in perspective would mean revising your thesis to take this new idea into account.

If you find any of these problems, make sure you revise your thesis before you go on, or you will not have a focus for the rest of the revision process.

Step 3   Revising Essay Structure

Once you have checked and, if necessary, revised your thesis, your next step is to assess the effectiveness of your paragraph divisions and paragraph order.

Checking Paragraph Divisions

In Chapter 1 we discussed the fact that, in essays, each paragraph constitutes or contributes to one specific point. The left-hand column of the revision outline, if you have made one, gives you a convenient way of seeing whether your paragraphs are focused on single points and whether these points support your thesis.

Your revision outline may reveal one or more of these problems with essay structure:

Failure to paragraph   In the process of writing you may get carried away by your ideas and simply move from one point to the next without starting new paragraphs. Remember that paragraph breaks are useful signals to your reader of the stages in your reasoning. Indicate on your draft and on your revision outline where each new point begins, and divide your material accordingly.

Paragraphs too long   You may find that your paragraph divisions correspond to the points outlined in your thesis but that your paragraphs are still uncomfortably long for a reader. Most paragraphs in academic essays are about one-half to three-fourths of a typed page. If one or more of your paragraphs is longer, you may be trying to cover too much at once. In discussing points of style, for example, you may find that you have taken two or three pages to talk about diction, sentence structure, and figurative language. Rather than trying to cover all these aspects in one paragraph, you could divide the material into three paragraphs.

Paragraphs too short   If you are someone who stops to think before writing each sentence, you may find that you also tend to start new paragraphs every sentence or two. Short paragraphs are common in newspapers but hard to follow in academic writing, where readers expect ideas to be fully developed and the connections among ideas to be clear. If you need to gather your sentences together into longer units, make notes to that effect on your draft and on your revision outline. If your paragraphs are short because you have not explained your points fully, see Chapter 8, Revising Individual Paragraphs.

Paragraphs contain unrelated points   A common problem with middle paragraphs is that the writer mentions two or three points but does not develop any one point fully. Note where you may need to make new paragraphs so that each one focuses on a single point.

Paragraphs not relevant to thesis   When you check your middle paragraphs against your revised thesis, you may decide to eliminate paragraphs because you have wandered away from your main points.

Sometimes paragraphs no longer support your thesis or you have better material to add. Note any changes you intend to make in the right-hand column of your revision outline.

Checking Paragraph Sequence and Transitions

You can also use your revision outline to determine whether you have followed the order you intended and whether that order still seems appropriate. Awkward transitions between paragraphs may be a problem of style (which is covered in Part 2, Handbook, Using Transitions to Connect Ideas), but they may also indicate that you need to rethink paragraph order. Enter the new order on your revision outline. For an example of how to use a revision outline, see the sample topic below.

Sample Topic: Colonialism in Frederic Raphael's "Special English"

In Chapter 6 we showed how you would draft a textual analysis essay on the treatment of colonialism in Frederic Raphael's "Special English." Here you will follow the process of revising thesis and essay structure in that draft.

Step 1 Making a Revision Outline

Outlining the draft and recording the changes you need to make will give you a systematic way of revision. You might outline the draft essay on "Special English" as follows.

THESIS: In "Special English" Frederic Raphael shows that the masculine ideals of control and detachment that destroy a relationship between a man and a woman are, in fact, the same as the colonial attitudes responsible for the war in which this story is set.

MIDDLE PARAGRAPH 1. Point: Story is set on a remote island while a colonial war is going on. Man seems to think that woman is his colony

MIDDLE PARAGRAPH 2. Point: Lacks specific details, but man sees woman as a "prize," not as an individual

MIDDLE PARAGRAPH 3. Point: Language is formal, complex, remote—just like the man. Their rela-

tionship is "stained" by the news of
the colonial war

MIDDLE PARAGRAPH 4. Point: POV is actually his; we see the
woman through his eyes. He hates
her when she is no longer his possession, his colony

Entering changes as you decide on them will give you a **revision
outline**.

Step 2   Revising the Thesis

Checking for opinion and support   Is the thesis an opinion with
reasons? The thesis for the draft essay says that Raphael establishes a
parallel in this story between masculine attitudes and colonial attitudes. This is clearly an interpretative opinion, not a fact about the
story, such as "This story was first published in 1979."

Although the thesis states the similarity between masculine and
colonial attitudes, it does not explain how both are destructive. A more
complete thesis would clarify the connection between the man's growing hatred of the woman and the hatred expressed in the colonial war
and might read something like this:

> Through setting, characterization, style, and point of view,
> Raphael establishes parallels between masculine attitudes
> and colonial attitudes. In a man's growing hatred of the
> woman he brings to a remote island, we see the hatred of the
> colonizer for the colonized.

Checking the fit between thesis and middle paragraphs   If you
look carefully at the outline of the draft, you will see that the points on
setting, characterization, style, and point of view are not clearly connected with the thesis. All the paragraphs should focus on the parallels
between masculine and colonial attitudes. You would revise each paragraph to make sure that it supports the thesis.

The paragraph on style, for example, makes several points about
language: that it is rather formal, controlled, and complex and that the
metaphor linking the news broadcasts with the couple's relationship is
interesting. Although these are valid points about the style of "Special
English," it's not yet clear how this analysis of the style supports the
thesis. The connections between the material in the other middle paragraphs and the thesis also need to be spelled out and all the paragraphs
need more evidence. Before you fill in these details, however, you need
to consider the structure of the essay as a whole.

Step 3   Revising Essay Structure

Checking paragraph divisions Each middle paragraph should discuss one aspect of your subject. Even if all your material is on a single aspect of the work you are analyzing, you may need to subdivide paragraphs longer than one-half to three-quarters of a page (typed, double spaced) or to combine short paragraphs. All the middle paragraphs in this draft focus on a single aspect of the story and are about the right length. They need to be developed more effectively, however (see Chapter 8).

Checking paragraph sequence As you can see, the order of setting, characterization, style, point of view works well because it leads up to point of view, the most important aspect of the story.

Step 4   Entering Changes on the Revision Outline

Having checked the paragraph order, you are now ready to enter the changes in essay structure onto your revision outline.

[From draft]	[Proposed revision]
MIDDLE PARAGRAPH 1: SETTING	
Point: remote island, colonial war, woman = colony	Point: setting introduces colonial issues
MIDDLE PARAGRAPH 2: CHARACTERIZATION	
Point: lacks specific details	Point: lack of details strengthens connection between masculine attitudes and colonialism
MIDDLE PARAGRAPH 3: STYLE	
Point: language is formal and complex, just like the man	Point: parallel between masculine and colonial attitudes reinforced by style
MIDDLE PARAGRAPH 4: POINT OF VIEW	
Point: we see the woman through his eyes	Point: colonizer–colonized relationship between man and woman is conveyed through POV

If you record changes at each stage of the revision process, you will end up with a good framework for improving your essay. For a detailed examination of the process of revising middle paragraphs, introductions, and conclusions, see Chapter 8.

Working on Your Own Assignment

When you revise, your focus shifts from writing for yourself, as you work out your ideas, to writing for your readers. You begin by checking for fundamental problems with your thesis and essay structure.

- Turn your draft outline into a revision outline by noting necessary changes in the right-hand column.
- Check your thesis.
  - Does your thesis state an opinion or idea and provide reasons to support it?
  - Do you need to revise your thesis because of new ideas that occurred to you as you wrote your draft?
- Check your paragraph divisions.
  - Do your paragraph divisions correspond to the major categories of your analysis?
  - Do you need to combine short paragraphs on a single point? Or to subdivide long paragraphs?
- Check your paragraph sequence.
  - Is your basic structure deductive, inductive, or a mixture? Is the structure appropriate for your subject and audience?
  - Are the paragraphs arranged in a logical sequence? Are they arranged in an order of ascending interest? Is the sequence appropriate for the subject and audience?
  - Have you used transitional devices to show how paragraphs are related?
- Practise your revision skills by exchanging drafts with your classmates.

EXERCISE

Decide whether each of the following is a valid thesis statement for an analysis essay and explain your decision.

1. Essay topic: Discuss the treatment of eating disorders in Laura Robinson's "Starving for the Gold."

   THESIS: Laura Robinson's "Starving for the Gold" is a discussion of eating disorders among female athletes.

2. Essay Topic: Explain how Swift uses irony as a persuasive strategy in "A Modest Proposal."

   THESIS: Economic conditions in Ireland in 1729, when Swift wrote "A Modest Proposal," were terrible.

3. Essay Topic: What does the elephant symbolize in George Orwell's essay "Shooting an Elephant"?

    THESIS: By examining the sequence of events, the use of descriptive details, and the tone of "Shooting an Elephant," we can see what the elephant symbolizes.

4. Essay Topic: How does Judith Fetterley develop her interpretation of Faulkner's story "A Rose for Emily"?

    THESIS: According to Fetterley, "A Rose for Emily" shows us that the definition of the "lady" is both grotesque and dehumanizing.

5. Essay topic: Analyze the theme of self-deception in Margaret Laurence's novel *The Stone Angel.*

    THESIS: Hagar's inability to understand either herself or others is a major theme in ***The Stone Angel***.

chapter 8

Revising Individual Paragraphs

When you have checked your thesis and essay structure, you are ready to consider changes to individual paragraphs. Do you give enough evidence to support your points? Have you provided enough context for your discussion? These are the kinds of questions we examine in this chapter. First we discuss the general principles of revising middle paragraphs, introductions, and conclusions. Then we show how you might make changes to individual paragraphs in the draft essay on the short story "Special English."

Step 1   Revising Middle Paragraphs

Checking Topic Sentences: Content

A topic sentence functions as a mini-thesis, controlling the content of the paragraph and showing how the paragraph relates to the thesis. Is there a sentence that announces the *subject* of each paragraph and makes a *point* about that subject? Does that point support some aspect of your thesis?

Imagine, for example, that you are writing an essay on the effects of alcoholism. A good topic sentence for the first middle paragraph might read something like this: "The physical effects of advanced alcoholism are well known, but many people are unaware of the early symptoms of physical dependency." This sentence works well as a topic sentence because it identifies the subject of the paragraph (physical effects) and makes a point about it (the invisibility of early physical symptoms). The subject is an aspect of the overall subject of the essay (effects of alcoholism) and the point helps support and develop the thesis (the lack of visibility of these effects).

Problems with content

No topic sentence   A topic sentence should be at a higher level of generality than other sentences in your paragraph. Occasionally you may discover a draft paragraph that is full of specific examples and other details but has no topic sentence explaining their significance.

Or you may find that two or more sentences make points without identifying the more general aspect of the subject to which they refer—for example, from the assignment on alcoholism, "Alcoholism may cause malnutrition" and "It may also cause cirrhosis of the liver." Both these sentences make points, but the points are at the same level of generality. There is no mention of their common subject, physical effects, to show how this paragraph develops the thesis.

No point made about the subject of the paragraph   Sometimes the first sentence of a paragraph may state its subject, as in "Another major factor in alcoholism is its psychological effects," without making a point. If you use a sentence like this as a transition, check to see that your paragraph also contains a topic sentence that makes a point.

Point not connected to thesis "The physical effects of alcoholism are obvious to anyone who cares to look." This point obviously contradicts the thesis; in other cases, you may simply need to make the relation between point and thesis clearer.

Checking Topic Sentences: Placement

Like essays, paragraphs can be organized either deductively or inductively. If your essay is organized deductively, your reader will expect your paragraphs to be organized deductively, with your topic sentence at or near the beginning of the paragraph (a transitional sentence may come first). If your essay is organized inductively, many of your paragraphs may be as well, with your topic sentence at or near the end of each paragraph.

Problems with placement You may have a good topic sentence, but it may be buried in the middle of the paragraph and need to be moved to the beginning or end. Or you may end paragraphs with the topic sentence for the next paragraph. This practice is confusing for readers and should be avoided.

"Umbrella" topic sentences Sometimes, as noted in Chapter 7, you may have more material on one aspect of your subject than you can comfortably fit into a single paragraph. If a paragraph has become too long (more than three-quarters of a page), you can often divide it and then use an "umbrella" topic sentence to tie related paragraphs together, as in the following example:

"Umbrella" topic sentence	Although some of the social effects of alcohol abuse are well known and highly publicized, such as the role of alcohol in family violence and in traffic accidents, other effects are less obvious.
Topic sentence for paragraph A	Alcohol has been shown to be a factor in X percent of incidents of family violence. [paragraph on alcoholism and family violence]
Topic sentence for paragraph B	The role of alcohol in traffic accidents, with their effect on the costs of insurance and health care, is also well established.
Topic sentence for paragraph C	Most people, however, are unaware that absenteeism is an early sign of alcoholism and that absenteeism has a significant effect on economic productivity.

Checking Supporting Details

To be convincing to your reader, the point in your topic sentence needs the support of specific details. In drafting your middle paragraphs, you are likely to use a variety of specific details from the material you have gathered: facts and figures (such as names, dates, statistics); examples (such as representative instances, case studies, hypothetical examples); and references to authorities. To support your point about the invisibility of early physical symptoms of alcoholism, for instance, you might refer to a statistical survey, to examples of unrecognized symptoms, to the statements of a medical expert, or to a combination of these sources.

Two problems to watch for as you are revising individual paragraphs are inadequate detail and misleading or irrelevant detail.

Inadequate detail   You may find that one of your paragraphs consists of a series of points with no examples or evidence to support any of them. For instance: "Alcoholism has many physical effects. Several of these are very serious. The alcoholic is often unaware of these effects. The general public is unaware of many of these effects too. The level of awareness concerning the physical effects of alcoholism is quite low."

Misleading or irrelevant detail   If you want to make a point about the effects of alcoholism but you give an example that illustrates its causes, your paragraph will obviously not be convincing. But you also need to check for more subtle problems with evidence, such as misleading statistics, unrepresentative examples, and misused authorities. You will find a discussion of these issues in Chapter 10, Gathering Material for Evaluation Essays.

Checking Explanations

A paragraph may be full of detail but still not work because the connection between the detail and the point it should support is not clear. This problem is particularly common in essays about literature, where the writer may think a simple quotation or reference to the text is enough to support a point. Take the following sentences: "Joy Kogawa's *Itsuka* is about overcoming both individual apathy and past injustice. By becoming involved, Naomi learns many things about herself and about the past." There is a missing connection here, the explanation of exactly what Naomi is involved in, and how this involvement relates to past injustice.

Step 2   Revising the Introduction

Your introduction gives your readers a chance to prepare, emotionally and intellectually, for the essay that is to follow. Readers expect to find out what your subject is, why you think it is important, and what you intend to say about it. Ensure a good first impression by revising your introduction carefully.

Checking Subject and Context

In the opening sentences of an essay, you identify your subject and provide the context for your thesis. Keep your introduction focused by limiting your subject to the one specified in your essay topic—not "the concept of heroism" in general, but the "female hero in Alice Walker's *Possessing the Secret of Joy* and Toni Morrison's *Sula*." For other textual analysis essays, your subject might make it appropriate to discuss the genre of the work or its social or historical setting. Make sure you mention the author and title of all works you will discuss. For essays in other academic disciplines, you might begin with factual information about historical events or the theoretical framework of a concept you plan to analyze. If you were writing on Freud's theories of sexuality, for instance, you might outline the current debate about the theories or give the historical situation within which they were developed.

Check your opening sentences for the following problems:

Pretentious and irrelevant claims If you begin an essay on blindness in *King Lear* by claiming that "Shakespeare is the greatest dramatist who ever lived," or that "*King Lear* is the greatest of all Shakespeare's plays," you are likely to disappoint rather than impress your readers. First, readers will have only a vague idea of your subject—is it great dramatists? great Shakespearean plays? Second, they are likely to find such statements pretentious, since claims like these imply that you have read all dramatists or all of Shakespeare's plays, a claim you probably don't intend to support.

It is far better to gear your opening statement to your specific subject. If you were writing on blindness in *King Lear*, for instance, you could provide a context for your thesis by discussing the critical controversy over the meaning of blindness in this play or the use of blindness as a metaphor in other literary works.

Too much detail Your statement of context provides a framework for your thesis (in deductively organized essays) or for the question you will explore (in inductively organized essays). It is not the place to explain your points fully or to give examples. If your discussion of context is longer than two or three sentences, you may need to omit some material or move it into the body of the essay.

Checking Thesis

If you organize your essay deductively, the common practice for academic essays, end your introduction with your thesis. There are two reasons for ending with your thesis. First, beginning with your thesis, before you have established a context for it, may encourage your readers to think of objections. Second, putting your thesis at the end will help both you and your readers to focus on your main idea.

In the first draft, you may have introduced your thesis with statements such as "In this essay I will discuss..." or "My purpose in this paper is to compare...." Statements such as these can help you get started, but you can omit them when you revise.

A more polished way of setting out the purpose and scope of your essay is by stating the reasons for your opinion, or the aspects of your subject that you will cover, in the order you will discuss them. You might end the introduction to an essay on alcoholism, for example, with this thesis: "The physical, psychological, and social effects of alcoholism all share a single feature: their invisibility in the early stages of the disease." Your opinion here is that the early effects of alcoholism are often invisible; by naming the aspects of the subject you plan to discuss—physical effects, psychological effects, and social effects—you define the scope of your essay and provide a guide to its structure.

Make sure that the order of points in your introduction corresponds to the order of points in your middle paragraphs.

Step 3   Revising the Conclusion

The conclusion is an opportunity for both you and your reader to step back from the specific points you have made to consider their larger significance. Here are some suggestions on how to revise your conclusion to achieve this purpose.

Checking for Restatement of Thesis

If you have developed your points fully in your middle paragraphs, your conclusion should confirm your thesis by clarifying or extending it in some way. For example, if you have argued that blindness in *King Lear* is linked to egotism and lack of spiritual vision, and your middle paragraphs have shown how this link is made in characterization, setting, and action, you can draw all these strands together in the restatement of your thesis.

Look for the following problems when you revise conclusions:

Pretentious and irrelevant claims Vague claims and sweeping generalizations are as inappropriate in conclusions as they are in introductions. Often writers are led to vague and pretentious conclusions because something has gone wrong with the middle of the essay. If, for instance, your essay analyzing a Wordsworth sonnet ends with a statement such as "Wordsworth is the most interesting Romantic poet I have read," check whether you have actually made connected points about the sonnet in your middle paragraphs.

Mechanical repetition of thesis Repeating your thesis exactly sounds mechanical and suggests that your middle paragraphs have not contributed much to the essay. The minimal solution to this problem is to use synonyms for key words and to change the structure of your original thesis statement. A better solution is to incorporate the main points of your middle paragraphs into your restatement of thesis. Thus, for example, in the essay on the effects of alcoholism referred to earlier, your restatement and extension of thesis might read: "The partial invisibility of the physical, psychological, and social effects of alcoholism seems due to deliberate self-deception, both by the alcoholic and by the public." The thesis statement noted the partial invisibility of the effects of alcoholism; this sentence adds a statement of cause (deliberate self-deception) that emerged from the middle paragraphs.

Checking for Statement of Wider Implications

Concluding with a statement about the wider implications of your essay gives you a chance to emphasize the significance of your subject. A statement of wider implications often involves a shift in perspective or frame of reference, as though a camera had moved from close-ups to a panning shot. Here are some possibilities:

- Move from the specific case you have discussed to the general category to which it belongs. It would seem valid, for example, to conclude an essay analyzing a Wordsworth sonnet with a statement about the possible implications for other Wordsworth sonnets, possibly for the Romantic sonnet in general, or just for the sonnet form. It would not seem valid to make sweeping generalizations about Wordsworth's stature as a poet or the value of Romantic poetry.

- Move from immediate causes and effects to more distant causes or long-term effects. You might end an essay on the effects of drought and depression on prairie farmers with a sentence like this: "Together, drought and depression taught prairie farmers two lessons they have never forgotten: to conserve their land and to distrust the economic policies of the federal government."

- Briefly compare your subject with one more familiar to your readers. To conclude an essay analyzing the economic boom of

1979 to 1980, for example, you might suggest the similarity between this period and the "gold fever" of 1849.

- Return to the broader context you established in your introduction. If you introduced your essay on blindness in *King Lear* by commenting on blindness in other literary works, for example, you might remind your readers of the metaphorical meanings of blindness in these works.

Sample Topic: Colonialism in Frederic Raphael's "Special English"

Step 1   Revising Middle Paragraphs

If you reread the draft essay on "Special English" (see Chapter 6, pp. 69–70), you will see that all the middle paragraphs exhibit similar problems with topic sentences, detail, and explanation. You would note on your revision outline the specific changes to make in each paragraph. We have chosen the paragraph on style as our example of how to revise middle paragraphs. Here is the draft paragraph:

> The language in "Special English" suggests someone who is well educated. The narrator uses formal words and phrases like "saline rail," "tempo," "distinct variations," "kindled," "enhanced," "eloquent." Most of the sentences are quite complex, with many subordinate clauses and qualifications, giving the impression of a thoughtful and controlled style. The most interesting metaphor in the story is that of the news broadcasts of the colonial war staining "the vocabulary of their understanding . . . with the world's blood" (70).

Checking topic sentences   As you have seen, a good topic sentence should state the main idea in the paragraph and show how the material in it supports the thesis. The topic sentence for this paragraph should therefore link style with the masculine desire to control both women and colonies. It could also usefully include a transition to link this analysis of style with the previous paragraph. A revised topic sentence might look something like this:

> The parallel between masculine attitudes and colonial attitudes is further developed by the diction and imagery of "Special English."

Checking supporting details The examples of diction support the idea that the style of the story is formal and controlled. The same point is made about sentence structure, but there are no examples to support it. More significantly, there are no examples that link the man's desire for control to masculine and colonial attitudes. The best support for this connection is the metaphor *prize* in the second sentence: "He took her, his prize, to a remote island...." A prize is something won in a competition; it is also something seized or captured in war. The word "prize" thus suggests a parallel between women and colonies as possessions controlled by English-speaking men.

Checking explanations The draft paragraph says that the metaphor comparing the news of the colonial wars to blood is the most interesting stylistic element in the story, but fails to explain why it is interesting. If you were revising this paragraph, you would need to explain this point.

With a revised topic sentence, additional details, and rewritten explanations, the paragraph on style might look like this:

SAMPLE WRITING

The parallel between masculine and colonial attitudes established by the setting and characterization in "Special English" is developed by its diction and imagery. The formal words and phrases—"saline rail," "tempo," "distinct variations," "enhanced" and "eloquent"—are reinforced by the vocabulary of teaching and learning in phrases like "instructively simple," "the vocabulary of their understanding," "her newly educated vanity," and "special English." This intellectual, detached diction pretends to be objective and inclusive: to present the woman's perceptions as well as the man's. We gradually see, however, that the man's language is that of the colonizer who assumes that his perception of reality fits both of them and that she exists to meet his needs. She is his "prize" but as remote from him as the island where he has taken her. Finally, the metaphor of the colonial war "staining the vocabulary of their understanding...with the world's blood" (386) merges the colonial war and the male–female relationship.

Step 2 Revising the Introduction

Here is the draft introduction with the revised thesis:

SAMPLE WRITING

Colonialism and masculine attitudes are linked in Frederic Raphael's short story "Special English." The setting, characterization, style, and point of view reinforce this connection. Raphael shows that the masculine ideals of control and detachment that destroy a relationship between a man and a woman are, in fact, the colonial attitudes responsible for the war in which this story is set. In a man's growing hatred of the woman he brings to a remote island, we see the hatred of the colonizer for the colonized.

Checking subject and context   The first sentence of this introduction announces that Raphael links masculine attitudes and colonialism, a point that is then repeated in the next three sentences. A stronger introduction would eliminate this repetition and give readers a better orientation to Raphael's story by noting that Raphael explores the parallels between traditional masculine attitudes and colonial attitudes in order to show how destructive both are.

A revised introduction might look like this:

SAMPLE WRITING

Frederic Raphael's "Special English" is a very short short story that appears to be about male–female relationships. We fail to grasp the significance of the story, however, unless we also recognize it as a critique of colonialism. Through setting, characterization, style, and point of view, Raphael establishes parallels between masculine attitudes and colonial attitudes. In a man's growing hatred of the woman he brings to a remote island, we see the hatred of the colonizer for the colonized: hatred that erupts in a brutal colonial war.

Step 3   Revising the Conclusion

Here is the draft conclusion:

SAMPLE WRITING

In "Special English" Frederic Raphael shows the similarities between the masculine attitudes that destroy a relationship between a man and a woman and the colonial attitudes responsible for the war. The setting emphasizes the man's preference for what is remote and easily controlled. His actions reinforce these qualities as does the style. A close examination of the narrative perspective shows us that what seemed neutral and objective is actually the man's point of view. His ideas about what the woman thinks and feels are flattering but also hateful and threatening to him.

Checking for restatement of thesis If, as often happens, you have changed your thesis during the process of revising your introduction and middle paragraphs, you need to make sure that your conclusion fits with these changes. Because the thesis now links masculine attitudes and colonial attitudes, the restatement of the thesis in the conclusion must reflect this important change.

Checking for summary of major points It's a good idea to sum up your main points at the end of your essay. The draft conclusion tries to do this, but the points about setting, characterization, style, and point of view are not clearly connected to the similarities between colonial and masculine attitudes. These points therefore need to be revised so they are more clearly connected with the revised thesis.

Checking for statement of wider implications There is no statement of wider implications in the draft conclusion. You could establish a wider context, however, by raising some questions about Raphael's choice of point of view. Why does the point of view seem omniscient at first, as though an impartial narrator were revealing the truth about both characters? Why is it hard to see that the story is presented from the man's point of view and that the style of the story is actually a distinctively masculine style? A possible answer to these questions is that both the masculine and the colonial point of view claim to be objective, so it is harder for readers to see the biases involved. By raising this issue, you could suggest wider implications for the parallels between colonialism and masculinity that Raphael explores in this story.

If you revised your conclusion to include these changes, you might come up with a paragraph like this:

SAMPLE WRITING

The parallels between masculine and colonial attitudes are developed gradually in "Special English." Although the setting and characterization establish the concern with colonialism quite explicitly, Raphael makes the most interesting connections between colonialism and masculinity through the style and the point of view. Both attitudes present a dominating masculine world view; both are destructive. An analysis of "Special English" suggests that both masculinity and colonialism present a view of the world that seems objective: it takes careful reading to detect the biases behind this objectivity. To question these seemingly objective attitudes towards women and those who are colonized may be the most important lesson we learn from "Special English."

In showing you how to revise this draft, we have focused on the larger elements of the essay: thesis, essay structure, and the content of individual paragraphs. When you have revised these elements of your draft, you are ready for final editing. For information on how to eliminate common errors in grammar, sentence structure, punctuation, and spelling, see Part 2, Handbook. This part of the text also contains tips for using quotations more effectively and information on essay format (margins, title pages, and such), quotation format, and the format of in-text citations and bibliographical entries.

Working on Your Own Assignment

In revising individual paragraphs, you focus on providing readers with a context for your essay, good explanations and details to support your points, and a clear relationship between your thesis and topic sentences.

- Use your revision outline to record necessary changes.
- Check middle paragraphs for
  - *Topic sentence*: What point are you making in each paragraph? How does the material in the paragraph support your thesis? Make sure your topic sentence answers both questions.
  - *Supporting detail*: Have you included sufficient evidence (examples, quotations, facts, statistics) to support your point?
  - *Explanations*: Have you explained how your evidence supports your point?
- Reread your introduction.
  - Is it focused on your essay topic?
  - Does it provide a context that prepares your reader for your thesis?
  - Should you eliminate any claims that now seem pretentious or irrelevant?
  - Does your thesis still fit the body of the essay?
- Reread your conclusion.
  - Does your conclusion reinforce your thesis (without mechanically repeating it)?
  - Does it remind your reader of your main points (without mechanically summarizing them)?
  - Does it suggest the broader implications of your thesis?

— Do you need to remove vague claims and sweeping general-izations? Have you introduced new ideas that seem to belong in the body of the essay?

- Practise your revision skills by exchanging drafts with your classmates.

EXERCISES

A. Decide whether each of the following is an effective topic sentence.

1. Within the next ten years, poachers may have slaughtered nearly all Indian tigers.

2. Southern plantation owners built houses like Greek temples because they wished to proclaim their connections with Classical civilizations.

3. NATO now includes a number of eastern European countries.

4. Here are some simple techniques to demonstrate to your dog that you are in charge.

5. Margaret Laurence uses setting effectively in her story "The Loons."

B. Read the paragraph below; then answer the questions that follow.

In tough economic times, provincial governments are likely to want more control over tax–supported colleges and universities. Each government might allocate money directly to faculties producing graduates with employment skills in current demand and give less money to faculties with low employment opportunities. Students would know they had a job in their field when they graduated and could thus make plans for the future with more confidence. They wouldn't graduate thousands of dollars in debt and with no immediate prospect of a job. Tuition could be waived for students taking government-approved courses. By the use of financial pressure, the government could insist on more practical content in courses. Less emphasis on research and theoretical knowledge could result in fewer ideas being generated. Government-controlled colleges and universities would be less willing to criticize government policies. There would be fewer unemployed and underemployed graduates.

1. What is the overall point of this paragraph? Write a topic sentence that states this main point.

2. What are the main subpoints? Are they presented in an effective sequence?

3. Is there enough evidence to support these subpoints? What other sorts of evidence are needed?

4. Are connections between details and points sufficiently explained? What transitions would be helpful?

C.   Revise the above paragraph. You may need to expand it into two paragraphs. If so, use an umbrella topic sentence to cover both paragraphs.

D.   If you drafted a paragraph analyzing "Love Lessons" or one of the essays in Part 3, Readings (see Exercises in Chapter 4), make a revision outline for the paragraph and then revise it. Or trade paragraphs with a classmate, make suggestions for changes, and then revise your own draft.

E.   Suppose that you have been asked to write an essay analyzing the theme of Robert Frost's poem "Stopping by Woods on a Snowy Evening." Here is the poem.

PUBLISHED WRITING

STOPPING BY WOODS ON A SNOWY EVENING

Whose woods these are I think I know.
His house is in the village though;
He will not see me stopping here
To watch his woods fill up with snow.

My little horse must think it queer
To stop without a farmhouse near
Between the woods and frozen lake
The darkest evening of the year.

He gives his harness bells a shake
To ask if there is some mistake.
The only other sound's the sweep
Of easy wind and downy flake.

The woods are lovely, dark and deep;
But I have promises to keep,
And miles to go before I sleep,
And miles to go before I sleep.

I. Cross out all the irrelevant statements in the following introduction to an essay analyzing the theme of this poem. You will be left with three sentences that (1) establish an appropriate context for an analysis of the poem; (2) outline the principal areas the essay will cover; (3) state the thesis of the essay. Label these three sentences. HINT: Pick out the thesis first. Then look for key words from the thesis in the sentences that lead up to it. This strategy will help you eliminate sentences that are either too general or too specific.

INTRODUCTION

Robert Frost is a very famous American poet. This poem has been quoted on many American state occasions, such as presidential inaugural addresses. People like this poem because, like all poetry, it is simultaneously auditory and visual. In many of his poems, Robert Frost wrote about the beauty of the pastoral New England landscape, but his poems are not just a simple celebration of nature. Life is often presented symbolically as a journey, just as Frost presents it in this poem. Through the imagery, rhythm, sound patterns, and structure of "Stopping by Woods on a Snowy Evening," Frost presents a human dilemma most readers can identify with. In the second stanza, Frost contrasts the speaker's desire to stop with the horse's surprise. The result is a deceptively simple pastoral lyric in which Frost presents the tension between meeting obligations and longing for a respite from them. With poems as good as this one, it's no wonder that Frost won four Pulitzer Prizes.

2. Cross out all the irrelevant statements in the following conclusion to an essay analyzing the theme of "Stopping by Woods on a Snowy Evening." You will be left with three sentences that (1) restate the thesis; (2) summarize the main points of the essay; (3) suggest the wider implications of the essay. Label these sentences.

CONCLUSION

Like all good nature poets, Frost conveys his enjoyment of the landscape he describes very powerfully. It's obvious, however, that Frost never experienced a Canadian winter, where yielding to the desire for a rest might lead to that all-too-common Canadian experience: death in the snow. As we have seen, "Stopping by Woods on a Snowy Evening" deals with that common human desire to rest both the body and the spirit before tackling responsibilities once again. Other poets we studied this term also deal with universal themes, but their poetry is much harder to understand than Frost's. Our analysis of the technical features of this poem—the hypnotically regular rhythm, the soothing sound patterns, the images of the silent, frozen landscape, and the overt clash of desires in the last stanza—confirms that Frost's apparently simple celebration of the New England landscape is really a subtle exploration of the human condition. In the last stanza, especially, we feel the pull of the darkness and the woods through the alliteration of *dark* and *deep*. "Stopping by Woods on a Snowy Evening" is thus a good example of Frost's ability to reach a wide audience through poetry that never parades its technical and moral sophistication. "Stopping by Woods on a Snowy Evening" is a great poem and I enjoyed reading it very much.

chapter 9

Writing Comparison Essays

A special type of analysis essay you may be asked to write in many college and university courses is the comparison essay. You may be asked, for example, to compare two poems, two models of moral development, social organization in two tribal societies, or two accounts of the same historical event. Whatever your subject, the purposes of comparison remain the same: to help you and your reader better understand both the things you are comparing and the more general concept that is the basis for the comparison. Let us look at these two purposes.

Comparison is a process basic to thinking. We continually try to understand things by seeing how they are similar to and different from other things. Let's take wealth as our **basis of comparison**, that is, the common element in terms of which we will compare something. Is someone with an income of thirty thousand dollars a year a wealthy person? Our answer would vary depending on whom we compared this person to. We might consider the person wealthy compared to someone whose income was five thousand dollars, but not wealthy compared to someone whose income was eighty thousand. Without comparison, the term wealth is virtually meaningless.

But our understanding of the concept of wealth will remain fairly superficial unless we take the comparison further. As we work through the similarities and differences between the situations of people with different incomes, we are forced to think not only about those specific instances, but also, and perhaps more significantly, about our own ideas of what constitutes wealth. What standard of living does each person have? How many people does the income support? How much of the income is disposable income—that is, money that does not have to be spent on necessities such as food, clothing, and housing? For instance, a teenager living at home and earning five thousand dollars working part-time may have more disposable income than a single parent earning thirty thousand. Does that make the teenager a wealthier person? Writing an analysis essay comparing the economic positions of the teenager and the single parent would thus help us understand both the concept of wealth and the specific things we were comparing.

This chapter emphasizes the most problematic aspects of making comparisons: choosing a basis of comparison, arriving at a thesis, and organizing your material. To illustrate the stages in writing and revising comparison essays, we focus on a sample topic, a comparison of two historical accounts of a U.S. cavalry attack on a Cheyenne village.

Stage 1 Clarifying Comparison Topics

Step 1 Checking for a Basis of Comparison

Check to see whether your topic gives the basis upon which you are to compare things. Can you put the topic in the form "Compare X and Y in terms of Z"? If so, the topic gives the basis of comparison, Z.

> On the basis of material in your textbook, compare the social organization of the !Kung San and the Mutayr. (Social organization is the basis of comparison.)

> Compare the use of setting [basis of comparison] in James Joyce's "Araby" and John Steinbeck's "The Chrysanthemums."

Other assignments do not indicate a basis of comparison.

> Compare Wilfred Owen's poems "Anthem for Doomed Youth" and "Dulce et Decorum Est."

> Compare Piaget's and Vygotsky's theories of child development.

If your topic does not specify a basis of comparison, you will need to decide upon one before you begin gathering material (see below).

Step 2 Looking for Similarities and Differences

Remember that "compare" always means "compare and contrast." Look for both similarities and differences in the things you are comparing.

Stage 2 Gathering and Categorizing Material

Step 1 Deciding on a Basis of Comparison

A basis of comparison provides a focus for your essay and so indicates what material is relevant and what is not. For example, if you tried to compare every aspect of two very different tribal societies, such as the !Kung San and Mutayr, you would have to write a book rather than an essay. Using social organization of the two societies as a basis of comparison, in contrast, would limit the scope of your essay.

In addition to providing a focus for your essay, your basis of comparison will often help you decide which categories will be most useful to you as you gather material. If you were writing on social organization in the !Kung San and Mutayr tribes, then your categories would all be aspects of social organization, such as family structure, work organization, and political structure. Language would not be a relevant category. If you were comparing setting in two short stories, you would focus on questions about the settings, but also consider how the element of setting relates to other categories of textual analysis: Do changes of setting serve a structural purpose, as in the movement from country to city? What elements of style are noticeable in the depiction of setting? Are settings a reflection of the characters that inhabit them?

If your essay assignment does not specify a basis of comparison, gather material in the categories that seem most appropriate to the assignment and then see what basis of comparison will best illuminate the similarities and differences between your subjects. For example, to compare Wilfred Owen's poems "Anthem for Doomed Youth" and "Dulce et Decorum Est," you would first gather material using the categories for poetry analysis (see Part 4, Resources for Writing). Your analysis might reveal similarities and differences in style, tone, and point of view that you could best explain by showing how these elements convey similar themes about the futility of war. You would thus make theme your basis of comparison. If you need to practise finding a workable basis of comparison, see Exercise A at the end of this chapter.

Step 2 Gathering Equivalent Material in Matching Categories

The second concern in gathering material is that your categories *match* and that they contain roughly equivalent amounts of material. If you are comparing an electric car with a gasoline-powered one, for example, and you have information on the durability and environmental impact of one, and the speed and carrying capacity of the other, you have two analyses, but no comparison. You would need to find equivalent information for both types of cars.

Similarly, if you have a great deal of information about a particular aspect of one subject but very little about the other, you must decide whether to drop the material, to find more material, or to explain the imbalance. Let's suppose, for instance, that in comparing the style of E. M. Forster's essay "My Wood" with the style of W. S. Merwin's essay "Unchopping a Tree," you discover that Forster uses many allusions, Merwin almost none. Do you decide not to discuss Forster's allusions? Comb Merwin's piece for the remotest echoes of other writers? In this case, your best bet would be to try to explain the imbalance. What purpose do the allusions serve in Forster's essay? Does Merwin achieve the same purpose (such as giving his position moral authority) by other means?

Stage 3   Formulating a Comparison Thesis

Step 1   Forming an Opinion about Each Set of Material

You arrive at a comparison thesis in much the same way that you arrive at a thesis for other analysis essays. But since you gather material in two sets of categories, there is an additional step involved. First you see what point the material in each set of categories makes about the basis of comparison. Suppose, for instance, that you are comparing the concept of heroism (basis of comparison) in novels by Ernest Hemingway and Saul Bellow. What does your material say about Hemingway's concept of heroism? What does your matching material say about Bellow's concept of heroism?

Step 2   Forming an Opinion about Overall Similarities and Differences

Next you make an overall point about the relationship between the two: Are they similar or different? What generalization can you make about the similarities and/or differences? From Hemingway's emphasis on well-performed action and ritual, you might conclude that heroism in his novels consists of courageous and knowledgeable physical action. In contrast, Bellow's emphasis on thinking heroes suggests a concept of heroism as courageous self-knowledge.

Step 3   Supporting Your Opinion about Similarities and Differences

Just as you use matching categories for gathering material about the things you are comparing, so you support your opinion by giving reasons drawn from matching categories. You might support your thesis about the novels of Hemingway and Bellow, for example, by stating that differences in plot, characterization, and style reflect differences in the authors' concept of heroism.

Similarly, if you were comparing the !Kung San and Mutayr tribes, you might decide that you could best explain their differences in social organization by the differences in their environments. Your thesis might be something like this:

> Social organization [the basis of comparison] among the
> !Kung San is flexible and egalitarian [opinion derived from
> material] because of the easy availability of the means of
> subsistence in their environment [supporting reason],
> whereas social organization among the Mutayr is rigid and
> hierarchical because of the difficulty of surviving in a harsh
> environment.

Stage 4 Drafting

Steps 1 and 2 Selecting Material and Making Points

Usually the categories of material you found relevant in working out
your thesis will become the basis for your middle paragraphs, just as in
other analysis essays. There are two points you need to keep in mind,
however. First, because you have matching categories of material for
two or more subjects, you may need to limit the number of categories
you use. If, for instance, you were comparing two poems, one a sonnet
and one not, you would likely drop the category of structure, since
there would not be much point in "proving" the obvious differences between the two.

Second, you should have roughly equivalent amounts of material
for each of the things you are comparing.

It is especially important to note on your draft outline the point
you intend to make about each category you use. Otherwise you may
find yourself merely repeating that the things you are comparing are
similar or different.

Step 3 Organizing Comparisons

Probably the most common problem in writing comparison essays is
finding an effective method of organization. There are two basic methods of organizing comparisons: the block method and the point-by-
point method.

Block method When you use the *block method*, you say everything
you have to say about one subject before you discuss the other. This
method can be effective for very short essays in which overall similarities and differences are more important than detailed comparisons (as
you might find, for instance, in a personal essay comparing good teachers and bad teachers). The block method is also useful for in-class essays and essay exams when you are developing a few main points
without extensive quotations or facts and figures as evidence.

Point-by-point method When you use the *point-by-point method*, you compare things one aspect at a time. In an essay comparing social organization in the !Kung San and Mutayr tribes, for instance, you might discuss family structure in both tribes, then work organization in both tribes, and then political structure. The point-by-point method is usually better for essays over 500 words and for detailed comparisons because you can explain the significance of similarities and differences as you go along. You don't risk leaving them unexplained or having to add another section to explain them.

Sample Topic: Comparing Two Historical Accounts

Textual analysis extends beyond literature classes, so let's assume that in your history class you have been discussing the fact that historians are interpreters, not merely recorders, of events. To emphasize this point, your instructor has asked you to write a 750-word essay on this topic:

> Compare the accounts reprinted below of the clash between the U.S. Cavalry and the Northern Cheyenne at Dull Knife's village in 1876.

Stage 1 Clarifying Comparison Topics

The assignment does not specify a basis of comparison. It does, however, provide you with your material: the two accounts of the same historical incident. Since the accounts cover the "same" event, you would focus on differences between them.

Here is Ernest Wallace's version of the incident.

PUBLISHED WRITING

With the reservation quiet, General George Crook, commanding the Department of the Platte, placed Mackenzie in command of a winter campaign, known as the Powder River Expedition, against a large band of Northern Cheyennes under Chief Dull Knife, who had fled the Red Cloud Agency in time to participate in the slaughter of Custer's troops. In a blinding snowstorm on November 14, Mackenzie with 1,552 men, 6 surgeons, almost 400 Indian scouts, and 168 supply wagons rode out of Fort Fetterman on the upper North Platte for the Powder River, one hundred miles to the north. Eight days later scouts located Dull Knife's camp on the Red Fork of the Powder River. Packing rations for ten days and taking 363 Indian scouts and 818 troops, including his tough and reliable 4th Cavalry,

Mackenzie in subzero temperature marched for the village. When he attacked soon after daylight on the 25th, the surprised warriors rushed to a sheltered spot surrounded by an open stretch of level prairie. After Dull Knife refused to surrender, Mackenzie ordered his men to burn the village, with its 173 lodges, huge quantities of hides and robes, and "tons" of buffalo meat, and then with Cheyenne bullets flying all around him led the dangerous assault against the Indian stronghold. One officer, at least, concluded that Mackenzie deserved the star of a brigadier general for the courage and skill he demonstrated on that day. The band escaped, but in the fight it lost twenty-five known dead and about five hundred ponies, while Mackenzie in turn lost one officer and five enlisted men killed, twenty-six men wounded, and fifteen cavalry horses killed. General Crook reported that he could not commend too highly Mackenzie's "brilliant achievements"; his victory would be a terrible blow to the hostiles. (172–173)*

---

*Reprinted by permission of Texas A & M University Press. Wallace, Ernest. *Ranald S. Mackenzie on the Texas Frontier* (1964), pp. 172–173.

The second description is from *Bury My Heart at Wounded Knee: An Indian History of the American West* by Dee Brown.

PUBLISHED WRITING

The soldiers were looking for Crazy Horse, but they found a Cheyenne village first, Dull Knife's village. Most of these Cheyennes had not been in the Little Bighorn battle, but had slipped away from Red Cloud agency in search of food after the Army took possession there and stopped their rations. General Crook sent Three Fingers Mackenzie against this village of 150 lodges.

It was in the Deer Rutting Moon, and very cold, with deep snow in the shaded places and ice-crusted snow in the open places. Mackenzie brought his troopers up to attacking positions during the night, and struck the Cheyennes at first daylight. The Pawnee mercenaries went in first, charging on fast ponies Mackenzie had taken from the reservation Sioux. They caught the Cheyennes in their lodges, killing many of them as they came awake. Others ran out naked into the biting cold, the warriors trying to fight off the Pawnees and the onrushing soldiers long enough for their women and children to escape.

Some of the best warriors of the Northern Cheyennes sacrificed their lives in those first furious moments of fighting; one of them was Dull Knife's oldest son. Dull Knife and Little Wolf finally managed to form a rear guard along the upper ledges of a canyon, but their scanty supply of ammunition was soon exhausted. Little Wolf was shot seven times before he and Dull Knife broke away to join their women and children in full flight toward the Bighorns. Behind them Mackenzie was burning their lodges, and after that was done he herded their captured ponies against the canyon wall and ordered his men to shoot them down, just as he had done to the ponies of the Comanches and Kiowas in Palo Duro Canyon. (290–291)*

---

*From *Bury my Heart at Wounded Knee: An Indian History of the American West* by Dee Brown. Copyright 1970 by Dee Brown. Reprinted by permission of Henry Holt and Company, Inc.

Stage 2 Gathering and Categorizing Material

Step 1 Deciding on a basis of comparison

Since the point of the assignment is to demonstrate that history is not an objective record of events but someone's interpretation of those events, you would likely use as your basis of comparison the attitude the two historians display towards their subject.

Step 2 Gathering equivalent material in matching categories

You would make notes about each account, using the categories for textual analysis set out in Chapter 4. Then, because this is a comparison essay, you would put your categories together in matching pairs, making sure that you have roughly equivalent material for each account, as in this chart.

	WALLACE	BROWN
Subject	The battle at Dull Knife's village, 1876	Same
Structure	Begins with a long section on preparations for battle. Ends with commendation of Mackenzie.	Fewer preliminaries. More focus on the battle. Ends with Mackenzie killing the ponies.
Development	Precise details of numbers and quantities: 1,552 men, 6 surgeons, etc.	Few precise details; more evocative, sensory descriptions of "biting cold," "furious moments" experienced by Indians.
Style	Vocabulary is that of a military expert: "the hostiles"; Mackenzie's "brilliant achievement." Long detailed sentences.	Vocabulary is Indian: "Deer Rutting Moon," "Three Fingers Mackenzie." Sentences emphasize action.
Tone	Mackenzie presented as leading a dangerous assault	Mackenzie presented as finding the village by accident, attacking with

	against well-armed Cheyenne, taking just revenge for the slaughter of Custer's troops.	unfair surprise, taking brutal retribution; brave warriors "sacrificed their lives."
Thesis	The battle consisted of a well-planned, justified, and successful attack.	The battle consisted of a brutal, unheroic attack upon less well-equipped and defenceless Indians.

Stage 3   Formulating a Comparison Thesis

The material in your matching categories clearly indicates a difference in attitude: Wallace takes a favourable view of Mackenzie and is unsympathetic to the Cheyennes, whereas Brown's attitude is just the opposite. This statement can serve as the opinion part of your thesis. To support this opinion, you could give the elements of the accounts that convey these attitudes. You would then have a thesis statement something like this:

> If we compare the structure, development, and style of these accounts, it becomes clear that Wallace's account conveys a favourable attitude towards Mackenzie and an unfavourable attitude towards the Cheyenne, whereas Brown's account conveys the opposite.

Stage 4   Drafting

Steps 1 and 2   Selecting material and making points
The thesis suggests that the categories of structure, development, and style are most relevant to a comparison of these two accounts. Here are the points you might make about the similarities and differences in these elements:

Structure	Wallace's structure emphasizes justice of cavalry attack.
	Brown's structure emphasizes injustices suffered by the Cheyenne.
Development	Wallace's detail reflects military precision.
	Brown's detail reflects Indians' experience.
Style	Wallace's style emphasizes precise factual information and military vocabulary.
	Brown's style emphasizes action and Indians' sense-oriented vocabulary.

[handwritten annotations: "discription", "Emotion", "observess experience", "participants"]

Step 3   Organizing comparisons
If you were comparing the Wallace–Brown accounts on an exam, you might use the block method of organization. For an essay, however, you would use the point-by-point method so that you could more clearly show specific differences in structure, development, and style.

Stage 5 Revising Thesis and Essay Structure

Step 1 Revising the Thesis

A comparison thesis should do two things. First, it should make a point about the basis of comparison. This point should account for the major similarities or differences in the things you are comparing. Second, it should give reasons to support your point. Check to see whether your thesis fulfills both of these requirements.

The thesis for the Wallace–Brown comparison (see above) still seems valid since it makes a point about a main difference between the two accounts. This main difference, the writers' attitudes to the participants, is a clear basis of comparison.

The following theses would need to be revised:

- Wallace's account of the Powder River Expedition is quite different from Brown's. (mentions both things being compared, but does not make a point or indicate a basis of comparison)

- Wallace and Brown write about the same subject, but their accounts differ in structure, development, style, and tone. (mentions *how* the accounts differ, but not *why*—no point being made)

- Wallace's account is sympathetic to Mackenzie, but Brown's style is more descriptive. (points about each account, but no common basis of comparison)

For practice in evaluating theses for comparison essays, see Exercise A3 at the end of this chapter.

Step 2 Revising Essay Structure

Check to see whether

- your choice of block or point-by-point method of organization still seems appropriate
- your paragraphs correspond to the sequence implied by your thesis statement
- your discussion includes matching points about the things you are comparing
- your sequence of paragraphs still seems effective.

Stage 6 Revising Individual Paragraphs

Step 1 Revising Middle Paragraphs

Check to see whether

- you use topic sentences that clearly indicate your method of organization
- you use umbrella topic sentences when necessary to indicate the major divisions in your material
- you give roughly the same amount of space to developing points about each thing you are comparing.

If you were to outline the first draft of an essay on the Wallace–Brown passages, you might find that, though you have followed through on your plan for the sequence of paragraph topics—by analyzing structure, use of detail, and style—these topics are jumbled together in particular paragraphs. Your outline of one paragraph might look like this:

MIDDLE PARAGRAPH 3

Wallace's account has lots of details about exactly how many troops were in the battle, how many lodges were burnt, and so on. Brown mentions only one figure: 150 lodges. Wallace uses the language of the military historian. Brown uses the language of the Aboriginals.

OUTLINE

Middle Paragraph 3 Topics: development of detail; also diction (style).
Point: no overall point.
Topic sentence: none.

You would begin your revision by splitting this paragraph into two, one comparing the use of detail in both accounts and one comparing their style. You would then need to decide what point to make about the differences in detail and style and write topic sentences making these points. You would also need to gather more evidence from both accounts to support your points. You can see the result of these changes if you read middle paragraphs three and four in the final draft (see "Two Views of the Battle at Powder River" in Part 3, Readings).

Steps 2 and 3 Revising Introductions and Conclusions

Introductions and conclusions in a comparison essay need to reflect a *balance* of material. Begin your introduction by establishing the context for both things being compared. Remember that your conclusion should clarify your comparison thesis and its wider implications, rather than summarizing your points about one of your objects of comparison, or both separately. You may find it helpful to include notes on your introduction and conclusion in your draft outline.

Checking the draft of the Wallace–Brown essay, you might find these sentences leading up to the thesis:

> Ernest Wallace's *Ranald S. Mackenzie on the Texas Frontier* is a historical study of General Mackenzie's expeditions against the Cheyenne. One of these expeditions was the Powder River expedition of 1876 in which Mackenzie and his cavalry attacked Dull Knife's village. I will compare Wallace's account of this attack with Dee Brown's *Bury My Heart at Wounded Knee*.

The conclusion might be something like this:

> These two accounts are very different because Wallace and Brown have different attitudes. Both accounts are interesting, but they are very different.

The draft introduction establishes the subject well, but it is clearly unbalanced in favour of the Wallace account, and will need to include more on Dee Brown's book. The conclusion refers to both of the things being compared, but it needs much more development of the thesis and its implications. To see how these changes could be made, look at the introduction and conclusion to the revised essay, "Two Views of the Battle at Powder River" Part 3, Readings.

Working on Your Own Assignment

Your purpose in comparing is to illuminate the similarities and differences between two things in reference to a **basis of comparison**.

- Check your essay topic. Are you given a basis of comparison, or will you need to work out one?
- Gather material on both subjects by using the appropriate questions for content or textual analysis. Work on your subjects separately so that you don't distort them by trying to find similarities too soon.
- Arrange your material in matching categories that contain equivalent amounts of material, focusing on the categories most relevant to your topic.
- Examine your material to determine the main similarity and/or difference.

- Formulate a thesis by making a general point about this main similarity and/or difference and giving reasons to support it.

- Organize your material by the block method or the point-by-point method, depending upon the length and complexity of your essay. Your topic sentences should make clear which method you are using.

- When you revise your draft, check to see whether you have given equal attention to both subjects in your introduction, your thesis statement, your main points, and your evidence.

- For examples of comparison essays and essays that combine comparison and evaluation, see the following pieces in Part 3, Readings: Vivian Gornick, "Two Women of Science"; Joyce MacDonald, "The Problem of Environmental Costs: Suzuki vs. Merwin"; Karin Swanson, "Spontaneity and Enjoyment of the Natural World"; and "*The English Patient* Debate."

EXERCISES

A. Respond to the following questions in a sentence or two.

1. Choose two similar television programs (two talk shows, news programs, sitcoms, police or medical dramas). Figure out at least three different bases of comparison that you could develop in an essay comparing the two programs.

2. Briefly describe the most efficient strategy for gathering material for a comparison essay.

3. How effective is each of the following as a thesis for a comparison essay?

    a) Frederic Raphael and George Orwell present quite similar ideas on the nature of colonialism.

    b) The central similarity in "A Modest Proposal" and "Unchopping a Tree" is that both Swift and Merwin present their ideas through a persona who forces readers to examine their own attitudes and values.

    c) Laura Robinson's analysis of the causes of anorexia is much more convincing than Maggie Helwig's.

    d) In both *Casablanca* and *The English Patient*, the central character must choose between loyalty to a country and love for a woman.

    e) Although both Thoreau and Forster point out the spiritually deadening effects of owning property, the main difference between them is that Thoreau's desire to distance himself completely from the faults he criticizes makes many readers feel rather defensive, whereas Forster's willingness to admit these faults in himself makes many readers willing to accept his ideas.

4. What are the main advantages of using the **block method** to organize the body of a comparison essay?

5. What are the main advantages of using the **point-by-point method** to organize the body of a comparison essay?

B. Work out a basis of comparison and a thesis for a short essay on each of the following subjects. Compare your responses with those of your classmates.

> EXAMPLE: living at home and living on your own
>
> BASIS OF COMPARISON: sources of stress
>
> THESIS: Feeling that I was not meeting my parents' expectations was the main source of stress while I was living at home, whereas worrying about how to pay my bills is the main source of stress now that I am living on my own.

a. Studying at home and in a school library

b. Two places: coffee bars, pool halls, neighbourhoods

c. Two people in similar roles: parents, children, teachers, friends

C. Choose one of the following:

1. The essay "Two Women of Science: Carol Steiner and Sharlene George" is organized by the block method. Make an outline showing how you would organize Gornick's material using the point-by-point method. What would be the advantages and/or disadvantages of reorganizing the material in this way?

2. Karin Swanson organizes her comparison of Robert Frost's poem "Stopping by Woods on a Snowy Evening" and Edward Thomas' "Adlestrop" in the essay "Spontaneity and Enjoyment of the Natural World" by the point-by-point method. Make an outline showing how you would organize Swanson's essay using the block method. What would be the advantages and/or disadvantages of reorganizing the material in this way?

c h a p t e r   1 0

Gathering Material for Evaluation Essays

To evaluate something is to determine whether it is strong or weak, good or bad, beautiful or ugly, useful or impractical, right or wrong, logical or illogical, a cost or a benefit, an advantage or a disadvantage, to use some of the most common terms of evaluation. Judging the value of things and trying to persuade others to accept our judgments are important human activities, whether you are arguing with a friend about a movie or campaigning for a political candidate. Making judgments is equally important in academic disciplines, as you learn how to determine whether information, ideas, experiments, theories, works of art are useful or less useful, good or bad.

You will find writing evaluative essays easier if you are aware of the criteria for making evaluations. Although the specific criteria will vary depending upon whether you are evaluating cars or computers, friendships or foreign policy, there are four common *standards of evaluation* that provide a broad framework for making judgments. This chapter shows you how to gather material by using these common standards of evaluation. The next chapter illustrates the process of writing and revising an evaluation essay, using a type of assignment that many students find difficult—evaluating an argumentative essay.

Stage 2   Gathering Material: Analyzing and Evaluating

Step 1   Analyzing: Identifying Parts, Stages, Causes/Effects

Gathering material for an evaluation essay is a two-step process. First you analyze the subject by dividing it into its parts, stages, or causes/effects, using the appropriate categories of content or textual analysis. (See Chapters 3 and 4.) To evaluate the design of a new park, for instance, you would first analyze the park as a system of inter-connected parts, such as the playground, picnic area, public facilities, and landscaping. Similarly, to evaluate a tennis match, you might first divide it into stages according to who won the sets; or to evaluate proposed changes to the Young Offenders Act, you might begin by listing their possible effects. If you are evaluating two things, you begin as you would for making comparisons, by listing equivalent elements, such as aspects of lighting and direction in two films, or the roles of parents, children, and social workers in two kinds of dysfunctional families.

Step 2 Evaluating: Using Standards of Evaluation to Identify Strengths and Weaknesses

After you have divided your subject(s) into appropriate parts, stages, or causes and effects, you next identify the strengths and weaknesses of the material in each category by applying the appropriate standard(s) of evaluation.

Four common standards, as we mentioned in Chapter 2, are the aesthetic, the practical, the ethical, and the logical. By applying the guidelines that follow, you will learn to make reasonable judgments of strengths and weaknesses according to each of these standards of evaluation. When you write your essay, your judgments about strengths and weaknesses become arguments to support your thesis. Applying the aesthetic standard of evaluation thus gives you aesthetic arguments, applying the practical standard gives you practical arguments, and so on. You will also learn to recognize the strengths and weaknesses in someone else's evaluations and arguments, the subject of the next chapter.

Aesthetic standard The *aesthetic* standard is commonly used to judge works of art, or the "performance" aspect of any activity, such as a political candidate's speaking skills or a figure skater's technique. When you evaluate by an aesthetic standard, you ask one or more of these questions: Is it well constructed, beautiful, pleasing to the senses? Is it well performed? Is it a good example of its kind? Each of the following claims—that trees are beautiful, that a rock concert was electrifying, that a political speech was fumbling and ineffective—is based on an aesthetic standard. You can most easily find examples of aesthetic judgments in reviews of books, films, and theatre performances. A theatre reviewer, for example, may praise the acting and set design in a new play, but complain about poor direction and a weak script.

In making aesthetic judgments, we rely on two main criteria: coherence and comparison. When we ask whether something is well constructed, we are asking about its coherence. Do all the parts work together to make a satisfying whole? On these grounds, we might conclude that *Freddy's Dead: The Final Nightmare* is a good movie because it has interesting characters, a suspenseful plot, and good special effects.

A judgment that an object is a good one of its kind, or that one object is better than another of its kind, obviously rests on comparison. For example, if we claim that *The Silence of the Lambs* is a better horror film than *Freddy's Dead: The Final Nightmare*, we are comparing both films to our ideal model of the good horror film. As always, your basis of comparison should be clear and appropriate. If you merely say,

"That was not a very good performance of *Macbeth*," you do not indicate what your model of good performances is—the BBC production? Roman Polanski's movie version? Make sure you compare things of the same kind—it's hardly fair to decide that *Macbeth* is bad because it isn't as funny as a Woody Allen movie. And be aware of the limitations of your own experience. A claim that *Terminator 2* is the best movie ever made might convince readers who see only action films, but is not likely to convince readers with a wider range of experience.

Your judgments about aesthetic strengths and weaknesses will be more persuasive if you use both criteria.

Practical standard   When you use the *practical* standard of evaluation, you judge things by their feasibility and usefulness, according to criteria such as cost and efficiency. In assessing practical strengths and weaknesses, you ask one or more of the following questions: Will this work? Will it be useful? Does it have a relevant application? When Laura Robinson argues, in "Starving for the Gold" (Part 3, Readings), that "even an influx of women coaches" would not solve the problems faced by women athletes, she is evaluating the situation according to a practical standard.

Practical judgments connect the thing being evaluated (whether an idea, a technique, an object, a person) with the social situation or context in which it will be applied, or the purpose it will serve. Publishers consider not only whether a novel is well written, but whether it will sell. Consumers complain about products that don't work properly. Voters question whether building a new city hall is an efficient use of their tax money. The novel, the products, the proposal to build a new city hall are all being judged by a practical standard.

You can ensure that your judgments about practical strengths and weaknesses are reasonable by pinpointing specific parts that do or do not work and by considering as many aspects of the context as possible. To acknowledge that a new city hall would create more working space and yet criticize the cost, for example, would give you a more balanced judgment than to conclude that the proposal was totally impractical. In thinking about the context, you should ask yourself questions like these: "workable" for whom? for doing what? in what circumstances? with what short- and long-term effects? If you were trying to judge the practical value of Paolo Freire's ideas about teaching, for instance, you would have to ask questions like these: Would methods that worked with South American peasants work with urban children? with school dropouts? What changes would be required in the way schools are organized? in the relationship between teacher and students? What would be the practical consequences for students learning to read and write? in students' later lives?

Ethical standard   When you use the *ethical* standard, you judge things by their moral worth, their rightness or wrongness according to particular moral, ideological, or religious values. In identifying ethical strengths and weaknesses, you will ask questions like these: Is this right or wrong? Is this a position worth believing in? Is this a behaviour worth imitating? Is this a course of action worth following? When Maggie Helwig argues in "A Certain Hunger" (Part 3, Readings) that "a society devoted to consumption" is a destructive society, she is making an ethical judgment. She does not say that such a society does not function well (which would be a practical argument); instead she argues that consumerism creates spiritual starvation, implying a system of values in which "spirit" plays a major role.

Ethical judgments are based on systems of values that vary widely. Among the most common are religious beliefs about the teachings of a Supreme Being; secular beliefs about the rights of the individual and the value of progress; and what we might call communitarian beliefs about such values as altruism, tradition, collective responsibility, justice, and the rule of law.

When you are evaluating ethical strengths and weaknesses, make sure that you are aware of the system of values you are invoking and that those values are appropriate to your subject. In "It Always Costs" (Readings) David Suzuki makes his argument more convincing by admitting to a change in his system of values, from a belief in the value of technological progress to a belief in collective responsibility for the environment.

Your ethical judgments may be weak if you do not state your position explicitly enough, or if readers perceive your system of values as inappropriate or irrelevant to your subject. In "An Image of Africa" (Readings) Chinua Achebe argues that Joseph Conrad's *Heart of Darkness* expresses a racist vision. Is Achebe's ethical argument strong or weak? Achebe's position is certainly explicit, and many readers would agree with his argument. But other readers may reject it on the grounds that moral–political judgments should not be made about literary works, or argue that Conrad's work should be judged by a different system of values.

Logical standard   The *logical* standard is used to judge the validity of reasoning and evidence in stated or implied arguments. You may be asked to assess the logical validity of a persuasive essay, a theory, a proposal, a piece of research—in all of these cases, the arguments are explicit. You could also evaluate the implicit arguments made in a film such as *JFK*, which promotes a conspiracy theory of Kennedy's assassination.

When you identify strengths and weaknesses in logic, you ask two types of questions:

1. **General questions** about the assumptions underlying the arguments you are evaluating and about the quality of thought they reveal. These questions are an extension of those you ask about context whenever you analyze nonfiction (see Chapter 3).

   a. What assumptions does the speaker/writer/director make? What perspective(s) does the piece represent? Does it reflect the values and concerns of a particular cultural, political, religious, sexual, racial, philosophical, or theoretical orientation? Are these valid perspectives to bring to this subject?

   b. What is the overall quality of thought? Does the thinking suggest, for example, a superficial or an intelligent grasp of complex issues, a sensible or visionary approach to everyday problems, a significant concern that deserves better treatment?

2. **Specific questions** about the writer's reasoning and evidence.

The following guidelines will help you evaluate the logic of someone else's work—or your own.

Evaluating Reasoning   When you evaluate a writer's argument, you look critically at the thesis and main points. Your purpose is not to determine whether these ideas are true—that may be a matter of opinion—but whether they are free of errors in reasoning. Here are the major types of arguments and the common problems to watch for.

Deductive Argument   Any argument that moves from general principles to make a judgment about more particular cases could be called a deductive argument. The most rigorous kind of deductive argument is the *syllogism* where a general statement, called the *major premise* ("all lawyers are trustworthy"), is linked to another statement, called the *minor premise* ("Joan is a lawyer"), to produce a *conclusion* ("therefore Joan is trustworthy").

As you can see from this example, problems can occur in deductive arguments if the major premise is untrue (not all lawyers are trustworthy), the minor premise is missing, or the conclusion does not follow ("therefore Joan would make a good candidate for mayor"). Be skeptical of sweeping generalizations: "Throughout history humans have struggled for perfection." "Men have more power than women." "Hard work leads to success." They are often based on a major premise that is questionable or untrue.

Causal Argument Reasoning from cause to effect is an important form of logical reasoning. You are using such reasoning when you claim that cutting spending for education will lead to more delinquency, or that creating jobs will reduce the number of people on welfare. When David Suzuki in "It Always Costs" argues that technology brings with it enormous costs as well as enormous benefits, he is making a causal argument about the effects of technology.

Problems in causal reasoning include circular reasoning, where the point that should be proved is assumed to begin with; for example, "I will show that this dreadful practice of abortion, child murder, is morally wrong." Other problems in causal reasoning occur when an effect is assumed, but not proven, to arise from a particular cause. For example, "This increase in murders is the result of the suspension of the death penalty" is a claim that requires further evidence, since many factors affect the homicide rate.

Evaluating Evidence Anything used to show a statement is true or false is considered evidence. The most common types of evidence are examples, facts and figures, and references to authorities. Analogies, which may be helpful in explaining concepts, are more problematic as evidence to support an argument. In evaluating the evidence used to support points, you should keep these considerations in mind.

Examples In using examples, you choose something small and detailed, like a line from a poem, a scene from a play, a case of delinquency, or an event from history, to support a point about a larger whole, such as the theme of a poem, the meaning of tragedy, the reasons for delinquency, the validity of a historian's interpretation. In "An Image of Africa" Achebe gives many examples of language from *Heart of Darkness* that he thinks reflect Conrad's racism.

Problems in using examples arise when there is a questionable connection between the particular example and the general point it should illustrate. Examples can be irrelevant or unrepresentative: "The statements of this teenage girl prove that the values of adult society are in crisis." More commonly still, generalizations can be based on too few examples: "My neighbour's parties have kept me awake three nights in a row; clearly consideration for others is disappearing in today's society."

Facts and Figures Another kind of evidence is sometimes called "hard" evidence: statistics, research studies, scientific observation and the like. In "Profits by the Truckload" (Readings), Ross Laver offers many facts and figures to support his points about the popularity of sport utility vehicles.

Although "hard" evidence is potentially the most convincing evidence of all, problems do arise. Statistics and other "facts" can be manipulated. Problems in using "hard" evidence arise when the sources of evidence are not current, when the evidence does not come from a reliable or appropriate source (as when statistics from the United States are assumed to apply to Canada), or when evidence is selectively cited.

References to Authorities   The opinion of someone who is knowledgeable about your subject is a valid kind of evidence. In "Sensual Education" (Readings), Robert S. Root-Bernstein cites a long list of chemists, physicists, mathematicians and other scientists who have attested to the sensual component of scientific discovery. Within academic disciplines, you are often expected to locate your own ideas within a tradition of thinking about your subject. Argument by authority is thus important when you write academic essays, especially research essays.

Problems result from citing authorities who are not relevant to your subject. A famous chemist is a valid authority for an essay on chemistry, but not for an essay on juvenile delinquency. Other problems are vague and unsupported references to authorities ("experts claim," "research shows") and overreliance on authorities. For suggestions about integrating other opinions with your own analysis, see Chapter 13.

Analogies   An analogy is a likeness. If you say that dropping out of school is like deserting the army, you are using an analogy. When you use an analogy as part of an argument, you are usually arguing that a situation is like another situation, and will have the same outcome (good or bad). You might argue, for instance, that recent acts of anti-Semitism in Western Europe are like those that occurred before Hitler took power, and will have the same consequences.

Arguing by analogy is tricky, because an analogy that seems valid to one reader may not seem so to another. If you claimed that the United Nations' intervention in troubled areas of Europe is just like the United States' intervention in Vietnam, for instance, you would have trouble convincing some readers, because of the significant differences between the two situations.

Evaluating Emotional Appeals   Almost anything you might evaluate appeals to your emotions or intuitions as well as to your capacity for logical reasoning. When you look at the emotional appeals made, for example, by an advertisement, a movie, or an essay, you identify strengths and weaknesses by the same criterion that you use for logical reasoning: can these emotions reasonably be said to follow from the situation? When the emotions seem excessive, we may judge the advertisement as manipulative, the movie as melodramatic, the essay as bad-tempered. When the emotions seem reasonable, we are likely to feel an identity of interest or response. Then the advertisement may seem funny, the movie gripping, the essay forceful.

By themselves, emotional appeals are usually persuasive only to the already convinced, who will not feel that the emotions aroused are excessive. In academic essays, emotional appeals need the backing of arguments and evidence, which readers can weigh more dispassionately.

Evaluations you make according to a logical standard, like all other kinds of evaluation, will be tinged by your personal likes and dislikes, since it is impossible to be purely "objective." However, try not to let the fact that you agree or disagree with the position put forward, or like or dislike the way it is presented, blind you to the strengths and weaknesses of its logic. You may agree wholeheartedly with a proposal that is very badly argued, or you may dislike the style of a piece that is argued very well. It is better to admit these conflicting judgments than to try to ignore or disguise them. You will find a sample evaluation of the logic of an essay in Chapter 11.

Step 3   Categorizing Strengths and Weaknesses

You will find it easier to formulate an evaluative thesis if you make a chart identifying the parts of your subject and setting out strengths and weaknesses in matching columns. If you were evaluating a propsal to build a rapid transit system, for instance, your chart might look like this:

	STRENGTHS	WEAKNESSES
Personal Effects	• reduction of traffic congestion • reduction of traffic accidents	• lack of convenience • lack of public interest
Economic Effects	• less land required for parking • stimulation of downtown business	• rise in taxes
Environmental Effects	• reduction in air pollution • conservation of energy	

Make a separate chart for each standard of evaluation you use. You can then combine your independent judgments about each set of strengths and weaknesses to formulate a thesis about overall strengths and weaknesses.

Step 4   Choosing Standards of Evaluation

Sometimes your subject may limit you to a single standard of evaluation (such as the aesthetic merits of a ballet); sometimes your essay topic may specify a single standard ("What are the practical advantages and disadvantages of graduated driver's licences?"). If you are working with a single standard, make notes on each part, stage, or cause/effect and then assess its strengths and weaknesses in relation to your standard of evaluation.

You will be able to gather more material and produce a more complete evaluation of your subject by using as many standards of evaluation as seem relevant to your subject and your topic. If you were considering books on sibling rivalry to buy for an elementary school library, for instance, you could evaluate their aesthetic merits (such as the quality of the story and illustrations), their practical merits (such as cost and availability), and ethical merits (such as their avoidance of stereotypes and treatment of violence).

Working on Your Own Assignment

When you evaluate something—a play, a proposal for a group home, a government policy, or a scientific theory—your main purpose is to determine its strengths and weaknesses according to one or more *standards of evaluation.*

- Use the appropriate questions for content or textual analysis to gather information on your subject(s).
- Identify the strengths and weaknesses of each part, stage, or cause/effect into which you have divided your subject, using the appropriate standard(s) of evaluation.
  - *Aesthetic standard*: Is it beautiful, well constructed, well performed, a good thing of its kind?
  - *Practical standard*: Is it workable, useful, applicable in this context?
  - *Ethical standard*: Is it right or wrong, good or bad, according to a relevant system of values?
  - *Logical standard*: Is it well thought out, sound in reasoning, supported by appropriate evidence?
- To see how different standards of evaluation may be applied to the same subject, read "The *English Patient* Debate" in Part 3, Readings.

EXERCISES

A.   Answer each of the following questions.

1. What standards of evaluation could you use if you were assessing the strengths and weaknesses of a proposal to include the cost of a lap-top computer in every college or university student's tuition fees?

2. List the main advantages and disadvantages of this proposal. Be sure to use more than one standard of evaluation.

3. What kinds of evidence would you include if you were writing an essay evaluating this proposal?

B. Write one paragraph on each of the following questions.

1. What standards of evaluation does Forster use in "My Wood" to assess the advantages and disadvantages of owning property?

2. What standards of evaluation does Thoreau use in "Economy" to assess the disadvantages of owning property?

3. Which writer, in your opinion, presents the stronger defence of his position? Be sure to make your own standard(s) of evaluation clear.

chapter 11

Writing
Evaluation Essays

In Chapter 10 you saw the important role that standards of evaluation play in gathering material for evaluation essays. The most common standards, you will recall, are ethical, aesthetic, practical, and logical. One or more of these standards provide the basis for the evaluation essays you read and write. In "The Moral Superiority of *Casablanca* over *The English Patient*" (Part 3, Readings), for example, Thomas Hurka evaluates the two films according to the *ethical* position that political causes are more important than personal relationships. The replies to his article (Readings) also evaluate the film on ethical grounds, asserting that relationships are just as important as, or more important than, politics. None of these writers focus on the *aesthetic* standard of evaluation, but you could reasonably judge the films on how successfully direction, use of setting, camera angles, and so on convey theme and meaning. The *practical* standard of evaluation is harder to apply in this case, although perhaps if you were a travel agent you could evaluate the films according to which gives the most practical tips on living abroad!

You are likely quite accustomed to making judgments on ethical, aesthetic, and practical grounds, in everyday conversation if not in writing. You probably have less experience applying a *logical* standard of evaluation. And yet throughout your courses you will be expected to assess the validity of research studies, philosophical arguments, political theories, and similar material. So to demonstrate the process of writing an evaluation essay, we will use a type of assignment that students often find difficult: evaluating the logic of an argumentative essay. Here is the topic: "Write an essay evaluating strategies of argumentation in Barbara Amiel's 'How to Preserve the Health-Care Safety Net.' " You will follow the example more easily if you read her essay first (reprinted in Part 3, Readings).

When you gather material for evaluation essays, as we emphasized in Chapter 10, you need to consider both the strengths and weaknesses of whatever you are evaluating. As you will see, this principle also applies to formulating a thesis and presenting your arguments.

Stage 1   Clarifying Evaluation Topics

Step 1   Deciding What to Evaluate

In an evaluation assignment, you may be asked to assess a single subject (such as a business proposal, the choreography of a musical, an essay). Or you may be asked to compare the strengths and weaknesses of two subjects (such as the use of setting in two short stories, the validity of two theories, the practicality of two designs for electric cars). In evaluating Amiel's essay, you have a single subject.

Step 2   Identifying the Standard(s) of Evaluation

Most evaluation assignments imply, rather than spell out, the standards by which you are to evaluate your subject. For example, the topic "Discuss whether Paolo Freire's methods of teaching literacy are applicable to North America" implies a practical standard of evaluation. Similarly, "Is the film version of *The Handmaid's Tale* better than the novel?" suggests an aesthetic standard. If your assignment does not make clear which standard(s) to use, you will have to decide what kinds of judgments would be appropriate for your topic. For practice in doing so, see the first exercise at the end of this chapter. The assignment on Barbara Amiel's essay mentions "strategies of argumentation," and so indicates that you would use a logical standard of evaluation.

Stage 2 Gathering Material: Analyzing and Evaluating Your Subject

Step 1 Analyzing: Identifying Arguments and Evidence

Before you can evaluate, you need to make sure you understand what the writer is saying. So begin by analyzing the content of the piece according to the suggestions in Chapter 3. In analyzing a persuasive essay like Amiel's, you would focus on the writer's thesis, the arguments that develop the thesis, and the evidence that supports each point. You might summarize Amiel's thesis as follows:

Amiel's thesis

> Amiel argues that to address problems resulting from socialized medicine, especially problems of "stratospheric health-care costs" and poor service, we need to return to a system that allows private insurance and "private medicine to co-exist with a public safety net."

Since most arguments are based on the standards of evaluation discussed in Chapter 10, you can use these standards to help you identify the kinds of arguments a writer makes. Are Amiel's arguments ethical, practical, or aesthetic ones, or a combination? What evidence is used to support each argument? Employing this framework, you may come up with the following analysis:

Arguments and evidence

Practical Arguments

Problem: Socialized medicine creates a free health-care system, with the following negative results:

1. The system is abused.

> Examples: People going to the doctor for colds; middle-class women going to psychiatrists to discuss their love lives.

2. Government coercion is required to stop doctors from opting out or migrating to urban centres.

> Example: Ontario's plans for "coercive measures against doctors."

3. Government is unable to contain the soaring costs of medical technology and of hospital workforces in the face of a "bulge" in demand from older people.

> Examples: Sewing back amputated limbs; "multi-million-dollar diagnostic machines."

4. The medical bureaucracy grows and, rather than cutting its own size or costs, cuts services, with negative economic results.

> Examples: "Brain drain" of doctors; wealthy leave country for heart surgery.

Solution: Return to private profit-making insurance, independent doctors, and an officially approved two-tier system of health care.

Ethical Arguments

1. Socialized medicine's inability to contain technology and workforce costs creates not only economic but also "ethical problems" concerning the allocation of resources.

> Examples: Who receives transplant organs, dialysis, CAT scans?

2. Reduction of services "dehumanize[s]" people when they are "at their most vulnerable and needy."

> Example: Patients need "a bedpan or an understanding nurse" but get instead "endless waiting, harassed staff."

Step 2   Evaluating: Identifying Strengths and Weaknesses

To identify strengths and weaknesses in argumentation, consult Logical Standard in Chapter 10. Evaluating Amiel's arguments in this way, you might come up with the following:

Causal reasoning   Amiel's arguments are organized into a problem–solution structure:

1. Problems of costs present in the late 1970s are still present in 1996.

2. These problems have two causes: a) the costs of new medical technology, and b) the huge bureaucracy that results from socialized medicine.

3. The solution to these problems is to return to a two-tier system.

There is an obvious weakness in causal reasoning in this sequence. Eliminating socialized medicine cannot be the whole solution to the soaring costs of health care, because, as Amiel admits, one cause—the costs of new medical technology—"has absolutely nothing to do with socialized medicine."

Evidence: Examples Amiel uses a number of examples to support her account of problems, examples like people going to the doctor with a cold, the costs created by "million-dollar diagnostic machines," the wealthy leaving the country for heart surgery, the "endless waiting." None of these examples refer to specific or identified cases, but readers aware of the crises in health care may find them typical enough to be convincing.

The only example relevant to Amiel's proposed solution, however, is the example of the way that Amiel was treated in the public ward of Toronto General Hospital in the 1950s. From this single example, Amiel deduces that

> All the nightmarish preconceptions that the British held
> about North American health care were a lie. Today, the
> nightmarish conceptions that Canadians hold about the no-
> tion of "two-tier" medicine are equally a lie.

A single experience that happened over forty years ago is surely insufficient support for her proposed solution to contemporary problems. Furthermore, although Amiel refers to North American health care, she presents not a single example from health care in the United States, the home of a decidedly two-tier system. Thus, though Amiel's use of examples of problems is reasonably effective, her use of examples to support her proposed solution is quite inadequate.

Evidence: Facts and Figures There are no facts and figures at all in the essay. The lack of facts and figures may not be a disadvantage when describing problems that readers are familiar with. But it's a distinct disadvantage when proposing solutions, since readers are likely to want some assurance that the solutions are practical.

Evidence: Authorities The authorities mentioned in the essay—Monique Bégin, Pierre Trudeau, Bill Davis, Bob Rae—are politicians Amiel sees as guilty of "mismanagement" of the health-care system. This repudiation of authorities is appropriate to Amiel's argument against government bureaucracy.

Emotional Appeals Amiel uses strongly evaluative and emotive diction in her essay, referring to the "horrors of British socialized medicine," the "fantastic" benefits received from private insurance, the "nightmarish preconceptions" that make up a "lie." Since none of these views are backed up by argument, this diction will only appeal to readers who already share Amiel's position.

A more effective emotional appeal is the way Amiel presents herself in the essay. By mentioning that she has made "some significant miscalculations" in her predictions and that she was once a student who "couldn't afford [her] insurance," Amiel emphasizes her vulnerability. This gives more credibility to her claims of sympathy with patients who are "vulnerable and needy" and with the "indigent" who need public health care.

Steps 3 and 4   Categorizing Strengths and Weaknesses and Choosing Standards of Evaluation

You will find it easier to formulate a thesis if you set out strengths and weaknesses in columns like this:

Part	Strengths	Weaknesses
Causal reasoning	Clear problem–solution structure	Solutions don't flow from problems
Evidence: examples	Examples of problems reasonably effective	Examples of solutions very weak
Evidence: facts and figures	None used	Absence makes solutions less convincing
Authority	Attacks on government authority fit case; will be convincing only if rest of case is	
Emotional appeals	Allows identity with "vulnerable"	Evaluative diction not supported

Stage 3   Formulating an Evaluative Thesis

Step 1   Forming an Opinion about Strengths and Weaknesses

The first step in formulating an evaluative thesis is to decide whether strengths outweigh weaknesses, weaknesses outweigh strengths, or the two are roughly equal. For example, if you are evaluating a dramatic performance, you may have to decide whether an unimaginative set design ruins the impact of the play, or whether good acting offsets the poor staging.

Looking at the material you have gathered on Barbara Amiel's essay, you may decide that the essay is strong on describing problems, but weak on presenting solutions, and that the weakness in presenting solutions is finally more important. You can then formulate a thesis about this relationship between strengths and weaknesses in the following way:

> While Barbara Amiel's essay effectively conveys a sense of the problems confronting Canada's health-care system, her proposed solutions to these problems are much less convincingly presented.

This thesis has the right focus because it is an opinion about the strengths and weaknesses in Amiel's strategies of argumentation, as the assignment required. The thesis would not fulfill the demands of the assignment if it merely restated Amiel's opinions about the health-care system, or if it focused on a different standard of evaluation ("Barbara Amiel's views on health care are morally corrupt").

Step 2   Supporting Your Opinion and Indicating Your Standard(s) of Evaluation

You can draw the reasons to support your opinion from your chart of strengths and weaknesses. If you have listed more strengths and weaknesses than you can discuss adequately in your essay, choose the most important points or combine small points under a broader category. Since your reasons are based on one or more standards of evaluation, you may need to mention the relevant standards explicitly in your thesis or elsewhere in your introduction. You may also need to explain why a particular standard is appropriate to the subject you are evaluating, as Chinua Achebe does in "An Image of Africa" (Readings) when he judges Conrad's *Heart of Darkness* by an ethical standard.

Adding reasons to support the opinion about Amiel's essay results in the following thesis:

> The strengths of Amiel's essay, according to a logical standard of evaluation, are its unspecific but effective examples of problems, and the emotional appeal of a writer who seems to be able to put herself in the patient's place. These strengths, however, are more than offset by the essay's weaknesses in presenting solutions, namely its defective causal reasoning and its lack of convincing examples of a practical and humane alternative.

This thesis outlines the arguments to be made in the essay, a useful guide to readers.

Stage 4 Drafting

Steps 1 and 2   Selecting Material and Creating Arguments

Just as you consider both strengths and weaknesses when you work out an evaluative thesis, so you should include both strengths and weaknesses in the body of your essay. Present this material in the form of *arguments*: each point is an evaluative point, and each point needs evidence to support it.

Step 3 Organizing Evaluation Essays: Presenting Arguments For and Arguments Against (Pro/Con)

Arguments for your case are called *pro* (Latin for "for") arguments; arguments against it are called *con* (Latin for "against") arguments. Usually the best plan is to put the *con* arguments first, then follow these with the *pro* arguments. That way, the arguments supporting your position are freshest in your reader's mind when you reach your conclusion.

Don't merely state the *con* arguments, however. Doing so would confuse your reader. Instead, you either *refute* opposing arguments or *concede* their validity. When you *refute* an argument, you state the opposing point and then give reasons or evidence that casts doubt on its validity. For example, in "To Peacekeep or Not to Peacekeep" (Readings), James Ash starts his essay by presenting the *con* argument that peacekeeping takes troops away from territorial defence, and then refutes this argument by claiming that territorial defence is unnecessary for Canada.

Sometimes opposing arguments are valid. Critic X, or your own good sense, may tell you that a movie is predictable, but you love it anyway. Then what do you do? Don't ignore strengths or weaknesses that may seem to undermine your position. Your judgment will seem more balanced, and therefore more believable, if you *concede* valid arguments on the other side. Chinua Achebe is making a concession when, in "An Image of Africa" (Readings), he acknowledges that he is drawing from "rather trivial encounters rather heavy conclusions which at first sight might seem somewhat out of proportion to them."

The thesis on Amiel's essay states that weaknesses outweigh strengths. The strengths of Amiel's essay would thus become the *con* arguments (arguments against your position), and the weaknesses would become the *pro* arguments (arguments for your position). In structuring the draft, first concede the logical strengths of the essay, and then focus on its weaknesses.

Stage 5 Revising Thesis and Essay Structure

Step 1 Revising the Thesis: Checking for an Evaluative Point

The draft thesis on Amiel's essay is effective because it has an evaluative point ("strengths are more than offset by...weaknesses") with support ("effective examples of problems, and...emotional appeal...[but] weaknesses in presenting solutions").

Step 2 Revising the Structure: Highlighting Arguments For and Arguments Against

In looking at the overall structure of your draft, you check whether concessions and refutations are followed by arguments for your case, and whether these *con* and *pro* arguments are clearly identified by topic sentences. Topic sentences are particularly important in evaluative essays, because your reader can easily become confused about which arguments you are refuting and which ones you are presenting as your own.

To check the effectiveness of your paragraph sequence and topic sentences, it is a good idea to make an outline of your draft, identifying subject and point in each paragraph. Once you have made the outline, you can check whether you have topic sentences that successfully indicate the movement of your argument. An outline for your draft of the Amiel essay may look like this:

PARAGRAPH 1 (Concession): Amiel's use of examples of problems (subject) is effective (point)

PARAGRAPH 2 (Concession and refutation): Amiel's use of emotional appeals (subject) is partly effective, but partly not (point)

PARAGRAPH 3 (*Pro* argument): Amiel's causal reasoning (subject) is flawed (point)

PARAGRAPH 4 (*Pro* argument): Examples of solutions (subject) are lacking (point)

Looking at your draft and this outline, you may decide that the paragraph sequence seems appropriate: concessions and refutations come before your *pro* arguments, and the stronger of these comes last. However, the topic sentences may seem less effective. For example, the topic sentence for paragraph 2 might read: "Amiel's emotional appeals are quite a good way to arouse the reader's interest." This sentence focuses on the right subject and does present the *con* argument;

however, the outline indicates that you also intend to criticize Amiel's use of emotional appeals. So you might revise the topic sentence like this: "Amiel reinforces her examples of problems with emotional appeals, but these emotional appeals are only partly effective."

Stage 6   Revising Individual Paragraphs

Step 1   Revising Middle Paragraphs: Checking for Problems in Argument

Since an evaluation essay is a series of arguments, you need to make sure that your own arguments are not flawed by problems such as faulty use of evidence or appeals to irrelevant authorities (see Chapter 10). For example, the draft version of the paragraph on the weaknesses in Amiel's causal reasoning may look like this:

> The weaknesses in Amiel's argument are first evident in her causal reasoning, which is distinctly flawed. Amiel claims that a return to private insurance and private medicine would solve health-care problems, but there are elements in the essay that contradict this causal connection. So the connection she claims is unconvincing.

This paragraph focuses on a single point introduced in the topic sentence, but offers no evidence to support this point. If you specify what the "elements in the essay that contradict this causal connection" actually are, you may come up with a revised paragraph like the following:

> The weaknesses in Amiel's argument are first evident in her causal reasoning, which is distinctly flawed. Amiel claims that a return to private insurance and private medicine would solve health-care problems. However, she has already argued that there are "two main problems with modern medicine" and that one of these—the cost of medical technology and a trained workforce—"has absolutely nothing to do with socialized medicine." Even if the reader accepts Amiel's argument that socialized medicine is the other half of the problem, it is obvious that eliminating it can only be half a solution.

Step 2   Revising Introductions and Conclusions: Including the Audience

The beginning and end of your essay are important places to establish your fair-mindedness and consideration for your readers. These are important qualities in an evaluation essay, because not all your readers will share your views. If you do not seem to take alternative opinions seriously, your readers may not take your opinions seriously.

In your *introduction*, you can show your fair-mindedness by offering your readers an independent perspective on the subject. Your readers will be less likely to dismiss your thesis if you begin by outlining views that differ from your own or by summarizing the issue or its history.

If you forget the need to take other views into account, you may write the beginning section of your draft introduction as follows:

> In a essay for *Maclean's* entitled "How to Preserve the Health-Care Safety Net," Barbara Amiel argues for changes in the Canadian health-care system. I do not find her case very convincing.

Bringing in your response before you have said anything more about the essay will likely not persuade a reader who generally likes Barbara Amiel's writing, or who is not familiar with this particular essay. So to give your reader some independent perspective on the issue, you can begin your introduction by stating the main point of Amiel's essay non-evaluatively:

> In an essay entitled "How to Preserve the Health-Care Safety Net" (*Maclean's,* December 2, 1996, 13), Barbara Amiel argues that to address problems resulting from socialized medicine, especially problems of "stratospheric health-care costs" and poor service, we need to return to a system that allows private insurance and "private medicine to co-exist with a public safety net." How convincing is this argument?

Having shown that you understand Amiel's thesis well enough to summarize it, you can then move to presenting your own thesis in the rest of the introduction.

Similarly, in your *conclusion* you can reinforce the impression of fair-mindedness by reminding your readers that you have dealt with the *con* arguments as well as the *pro* arguments.

Your conclusion would not be very effective if it was too one-sided, like this one:

> The health-care system is a very contentious issue for Canadians, and Barbara Amiel's proposed solutions to its problems are not very convincing because her causal reasoning is flawed and she offers virtually no evidence that her solutions would work.

You could improve this conclusion by adding an account of Amiel's strengths, while making sure your summary of your *pro* arguments is extended enough to counter the *con* case. Your revised conclusion might read as follows:

> We are probably all aware of problems with Canada's health-care system, and Barbara Amiel's essay does point to these problems and encourage sympathy for patients suffering from them. However, her acknowledgement that other factors besides socialized medicine are responsible for problems in the system makes her attack on socialized medicine unconvincing. Furthermore, her seeming inability to cite examples of a two-tier system working effectively damages her claims concerning solutions. For these reasons, Barbara Amiel's "How to Preserve the Health-Care Safety Net" fails to persuade us that private insurance and medicine could co-exist with a public safety net in a way that would provide a humane and effective health-care system.

Once you have revised your individual paragraphs and given your essay a final editing, you should have an effective evaluative essay. For the full version of the revised essay on Amiel, see C. Smith, "What Does the Canadian Health-Care System Need?" (Part 3, Readings).

There's no guarantee that an evaluation essay, however well organized, will persuade a reader. But if you gather and evaluate your material with clear standard(s) of evaluation in mind, and if you include both *pro* and *con* material as you write and revise the essay, then your argument will be taken seriously, even by a reader with quite different views.

Working on Your Own Assignment

Your main goal in writing and revising an evaluation essay is to present a balanced assessment of the strengths and weaknesses of your subject.

- Decide which standard or standards of evaluation are required by your topic or are most relevant to your subject.
- Identify the strengths and weaknesses of each part, stage, or cause/effect into which you have divided your subject, using the appropriate standard(s) of evaluation.
- Formulate a thesis that states an opinion about this relationship between strengths and weaknesses, gives reasons to support your opinion, and indicates your standard(s) of evaluation.
- Write a draft, organizing your material into a series of *con* and *pro* arguments. Include evidence (reasons, examples, facts and figures) to back up all your points. If you use evidence from other sources, give the appropriate documentation.

- Outline your draft. Use the outline to check that you have put *con* arguments first and have led towards your strongest *pro* argument. Also check that your topic sentences effectively identify *con* and *pro* arguments.

- Check your draft to make sure that your arguments are not flawed by illogical causal connections, misleading examples, inaccurate or misleading statistics, appeals to irrelevant authorities, or excessive emotional appeals.

- Make sure that your introduction provides an independent perspective by summarizing the issue, its history, and/or opposing views nonjudgmentally. In your conclusion, remind your reader that you have considered the arguments both for and against your position.

- For examples of evaluation essays, see in Part 3, Readings: Chinua Achebe, "An Image of Africa"; Charles Gordon, "Achieving Virtue Through Stinginess"; David Suzuki, "It Always Costs"; Henry Thoreau, "Economy"; James Ash, "To Peacekeep or Not to Peacekeep"; Joyce MacDonald, "The Problem of Environmental Costs: Suzuki vs. Merwin"; C. Smith, "What Does the Canadian Health-Care System Need?"

EXERCISES

A. Identify the standard(s) of evaluation implied or stated in each of the following essay assignments.

1. Argue for or against the position presented by James Ash in "To Peacekeep or Not to Peacekeep."

2. Compare the use of flower symbolism in Steinbeck's "The Chrysanthemums" and Faulkner's "A Rose for Emily."

3. Which of the major psychoanalytic theories—Freud's, Jung's, or Adler's—is most useful for family social workers?

4. From your study of different types of social organization, which one(s) could most effectively help us cope with the problems of the 21st century?

B. Write a sentence or two evaluating the following as thesis statements for evaluation essays.

1. Although there is a lunatic fringe that opposes a woman's right to abortion, I will argue that the right is justified on medical, legal, and religious grounds.

2. In *The Hazards of Being Male*, Herb Goldberg argues that pressures to conform to a stereotyped image of masculinity force many men to live like emotional zombies.

Goldberg's thesis may be correct, but there is a problem with the narrow range of examples he uses and the logic he adopts to argue his case.

3. Toni Morrison's *Sula* is very good in its treatment of the need for sisterhood. This is a really good book; Morrison is the best black woman writer I have read.

C.   Decide what point the writer of the following paragraph is trying to prove. State that point in a topic sentence. Then reorganize the paragraph, putting the *con* arguments first and then the *pro* arguments. Compare your paragraph with your classmates'.

> An improved public transportation system will reduce traffic congestion. Of course, these improvements will cost money and taxes will go up. Even an improved public transportation system will never seem as convenient to most people as driving a car. With fewer cars on the road, traffic accidents will be reduced. Our concern for the environment ought to lead us to support a proposal that will conserve energy and reduce air pollution. A better public transportation system will stimulate downtown businesses and thus improve the business climate in the city.

D.   How effective are the following as introductory paragraphs for evaluation essays?

1. Childhood is one of the oldest subjects discussed in literature. Both Alice Munro's "Royal Beatings" and Frank O'Connor's "My Oedipus Complex" are stories about being a child. I think that Munro's story is better.

2. The most important context for discussing environmental problems is world population. This problem must be discussed now because the bigoted traditional attitudes of some churches and the misguided chauvinism of most Third World men are leading us into a disastrous situation. I will argue for three practical measures for reducing world population over the next forty years.

E.   Evaluate strategies of argumentation in Charles Gordon's essay "Achieving Virtue Through Stinginess" (Part 3, Readings). Follow the steps in this chapter for gathering material and formulating a thesis. Then make a draft outline, indicating the sequence in which you will treat strengths and weaknesses in order to support your thesis.

F.   Draft and revise a short essay evaluating Amiel's "How to Preserve the Health-Care Safety Net" (Readings) according to an ethical, aesthetic, or practical standard.

c h a p t e r   1 2

Gathering Material for Research Papers

As you take courses in a variety of academic disciplines, you will discover that methods of conducting research and writing about the results differ from field to field. The research papers you are asked to write will also differ in organization, style, and documentation. Nevertheless, research papers are basically extended versions of analysis, comparison, or evaluation essays. The special skills you need are those of finding research material and integrating it with your own ideas. Those are the skills we emphasize in this chapter. You can adapt the process of gathering material that we outline here to suit any research paper.

Research papers serve three purposes.

1. To increase your understanding of a subject covered briefly in class. A sociology instructor who can spend only one class on family violence, for example, might assign research papers on various aspects of this subject.

2. To acquaint you with the procedures and categories, the general ways of working, of a particular discipline. In doing a research paper in psychology, for example, you would learn how to use *Psychological Abstracts*; which journals to consult for research on a particular subject; and how experiments in psychology are conducted and reported.

3. To encourage you to synthesize information and integrate it with your own ideas. A research paper is not merely a summary of other writers' work; it is an essay in which you develop your own opinion on your subject and use your research material as evidence to support that opinion.

This chapter focuses on two important steps in writing research papers: how to find secondary sources and how to combine your own analysis with material from secondary sources. Our sample topic is the dramatic function of the graveyard scene in Shakespeare's *Hamlet*. In Chapter 13 we demonstrate how you would write and revise a research paper, again using this sample topic.

Stage 1   Clarifying Research Topics

Step 1   Defining Unfamiliar Terms

Since research papers are usually on specialized topics, you should be alert to the specialized use of terms. If you were writing a psychology paper on the development of the concept of narcissism, for example, you would begin by checking the definition of narcissism in your textbook and in a specialized dictionary such as the *Dictionary of Psychology*

(New York: Dell, 1985). You will find an annotated guide to such reference sources in Part 4, Resources for Writing.

Step 2 Understanding Directions

A research paper is not merely a compilation of information and opinion about your subject. In writing on a content topic, you will need to analyze, compare, and evaluate your research material. In writing on a textual topic, you will need to analyze (and perhaps compare and/or evaluate) your primary text(s) as well as secondary sources.

Step 3 Choosing a Topic

If you haven't had much experience writing research papers, you will probably want to choose a topic that seems both interesting and relatively straightforward. Because topics are sometimes more (and sometimes less) complex than they appear, it is a good idea to spend a few minutes brainstorming about each topic when you receive the assignment. If you decide on your topic well before the due date, you give yourself more time to think about it, even when you are not actively engaged in research and writing.

Step 4 Limiting Your Topic: Defining a Research Question

One of the most important preliminary steps is turning your research topic into a research question, that is, a central question that your paper will answer. For topics that are specific in focus, you can simply put your research topic into the form of a question. "The impact of the Free Trade Agreement on Canadian auto manufacturing," for instance, would become "What has been the impact of the Free Trade Agreement on Canadian auto manufacturing?" The question form will remind you that there are many possible answers, depending upon the point of view of the writers you consult.

When you are given a broad topic, you are free to select your own focus. But the wealth of information available means that it is easy to get bogged down or sidetracked. You will find it easier to locate material, and to make decisions about its usefulness, if you begin with a well-defined research question. Use brainstorming, freewriting, or tree diagramming (see Chapter 2) to develop a broad range of questions about your subject. If you tried brainstorming about the broad topic of eating disorders, for instance, you might come up with the following research questions: What causes eating disorders? What are the physical, psychological, and/or social effects? What are the current treatments? Although you might be tempted to try to answer all of these questions, your resulting paper could be rather superficial. You would be better off to choose one of these questions and explore it fully. Keep the other possibilities in mind in case you cannot find enough material to answer your original question. If you are concerned that your research question may narrow the topic inappropriately, check with your instructor.

Step 5   Choosing Material: Primary and Secondary Sources

As we indicated in Chapter 2, research papers include both *primary* sources (such as written documents, performances, experiments, and interviews) and *secondary* sources (such as articles and books written about your subject by others). If you were writing a research paper on *Hamlet*, the play would be your primary source; works about *Hamlet* would be your secondary sources.

One of the reasons for writing research papers is to learn to evaluate and integrate different sources of information. You should therefore try to use secondary sources that represent the range of information or opinion about your subject. Be careful not to base your essay on a single author's point of view, a single experiment, or a single survey. The number of references considered adequate will depend on the discipline, the instructor, the length of the assignment, and the amount of material available on your topic. A good rule of thumb is to use at least six reference sources in the final draft of a short research essay. Your working bibliography will likely contain two or three times as many entries as you actually use.

Clarifying research topics: The dramatic function of the graveyard scene in *Hamlet* Let's suppose that from the list of topics for a 2000-word research paper in your first-year English course, you have chosen this one:

> Using several critical discussions of the play, explore the dramatic function of the graveyard scene in *Hamlet*.

This topic obviously requires textual analysis, since you are asked to focus on how a particular part of the play "works." You might need to clarify the term "dramatic function." The term suggests that you should consider why the scene comes where it does in the structure of the play, rather than focus solely on the ideas it presents. You might formulate your research question like this: What does this scene contribute to the structure and meaning of the play? The topic suggests that you should use several secondary sources to clarify and enrich your interpretation of the scene and of the play. Since 2000 words is fairly short for a research paper, six sources should be adequate. You would thus aim for a working bibliography of about eighteen references.

Stage 2 Gathering Primary and Secondary Material

Step 1 Exploring Preliminary Sources of Information

Getting an overview of your subject If you are unfamiliar with your subject, you may need to do some preliminary investigation before you can plan an efficient research strategy. Here are some suggestions:

- For content analysis topics, read an overview of your subject in your textbook or an encyclopedia. For textual analysis topics, the best source may be one of the short introductory books published on most authors, genres, and literary and film topics. For both kinds of topics, reference materials such as the "Macropedia" section of the *Encyclopaedia Britannica*, or indexes like the *Index to Book Reviews* or the *Citation Index*, will help to give you a sense of the key writers on your subject. Bibliographies handed out in class and references in textbooks also often supply good starting points.

- Discuss your topic with your instructor, your classmates, or other people who know something about it. Reference librarians are an invaluable resource for helping you plan an efficient research strategy.

Analyzing your subject You will be better able to keep your research material in perspective if, as far as possible, you produce your own analysis, comparison, or evaluation before you consult secondary sources. Here are some suggestions:

- First, jot down what you already know and think about the subject, using one of the discovery techniques discussed in Chapter 2.

- For content analysis, use the general categories of systems, process, and/or causal analysis (see Chapter 3) to organize your notes and to clarify the kinds of secondary material you need to look for. For instance, you may know something about the *kinds* of treatment available for eating disorders, but discover that you don't know anything about the actual *process* of treatment. Or if you have read an overview that suggests key issues about your subject, use these issues as categories to organize your research and note-taking.

- For textual analysis, make notes in the appropriate special categories for analyzing texts (see Resource 6 in Part 4). Or if some issues suggested by your preliminary reading or discussion seem particularly relevant to your topic, use those issues as organizing categories. For instance, from class discussion of Joy Kogawa's *Itsuka*, you might have a sense of the questions to ask when you analyze the relation between fact and fiction in a different novel.

Writing down this material will help you to keep track of which ideas are yours and which ones come from secondary sources, and to prevent accidental plagiarism. It may also help you change or refine your research question.

Gathering material: Getting an overview of *Hamlet* Before you read the critics, you need to have some idea of what *Hamlet* as a whole is about and to work out a preliminary analysis of the graveyard scene. If you have not discussed the play in class, you might find it useful to begin by skimming an introductory book such as Keith Sagar's *Hamlet (Shakespeare)* (Oxford: Blackwell, 1969), which gives a scene-by-scene explanation of the action. On rereading the play, you might decide that *Hamlet* is about the prince's search for the proper action to take in a world where his high standards for determining the truth come into conflict with the corrupt Danish court.

Gathering material: Analyzing *Hamlet* Your next step would be to reread the graveyard scene carefully, taking notes according to the special categories for analyzing drama (see Resource 6 in Part 4).

NOTES ON *HAMLET*

Subject and Genre: What is the scene about? Does this play belong to a particular genre (kind) of drama?

Subject: death—conversation between two gravediggers about Ophelia's burial, Hamlet's jests with gravedigger about corpses and speculations about human mortality, Ophelia's funeral procession, Hamlet's quarrel with Laertes in the open grave, Claudius' decision to put his plot against Hamlet into action.

Genre: tragedy—according to my class notes, Shakespearean tragedy involves the fall of a hero of high estate as a result of both circumstances outside the hero's control and actions that stem from a flaw in his character. Because the flaw is also what makes the hero great, his death produces emotions such as sympathy, pity, fear, awe, and a sense of waste.

Dramatic Structure: What is the principle behind the selection and arrangements of events ("action")?

> *Structure of scene:* two distinct episodes—gravediggers and confrontation with Laertes. Why does Shakespeare include the gravediggers? Why does he have Laertes and Hamlet leap into Ophelia's grave?
>
> *Relation of scene to play:* Act V, scene i—only one more scene in play. Hamlet's last appearance was at the end of IV.iv., where he encounters Fortinbras' forces as he is leaving for England after killing Polonius. The intervening scenes focus on Ophelia's madness, Laertes' return to avenge his father, Claudius' plot for killing Hamlet, and the news of Ophelia's suicide. The graveyard scene thus sets the stage for the final confrontation between Hamlet and his foes.

Dramatic Setting: What is the place, time, and social environment within which the action takes place?

> *Place:* church graveyard.
>
> *Time:* day after Ophelia's death, news of Hamlet's return (see IV.vii.)
>
> *Social environment:* marked contrast in social position between gravediggers and the court. The gravediggers conclude that Ophelia is to be given a Christian burial only because she is a gentlewoman; Hamlet contrasts the gravedigger's insensitivity with the "daintier sense" of those who don't work for a living (V.i. 65–66).
>
> *Relation of scene to play:* graveyard setting connects this scene with others associated with death, such as Ghost's revelations, play within a play, murder of Polonius, Ophelia's death. The setting makes Hamlet's preoccupation with death part of the climax of the play.

Characterization: What are the characters like? How are various techniques, including dialogue and acting, used to portray them?

> *First Clown (Gravedigger):* witty, cynical, down to earth; not awed by death or by the nobility.
>
> *Hamlet:* presented in the first half of the scene as philosophical about death, not morbidly obsessed as he was at the beginning of the play. Begins to rant in response to Laertes' lamentations about Ophelia, but also declares his love for her and for Laertes.
>
> *Other characters:* Laertes is the other major character in the scene. What is the purpose of his excessive show of grief?

Diction, Images and Symbols, Pacing: What do I learn from usage level and word choice? What do images and symbols convey? What is the rhythm of dialogue and action?

> *Diction:* gravediggers' speech colloquial, comic, matter of fact; language of the court mainly informal, except for Laertes', which is formal and pretentious. Hamlet's language moves between these levels, sometimes in the same sentence: the lawyer's "fine pate" is "full of fine dirt" (V.i. 100); and the "noble dust of Alexander" can be found "stopping a bunghole" (V.i. 191–192).

> *Images and symbols:* many associated with death—skulls, grave.

> *Pacing:* language shifts from conversational prose in gravedigger episode to blank verse in burial scene; verbal "fight" between Laertes and Hamlet is the most distinctive use of sentence structure. Action shows similar shift from slow pace of first half of scene to unexpected twist as Hamlet and Laertes fight in the grave. Doesn't this behaviour seem a bit ridiculous?

Tone: What attitude to subject or audience is evident?

> The tone of the early part of the scene is playful, meditative, probing; the tone of the later part is emotional and dramatic.

Theme: What is the central idea?

> The scene shows Hamlet reacting to death in two violently contrasting ways. He is playful and self-possessed, somewhat distant when he thinks of death in abstract terms; but he is much more emotional when death becomes personal (Yorick's skull, Ophelia). How does this conflict relate to his search for proper action?

These notes will help you to determine whether the critics you consult are relevant to your topic.

Step 2   Compiling a Working Bibliography

A working bibliography is a preliminary list of books and articles that, from their titles or other information available to you, seem relevant to your research question.

For each reference you will need to take down complete bibliographical details, in the form discussed below. This information will enable you to locate material in your library and to identify in your paper the sources you have used. If you record full publication data as you collect your initial references, you will save yourself return trips to the library for missing information. You will also protect yourself against unintentional plagiarism: the use of ideas and information from sources that are not identified. You will find a fuller discussion of this issue in the next chapter.

Recording each reference on a separate file card, on a separate page of a small research notebook, or in a computer file will enable you to add or discard items easily. You will find sample bibliography entries below.

Locating references

Library Catalogues Today, most libraries provide access to the materials in their collections through on-line catalogues, although some retain card or microfiche catalogues. Whatever system your library uses, you can generally search for books by author, title, or subject. If you are looking for books *by* a particular author, use the author search option. If you are searching for resources *about* an author, however, you must use the subject search option. Subject searches are often the most fruitful, but can be frustrating if you do not choose the most appropriate search terms. If you don't find any listings under the first subject heading you try, consult the two-volume *Library of Congress Subject Headings*. This catalogue is especially useful for topics that might appear under several different headings. If you are looking for information on vitamin deficiencies, for example, you might not find any references under that heading. The *Library of Congress Subject Headings* catalogue would refer you to headings such as "Nutrition." You would then look for material under these headings. A reference librarian can help you define and limit your search.

Your library may contain relevant books that do not turn up during your search of the catalogue. When you go to the stacks, take a few minutes to scan titles and check indexes of books nearby. You may discover two or three useful sources.

Annual Bibliographies and Periodical Indexes Another useful source of references is annual bibliographies, which compile lists of both books and articles published in given areas over the course of a year, organized under appropriate subject (and sometimes author) headings. Periodical indexes are similar, but list only articles. The following list suggests the wide range of works available.

General Indexes
Canadian Periodical Index
Essay and General Literature Index
Readers' Guide to Periodical Literature

Specialized Indexes
Applied Science and Technology Index
Arts and Humanities Citation Index
MLA International Bibliography (modern languages and
literature)
Philosopher's Index
Psychological Abstracts
Religious and Theological Abstracts
The Year's Work in English Studies

If you are not sure which periodical index or annual bibliography
to consult for your topic, ask a librarian. Indexes with the word "abstract" in the title offer a summary of the books and articles they cite,
as well as giving publication details.

Many annual bibliographies and periodical indexes are available in
both print and CD-ROM versions, and some may also be accessed on-
line. Most people prefer to consult the electronic versions of these
texts, where available. Complex searches can be completed in seconds
on the computer, and in most libraries the list of useful citations you
discover can be downloaded onto a disk or printed off free of charge.
It's well worth your time, therefore, to familiarize yourself with your library's holdings of the electronic versions of those bibliographies and
indexes most relevant to your discipline. You should be aware, though,
that the electronic versions of these texts are very popular. You may
need to book an appointment to use them well in advance.

How to Use Print Versions The other solution to this problem is, of
course, to conduct your research by using the print versions of the bibliographies and indexes you wish to consult.

The most efficient way to use a periodical index or annual bibliography is to start with the current volume and work backwards until
you have enough references. Copy down references exactly as they
appear and then consult the key to abbreviations in the front of the
volume to decipher the entries. If you were looking in the *1992
Applied Science and Technology Index* for references on forest management, for example, you would find this entry under the heading
"TIMBER":

> The tropical timber trade and sustainable development. J. R.
> Vincent. bibl diags Science 256:1651–5 Je 19, 1992

Checking the key to abbreviations for this index, you would discover that this article by J. R. Vincent was published in the periodical
Science, volume 265, pages 1651–1655, on June 19, 1992, and that the
article includes a bibliography and diagrams.

For research on Shakespeare, you might consult the comprehensive annual bibliography published in *Shakespeare Quarterly* or the Author Index volumes of the yearly *MLA International Bibliography*.

How to Use CD-ROM and On-Line Versions   As in the case of using most electronic bibliographies and indexes, using the *MLA International Bibliography* on CD-ROM is much the same as using the print version.

First you must establish the terms you will use to search for information. Just as with the printed bibliography, you may search by title, author, or subject. Searching by subject is most likely to yield results. If you were writing a paper on the significance of the graveyard scene in *Hamlet*, for example, you would likely begin with the most obvious term—"Hamlet." The search takes only seconds and yields 915 entries—far too many to sift individually. You must narrow your search by cross-referencing with another term. Using "Hamlet" and "death," the computer will retrieve a list of 18 entries. One of the articles, "The Gravedigger's Scene: A Unifying Thread in *Hamlet*," by William E. Bennett, did not appear on the list of articles retrieved when using "Hamlet" and "graveyard" as subject terms. The computer is quite literal and "graveyard" is not the same as "gravedigger's." If you expand your search to related subjects—Ophelia, for instance—a quite different list is generated.

Because these lists require only seconds to retrieve and transcribe using CD-ROM technology, it is easy to assume that the computer is doing your searching for you. Such is not the case. Just as your automobile cannot get you where you want to go unless you steer it, so CD-ROM cannot produce the best results unless you guide it. You must direct the machine to the appropriate listings, using foresight and intelligence.

Advantages and Disadvantages   There are several advantages to using periodical indexes and annual bibliographies to find articles for your working bibliography.

1. Articles are more specialized than books; you are therefore more likely to find articles directly related to your research question. If you want material on the economic causes of the First World War, for instance, the titles of articles will tell you whether they cover your topic, whereas many book titles would not—you would have to locate the book and consult the index to find out.

2. Current research in many fields appears in articles several years before it is available in books. Periodicals are therefore a much better source of information in new and rapidly developing fields such as East Asian studies and gender studies, as well as in the sciences.

3. If all the relevant books on your topic are checked out, you can still find material in magazines or scholarly journals.

There are also potential disadvantages in using periodical indexes. One is that you may record a number of articles, only to discover that your library does not subscribe to some of the journals. You can cut down this risk by listing only works published in major scholarly journals. Note that many libraries compile information about their periodical holdings (newspapers, magazines, scholarly journals) in what is called a **serials list**. The serials list is the most efficient way of determining whether your library has the articles you need, since you can look up all the journal titles at the same time. Another potential disadvantage is that if you rely solely on these sources, you will likely miss important earlier work on your subject. You can usefully supplement periodical indexes by finding an annotated bound bibliography, if there is one for your subject. Consult the appropriate subject heading in your library's card or on-line catalogue. For Shakespeare you would find this entry:

> Champion, Larry S. *The Essential Shakespeare: An Annotated Bibliography of Major Modern Studies*. Boston: Hall, 1986.

The Internet If you have access to the Internet and are a regular visitor to cyberspace, you are probably aware that a simple Internet search can link you to a great deal of potentially valuable information on your topic, in the form of newsgroup postings, listserv messages, electronic journals, and files available for viewing and downloading via sites on the World Wide Web. As in the case of all on-line searches, choosing the most appropriate search terms will be vital to your success. You may need to experiment with several combinations to provide the best and most thorough results. Unlike library catalogues, Internet information has no common set of subject terms assigned to it, and consequently finding valuable sources on the Internet is often hit and miss. Experimenting with different search engines is also a good idea. Some, such as Yahoo!, are organized by subject and can therefore help you weed out much of the irrelevant information that Internet searches often produce.

One problem with using the Internet as a research tool lies in the unvetted nature of much of the material you will find on it. Unlike print sources, which generally receive the scrutiny of an editor and publisher before they reach your library, only some Internet publications (primarily electronic journals) are subject to such a process of critical evaluation. Consequently, the trustworthiness and scholarly value of Internet sources is much less easy to verify. For this reason, it is usually not a good idea to rely exclusively on Internet sources in your essay.

When you discover a site or document that you believe will be useful, create a bookmark for it so that you can return to it easily. Andrew Harnack and Eugene Kleppinger, in their handbook *Online!: A Reference Guide to Using Internet Sources* (New York: St. Martin's, 1997, 55), list the following as important information to record about sources:

Author(s)

Title of document

Electronic address

Date of publication

Date of access

Part or section heading or number

Other important information (that is, type of e-mail message)

Bear in mind that it will often be impossible for you to find some of this information—record as much of it as is available for each of your sources. For more information on finding, evaluating, using, and documenting Internet sources, consult Harnack and Kleppinger's book or visit their Web site at <http://www.smpcollege.com/online-4styles~help>. A brief guide to documenting the most common type of Internet sources appears in Documentation in Part 2, Handbook for Final Editing.

One final research option is to request a professional on-line search. These searches, conducted by a librarian according to the search terms you provide, cover commercial databases not available on CD-ROM. A fee is usually charged for such searches, however, and you may find that you end up with more material than you have time to evaluate.

Recording bibliographical information For each reference you include in your working bibliography, record complete bibliographical information so that you can find the work in your library, and, if you use it in your essay, include the appropriate citation.

- Record the following information, in the order given, for each secondary source:

  a. For *books*: Complete name of author(s), last name first; title; place of publication, publisher, and date of publication.

     King, Walter N. *Hamlet's Search for Meaning*. Athens, GA: U of Georgia P, 1982.

  b. For *articles*: Complete name of author(s), last name first; title of article; magazine or journal in which the article appears; day, month, and year of publication (for weekly and monthly magazines) or volume, issue number, and year (for journals); page numbers.

Cohen, Michael. " 'To what base uses we may return': Class and Mortality in *Hamlet* (5.1)." *Hamlet Studies* 9:1–2 (Summer–Winter 1987), 78–85.

    c. For *Internet and other sources*: See the discussion of Internet sources above and in Documentation, Part 2, Handbook for Final Editing.

- A the bottom of the entry, note the bibliography, index, or catalogue in which you found the reference, in case you discover you have not recorded it accurately.

- From your library's on-line, microfiche, or card catalogue, copy the call number for each book or journal, and, if your college or university has more than one library, note the locations of copies. If you fail to find some of your references, note "not in library" or "volume missing" on your entry.

Sample entries in your working bibliography, with a call number for the Library of Congress classification system, might look like this:

ENTRY FOR A BOOK

Mitchell, James. *Anorexia Nervosa and Bulimia: Diagnosis and Treatment*. Minneapolis: U of Minneapolis P, 1985. Health Sciences Lib. RC 552/A5/A623. [Source: on-line catalogue].

ENTRY FOR AN ARTICLE

Gikandi, Simon. "Chinua Achebe and the Post-Colonial Aesthetic: Writing, Identity and National Formation." *Studies in Twentieth Century Literature* 15.1 (1991): 29–41. [Source: MLA International Bib. (1992)]

Step 3   Evaluating Secondary Sources and Taking Notes

Evaluating secondary sources   Before you start taking notes, spend a few minutes evaluating each of your references. For books, check the table of contents and the index and skim the pages most relevant to your research question. Read the introductory and concluding paragraphs of articles.

    If you decide to discard a reference because its focus seems different from your own, make a note on your file entry saying so and indicating what its focus is. References you discard at this stage may prove to be useful later on if you change the direction of your research.

Taking notes   For books, articles, and Internet sources that address relevant issues or provide useful factual information, take notes on these points:

- The issue or problem that the writer identifies.
- The main point the writer makes about the issue.
- The context of this issue. Does the writer give background information or summarize the viewpoints of other writers?
- Key points in the development of the explanation or argument and key pieces of evidence cited.
- The writer's conclusion.
- Your own reactions to and evaluation of the reference.

Summarizing Summarize or paraphrase most material. Use point form to avoid inadvertent plagiarism and include the page reference for each point and detail.

Quoting Use direct quotation when the precise wording may be important to your discussion, as in definitions of concepts or particularly effective ways of making a point. Try not to quote more than a sentence at a time; quote the whole sentence so that you will have the context (you can shorten quotations when you edit); copy the quotation *exactly* as it appears in the original (including spelling and punctuation); put quotation marks around everything you quote, however short; indicate the exact page on which each quotation occurs. If a quotation is continued from one page to another, use a slash mark to indicate the page break in case you decide to omit part of it.

Evaluating Conclude your notes on each reference with your own evaluation of the ideas and evidence it presents, your comments on its relation to other references, and/or your notes on its place in your essay. To avoid possible confusion, put your own comments in square brackets or use some other way of identifying them.

Step 4 Categorizing Material: Combining Preliminary Analysis and Research Material

Now you have your preliminary notes, which may include your analysis of primary sources, and your notes on secondary sources. In order to synthesize and integrate the two, you need to complete these steps:

- Choose the most relevant categories of preliminary material.
- Establish appropriate categories for the secondary material.
- Put the two sets of material together so that you can see where they do and do not match.

Through this process a general point will begin to emerge that you can refine to make your thesis. To demonstrate this final step in the process of gathering material, let us look at the sample topic.

Choosing material from your preliminary analysis All your original material may still seem relevant, or some categories may seem more relevant than others, perhaps because they form a distinct pattern, or because you now understand the assignment or the subject better.

If you review the preliminary analysis of *Hamlet* (pages 143–45), the material in the categories of dramatic structure and characterization seem to form the most distinct pattern. In each category there is a striking contrast between elements that are down-to-earth and witty (Hamlet conversing with the gravediggers; the first gravedigger) and elements that are emotional and dramatic (Hamlet discussing Ophelia and struggling with Laertes; Laertes). What dramatic function can a scene with such contrasting elements fulfill in the play as a whole?

Establishing categories for secondary material When you read literary criticism, you will often find that critics organize their material according to issues or theories rather than by the categories we suggest for textual analysis.

Nevertheless, as you will see when you combine the two sets of material, these categories of textual analysis underlie much critical commentary. Few of the critics writing about the graveyard scene have anything to say about its dramatic function; instead, they focus on what the scene shows about the development of Hamlet's attitudes towards death, an aspect of characterization. You can divide their views into three categories:

- The scene shows Hamlet developing a Christian acceptance of death (Walter King, Maynard Mack). *OR*
- It shows Hamlet developing a secular and fatalistic attitude (G. Wilson Knight, Richard Levine). *OR*
- It shows a mixture of these two attitudes (Peter Philias).

Combining material The most effective way to bring preliminary material and research material together is to use columns that make it clear where the two sets of material match and where they do not. You might set out the *Hamlet* material in columns as follows:

PRELIMINARY ANALYSIS	SECONDARY MATERIAL
Dramatic Structure	
2 contrasting episodes: gravediggers and Hamlet Hamlet and Laertes	Scene "bring[s] into dramatic focus parts… seemingly disparate" (Bennett, 160)
	Laertes' "ranting" creates sympathy for Hamlet (Cheadle) Bending over Ophelia creates sympathy for Hamlet (Cheadle)

Characterization

First gravedigger: witty,   "ranting" (Cheadle)
cynical, down to earth

Laertes: dramatic, elevated
language

Hamlet: Hamlet's Attitude to Death:
lst episode: witty, less   Move to Christian acceptance
metaphysical   (King, Mack)
2nd episode: feeling, dramatic   Move to fatalism
                                              (Knight, Levine)
                                              Mixture of above (Philias)

As you can see, placing this material in columns reveals at a glance that both the preliminary analysis and the secondary material comment on the Hamlet–Laertes episode. The columns do not match, however, when it comes to the characterization of Hamlet. You can thus see more clearly what you have to contribute to the interpretation of this scene—your reasons for the shift in Hamlet's character.

Once you have brought your preliminary analysis and your research material together in a systematic way, you are ready to move on to the next stages of writing a research paper: formulating a thesis and writing and revising a draft. We will discuss these stages in Chapter 13.

Working on Your Own Assignment

Preliminary thinking and writing about your research paper topic will help you to plan and carry out an efficient strategy for gathering material.

- Spend a few minutes freewriting or brainstorming about each possible topic so that you understand what each one demands.

- Choose a topic that interests you and narrow your focus to one or two specific research questions.

- Use appropriate categories for content analysis or the special categories for textual analysis to explore and develop your approach to your topic (see Part 4, Resources for Writing).

- Compile a working bibliography of secondary sources by using periodical indexes and annual bibliographies (print, CD-ROM, or on-line versions) and catalogues of your library's holdings. You might also search the Internet for possible sources.

- For each secondary source, take down complete bibliographical information.

- Make most of your notes in point form, with short, carefully selected quotations for key ideas. Include page numbers for both quoted and paraphrased material.
- Reorganize your notes into matching columns, with your ideas on one side of the page, ideas and information from secondary sources (with references) on the other. This integration of primary and secondary material will help you with the next stage of the process, working out a thesis that answers the most important questions posed by your topic.

EXERCISES

A.   Respond to each of the following questions in a sentence or two.

1. How is a research essay different from a research report?

2. If you were writing an essay on Charles Dickens' novel *Great Expectations*, what would be your primary source of information? What kinds of material would be secondary sources?

3. Why should you work out your own ideas about your subject before you begin to do research?

4. How would you find these four sources of information for a research essay on juvenile arthritis: a book, a scholarly article, an article in a popular magazine, an electronic publication?

5. What is the most efficient way to take good notes on secondary sources?

B.   Gather material for a mini-research paper on one of the topics below by (1) formulating a research question; (2) making notes about your own ideas on the subject; and (3) using three or four essays from Part 3, Readings, as your secondary material. Keep your notes on this material for an exercise in Chapter 13.

- attitudes towards eating
- attitudes towards science and/or technology
- attitudes towards cultural differences
- attitudes towards creativity

chapter 13

Writing Research Papers

A research paper is the longest and most time-consuming project in most courses, and so it's especially important to plan your time carefully. This chapter will be much more useful if you have worked through all the steps in Chapter 12: Gathering Material for Research Papers, which explains the following:

- How to choose a research topic.
- How to formulate a research question.
- How to compile a working bibliography.
- How to take notes on secondary sources and document them.
- How to organize your notes to reveal the similarities and differences between your ideas and the ideas you find in other sources.

In this chapter we discuss the remaining stages in writing and revising a research paper, from finding a thesis to revising individual paragraphs. As you will see, the most important issue is working out a clear relationship between your own ideas about your subject and the ideas and information in your research material.

The first part of this chapter focuses on common problems you may encounter in writing research papers. The second part takes you through the process of writing a research paper with our sample topic: the function of the graveyard scene in *Hamlet*.

Stage 3   Formulating a Thesis: Answering Your Research Question

Step 1   Forming an Opinion

Because a research paper is an essay, it must have a thesis: your main point about your subject. As you look over your notes, try to find a pattern that unites your categories of material. If you have gathered material on characterization in *Macbeth*, for instance, you may find that you can connect several points by focusing on the destructive effects of gender stereotypes. Or your research into alcoholism may suggest weaknesses with the disease model that you can make central to your paper.

If you have trouble seeing connections among your categories of material, ask yourself these questions:

- What was my research question?
- What issues did I find in my research material?

- What are the connections between these issues and my research question?

The answers to these questions should lead you to an opinion about your subject. Check your opinion against your essay topic to make sure that you have not been led off-topic by your research material.

Step 2   Supporting Your Opinion

Your opinion about your subject may not differ from the views of other writers you have consulted. If you were researching Britain's entry into the First World War, for example, you might conclude, along with the historians you had consulted, that the British were initially disorganized and inefficient. You might wonder, then, how your thesis could be any more than a summary of the research you had done.

The answer is that the reasons you give to support your opinion will be your contribution to the debate. In your reading about Britain's war effort, for example, you may find one historian who blames the slow start on Prime Minister Herbert Asquith's indecisiveness; another who blames the arrogance of Field Marshall Earl Kitchener; and a third who blames the British class system and capitalist economics. In order to give reasons for your opinion, you will have to reach your own conclusions about the relevance of each of these factors. Through this process you develop the intellectual framework for your essay, instead of depending upon the framework provided by your sources.

When you revise, make sure you check your thesis against the possible problems outlined in Chapter 7. If you have trouble revising your thesis satisfactorily, review the process of finding a thesis in Chapter 5.

Stage 4   Drafting: Making a Formal Outline

When you are writing short essays, you may plan your piece by jotting down your points in a draft outline (see Chapter 6). When you are writing a research paper, however, you may be asked to hand in a **formal outline** as a guide for your reader. Some writers finish the paper first and then write an outline. You can also make a formal outline before you write your draft to work out the relationship among your major points, minor points, and supporting evidence. You can also use the outline to check the balance between material you've found in your sources and your own analysis.

To make a formal outline, write your thesis at the top of a page. Then list your major points with Roman numerals, your subpoints under each heading with capital letters, and evidence to support each subpoint with Arabic numerals. If you need a fourth level, use lower-case letters. Your outline will look something like this:

THESIS: main idea of the whole essay

I. Major Point

    A. Minor point
        1. Evidence (writer A)
        2. Evidence (your analysis)

    B. Minor point
        1. Evidence (your analysis)
        2. Evidence (quotation from writer B)

II. Major Point

    A. Minor point
        1. Evidence (facts and figures from writer C)
        2. Evidence (your analysis)

    B. Minor point
        1. Evidence (your examples)
        2. Evidence (examples from writer D)
        3. Evidence (quotation from writer E)

Since an outline is a way of classifying information by dividing it into smaller units, you should have at least two items at each level. That means if you have an A, you must have a B; if you have a 1, you must have a 2. Difficulties in filling in your outline may indicate important gaps in your material or a need to combine small points under a broader heading.

Your formal outline will be more useful to you and your reader if you state the ideas you intend to express, not just the subject of each section or paragraph. A heading like "Hamlet and Laertes in the grave," for instance, is less useful than one like "Hamlet's grappling with Laertes in the grave foreshadows their duel and deaths." You can easily turn headings that make a point into topic sentences for your middle paragraphs. You will find an example of a formal outline in the sample topic below.

Stage 5 Revising: Integrating and Documenting Research Material

As you draft your research paper, keep the same principles in mind as for other kinds of essays. When you finish, make a revision outline and check your thesis, essay structure, and individual paragraphs. You will find an example of this process in the sample topic that concludes this chapter. Here we will focus on the problems specific to research papers: integrating and documenting your research material.

Step 1 Integrating Research Material

When you use research material, keep the following principles in mind.

- Your main purpose in a research essay (as in any essay) is to present *your* views on a subject. Use ideas and factual information from other writers to provide additional support for your views or to provide alternative views that you will argue against.

- Write clear, focused topic sentences that guide your readers through each step of your argument or analysis.

- Make clear distinctions between your ideas and those of your sources by using appropriate transitional words and phrases (Wong's study provides further support...; on the other hand, Friedman argues...).

- If your subject is a work of literature, be sure to provide your own evidence from the work to explain why you agree or disagree with another writer's interpretation. Don't rely on quotations from critics to make important points for you.

- Keep quotations short and in appropriate format (see Quotations in Part 2, Handbook for Final Editing).

- Include explanations that make the significance of details apparent to your reader.

When you are trying to pull together material from a wide variety of sources, it's easy to get caught up in details and lose sight of the points those details are meant to support.

In the following paragraph, for instance, the writer draws on three sources: J. M. Bynner, *The Young Smoker* (London: Her Majesty's Stationery Office, 1969); Bernard Mausner and Ellen S. Platt, *Smoking: A Behavioral Analysis* (New York: Pergamon, 1971); and Richard Olshavsky, *No More Butts: A Psychologist's Approach to Quitting Cigarettes* (Bloomington: Indiana UP, 1977). The paragraph provides adequate *details* in a mixture of summary and quotation. It is very confusing, however, because it does not provide enough *explanation* of the relationship between the topic sentence and the various studies; indeed, one of the studies seems to contradict the others.

> The social causes of smoking have been established in a number of studies. According to B. Mausner and E. Platt, many smokers reported that they thought of smokers as daring and sophisticated and of non-smokers as sensible and

careful (7). According to Richard Olshavsky, advertising does not seem either to inhibit or to promote cigarette smoking (98). In his study of the smoking habits of British schoolboys, J. M. Bynner discovered that "Boys who smoke thought of themselves as being fairly tough but not as tough as they would like to be. They, more than any other group, saw non-smokers as completely lacking in toughness, and thus the act of giving up smoking involved identification with a group which had a very unattractive characteristic" (93).

Notice how the revised version links the topic sentence with the research details, explains the apparent contradiction in the studies, and maintains the mixture of summary and quotation:

The social causes of smoking have been established in a number of studies. Although the image of smokers conveyed by advertising may not be important, since, as Richard Olshavsky points out, advertising does not seem either to inhibit or to promote cigarette smoking (98), there is good evidence that the image smokers have of themselves is very important. In his study of the smoking habits of British schoolboys, J. M. Bynner discovered that "Boys who smoke thought of themselves as being fairly tough but not as tough as they would like to be. They, more than any other group, saw non-smokers as completely lacking in toughness, and thus the act of giving up smoking involved identification with a group which had a very unattractive characteristic" (93). Adults seem to share this kind of thinking. According to B. Mausner and E. Platt, many smokers reported that they thought of smokers as daring and sophisticated, and of non-smokers as sensible and careful (7).

Step 2   Documenting Research Material

Whenever you use ideas or information from another source, you must tell your readers where the material came from, whether you quote directly or paraphrase.

Failure to give credit when you use someone else's work is **plagiarism**.

Plagiarism is using the words or ideas of another writer as though they were your own. It is a form of stealing for which there are severe academic penalties, ranging from receiving a failing grade on the paper or in the course to being expelled.

One kind of plagiarism is deliberately stealing someone else's words. Students occasionally copy a friend's paper or a published source and attempt to pass the work off as their own. This type of plagiarism is usually easy to spot because instructors are familiar with the original or with the student's other work.

A more common kind of plagiarism is using someone else's words or ideas without adequately documenting the source. Although plagiarism of this type usually occurs as a result of sloppy note-taking rather than intentional deceit, the penalties may be almost as severe. You are responsible for distinguishing your own insights and ideas from the material you find in published sources. The following examples illustrate how to do so.

Here are the general principles to keep in mind:

- Make clear which ideas are yours and which come from secondary sources.

- Put quotation marks around any three or more consecutive words you use from a primary or secondary source. You will find guidelines for using quotations effectively and for quotation format in Quotations, Part 2, Handbook for Final Editing.

- Give references for both paraphrased and quoted material.

- Follow the proper format for in-text citations and bibliographical entries. You will find guidelines for both the MLA and APA systems of documentation in Documentation, Part 2, Handbook for Final Editing.

To illustrate these principles, let's look at an example.

Imagine that in doing research on the graveyard scene in *Hamlet*, you came across the following passage in Michael MacDonald's article "Ophelia's Maimed Rites" (*Shakespeare Quarterly*, 37:3 [Autumn 1986], 309–17. Reprinted by permission of *Shakespeare Quarterly*.) This passage describes the contradictory attitudes towards suicide that Shakespeare dramatizes.

PUBLISHED WRITING

It would be hard to think of a case better suited to illuminating the problems that identifying suicides and burying their bodies presented than the passive drowning of a madwoman of high birth. Nothing in V.i simplifies the difficulties that surround Ophelia's death. The quibbling of the clowns is effective satire because it pointedly calls attention to the arbitrary and subjective methods of coroners' juries. The hard words of the churlish priest highlight the failure of ecclesiastical law to provide guidance in such cases. Laertes's angry protests echo the desperation and humiliation displayed by hundreds of families whose loved ones killed themselves, families who then attempted to conceal the suicide or escape its consequences. In the argument between the priest and the bereaved brother, both parties were justified, and both parties would have claimed a share of the audience's sympathy. (316)

In taking notes, you might paraphrase the passage this way:

SAMPLE WRITING

Shakespeare dramatizes the contradictory attitudes towards suicide among his contemporaries without reconciling them. The death and burial of Ophelia reveal all the ambiguities surrounding cases of suicide. The gravediggers' jests underscore the arbitrary nature of the rulings made by coroners' juries. The exchanges between Laertes and the priest reflect on the one hand the anger and humiliation of the suicide's family, and on the other the lack of clear guidelines in church law. Shakespeare's audiences would have felt sympathy for both positions.

If you included this paragraph in your paper without indicating the source of the ideas, you would be guilty of plagiarism, even though the wording is different.

Adding a citation will identify the source of paraphrased material, but it may not clearly distinguish between another writer's ideas and your own. If you add the parenthetical reference (MacDonald 316) to the end of the paraphrase, for example, a reader would still not be sure whether all of the ideas are MacDonald's, or merely the point about Laertes and the priest. Putting MacDonald's name at the beginning of the paragraph, with the page reference at the end, would clearly establish whose ideas these are:

As Michael MacDonald points out, Shakespeare dramatizes attitudes towards suicide among his contemporaries.... Shakespeare's audiences would have felt sympathy for both positions. (316)

Sample Topic (Research): The Dramatic Function of the Graveyard Scene in *Hamlet*

In Chapter 12 we examined the first two stages in writing a research paper on the dramatic function of the graveyard scene in *Hamlet*, clarifying the topic and gathering material. Now we will show the remaining stages in writing and revising this research paper: formulating a thesis, drafting, revising thesis and essay structure, and revising individual paragraphs.

Stage 3   Formulating a Thesis

Step 1   Forming an opinion If you review the secondary material on the graveyard scene at the end of Chapter 12, you will notice that little of it directly addresses the question of dramatic function—that is, the purpose the scene serves at this point in the play. One critic who does address this issue is B. D. Cheadle. Cheadle comments that Shakespeare uses the contrast between Hamlet and Laertes to re-establish our sympathy for Hamlet before his impending death. This comment raises the possibility that other aspects of the scene serve the same dramatic function.

Re-examining the material, you might determine that other aspects of the scene do engage our sympathy for Hamlet, forfeited by his killing of Polonius and Ophelia's death. In the first half of the scene, the gravediggers criticize the court's using its power to ensure a Christian burial for Ophelia. Here the gravediggers provide a bridge for the audience between seeing events from the court's perspective and seeing them from Hamlet's perspective. When Hamlet enters, his first remark is on the insensitivity of the gravedigger, who sings while he works. This comment makes us feel that Hamlet has finer feelings. His exchanges with the gravedigger and his speculations about the dead seem almost comic, and yet we know, as Hamlet doesn't, that the grave being dug is Ophelia's. The dramatic irony of this situation would certainly make us more sympathetic to Hamlet.

In the second half of the scene, Hamlet's declaration of love for Ophelia and for Laertes would engage our sympathy, especially since we know that Laertes has agreed to Claudius' plot to kill Hamlet. The tussle in the grave seems to foreshadow the duel between Hamlet and Laertes and its outcome. This sense of impending doom would also make us sympathetic to Hamlet.

Several aspects of the scene do seem to confirm this interpretation. Your statement of opinion, then, might be something like this:

> The dramatic function of the graveyard scene is to engage
> the audience's sympathy for Hamlet before his death.

This opinion addresses the issue set out in the essay topic, and is therefore a suitable basis for a thesis.

Step 2   Supporting your opinion To give reasons for your opinion, you would return to those aspects of the scene that support your interpretation. You could complete the thesis about the dramatic function of the graveyard scene by showing how Hamlet's relations with the gravediggers, with Ophelia, and with Laertes affect the audience:

> The dramatic function of the graveyard scene is to engage the audience's sympathy for Hamlet before his death. The scene accomplishes this purpose in three ways: by using the gravediggers as a means to shift the audience's perspective from the court to Hamlet; by clarifying Hamlet's relationship with Ophelia; and by symbolically foreshadowing the outcome of the duel between Hamlet and Laertes.

Stage 4   Drafting

Steps 1 and 2   Selecting material and making points With research papers it is sometimes easy to focus on the criticism and lose sight of your own analysis of the text. One way you can maintain a balance is to synthesize the most relevant research in a paragraph or two at the beginning of your paper and then to develop your own analysis in detail, using references to critics to support specific points.

Step 3   Organizing material: Constructing a formal outline Once you have decided what material to use and what points to make, you can organize your material by making a formal outline something like this:

THE GRAVEYARD SCENE IN *HAMLET*

Thesis: The dramatic function of the graveyard scene is to engage the audience's sympathy for Hamlet before his death. The scene accomplishes this purpose in three ways: by using the gravediggers as a means to shift the audience's perspective from the court to Hamlet; by clarifying Hamlet's relationship with Ophelia; and by symbolically foreshadowing the outcome of the duel between Hamlet and Laertes.

I. Philosophical interpretations of the scene
   A. Scene shows Hamlet's Christian acceptance of death
   B. Scene shows fatalistic resignation in face of death
   C. Scene shows mixture of both these ways of viewing death
   D. Inadequacy of philosophical interpretations

II. Dramatic functions of the scene
   A. Encounter with gravediggers shifts sympathy from court to Hamlet
      1. Audience sympathizes with court in preceding scenes
      2. Hamlet presented as more sensitive than singing gravedigger
      3. Jests about death show Hamlet as neither morbidly preoccupied with death nor overly sentimental, but accepting its reality

    B. Last half of scene resolves ambiguity of Hamlet's feelings for Ophelia
      1. Earlier scenes show ambiguity in Hamlet's relations with Ophelia
      2. Hamlet regains sympathy by declaring his love for Ophelia

    C. Hamlet's grappling with Laertes in the grave foreshadows their duel and deaths

Step 4   **Sketching introduction and conclusion** To establish a context for the thesis about the graveyard scene, you might remind readers about its place in the action of the play as a whole. You might decide not to worry about a conclusion, since developing the body of a research paper is itself a considerable task, and merely say something about Hamlet as a tragic hero.

Step 5   **Writing the draft** You will find the final version of the research paper on the graveyard scene in Part 3, Readings. In the section below we will show how you would identify problems specific to research papers and make the appropriate revisions.

Stage 5   Revising Thesis and Essay Structure

Step 1   **Revising thesis** The idea of Hamlet as a tragic hero does not appear in the original thesis. Yet this point would help to explain *why* Shakespeare wants to engage our sympathy for Hamlet in this scene. You might therefore add this point to your thesis:

> Without a change in character, Hamlet would not achieve
> the stature of a tragic hero, because his death would not
> arouse the pity, fear, awe, and sense of waste common to
> Shakespearean tragedy.

Step 2   **Revising essay structure** If the draft follows the order of the formal outline, the structure as a whole should be satisfactory. You might discover a problem with paragraph divisions, however, such as a middle paragraph that is far too long and contains a confusing mixture of points about Hamlet's relation to Ophelia and to Laertes. You would note the changes needed on your revision outline.

Stage 6   Revising Individual Paragraphs

Step 1   Revising middle paragraphs

Checking Topic Sentences You may find that topic sentences in the draft are not very clear. Here, for example, is the original topic sentence for the second middle paragraph: "But our emotional response to the scene is shaped by the fact that it opens not with the funeral procession but with the gravediggers debating the decision to give Ophelia a Christian burial." This sentence does not make the point indicated on the outline: that the encounter with the gravediggers shifts the audience's sympathy from the court to Hamlet. You could make this point more clearly, and link it to Hamlet's role as a tragic hero, like this:

> The graveyard scene opens not with Hamlet's entrance but with the conversation between the gravediggers. This opening allows for a gradual shift in sympathy from the court to Hamlet and humanizes the prince by making death a personal rather than a metaphysical concern.

Integrating Research Material   A major task of revising research papers is clarifying the connections between your analysis and others' views. This excerpt from the draft illustrates this difficulty.

> After trying to figure out how a coroner might have reached a verdict of drowning in "self-defence," the gravediggers conclude that only her social position has secured Ophelia burial in consecrated ground, a burial that would have been denied a social inferior. The effect of this debate, as Peter Philias points out, is to shift attention away from the religious question of salvation and damnation that had been so powerful in Hamlet's own considerations of suicide (Philias 231). The reduction of death from a metaphysical to a human concern is further emphasized by the first grave-digger's actions: he tosses skulls about and sings while he works.

Here it is not clear how Ophelia's burial or Philias' explanation relates to the point about the audience's shifting sympathies. Furthermore, the last sentence introduces a new point.

In the revised version (middle paragraph 6), the connections are spelled out:

> But the graveyard scene does not merely shift the point of view from the court to Hamlet. It also humanizes Hamlet by making death a personal rather than a metaphysical concern. The gravediggers' debate over Ophelia's burial, as Peter Philias points out, shifts attention away from the religious questions of salvation and damnation that were so powerful when Hamlet himself was considering suicide, because the gravediggers focus on the social issues of power and status (231). The reduction of death from a metaphysical to a human concern is further emphasized by the gravedigger's actions as he tosses skulls about and sings about the human cycle of love, age, and death.

Acknowledging Sources In writing your draft, you might attempt to synthesize views about Hamlet but, as in this example, fail to indicate who holds each position:

> Many critics have suggested that the episode with the gravediggers indicates a change in Hamlet's character, though they have not agreed about the meaning of that change. Some see Hamlet coming to a Christian acceptance of death; others see his attitude as that of fatalistic resignation; others argue that the scene is a mixture of both these ways of viewing death.

In revising, you would need to discuss these views in more detail and to document your sources. In the final version, this paragraph has expanded into two, the first on the Christian interpretations and the second on the other interpretations. Here is the expanded material on the Christian interpretations, with the appropriate in-text citations:

> Maynard Mack and Walter King are representative of those who favour a Christian interpretation. According to Mack, Hamlet by the last act of the play has "learned, and accepted, the boundaries in which human action, human judgment are enclosed" and therefore no longer assumes he must single-handedly set the world to rights (521). Similarly, King argues that the graveyard scene presents "affirmation of life and love as a viable center of values in a God-created and God-centered universe," but within the context of a world in which these values "are perennially in danger of being snuffed out" (146).

Steps 2 and 3 Revising the introduction and conclusion In drafting your introduction, you might remind readers of previous events in the play. In revising, however, you may decide that some of this detail is excessive. The revised introduction shows how the analysis relates to the criticism and includes the point about Hamlet as a tragic hero.

You might have concluded your draft by saying something like, "In these ways, then, Shakespeare uses the graveyard scene to give Hamlet the qualities appropriate to his status as a tragic hero." The revised conclusion draws together the points made in the essay and again places this analysis within the context of other criticism.

Once you have written a revised draft, you are ready to give your research paper a final editing. Pay particular attention to quotations that are too long, poorly introduced, or inadequately explained and to the form and adequacy of citations. Aside from quotations and documentation, you are likely to have many of the same problems with sentence structure, grammar, and punctuation in research papers as in your other essays. Check the relevant sections of Part 2, Handbook for Final Editing. Make sure you have followed the guidelines for essay format and give your paper a final proofreading.

Working on Your Own Assignment

In writing and revising a research paper, your goal is to produce a coherent essay in which you integrate your own ideas about your subject with information and ideas drawn from secondary sources.

- Formulate a thesis by reviewing your notes to find *(a)* the connections between the material you have gathered and your research question and *(b)* the most important similarities and differences between your ideas and the information in your secondary sources.

- Organize your material by making a formal outline that sets out the main ideas in the paper. Indicate in the outline where you want to bring in secondary material and the point you want to make about it.

- As you write your draft, keep track of your sources by putting the author and page number in parentheses after each quotation and after any paraphrased material (for APA style, include the year of publication).

- Check the thesis and overall structure of your draft against your formal outline. Watch for paragraphs that are too long. You may need to subdivide them, to shorten quotations, or to delete unimportant or irrelevant material. Make a note of any necessary changes.

- As you read through each middle paragraph, ask yourself two questions: What is the main point? How does this material support my thesis? If your topic sentence does not answer these questions, revise it. Put all the important points in your own words and include quotations, references, and other evidence to support them. Make clear why you agree or disagree with the opinions of other writers.

- Make it easy for readers to see which ideas are yours and which come from other sources by introducing and giving citations for both quoted and paraphrased material.

- In both your introduction and your conclusion, connect your own thinking with your research material.

EXERCISES

A. Respond in a sentence or two to each of the following questions.

1. What are the key characteristics of an effective thesis for a research paper?

2. What should the outline for your research paper include?

3. Define the term **plagiarism**. What are the best strategies to avoid accidental plagiarism when you are writing a draft of your essay?

4. What does it mean to **integrate** research material? How can you integrate research material more fully into your essay?

5. Where in this text can you find information on the format for in-text citations? format for entries on a Works Cited page? format for long and short quotations of poetry and prose? guidelines for using quotations more effectively?

B. Write and revise a research essay on the topic you chose for Exercise B in Chapter 12.

Handbook for Final Editing

part two

Strategies for Final Editing

This is your last chance to eliminate the kinds of errors that can distract and annoy your reader. Here are some tips.

1. Wait at least a day after you have finished writing your essay. If you try to edit immediately, you will miss errors.

2. Use spelling checkers and other editing software to pick up errors. Then print out a hard copy and edit it. You will notice errors that you would miss on screen.

3. Make a list of the kinds of errors you frequently make (such as problems with pronoun agreement, apostrophes, commas) and watch particularly for them.

4. Begin editing with the last sentence in your conclusion. Read each sentence separately and work your way back to the first sentence in your introduction. This procedure will help you to see what you have actually written, not what you have have memorized.

The chart on the following pages lists in alphabetical order the most common errors in sentence structure, grammar, mechanics, and format. This chart also includes common marking symbols, an example of each error, and page references to explanations and exercises in the handbook. When you get an essay back, note your errors on the chart and keep the chart handy when you edit your next essay.

Identifying Common Problems

Term	Marking Symbol	Example of Common Error	Page Reference
abbreviation	*Abbrev*	The **pres.** of the company will visit **AB & SK** this **yr**.	258
apostrophe	*(ˀ)Apos*	We have an exciting new season in **childrens'** programs.	239
capitalization	*Caps*	My **Mother** and I lived in the **north** for seventeen years.	257
colon	⊙/⋀	The camp offered a number of activities such as: canoeing, swimming, and tennis.	248
comma	⊙/⋀	Bill enjoys tennis, and football.	242
comma splice	*CS, CF*	Loons are an endangered species, pollution is destroying their habitat.	183
dangling modifier	*DM*	**After running a marathon,** exhaustion is inevitable.	187
dash	⊖/⋁⁻	The storm ripped and scattered all the shingles—**on the new roof.**	249
diction	*Dic*	Alison decided **to partake in** the volleyball game.	208
documentation	*Doc*	Macbeth echoes the witches' opening words when he says, "So foul and fair a day I have not seen." **(no in-text citation)**	272
essay format	*EF*	Gender stereotypes in *Macbeth*.	175
faulty coordination	*F Coord*	Adam was terrified **and** he burst into laughter.	191
faulty subordination	*F Subord*	**Although** Irene wanted to stop smoking, **however**, she lacked the willpower.	192
fragment	*SF, Frag*	**Which is the main reason for Allan's success.**	182
fused sentence	*FS*	The baby is hot ⋀ she must have a fever.	185
hyphen	⊖/⋁⁻	The well⋀prepared athlete must be mentally and physically fit.	255
italics	*Ital.*	This summer I plan to read Tolstoy's novel **War and Peace** while I'm on holidays.	253
misplaced modifier	*MM*	I **hardly** have any money.	187
mixed construction	*Mix*	One reason he is often late **is because** his car has chronic battery problems.	194

numbers	*Num*	**15** employees refused to join **three hundred and forty seven** of their co-workers in signing a petition.	257
parallelism	*//ism*	Our servers must be hard-working, intelligent, **and they can't insult the customers**.	189
parentheses	*(/)(/)*	During the second period, (the fans were holding their breath,) our team scored the winning goal.	250
passive voice	*Passive*	After **the ghost was seen by Hamlet**, he hated his uncle more intensely.	225
possessive pronouns	*P Poss*	The jury made **it's** decision.	235
pronoun agreement	*P Agr*	**Every student** must check **their** bag at the door.	232
pronouns of address	*P Add P Shift*	By the end of the movie, **you** could see that The hero had matured.	228
pronoun case	*P Case*	**Her** and I have been married almost twelve years.	234
pronoun reference	*P Ref*	Fred doesn't know whether to to get married or join the navy **which** makes him uneasy.	236
quotation format	*Quot F*	Hamlet's despair is clear when he says, "O that this... into a dew."	267
quotation introduction	*Quot*	"The woods are lovely, dark, and deep." The speaker wants to rest.	265
quotation marks	*(")\w/*	Following the discussion of Alice Munro's story Boys and Girls, the class wrote an essay.	252
semicolon	*(;)\;*	When the movie ended; the audience burst into applause.	245
sentence length and structure	*S Var*	Hamlet misses his father. He is angry at his mother. He hates his uncle.	198
spelling	*Sp ()*	Elizabeth was **to** angry to speak.	261
split infinitive	*Split*	The rebels struggled **to strongly resist** the government forces.	188
subject–verb agreement	*S/V Agr*	The director's **use** of gimmicky special effects **were attacked** by the critics.	223
transitions	*Trans*	Peter wants to lose weight. ^ He refuses to diet.	204
verb forms	*VF*	After Sophy **had drank** the last beer, she **laid** on the couch and fell asleep.	219
verb tenses	*T, Tense*	Hamlet **grieves** for his father, but he **concealed** his feelings.	221
wordiness	*Wordy*	**Due to the fact that** the tickets sold out in the first half hour, many fans were disappointed.	216

1 Essay Format

Be sure to consult with your instructor if you have any questions about essay format. These are the most common conventions for the format of the essay and the title page.

Manuscript Conventions

1. Use white, standard-sized paper (not note-sized paper or over-sized computer sheets). Use ruled paper if you write longhand and write on only one side of the page.

2. Write in blue or black ink. If you use a dot-matrix printer, make sure the print is legible. Use a standard 12-point font. Do not set quotations in smaller type. If you wish to use a special font for a particular effect, check with your instructor.

3. Double-space typed essays. Check with your instructor about single- or double-spacing handwritten essays.

4. Leave generous margins, both to improve appearance and to provide space for comments. Margins should be about 3.5 cm (1 1/2 inches) on the left and at the top, and about 2.5 cm (1 inch) on the right and the bottom.

5. If you are using a word processor, check page breaks to make sure a heading doesn't appear at the bottom of a page.

6. Number the pages. Do not number the title page or the first page. Number the second page of your essay -2-. Place this number in the centre of the top margin.

7. Staple or clip the pages together. Do not fold corners or use pins.

8. Do not fold the essay or put it in a folder unless instructed to do so.

9. Keep a copy of your essay.

Title Page

1. At a minimum, the title of your essay should make clear which topic you are addressing. Avoid titles like "Essay 1." Good titles are usually a short form of your thesis.

2. Centre the title in the middle of your title page. Use normal-sized letters. Capitalize the first word and all other words except articles (*a, an, the*) and short prepositions (*on, at, in, of, for*).

3. Do not underline the title of your essay. Do not put quotation marks around it. Do not put a period after it. If your title includes the name of the work you are analyzing, follow these rules.

   a) If the work has been published separately (within its own covers), italicize (or underline) the title of the work. Titles of plays, films, magazines, and books are italicized.

   False Pride in Dickens' *Great Expectations*

   b) If the work has never been published within its own covers, put quotation marks around the title. Titles of short stories, poems, essays, and articles have quotation marks around them.

   The Theme of Possession in D. H. Lawrence's
   "The Rocking Horse Winner"

   Within your essay, follow the same rules for italicizing titles or putting quotation marks around them.

4. Put your name, the name of the course, the section number, the date, and your instructor's name (spelled correctly) in the lower right hand corner.

   Marco Deluca
   English 101 (08)
   January 22, 1998
   Instructor: Dr. Aisha Mitchell

2 Understanding Sentence Structure

If you sometimes make errors in sentence structure, then the terminology in this section will help you to diagnose your problems and correct them.

Recognizing Clauses and Phrases

Knowing the difference between a clause and a phrase will help you to understand sentence structure and thus eliminate accidental sentence fragments, comma splices (sometimes called comma faults), and fused sentences from your writing. A *clause* is a group of words that contains a subject and a verb. A *phrase* is a group of words that does not contain a subject and a verb.

> MAIN CLAUSE We had eaten dinner. (subject: *we*; verb: *had eaten*)
>
> SUBORDINATE CLAUSE After we had eaten dinner (subject: *we*; verb: *had finished*)
>
> PHRASE After eating dinner (no subject, no verb)

You may think that *eating* is a verb in "After eating dinner," but words with -*ing* endings function as verbs only when they are used with auxiliaries such as *is, was, has been*. *Dancing,* for example, can be used as a noun (*Dancing* is good exercise), or an adjective (The *dancing* elephants delighted the crowd), as well as a verb (The elephants *are dancing*). For more information on verbs, see Solving Verb Problems.

Here are some common types of phrases:

SENTENCES

> PREPOSITIONAL PHRASES around the corner, through the woods, of mice and men
>
> PARTICIPIAL PHRASES while watching television, when driving on icy roads, before skiing down the slope
>
> INFINITIVE PHRASES to come home, to breathe deeply, to save money

Clauses often include phrases:

> They decided to walk home through the woods. (*to walk home* is an infinitive phrase; *through the woods* is a prepositional phrase)
>
> Rosa, after hearing a tentative scratch on the window, peeked through the curtain. (*after hearing a tentative scratch* is a participial phrase describing Rosa; *on the window* is a prepositional phrase)

EXERCISE I

Put parentheses around all the phrases in the following sentences. Be sure to include the phrases within clauses.

1. After struggling for half an hour to dig their companion out of the avalanche, the exhausted skiers slumped to the ground.

2. By the last period of the hockey game, the roar of excited fans in the arena had reached a crescendo.

3. On our last holiday in England, we went to see the Poets' Corner in Westminster Abbey.

4. While listening to the after-dinner speaker, I rearranged the silverware.

5. Before starting the climb, hikers were advised to fill their water bottles.

Recognizing Main Clauses and Subordinate Clauses

A main clause is a group of words with a subject and a verb that can stand alone as a complete sentence.

> MAIN CLAUSE We had washed the dishes.
>
> MAIN CLAUSE We went to a movie.

A subordinate clause begins with a subordinate conjunction. It has a subject and a verb, but it cannot stand alone as a complete sentence.

> SUBORDINATE CLAUSE After we had washed the dishes (*After* is a subordinate conjunction.)

If you can recognize a subordinate conjunction, then it's easy to distinguish between a main clause and a subordinate clause. Here is a list of the most common subordinate conjunctions:

after	if
before	unless
when	although
while	even though
during	because
as	provided that
as long as	in order that
since	until

Relative pronouns may also serve as subordinate conjunctions:

who	whomever
whom	which
whoever	that*

EXERCISE 2

Underline the main clause(s) in the following sentences. Put parentheses around subordinate clauses. Underline the subject of a main or subordinate clause once; underline the complete verb (the main verb + any auxiliaries) twice.

1. (While) the fighting persists, the airport will remain closed.
2. Many people will die of injuries and starvation (unless) we can get supplies to them.
3. I am worried about my parents, (who) are helpless victims of the civil war.
4. (Although) many attempts have been made to enforce a cease-fire, the fighting has increased.
5. Hopes for an early solution are fading (because) neither side will compromise.

Recognizing Simple, Compound, and Complex Sentences

Being able to identify simple, compound, and complex sentences will help you avoid common errors in sentence structure and use commas and semicolons accurately. If you understand the structure of these types of sentences, you can introduce more variations in the structure

---

* Occasionally *that* is omitted from sentences, as in "We thought [that] we might go to a movie."

of your own, and appreciate the skill with which other writers use them.

The Simple Sentence

This term describes the grammatical construction of a sentence, not its content. A **simple sentence** has one main clause. It may also have a number of phrases, as in this sentence:

> I noticed a little boy, probably two or three years old,
> crouched in the doorway of the filthy shack.

In this sentence, "I noticed a little boy" is the main clause. The phrases "probably two or three years old," "crouched in the doorway," and "of the filthy shack" add more information, but they are not clauses. This is a simple sentence.

The Compound Sentence

The **compound sentence** has two or more main clauses and no subordinate clauses. These clauses may be joined with a semicolon; a comma and coordinate conjunction (*and, but, or, nor, for, yet, so*); or a semicolon and a conjunctive adverb (*therefore, thus, however, nevertheless, furthermore*).

> Civil unrest increased; people attempted to protect themselves. (main clauses joined with a semicolon)

> Civil unrest increased, so people attempted to protect themselves. (main clauses joined with a comma and a coordinate conjunction)

> Civil unrest increased; therefore, people attempted to protect themselves. (main clauses joined with a semicolon and a conjunctive adverb)

The Complex Sentence

This term describes the grammatical construction of a sentence, not its content. A **complex sentence** has one main clause and one or more subordinate clauses. If the subordinate clause comes first, put a comma after it.

> Because the roads were terrible, the meeting was cancelled. (one subordinate clause at the beginning of the sentence)

> You may contact us in the evening if you are unable to control the dog. (one subordinate clause at the end of the sentence)

Although he wanted to speak to her before the evening ended, he continued to sit in the darkest corner of the restaurant. (two subordinate clauses at the beginning of the sentence)

EXERCISE 3

Label the following sentences simple, compound, or complex. Underline main clauses and put parentheses around subordinate clauses. Underline the subject of a main or a subordinate clause once; underline the complete verb (the main verb + any auxiliaries) twice.

1. Smoking in the hospital was prohibited, so patients huddled outside the doors in freezing temperatures. *compound*

2. *Othello* is the tragedy of a man who "loved not wisely, but too well."

3. As the runners surged towards the finish line, the crowd cheered wildly.

4. The distraught parents searched the campground, the lakeshore, and the surrounding woods for their missing child.

5. The weather, which had remained warm for several days, suddenly turned bitterly cold.

3 Correcting Common Errors in Sentence Structure

Correcting Sentence Fragments

As its name implies, a sentence fragment is an incomplete sentence. It may lack a subject, a verb, or both, or it may be a subordinate clause or phrase punctuated as a sentence. Occasionally a sentence fragment may be used effectively for emphasis, as in

Another victory for our side.

If your essay contains a mixture of intentional and accidental fragments, however, you will confuse your reader. Sentence fragments may also make your writing too informal.

To correct sentence fragments, supply the missing subject, missing verb, or missing main clause, or attach the fragment to the main clause.

FRAGMENT Given the choice of resigning or being impeached.

COMPLETE SENTENCE Given the choice of resigning or being impeached, the corrupt president left the country. (main clause added)

FRAGMENT Even though students had been warned that they would be expected to write an in-class essay. Many of them arrived late.

COMPLETE SENTENCE Even though students had been warned that they would be expected to write an in-class essay, many of them arrived late. (subordinate clause attached to the main clause)

FRAGMENT Shakespeare's play *Richard III* deals with fundamental human problems. Such as the conflict between good and evil.

COMPLETE SENTENCE Shakespeare's play *Richard III* deals with fundamental human problems, such as the conflict between good and evil. (phrase attached to main clause)

EXERCISE I

Revise the following sentences to correct sentence fragments.

1. Many students decide not to hold part-time jobs. Because they need time to study.

2. Although the benefits of pollution regulations outweigh the costs. Every regulation has an impact on the Canadian economy.

3. The pollution of prairie waters is mainly caused by agricultural insecticides. Whereas the pollution of the St. Lawrence Seaway is mainly caused by the industrialization of southern Ontario.

4. Fibre cables, on the other hand, which require repeaters about every twenty kilometres, depending on capacity demands.

5. In the Classical Age, Greek social life was dominated by the evolving institutions of the male social sphere. Excluding women, who were considered tied to nature and thus a lower order of being than men.

6. The artist Kirchner placing prime emphasis on feelings and experiences and distorting nature when this distortion was necessary.

7. Darwin's formulation of the theory of evolution had a profound impact on many areas of nineteenth-century thought. From history to economics to psychology.

8. People who want compensation for all the injustices they have endured and who will no longer accept the indifference of government bureaucracies.

9. Genetic manipulation could be useful in the treatment of some diseases. Such as diabetes.

10. In "My Last Duchess" where Browning criticizes the standards by which the Duke judges himself and other people.

Correcting Comma Splices

The comma splice (sometimes called the comma fault) occurs when only a comma is used to join two main clauses. There is no conjunction to show how the clauses are related. Each of the following sentences contains a comma splice.

1. The thinking behind the idea of the Divine Right of Kings is that God has invested the power of kingship in the king, whatever a king does is sanctioned by God.

2. Hamlet and Laertes have very different personalities, both are enough like us and the people we know to be believable.

3. We have high expectations of our leaders, we become cynical when they fail us.

4. He assumed the jewels were cheap fakes, therefore he believed his wife could buy them with her household money.

5. She wanted badly to win the prize, she practised hours every day.

Whenever you make two separate points, you need more than a comma to show how they are related. There are five ways to correct comma splices.

1. Separate main clauses with a period.

   The thinking behind the idea of the Divine Right of Kings is that God has invested the power of kingship in the king. Whatever the king does is sanctioned by God.

2. Join main clauses with a comma and a coordinate conjunction (*and, but, or, nor, for, yet, so*). Choose the conjunction that best expresses the relationship between the ideas.

   Hamlet and Laertes have very different personalities, but they are enough like us and the people we know to be believable.

3. Join main clauses with a semicolon.

   We have high expectations of our leaders; we become cynical when they fail us.

4. Join main clauses with a semicolon and a conjunctive adverb. Put a comma after the conjunctive adverb if it is more than one syllable (after *therefore,* but not after *thus*).

   Here is a partial list of conjunctive adverbs with indications of how they are used:

   conjunctive adverb.

   • to signal that one idea is a result of another: accordingly, consequently, therefore, thus, hence

   • to signal that one idea is added to another: furthermore, moreover, besides

   • to signal a contrast in ideas: nevertheless, however, otherwise, still

   To choose the appropriate conjunction, consider how the ideas are related. In this sentence, the second idea is a result of the first:

He assumed the jewels were cheap fakes; therefore, he believed his wife had bought them with her household money.

5. Change one of the main clauses into a subordinate clause.
   Notice that when the subordinate clause is first, it is separated
   from the main clause by a comma.

   Because she wanted badly to win the prize, she practised
   hours every day.

   She practised hours every day because she wanted badly to
   win the prize.

EXERCISE 2

Choose the most appropriate method to correct comma splices in the following
sentences.

1. Holden wants to be like the ducks, no one seems to notice them.
2. The premier met with his aides and advisors on several occasions, no word of their discussions has reached the press.
3. The southern half of the province has received very little rain for the third consecutive year, poor crops are expected.
4. She was constantly late, her work was sloppy.
5. It is no surprise that autistic children do not want to participate in reality, sensory stimuli distort their perceptions.
6. The competition in high schools is intense, some students use alcohol to escape from the pressure to succeed.
7. The decodable frequency range of copper is very small, it is quite economical to replace copper wiring with fibre optics.
8. Nuclear fusion is the power of the future, with it we may accomplish tasks never before dreamed of.
9. Violence on television gives us a sense of power, we see through the killer's eyes.
10. He studied all night for the exam, he did poorly.

Correcting Fused Sentences

Fused sentences (sometimes called run-on sentences) occur when the
writer tries to pack more information into a sentence than its grammatical structure can accommodate. Fused sentences have no punctuation to show how the clauses are related.

* Television networks make money by selling advertising time
  therefore programs must appeal to people who can afford the
  products advertised.

X Jeans are a status symbol in Russia they sell for hundreds of dollars on the black market.

Fused sentences can be corrected in the same way as comma splices. Be sure not to create a comma splice by merely putting a comma between main clauses.

EXERCISE 3

Revise the following fused sentences by adding conjunctions and adjusting punctuation as necessary.

1. It is easy to make this delicious dessert just follow these instructions.

2. Some adolescents are sullen, rebellious, and lazy others work to support themselves and to help their families.

3. Einstein abhorred the practical use of his theories by the military in the future we may find more humanitarian uses for his concepts.

4. In the spring of 1997, the Red River became the Red Sea many people in southern Manitoba lost their homes and businesses.

5. Democratic institutions are slow to change they respond to shifts in majority opinion.

REVIEW EXERCISE I

1. Correct all the fragments, comma splices, and fused sentences in the paragraph below.

Various staging effects in Arthur Miller's play *Death of a Salesman* help the audience to understand Willy Loman's thoughts. The music, for example, when it is used to indicate a change from the present to the past in Willy's mind. The musical instrument used is the flute, it helps the audience to understand this shift. Time changes also indicated by changes in lighting. The town has expanded and become more densely populated towering apartment buildings have replaced the trees Willy remembers. The lighting changes the scene from the present to the past. Fading out the apartment buildings and lighting up the trees. These staging effects help the audience to follow Willy's mental journey.

Correcting Misplaced and Dangling Modifiers

A modifier is a word, a phrase, or a clause that supplies further information about another word in the sentence. Modifiers can act as adjectives to describe nouns or pronouns or as adverbs to describe verbs, adjectives, or other adverbs.

> The dog barked loudly. (*Loudly* is an adverb describing "barked.")

> When the stranger entered the yard, the dog barked loudly. (*When the stranger entered the yard* is a subordinate clause functioning as an adverb to describe "barked.")

> The dog, barking loudly, attacked the stranger. (*Barking loudly* is an adjective phrase describing "dog.")

> The dog, who had been barking for hours, went to sleep. (*Who had been barking for hours* is a subordinate clause functioning as an adjective to describe "dog.")

For clarity, a modifier must be as close as possible to the word it modifies, and there must be a word in the sentence for it to describe. If these conditions are not met, the modifier is either **misplaced** or **dangling**.

Correcting Misplaced Modifiers

Misplaced modifiers are single words (especially *almost*, *even*, *hardly*, *just*, *merely*, *nearly*, *only*, *scarcely*), phrases, or clauses that are too far away from the word they describe to be clear.

> ✗ This film *only* runs fifty-eight minutes. (Is this the only film that runs fifty-eight minutes or does it run only fifty-eight minutes?)

> She told him *on Friday* she was quitting. (Did she tell him on Friday or is she quitting on Friday?)

> He *just* said he would be a few minutes late. (Did he say this very recently or did he only say that he would be a few minutes late?)

You can easily correct a misplaced modifier by moving it as close as possible to the word it describes.

> Only this film runs fifty-eight minutes. **OR** This film runs only fifty-eight minutes.

> On Friday she told him she was quitting. **OR** She told him she was quitting on Friday.

He said he would be just a few minutes late.

A special type of misplaced modifier is a **split infinitive**. An infinitive is *to* + a verb: *to walk, to think, to breathe*. An infinitive is split when a modifier (usually an adverb) is placed between *to* and the verb: *to seriously think.* Try to avoid splitting an infinitive when the resulting construction is awkward.

> SPLIT INFINITIVE Alex tried to carefully prepare for the exam.

> REVISED Alex tried to prepare carefully for the exam.

EXERCISE 4

Revise the following sentences to eliminate misplaced modifiers.

1. The Wongs were amazed to see a bear on the main street while vacationing in Jasper.

2. Selina needed time to mentally prepare for the lawyer's questions.

3. Tomas tried on the new clothes he had selected in the dressing room.

4. Peter nearly ate an entire pizza for breakfast.

5. Beena was just trying to rapidly read through the whole chapter before class.

Correcting Dangling Modifiers

A **dangling modifier** is a phrase, often at the beginning of the sentence, which has no logical connection with the rest of the sentence. The phrase dangles because there is no word in the sentence for it to modify.

> ✗Bitterly regretting his misspent youth, his days in jail seemed endless.

> When empty, return them to the store.

You can't eliminate a dangling modifier by moving it to another position in the sentence; instead, you need to revise the structure of the sentence itself. You can do this in two ways:

1. Expand the dangling modifier into a subordinate clause.

   > Because he regretted his misspent youth, his days in jail seemed endless.

   > When the bottles are empty, return them to the store.

2. Revise the main clause so that it contains a word for the introductory phrase to modify.

Bitterly regretting his misspent youth, the prisoner found his days in jail endless.

When empty, the bottles should be returned to the store.

EXERCISE 5

Revise the following sentences to eliminate all dangling modifiers.

1. Determined to finish her essay, all interruptions were ignored.
2. After hearing the manager's plans to reorganize the office, it was difficult for the workers to remain calm.
3. A lover of movies since childhood, his plan was to become an actor.
4. When recovering from major surgery, strenuous exercise should be avoided.
5. Just before starting school, Domingo's parents moved to Halifax.

REVIEW EXERCISE 2

Revise the following sentences to eliminate misplaced and dangling modifiers.

1. He scarcely knew anyone at the party.
2. Even after studying all night, many of the exam questions seemed unfamiliar.
3. After a hot, strenuous day of sightseeing, the hotel pool looked inviting.
4. By using a narrative introduction, the reader's attention can be caught.
5. Instead of working at a regular job, crime may seem an easier way to get a lot of money quickly.
6. When underage, Louis XIV's ministers had charge of the government.
7. By regulating the disposal of hazardous wastes, the environment will be preserved.
8. To successfully jump from this height, you'll need a special parachute.
9. One terrible night, while showing off my new car to my friends, the engine exploded.
10. In writing stories for popular magazines, the readers always want a happy ending.

Correcting Faulty Parallelism

Parallelism When sentence elements (words, phrases, clauses) are parallel, they have the same grammatical construction.

She was *lucky, intelligent,* and *brave.* (parallel adjectives)

Slowly and *painfully,* the lone survivor crawled towards the camp. (parallel adverbs)

> The riders made their way *over the mountain, through the valley,* and *into the town.* (parallel phrases)
>
> *What we say, what we think,* and *what we do* are often at odds. (parallel clauses)

Parallel sentence structure is especially important whenever you have a list (of steps in a procedure, for example) and when you join parts of a sentence with coordinate conjunctions (*and, but, or, nor, for, yet, so*) or correlative conjunctions (*neither...nor, either...or, not only...but also*).

> Before you leave, close the windows, turn off the lights, and lock the doors. (parallel steps)
>
> The cowardly fail because of their fear, but the courageous succeed in spite of their fear. (parallel main clauses joined with a coordinate conjunction)
>
> Your choice in this situation is either to finish the project or to fail the course. (parallel phrases joined with correlative conjunctions)

Faulty parallelism as its name suggests, occurs whenever sentence elements are not parallel. You can correct faulty parallelism by balancing words with words, phrases with phrases, and clauses with clauses.

> NOT PARALLEL To write an effective conclusion, restate your thesis, summarize your main points, and the broader context of your subject should be suggested.
>
> PARALLEL To write an effective conclusion, restate your thesis, summarize your main points, and suggest the broader context of your subject.
>
> NOT PARALLEL As a winner you will achieve success, and respect will also come your way.
>
> PARALLEL As a winner, you will achieve both success and respect.

EXERCISE 6

Revise the following sentences to correct faulty parallelism.

1. Gandhi, as he is portrayed in Richard Attenborough's movie, is intelligent, brave, and he showed total commitment to his cause.

2. Many children do poorly in school because of inadequate diet, poor instruction, and they are not very interested.

3. To prevent shock, cover the victim with a blanket, speaking reassuringly.

4. The transition from adolescence to maturity is marked by the acquisition of certain qualities: being less self-conscious, to be able to manage one's own affairs, and the ability to get along with people.

5. To clean this oven, I need either atomic weapons or ~~perhaps~~ a miracle ~~will happen~~.

Correcting Faulty Coordination and Subordination

Use **coordination** to join points of equal importance. To create coordination, join words, phrases, and clauses with coordinate or correlative conjunctions.

> Only those who have a diploma in Early Childhood Education or who have equivalent work experience need apply for this position.
>
> This will be a step out of the frying pan and into the fire.
>
> Your analysis of this problem is both thorough and creative.

Use **subordination** to join points of unequal importance. To create subordination, put your main point in the main clause and your less important point in a subordinate clause or phrase.

> Although everyone was aware of the problem, no one knew what to do about it.
>
> Before Marta set out on her journey, she had her car serviced.

Coordination and subordination help you to use the structure of the sentence to emphasize your main point. Remember, too, that the clause or phrase at the end of the sentence always gets more emphasis. Thus for maximum emphasis, put your main idea in a main clause and put that clause at the end of the sentence. Notice the difference in the emphasis given to the main clause in these two sentences.

> Although the meeting was well publicized, it attracted little interest. (Putting the main clause last gives it maximum emphasis.)
>
> The meeting attracted little interest although it was well publicized. (Putting the subordinate clause last evens the emphasis given to both clauses.)

Faulty coordination can occur when the elements you join are not grammatically parallel. (For an explanation of parallelism, see above.)

> NOT PARALLEL On the camping trip, Lewis learned to despise canned food, to loathe outdoor toilets, and he was afraid of bears.

REVISED On the camping trip, Lewis learned to despise
    canned food, to loathe outdoor toilets, and to fear bears.

Faulty coordination can also occur if you join ideas that are unrelated or not of equal importance.

UNRELATED IDEAS The movie was boring and pretentious
    and hundreds of people lined up for hours to see it.

REVISED Although the movie was boring and pretentious,
    hundreds of people lined up for hours to see it.

UNEQUAL IDEAS Hamlet is Prince of Denmark and he is disillusioned by his mother's hasty remarriage.

REVISED Hamlet, Prince of Denmark, is disillusioned by his
    mother's hasty remarriage.

Don't use *and* as an all-purpose conjunction. Although *and* can sometimes be a weak signal of causal connection (I was late and I missed the bus), it's best to use *and* only when you want to signal that what follows is a coordinate fact or idea.

NOT   Dan was chronically tired and he had anaemia.

BUT   Dan was chronically tired because he had anaemia.

EXERCISE 7

Revise the following sentences to correct errors in coordination.

1. Robert is an ardent gardener, and he is a specialist in vibrations, and he lives in Fredericton.

2. In the summer, Andrea enjoys working in the garden taking long walks, and she likes to read romances.

3. Marco forgot to pay a speeding ticket and he received a summons to appear in court.

4. To function effectively as a social worker, you need to be both knowledgeable and compassion is important.

5. As far as I can tell, Ingrid has no interest either in getting a job and school doesn't interest her.

Faulty subordination occurs when the structure of the sentence does not subordinate ideas of unequal importance. Here are the most common causes of this error.

1. Attaching the subordinate conjunction to the wrong clause.

FAULTY Although they missed the plane, they left in plenty
    of time to reach the airport.

REVISED They missed the plane although they left in plenty of time to reach the airport.

2. Using an imprecise subordinate conjunction (especially *since* and *as*). *Since* can mean "because," but *since* can also mean "from the time that." If these two meanings might be confused, use *because* to indicate a causal connection.

CONFUSING Since she broke her ankle, she has been housebound.

CLEAR Because she broke her ankle, she has been housebound.

CLEAR From the time she broke her ankle, she has been housebound.

As can be used to mean *because*, but it's best to use *as* to mean "while."

CLEAR As Felicity struggled to listen to the lecture, her mind began to wander.

CONFUSING As Raul is the manager, he thinks he should make all the decisions.

CLEAR Raul thinks he should make all the decisions because he is the manager.

3. Using two conjunctions that mean the same thing.

MIXED Because he did not want to pay a late penalty for his income tax, therefore he rushed to the post office just before midnight.

REVISED Because he did not want to pay a late penalty for his income tax, he rushed to the post office just before midnight.

OR He did not want to pay a late penalty for his income tax; therefore, he rushed to the post office just before midnight.

Excessive subordination This error occurs when you try to subordinate too many clauses in a sentence. Avoid beginning and ending a sentence with similar subordinate clauses.

EXCESSIVE SUBORDINATION Because she was afraid of a hail storm, she covered all the windows because the force of the hail might break them.

REVISED Fearing a hail storm, she covered all the windows to protect them from the force of the hail.

ERRORS

Excessive subordination can also occur if you put too many clauses beginning with *that*, *which*, and *who* into one sentence.

> EXCESSIVE SUBORDINATION The novelist who wins this contest which is sponsored by a major publisher will be taken on a cross-country tour that begins July 1.

> REVISED The novelist who wins this contest, sponsored by a major publisher, will be taken on a cross-country tour beginning July 1.

 ## EXERCISE 8

Revise the following sentences to eliminate faulty or excessive subordination. Write C beside a correct sentence.

1. Although Michael Henchard loves Lucetta, he feels obligated to marry Susan, his former wife, although he does not love her.

2. Since Karl had a seizure caused by an allergic reaction, he has been cautious about all medications.

3. Because the assistant manager is autocratic and arrogant, therefore no one wants to work with her.

4. As the main character ties his sense of masculinity to clan traditions, he feels threatened when these structures begin to crumble.

5. Although Amin desperately needed a job, he was determined never again to work for his father.

Correcting Mixed Constructions

A **mixed construction** will occur if you begin a sentence with one grammatical construction and complete it with one that is different and incompatible. Any of the errors listed below will produce an awkward sentence.

Putting a Subordinate Clause Before or After a Linking Verb Readers expect linking verbs, such as *is* and *was*, to be followed by a noun or noun clause, not by a subordinate clause that modifies the verb. Formulations like *an example of this is when* or *the reason for this is because* are typical of this sort of mixed construction.

> MIXED An example of his hostility is when he turns his homicidal bull loose on the mushroom pickers.

> MIXED One reason she dropped out of school is because she was in constant conflict with authority.

> MIXED Because Maria is pregnant with another man's child is
> one reason she is afraid of her husband.

You can revise these sentences by supplying the missing noun or noun clause.

> REVISED An example of his hostility is his decision to turn
> his homicidal bull loose on the mushroom pickers.

> REVISED One reason she dropped out of school is her con-
> stant conflicts with authority.

> REVISED Maria is afraid of her husband because she is preg-
> nant with another man's child.

Another way to revise these sentences is to replace the linking verb.

> REVISED He shows his hostility when he turns his homicidal
> bull loose on the mushroom pickers.

> REVISED She dropped out of school because she was in con-
> stant conflict with authority.

> REVISED Because Maria is pregnant with another man's
> child, she is afraid of her husband.

Omitting the Subject   Leaving out the subject typically produces sentences like this:

> MIXED In this documentary makes the point that gorillas are
> a seriously endangered species.

This sentence is confusing because the prepositional phrase *In this documentary*, which normally introduces a grammatically complete sentence, seems to be the subject of the sentence. You could revise by omitting the preposition.

> REVISED This documentary makes the point that gorillas are
> a seriously endangered species.

Or you could keep the prepositional phrase and add a subject to the main clause.

> REVISED In this documentary, the filmmaker makes the point that
> gorillas are a seriously endangered species.

Leaving Out Part of a Comparison   Sentences that begin with phrases such as *the more, the less, the worse, the further* suggest a comparison. You will confuse your reader if you fail to complete the comparison.

MIXED The less time I have, I have a lot to do.

You could revise this sentence by pairing *less* with *more*.

REVISED The less time I have, the more I have to do.

Mixing a Question and a Statement

MIXED The little boy plaintively asked his mother when will
she finish writing her essay?

You could revise this sentence by rephrasing the question as direct
speech.

REVISED The little boy plaintively asked his mother, "When
will you finish writing your essay?"

You could also make the question a statement.

REVISED The little boy plaintively asked his mother when
she would finish writing her essay.

EXERCISE 9

Revise the following sentences to eliminate mixed constructions.

1. In *A Man for All Seasons,* it shows that the reason Sir Thomas More becomes a
   martyr is because he is willing to die for his beliefs.

2. An example of her cunning is when she persuades her client not to consult another
   lawyer.

3. By denying that the government intended to raise taxes increased the credibility
   gap between the Minister of Finance and the public.

4. The more Yvette loathed her family, she did not want to live with them.

5. The frustrated mother asked her daughter when will she ever grow up?

REVIEW EXERCISE 3

Revise the following sentences to eliminate faulty parallelism, faulty coordination and
subordination, and mixed constructions.

1. To complete this degree, you could take three more courses or a thesis could be
   written.

2. Although he loved her, he didn't want to marry her although she was rich.

3. The more the accused man protested his innocence, the jury didn't believe him.

4. The frustrated customer demanded to know when could she speak to the manager?

5. Julia has travelled extensively in the Far East and she teaches dance.

6. Because the roads through the mountains were hazardous, he decided to fly home because he didn't want to drive.

7. They vowed to remain married for better and worse, for richer and poorer, and whether or not they were both healthy.

8. As Timothy was the last to be hired, he was also the first to be fired.

9. He had forgotten about the test until the class started, although he did well on it.

10. Jonathan Swift, who was a satirist who lived in Ireland during the eighteenth century and who wrote *Gulliver's Travels* and "A Modest Proposal," defined happiness as the state of being securely self-deceived.

REVIEW EXERCISE 4

Rewrite the following paragraph to eliminate sentence fragments, comma faults, fused sentences, dangling and misplaced modifiers, faulty parallelism, and mixed constructions. Do not omit any of the ideas in the paragraph.

Although drugs seem to offer a quick and easy method of treating emotional problems and can be used effectively. Their long-range benefits are often questionable. Prescribed by psychiatrists, patients often take drugs that alter their moods greatly. Patients cannot distinguish their real feelings from the feelings induced by the drugs they may think that their anxieties have been eliminated when they have been suppressed by only the drugs. An example of this is when a businessman who suffers from an overwhelming feeling of worthlessness takes psychic energizers. He may be capable under the influence of these drugs of going to work regularly, running his business efficiently, and to fulfill his social obligations for a few months or even a few years. He becomes more dependent on the drugs and on the psychiatrist who prescribes them, he becomes less and less aware of the misery within. These drugs have merely masked his underlying fears, they have not resolved them. These fears are likely to re-emerge, more overwhelming than before. Whenever the man is subjected to more stress than usual. Each breakdown leaves him more dependent on the drugs and to get help from his psychiatrist and others who treat the emotionally disturbed.

4 Using Sentence Structure and Length to Clarify Ideas

When all your sentences are about the same length and have the same structure, it is difficult for a reader to distinguish main points from supporting details. Consider, for example, this discussion of the narrator in the "Prologue" to Geoffrey Chaucer's *The Canterbury Tales*.

> The narrator's weakness is his amazing tolerance of all types of people. This is his strength. His fellow pilgrims have weaknesses and oddities. He rarely criticizes them. He treats everyone in a kind, genial manner. He observes that the French spoken by the Prioress is not Parisian French. He is not condescending about her accent. He doesn't condemn the kind Parson for the occasional harsh word. He kindly ignores the Wife of Bath's earlier amorous adventures. He does not make derogatory comments about the Pardoner's hypocrisy. The narrator tends to adopt the standards of those around him. He wants to think well of others. He is not self-interested. His tolerance of their weakness seems a virtue.

This paragraph is hard to understand for two main reasons.

1. All the sentences have the same basic structure and are about the same length. As a result, it's hard to distinguish the ideas from the examples that support them.

2. There are no transitions: no words, phrases, or clauses that establish relationships between sentences. As a result, it is hard to tell whether the writer intended a particular statement to reinforce, qualify, or contradict another statement or to suggest a cause and effect relationship.

By varying sentence structure and length and providing transitions, you can help your reader to understand the connections among your ideas. If you compare the paragraph above with the revised version, you can see just how big a difference these simple changes make.

> The narrator's greatest weakness, his amazing tolerance of other people, is also his greatest strength. Despite his awareness of his fellow pilgrims' weaknesses and oddities, he rarely criticizes and treats everyone in a kind, genial manner. He observes, for example, that the Prioress does not speak Parisian French, yet he is not condescending about her accent. He kindly ignores the Wife of Bath's earlier amorous adventures and does not make derogatory comments about the Pardoner's effeminacy. Thus the narrator's tendency to adopt the standards of those around him springs from his desire to think well of others rather than from self-interest.

Varying Sentence Lengths

Your main points will be clearer and more emphatic if you express them in short sentences. Use longer sentences to gather details, reasons, and examples that support and develop your main points.

> Although the narrator is aware of his fellow pilgrims' weaknesses and oddities, he treats everyone kindly (main point: 16 words). He observes, for example, that the French spoken by the Prioress is not Parisian French, yet he is not condescending about her accent (supporting detail: 23 words).

Varying Sentence Patterns

The basic sentence pattern in English is subject + verb + object (Jennifer hit the ball). If all of your sentences follow this pattern, however, your writing will soon become as monotonous as a grade-one reader. You will also make it more difficult for your reader to distinguish major and minor points.

Common Sentence Patterns

Here are the most common sentence patterns:

The Loose Sentence: Subject + Verb + Modifier

> The team lost money, despite better players and an improved stadium.

This is the most common sentence pattern and is thus the easiest for most readers to understand. The modifier gains emphasis because it is placed at the end of the sentence. Readers would expect the following sentence to focus on the improvement in players and the stadium.

The Periodic Sentence: Modifier + Subject + Verb

> Despite better players and an improved stadium, the team
> lost money.

Because we have to wait for the subject and the verb, this sentence pattern creates suspense and interest. It puts maximum interest on the fact that the team lost money, so readers would expect the next sentence to deal with this issue.

The Embedded Sentence: Subject + Modifier + Verb

> The team, despite better players and an improved stadium,
> lost money.

This sentence pattern slows the reader down because the subject and the verb are separated by a lengthy modifier. It is useful if you want to imitate the process of thinking through a problem. It also leads readers to expect that the following sentence will begin to explore the real reasons for the team's inability to make a profit.

Sentences with Parallel Elements

The balanced construction creates a compound sentence in which two closely related main clauses with the same structure are joined with a semicolon, a comma and a coordinate conjunction, or a semicolon and a conjunctive adverb. It is especially useful when you want to suggest a choice between two equal possibilities.

> Perhaps Dmitri will treat his relationship with Anna as one
> more casual affair, or perhaps he will fall genuinely in love
> for the first time.

Sentences containing a series of parallel words, phrases, or clauses arranged in an order of increasing importance are useful when you want to sum up a number of factors or details.

> By the end of *The Mayor of Casterbridge*, Henchard has lost
> his family, his home, his standing in the community, and his
> hopes for the future.

Effective Sentence Variety

Varying the structure of your sentences will help you to avoid monotony and to clarify the relationships among ideas, explanations, and details. On the other hand, if every sentence follows a different pattern, your reader will find your paragraph confusing. Here are some guidelines for varying sentence structure effectively.

1. Keep the structure of topic sentences fairly simple. When you are making major points, you don't want to lose your reader in elaborate sentence patterns.

2. Change your sentence structure when you introduce an explanation. If your explanation takes more than one sentence, keep the sentences in similar patterns.

3. When you shift from explanation to details, change your sentence pattern.

4. Keep similar sentence patterns for all your details.

The simplest and most obvious way to change the structure of your sentences is to experiment with different ways to begin a sentence. Here are some possibilities to consider.

VARIETY

Ways to Begin Sentences

1. With the subject: *John A. Macdonald* was a colourful prime minister.

2. With a prepositional phrase: *Before Confederation* he had proved his skill as a politician.

3. With single-word adjectives: *Bold*, *shrewd*, and *stubborn*, he had clung to power for over thirty years.

4. With a participial phrase: *Drinking heavily*, he nevertheless maintained a firm grip on his party and the country.

5. With a subordinate clause: *Because he helped to bring about the birth of the nation and presided over it in its infancy*, he is known as the Father of Confederation.

6. With an appositive: *A man with great historical importance as well as undeniable personal weaknesses*, Macdonald continues to fascinate historians and biographers.

[handwritten annotation: noun or noun phrases that name the preceeding noun]

As these examples demonstrate, you can create emphasis by paying careful attention to the length and structure of your sentences. Avoid using italics (underlining) or capitalization to create emphasis.

NOT   Hamlet is in deep despair. He feels totally *isolated*.

BUT   Feeling totally isolated, Hamlet sinks into despair.

EXERCISE I

Rewrite the following paragraph to make the relationship among points, explanations, and details clearer by varying sentence structure and length.

> Good classroom rapport depends upon the attitudes of teachers towards their students. Teachers are leaders. They set the goals and the pace for reaching those goals. Teachers should remember that they are dealing with people. They should be flexible. They should try to stay in tune with the needs and interests of their students. They should consider their students' limits. Teachers can establish friendly relationships. They can show a genuine understanding of their subjects and their students. They can show a commitment to both their subjects and their students. These attitudes create good classroom rapport. These attitudes make good human beings.

EXERCISE 2

Find a paragraph of your own writing that could be improved by varying sentence structure and length. Revise the paragraph and bring both versions to class for discussion.

5 Using Transitions to Connect Ideas

Transitional words and phrases are important for two reasons. They increase your reader's understanding of how your ideas are related. They also create a sense of continuity because one idea leads smoothly to the next, both within and between paragraphs .

Continuity Within Paragraphs

Sentence Hooks

Sentence Hooks are words and phrases used to create continuity between sentences. You can hook sentences together with pronouns, demonstrative pronouns, synonyms, and repeated words and phrases.

Pronouns After the first reference by name, use pronouns and possessive pronouns to indicate a continuity of subject. Make sure that the reference is clear (see Solving Pronoun Problems).

> Margaret Atwood has written several novels. *Her* most recent is.... *She* has also written...

Demonstrative Pronouns To avoid repeating your last point, refer to it with a demonstrative pronoun (*this, that, these, those*) and a noun that identifies the subject to which you are referring.

> During the Depression, prairie farmers suffered because of the severe drought. *This problem*...

> Macbeth murders Duncan and is responsible for the murder of Banquo and several others. *These acts* of violence...

Synonyms and Repeated Words and Phrases Keep your reader's attention on your subject by repeating key words and phrases or by using synonyms. Notice the continuity created by the repetition of "problem" and equivalent terms in the following paragraph.

> In the construction of the Imperial Hotel in Tokyo, Frank Lloyd Wright had to solve several architectural problems. First, he had to deal with difficulties created by earthquake tremors. Second, he had to correct the weak soil base of the hotel site. Third, he had to keep the building from cracking. To solve the problem of cracking, he created a hotel of many sections with expansion joints; to provide a solid base and prevent damage from earthquakes, Wright put concrete posts under the centre of each section and then cantilevered the floor slabs in all directions from the centre.

Transitional Words and Phrases

Transitional Words and Phrases are means of indicating relationships in time, space, and logic.

TRANSITIONS

RELATIONSHIP		SAMPLE TRANSITIONAL WORDS AND PHRASES
time		before, after, meanwhile, as soon as, during, until, then
space		on the right, near, farther away
logic	1. addition	and, another, a second, also, too, furthermore, moreover, not only...but also, first, second, etc.
	2. contrast	but, in contrast, yet, however, on the other hand, nevertheless, otherwise
	3. similarity	just as, like, likewise, similarly, in the same way
	4. examples	for example, for instance, to be specific, in particular, to illustrate
	5. cause and effect	therefore, thus, so, for, hence, because, consequently, as a result, accordingly

TRANSITIONS

6. concession and qualification	although, despite, while it is true that...
7. emphasis	most important, a crucial point, significantly, of overwhelming importance

Continuity Between Paragraphs

Paragraph Hooks

Paragraph Hooks are words and phrases that recall key ideas to create continuity between paragraphs.

1. Repeat single words or phrases or use synonyms to link the last sentence of one paragraph to the first sentence of the next.

    LAST SENTENCE OF PARAGRAPH 1 "His pride thus leads him to reject his friends' offers of help."

    FIRST SENTENCE OF PARAGRAPH 2 "His pride also prevents him from helping himself."

2. Use phrases, clauses, or occasionally whole sentences that briefly recall the ideas of one paragraph at the beginning of the next.

    FIRST TOPIC SENTENCE "Mackenzie King, Diefenbaker, and Pearson..."

    SECOND TOPIC SENTENCE "These three Prime Ministers were not the only ones to favour such a policy...."

Transitional Words and Phrases

Transitional Words and Phrases also indicate relationships in time, space, and logic between paragraphs.

Sample Topic Sentences with Transitions

TOPIC SENTENCE, PARAGRAPH 1 Opponents of rapid transit are quick to point out that the present city bus system loses money each year.

TOPIC SENTENCE, PARAGRAPH 2 It is true that any rapid transit is extremely expensive to build; thus for a few years our taxes will go up.

TOPIC SENTENCE, PARAGRAPH 3 If we invest sufficient funds to create a convenient, efficient rapid transit system, it will actually generate a profit.

EXERCISE I

Underline the transitional words and phrases in the following paragraph on the history of Fort Victoria.

Fort Victoria's early years were peaceful, apart from a few minor difficulties. These minor problems show, however, that if the Hudson's Bay Company had not fully supported the colony and if the problems had been handled less skillfully, much trouble could have developed. A year after the post was founded, Chief Factor James Douglas turned over the running of the post to his assistant, Roderick Finlayson. With a skillful use of diplomacy, Finlayson maintained good relations between the colonists and the original inhabitants of the area. Some, for example, became part of the settlement, aiding in the farming and being paid the same wages as other employees of the company. Finlayson was able to maintain these good relations and thus preserve the stability of the settlement even when trouble did arise between the settlers and the original inhabitants. When a group of Natives killed and ate some livestock and declared war on the fort, Finlayson, instead of declaring war in return, fired a cannon ball at a cedar lodge at the edge of their village. When a delegation came to the fort, Finlayson explained that he had enough arms to destroy them, but that he wished only to do good. The Natives paid for the cattle, the peace pipe was smoked, and vows of friendship were exchanged.

EXERCISE 2

Identify transitions in one of the following essays from Part 3, Readings. Then write a paragraph discussing the kinds of transitions the author uses and their effectiveness.

1. Laura Robinson's "Starving for the Gold"

2. George Orwell's "Shooting an Elephant"

3. David Suzuki's "It Always Costs"

EXERCISE 3

Use transitional words and phrases to clarify the relationships among ideas, explanations, and details in the following paragraph on Lizzie Borden, a character in Sharon Pollock's play *Blood Relations*.

Sharon Pollock presents Lizzie Borden as a victim of the demeaning treatment of women during the nineteenth century.

Lizzie does not want to continue living with her father and her stepmother. She does not want to get married. She wants freedom and independence. She needs money. Mr. Borden does not think that women can handle money and property. He changes his will and transfers both his money and his property to Lizzie's uncle. Mrs. Borden enthusiastically encourages him to do this. Lizzie's hatred for her stepmother increases. Tensions within the Borden household escalate. Lizzie tries to gain some freedom by getting a job. She offers to work in her father's factory. Her father rejects this suggestion as ridiculous. Lizzie can see no way to live the life she wants. She murders her father and her stepmother.

EXERCISE 4

Find a paragraph in your own writing that could be improved by better use of transitions. Revise the paragraph and bring both versions to class for discussion.

6 Solving Diction Problems

Diction refers to the individual words you use to express your ideas. These choices can make your writing sound breezy or bureaucratic, superficial or supercilious, confident or cantankerous. At one end of the scale is the very informal language characteristic of conversations among friends; at the other end is the highly formal language characteristic of specialists writing to other specialists (in legal documents, for example). Your diction should suggest that you are a friendly, serious, reasonable person writing to equally friendly, serious, and reasonable readers who might be less well informed or who might have different opinions about your subject. If your diction creates a different impression of your relation to your subject and readers, you can make the following revisions.

Correcting Problems with Your Level of Diction

1. Eliminate very informal language and slang that suggests you do not take your subject seriously.

    NOT   Hamlet was cheesed off by his mom's hasty marriage to his uncle.

    BUT   Hamlet was infuriated by his mother's hasty marriage to his uncle.

2. While the presence of some contractions (*don't, can't*) will give your writing a friendlier tone, too many contractions will make your writing seem too casual for a formal essay.

    NOT   Hamlet decides he'll feign madness while he's gathering proof that the ghost's telling the truth.

BUT Hamlet decides he will feign madness while he is gathering proof that the ghost is telling the truth.

3. Eliminate or define specialized vocabulary that may be unfamiliar to your reader.

 NOT Self-worth is affirmed when one's self-image is validated by one's significant others.

 BUT People like themselves better when their ideas and feelings about themselves are confirmed by those they care about.

4. Rewrite sentences that are too abstract or too grandiose.

 NOT The interpersonal interaction between volunteer counsellors and clients can provide the opportunity for both parties to gain a sense of self-worth and significance in the midst of our institutionalized society. (too abstract)

 BUT Meetings between volunteer counsellors and clients can help both to feel more worthwhile.

 NOT Throughout history man has struggled to understand his place in the ever-changing world in which he was only one infinitesimal link in the infinite chain of being. (too grandiose and sexist)

 BUT Men and women have always struggled to understand their place in the world.

5. Eliminate expressions that are too apologetic or argumentative.

 NOT I hope I will be able to show that some doctors over-prescribe medications because they want to meet their patients' expectations. (too apologetic)

 BUT Some doctors over-prescribe medications because they want to meet their patients' expectations.

 NOT Any fool can see that the emission of greenhouse gases is a worldwide problem.

 BUT The emission of greenhouse gases is a worldwide problem.

EXERCISE I

Rewrite the following paragraph so that its tone is appropriate for a university essay. You may need to check your dictionary to find replacements for some words.

I have actually found a variety of reasons for the bitching among the upper crust in Britain during the decades antecedent to the start of the civil war in 1642. The reigning

DICTION

monarchs, first James I and then his son Charles I, had abused Parliament for a long time. They had promulgated taxes without Parliamentary consent, they had stubbornly implemented unpopular political and ecclesiastical policies, and they had messed around with foreign trade. Any fool could see that the courts of James and Charles were absorbed in themselves, heedless of the welfare of the country and citizens, and only into their own advancement and enjoyment. It seems to the author of this paper that this antagonism between court and country was the principal cause of the brutal and agonizing civil war that pitted brother against brother, father against son, but I could be wrong.

Correcting Problems with Word Choice: Usage

Some diction errors are spelling mistakes (*there* instead of *their*) while others occur when one meaning of a word is confused with another (*realize* meaning "to make real" for *realize* meaning "to understand"). The term *usage* refers to the customary use of words, phrases, and expressions in English. Here is a list of the most common problems.

1. *A lot* is always spelled as two words. *Alot* is never correct. *A lot,* however, is quite informal. When possible, choose a more formal expression (such as *much, a great deal of, great, many*).

   Hyperactive children have a lot of trouble concentrating.

   Hyperactive children have great difficulty concentrating.

2. *Affect* and *Effect*

   a. *Affect* is usually a verb.

   The early frost affected the tomatoes.

   b. *Effect* is usually a noun.

   The effect of the early frost on the tomatoes was obvious.

3. *All right* is always spelled as two words. *Alright* is never correct.

   "All right," the bank manager said with a smile, "your loan has been approved."

4. *Allude* and *Elude*

   a. Use *allude* when you mean to refer to, as in an allusion to the Bible or the Koran.

   Forster frequently alludes to the Bible in his essay "My Wood."

b. Use *elude* when you mean to avoid or escape.

The clever thief eluded the police for seven years.

5. *Allusion* and *Illusion*

a. An *allusion* is a reference to a piece of literature, an historical event or figure, or to a popular movie or television show.

The speaker's frequent allusions to characters in popular television shows entertained the audience.

b. An *illusion* is something that deceives by creating a false impression. An *illusion* can also refer to the state of mind in the person who is deceived.

The use of perspective in the painting created the illusion of depth.

Alison clung to the illusion that Juan would never forget her.

6. *Among* and *Between*

a. Use *among* when you refer to more than two things.

Divide the candy canes evenly among all the Christmas hampers.

b. Use *between* when you refer to two things.

Divide the prize money between the two winners.

7. *Amount* and *Number* (See also *Less* and *Fewer*)

a. Use *amount* to refer to things considered as a mass.

Melt a small amount of butter in a pan.

b. Use *number* to refer to things that can be counted as individual units.

A small number of delegates attended the convention.

8. *Compare with* and *Compare to*

a. Use *compare with* when you examine the similarities and differences in things.

A comparison of the American Senate with the Canadian Senate strengthens the argument for electing senators.

b. Use *compare to* when you want to point out the similarities in two things.

I would compare her eating habits to those of a pig.

9. *Differ from* and *Differ with*

a. Use *differ from* to indicate that two things are unalike.

The stage version of the play differs enormously from the film version.

DICTION

b. Use *differ with* to express disagreement with a person.

> I wish to differ with your assessment of the mayor's voting record.

10. *Different from* (not *different than*)

> The effects of an expectorant cough syrup are different from the effects of a cough suppressant.

11. *Elusive* and *Illusory*

a. Use *elusive* when you want to describe something that is good at escaping or difficult to define or express.

> The elusive mouse disappeared in a crack in the wall.
> The specific implications of the new immigration policy remained elusive.

b. Use *illusory* when you want to describe something that is false or unreal.

> The benefits of the proposed tax reduction are illusory.

12. *Good* and *Well*

a. *Good* is usually an adjective.

> a good book, a good cookie

b. *Well* is usually an adverb.

> to drive well, to sing well

13. *Hopefully*. Some guides to usage accept *hopefully* as a sentence modifier meaning "I hope" or "perhaps."

> Hopefully, I can leave work early.

Some readers, however, find this usage confusing and insist that *hopefully* should be used only as an adverb meaning "full of hope."

> Dressed in Halloween costumes, the children shouted hopefully at the door.

Discuss this issue in class and see whether you can come to some agreement.

14. *Imply* and *Infer*

a. Use *imply* to mean "hint."

> His lack of response to her entreaties implied his refusal to grant her wish.

b. Use *infer* to mean "make an educated guess" or "draw a conclusion."

The detective inferred from the blood on the sheets that the victim had been murdered in his sleep.

15. *It's* and *Its*

   a. *It's* means "it is."

   It's raining for the third day in a row.

   b. *Its* is a possessive pronoun.

   The horse broke its leg.

16. *Less* and *Fewer*

   a. Use *less* to refer to things considered as a mass.

   Although I am earning more, I seem to have less spending money.

   b. Use *fewer* to refer to things that can be counted.

   Fewer students than expected signed up for this course.

17. *Lie* and *Lay*

   a. The principal parts of the verb to *lie* (to recline) are *lie, lay, lying,* and *lain.*

   She has been lying in the sun all afternoon.

   b. The principal parts of the verb to *lay* (to place) are *lay, laid, laying,* and *laid.*

   The soldiers are laying down their weapons.

18. *Like* and *As*

   a. Use *like* when you are not introducing a clause.

   He looks like his father.

   b. Use *as* to introduce a clause.

   That night she dressed as she did when she was a girl.

19. *Loose* and *Lose*

   a. *Loose* is usually an adjective (loose talk), but it can be used as a verb meaning "to let loose."

   Loose the dogs of war.

   b. *Lose* is a verb.

   She is afraid she will lose her job.

20. *Partake of* and *Take part in*

   a. Use *partake of* when you mean to have a share of something (usually a meal).

   The guests were invited to partake of the enormous turkey.

DICTION

b. Use *take part in* when you mean to join or participate.

Will you take part in our volleyball game?

21. *Principle* and *Principal*

a. *Principle* means a fundamental belief.

Most Canadians accept the principle of universal medical coverage.

b. *Principal* means most important, first in rank.

My principal objection is that cuts in services will inflict the most damage on the most vulnerable members of the community.

He is the principal dancer with the Royal Winnipeg Ballet Company.

22. *Realize*

a. *Realize* can mean "to make real," as in "to realize a profit."

b. *Realize* can also mean "to understand fully," as in "to realize that he was wrong."

You can avoid confusing these two meanings of *realize* if you use "realize that" when you mean "understand fully."

NOT   He realized his mother's unhappiness.

BUT   He realized that his mother was unhappy.

23. *There* and *Their*

a. Use *there* as an adverb or as a dummy subject.

Put the piano there.

There were many problems.

b. *Their* is a possessive pronoun.

their problem, their tough luck

24. *Uninterested* and *Disinterested*

a. Use *uninterested* to mean "not interested in."

I am uninterested in politics.

b. Use *disinterested* to mean impartial.

We need a disinterested third person to settle our dispute.

25. *You're* and *Your*

a. *You're* means "you are."

You're going to pay for this.

b. *Your* is a possessive pronoun.

Your car is in my parking space.

EXERCISE 2

Revise the following sentences to correct errors in usage. Most sentences contain more than one error.

1. From the noise in the lecture theatre, its reasonable to imply that a large amount of people were quite disinterested in the topic.
2. By now it should hopefully be obvious that acid rain has alot of affects on all of us.
3. Engineers must realize there responsibility to protect the environment.
4. Even on formal occasions, Ted dresses like he is going to a hockey game.
5. Cindy refused to partake in any of the celebrations connected with her mother's wedding.
6. Fred immersed himself in the allusion that his status as an outsider made him an uninterested party in the family dispute.
7. The principle difference in my two jobs is that I now work less hours and make more money.
8. The next command your going to learn is how to make your dog lay down on command.
9. "Alright," the driving instructor said, "this time you did good enough to pass."
10. The results of the medical tests were different than what the doctor had predicted.

7 Eliminating Wordiness

When you write a draft, you may find yourself repeating ideas, making false starts on sentences, and using inexact, wordy language because you are still working out your ideas. Sometimes the whole essay may be wordy because you have circled around ideas instead of including evidence to support them.

You can see both problems in the following draft paragraph from an essay comparing our economic system with that in William Morris's utopian novel, *News from Nowhere*. This paragraph seems substantial because it is long, but it makes only two points: people in Morris's society do not use money for business transactions and they have more freedom in determining how, when, and where they work. Instead of supporting these points with specific details, however, the writer merely repeats them.

> In Morris's society there is no monetary system or labour force. Everything is free. Nothing is paid for. People work as individuals; in other words, they do whatever work they want to do whenever they want to do it. People may wish to do no work at all and just enjoy a life free from all care and obligations. A labour position is open to a man or a woman on an equal basis. Our society has a monetary system and a labour force. Money is the basis of the way we carry out our business transactions. Various work forces are organized for various occupations. A person employed in one occupation must conform to the guidelines that are set out for that type of work, such as hours of work and fulfillment of responsibility.

Don't pad your essay with unnecessary words, phrases, sentences, and paragraphs just to reach the word limit. This strategy will only irritate your reader and weaken the force of your ideas. When you revise, try to eliminate unnecessary words and to rewrite wordy sentences and paragraphs. Here are some suggestions for writing more concisely.

1. Choose exact nouns, verbs, and modifiers.

   NOT   We walked slowly and quietly in the direction of the run-down little house. (13 words)

   BUT   We crept toward the hovel. (5 words)

2. Replace vague words, such as *very, somewhat, really,* and *rather* with a more exact word.

   NOT   They were really frightened by the ghost.

   BUT   They were terrified by the ghost.

3. Avoid carelessly repeating words and ideas.

   NOT   Entries to this competition are restricted to students only; no one else need apply. (14 words)

   BUT   Only students may enter this competition. (6 words)

4. Condense prepositional phrases to single words.

   NOT   She was dressed in a fashionable manner.

   BUT   She was dressed fashionably.

5. Don't overuse *there is/are* and *it is...that* to introduce sentences.

   NOT   There are a number of factors that we should consider before we make this decision.

   BUT   We should consider several factors before we make this decision.

   NOT   It is Hagar's pride that causes many of her problems.

   BUT   Hagar's pride causes many of her problems.

6. Combine several short sentences into one longer sentence by reducing sentences to clauses, clauses to phrases, and phrases to single words.

   Television cameras filmed the demolition of the Regency Theatre.

   The Regency Theatre was one of the most ornate movie-houses in western Canada.

   REVISED Television cameras filmed the demolition of the Regency Theatre, one of the most ornate movie-houses in western Canada.

WORDINESS

EXERCISE 1

Revise the following groups of sentences to make them more concise.

1. A study has been done on smokers. This study revealed that much smoking is an automatic response to certain activities. These activities might be driving, typing, reading, or drinking alcohol and coffee.

2. The book *A Circle of Children* and its successor, *Lovey*, are stories about a teacher of children who are emotionally disturbed. Mary MacCracken wrote an account of her experiences working with children with emotional problems and described her growth as a teacher. She began as a teacher's aide and gradually became a teacher who was fully qualified to work with emotionally disturbed children. The books show her development as a teacher.

3. Being a video game player, I find it my duty to give a good name to video games because I find them challenging. I would like to change people's attitudes towards video games by giving some information in the hope that many people will discard their belief that these are mindless games and learn that these games require many years of practice.

4. A society that maintained a balance between the needs of the society and the preservation of the environment would be the best kind of society. I would like to live in it.

5. He drove his car down the highway. He drove his car very fast. He was travelling about 150 km an hour. Suddenly he hit a very icy section of the road. The car went out of control and slid quite quickly in the direction of the ditch.

EXERCISE 2

Rewrite the following paragraph to make it more concise. Add specific examples to illustrate major points.

> Retirement for many people brings with it a reduction in the number of friends and acquaintances they socialize and share activities with. Because the friends they knew before they retired were often people they knew from work, retired people may not have so many friends after they stop working. People who have retired no longer share the same interests as people who are still working, and so they don't spend as much time together. If retired people don't have friends and acquaintances besides the people they worked with, they may feel very lonely when they stop working and have fewer contacts with people.

EXERCISE 3

Revise a paragraph of your own writing to make it more concise. Bring both versions to class for discussion.

8 Solving Verb Problems

Verb Forms

A **verb** is a word or group of words that expresses action, existence, possession, or sensation.

He **plays** hockey. She **has been playing** hockey. (action)

I **am** here. I **have been** here. (existence)

You **have** the measles. Soon we **will have** the measles. (possession)

The bread **smells** mouldy. Your hands **feel** cold. (sensation)

Main Verbs and Auxiliary Verbs

A verb phrase is formed by joining one or more auxiliary verbs to the main verb: **have been waiting, might be stolen**. The last word in the verb phrase is the main verb; the other words are auxiliaries. Here is a list of the most common auxiliary verbs:

1. forms of *to be*: *am, is, are, was, were, be, been, being*
2. forms of *to have*: *have, has, had*
3. forms of *to do*: *do, does, did, done*
4. others: *can, could, may, might, must, shall, will, should, would, ought to, have to, supposed to, used to.*

Principal Parts of Verbs

Principal Parts of Regular Verbs The four main parts of a verb are the present tense, the past tense (formed by adding *ed* to the present tense), the present participle (formed by adding *ing* to the present tense) and the past participle (formed by adding *has* or *have* to the past tense).

The present tense usually expresses habitual action (Every day I *walk* to school), whereas the present participle is used with an auxiliary to express ongoing action (I *am walking* to school now). The past participle is used to express action that began in the past and continues to the present (I *have lived* in Canada for twenty years) or to express action that began and ended in the past (I *had lived* in Germany for twelve years before I came to Canada).

To name a verb, give its infinitive form: *to walk, to fill*

PRESENT	PAST	PRESENT PARTICIPLE	PAST PARTICIPLE
walk	walked	walking	walked
fill	filled	filling	filled

Principal Parts of Irregular Verbs Regular verbs, as their name suggests, form their principal parts in a regular, predictable way. Irregular verbs, in contrast, form their principal parts in various unpredictable ways. Here are three different patterns of irregular verbs.

PRESENT	PAST	PRESENT PARTICIPLE	PAST PARTICIPLE
drink	drank	drinking	drunk
burst	burst	bursting	burst
steal	stole	stealing	stolen

The present participle of irregular verbs is always formed by adding *ing* to the present tense. It's the past tense and the past participle that may cause problems. You need either to memorize these forms or to check your dictionary. Here are some of the most troublesome irregular verbs to watch for in your writing.

Principal Parts of Troublesome Verbs

INFINITIVE	PAST TENSE	PAST PARTICIPLE
to be	was	been
to break	broke	broken
to choose	chose	chosen
to come	came	come
to cost	cost	cost
to go	went	gone

to lay (place)	laid	laid
to lie (recline)	lay	lain
to hang (a person)	hanged	hanged
to hang (a picture)	hung	hung
to lead	led	led
to rise	rose	risen

Note 1: Don't confuse *lose* and *loose*.

NOT   She is afraid that she will loose her mind.

BUT   She is afraid that she will lose her mind.

Note 2: Be sure to add the past tense ending to *use* and *suppose* when they are followed by an infinitive.

NOT   Rosa use to play soccer.

BUT   Rosa used to play soccer.

NOT   Alix is suppose to make dinner.

BUT   Alix is supposed to make dinner.

EXERCISE I

Correct any errors in verb usage in the following sentences. Put C beside a correct sentence.

1. Because he had laid in the sun all afternoon, he was horribly sunburnt.
2. I'll put my money in a safe place so I won't loose *lose* it.
3. After three months in her new job, she still wasn't sure what she was suppose *supposed* to do.
4. When the soldiers surrendered, they laid down their weapons in the sand.
5. The car loan *cost* costed more than he had anticipated.
6. I need to borrow your vacuum cleaner because mine is broken.
7. The clues have *led* lead the detective straight to the murder suspect.
8. I have a headache, so I think I'll *lie* lay down for an hour.
9. Their bubble of happiness finally burst.
10. After she had drank *drunk* all of the magic potion, she suddenly felt very tall.

Verb Tenses

Verb tenses indicate the time of existence, action, possession, or sensation. The basic tenses in English are the present, past, and future.

The tenses used in a sentence or series of sentences must accurately indicate the time relationships involved.

> She walks to the door. She opens her umbrella. She leaves.
> (all verbs in the present tense)

> She walked to the door. She opened her umbrella. She left.
> (all verbs in the past tense)

> When she finishes her meal (present tense), she will walk to the door, open her umbrella, and leave. (future tense)
> (change in tenses necessary to indicate time relationships)

Identifying Unnecessary Shifts in Tense

Unnecessary shifts in tense occur when the verb forms do not correspond to the time relationships. In the following sentence, the tense shifts are confusing,

> When she finished her meal, she walks to the door, opens her umbrella, and will leave.

Correcting Unnecessary Shifts in Tense

If you are caught up in the ideas you are trying to convey, you may switch from present to past or vice-versa without noticing. These suggestions will help you keep your tenses consistent.

1. When you are writing about literary works, keep your analysis and your account of events in the present tense:

   NOT In *Sons and Lovers*, D. H. Lawrence *describes* the poverty of English miners. The men's earnings *were determined* by the amount of coal they mine each week. If they *have* a poor spot, or if they *were injured*, or if the mine *was shut* down, they *will* not *earn* enough to feed their families. Lawrence *shows* that because of the uncertainty about the men's wages, some women *earned* extra money by knitting stockings and children often *go* to work at a very early age.

   BUT In *Sons and Lovers,* D. H. Lawrence describes the poverty of English miners. The men's earnings *are determined* by the amount of coal they *mine* each week. If they *have* a poor spot, or if they *are injured,* or if the mine *is shut* down, they *do* not *earn* enough to feed their families. Lawrence *shows* that because of the uncertainty about the men's wages, some women

VERBS

       earn extra money by knitting stockings and children
       often *go* to work at a very early age.

2. Use the simple present or past tense in preference to *-ing* verbs.

    NOT   Freud *is discussing* the relationships among the id,
              ego, and superego.

    BUT   Freud *discusses* the relationships among the id, ego,
              and superego.

3. If you sometimes omit verb endings, writing "he learn" instead of "he learns" or "he learned," check each verb.

4. If you know you have a problem with verb tenses, proofread your final draft a paragraph at a time, checking all verbs to make sure that (a) they are in the same tense, or (b) changes in tense are justified by the time relationships.

EXERCISE 2

Underline all the verbs in the following paragraph. Then correct unnecessary tense shifts. Do not make any other changes.

> People can plan for their retirement while they are still working. The most common way was through training programs initiated by employers at least ten years before the employee's retirement. These programs are providing information to the employees and help them to adopt a realistic view of the process of retirement. Most of these programs will contain information pertaining to pension planning, leisure time, and other issues.

Subject–Verb Agreement

Verbs must agree with their subjects in number: if the subject of the sentence is singular, the verb must be singular; if the subject is plural, the verb must be plural.

> The engine is hot. (singular subject, singular verb)
>
> The engines are hot. (plural subject, plural verb)

By the time you reach college or university, you probably won't make subject–verb errors very often. When you do, you may have lost track of the subject, as in the following cases.

1. Prepositional phrase between the subject and the verb.
Remember that the noun in the prepositional phrase (of the

children, between the *hedges*, beneath the *sheets*) is never the subject of the sentence.

NOT   The reaction to these incidents were quick and angry.

BUT   The <u>reaction</u> to these incidents <u>was</u> quick and angry.

2. Phrases that imply a plural subject when the actual subject is singular: *as well as, in addition to, along with, including.*

NOT   The cost, including parts and labour, were far more than the estimate.

BUT   The <u>cost</u>, including parts and labour, <u>was</u> far more than the estimate.

3. Indefinite pronouns that may seem plural but take a singular verb:

anybody	anyone	anything	each (of)
everybody	everyone	everything	either (of)
nobody	no one	nothing	neither (of)
somebody	someone	something	

NOT   Each of the passengers have a headphone.

BUT   <u>Each</u> of the passengers <u>has</u> a headphone.

NOT   Neither of the soldiers were wounded.

BUT   <u>Neither</u> [one] of the soldiers <u>was</u> wounded.

4. *There is/are* constructions

   In these constructions, the subject comes after the verb. *There* is never the subject of the sentence.

NOT   There is three important issues (subject) to consider.

BUT   There <u>are</u> three important <u>issues</u> (subject) to consider.

5. Singular subjects joined with *or*.

NOT   John or Carol are meeting you at the airport.

BUT   <u>John</u> or <u>Carol</u> <u>is meeting</u> you at the airport.

6. A combination of singular and plural subjects joined with *either...or, neither...nor, not only...but also.* With these constructions, the verb agrees with the subject closer to it.

NOT   Neither the students nor the teacher were satisfied with the test results.

BUT   Neither the students nor the <u>teacher</u> <u>was</u> satisfied with the test results.

Note: In these constructions, it is best to put the plural subject second.

Neither the teacher nor <u>the students</u> <u>were</u> satisfied with the test results.

EXERCISE 3

Underline the subject of the sentence. Then circle the correct verb form.

1. There (doesn't/**don't**) seem to be any books or articles on this subject.

2. Banff National Park, with its breathtaking scenery, its nature programs, and its plentiful campsites, (**attracts**/attract) millions of visitors every year.

3. Neither of the women (**was**/were) willing to vote for the candidate.

4. Not only the athletes but also the coach (**is**/are) tired at the end of the game.

5. The demand for luxury products (**is**/are) decreasing.

Active and Passive Voice

Verbs have two voices: active and passive. In the **active voice**, the subject of the sentence performs the action. In the **passive voice**, the subject is acted upon.

> ACTIVE Jasmine drove the car.
>
> PASSIVE The car was driven by Jasmine.

Uses of the Passive Voice

Usually the active voice is preferable because it is more direct and concise. Sometimes, however, the passive voice is necessary.

1. When the agent of the action is understood, unimportant, or unknown:

   I was born in Saskatoon.

   The roads were sanded regularly.

2. When you want to focus attention on the procedure and the results rather than on the agent.

   Ten milligrams of sodium chloride were placed in a beaker.

Passive constructions are often used in scientific writing to suggest that the steps and outcome will be the same no matter who performs the experiment. Researchers who place more emphasis on their own role in the experiments use the active voice more often.

Misuses of the Passive Voice

1. Avoid the passive voice when the active voice would be more concise, more direct, or more emphatic.

VERBS

NOT   It was reported to the president by the vice-president that an agreement was reached between the workers and the management.

BUT   The vice-president reported to the president that the workers and the management had reached an agreement.

2. Avoid mixing the active and passive voices in the same sentence.

NOT   Psychologists have found that more realistic estimates of control over future events are made by mildly depressed people.

BUT   Psychologists have found that mildly depressed people make more realistic estimates of their control over future events.

EXERCISE 4

Identify the verbs in the following sentences as active or passive. Revise sentences in which the passive voice is inappropriate or ineffective.

1. The desire by Swift in "A Modest Proposal" for better food, clothing, and housing for the Irish is expressed.
2. Their house was bombed during the war.
3. Skilled helicopter pilots lifted terrified flood victims from their rooftops.
4. The autopsy on the famous race horse was performed this morning.
5. The demand for better employment opportunities was forcefully expressed by the Métis in Alberta and Saskatchewan.

EXERCISE 5

Write a paragraph in which all of the verbs are in the active voice. Then rewrite the paragraph so that all of the verbs are in the passive voice. Bring both paragraphs to class for discussion. What are the strengths and weaknesses of each? Does a mixture work best?

REVIEW EXERCISE 1

Correct all problems with subject–verb agreement, tense shifts, troublesome verbs, and inappropriate use of the passive voice in the following paragraphs.

We were just getting use to the midnight sun and the lack of comforts in the bush camp when the animal come. We had no idea what was out there, but we knew it was coming towards us. Maybe a wolf or a small deer were foraging in the underbrush. A warning was given to us when the silence of the Arctic was broken by the crazed howling of our camp dog. With a sense of duty and pride, he flies into the bush towards the animal. Out of the thicket the dog came charging back, his eyes a picture of terror. He was refusing to leave his master's side, nor would he let us venture into the woods alone. This half-wild dog was trying to save us.

Although we couldn't hear it, we could feel the thing coming closer. The wild howling was began by the dog again. The camp geologist took this warning and runs for his rifle, a World War II surplus Winchester 303 with a shaky sight. Sixteen shells were loaded into two clips. We were ready and so was it. Finally a large female grizzly bear and her cub was in sight. The grizzly had two massive forelimbs swinging six feet off the ground. Her grey coat blended in with the charred trees as they were pushed over by her. The tiny grey cub playfully followed his fierce mother towards our camp. We had been seen by the huge bear, but she was not stopping. We were on the verge of panic, but we were ready. The canoe was ready, the motor having been attached and life jackets were thrown aboard. We could escape to the cold and windy lake.

REVIEW EXERCISE 2

Check your own writing for problems with subject–verb agreement, tense shifts, troublesome verbs, and inappropriate use of the passive voice. Bring examples to class for discussion.

9 Solving Pronoun Problems

Pronouns of Address

Using First-Person Pronouns: "I"

First-person pronouns (*I, we*) are appropriate when you want to draw attention to your own responses and experiences in personal writing. Because you want to keep your reader's attention focused on your subject, use first-person pronouns sparingly in most college and university essays. When you do want to refer to yourself, follow these guidelines.

1. To express agreement or disagreement with another viewpoint, use a phrase such as "I think" or "I believe." Make such phrases inconspicuous by putting them inside the sentence.

    NOT   I think Jones is right when she calls *The Merchant of Venice* a flawed play.

    BUT   Jones is right, I think, when she calls *The Merchant of Venice* a flawed play.

2. When you use a personal example to support a point, use "I" instead of awkward expressions such as "this writer."

3. Avoid using "I" when you intend your opinions to have a more general application.

    NOT   I had a hard time figuring out what these two lines mean. (implies it's your fault)

    BUT   The meaning of these two lines is hard to grasp. (implies that others would have the same difficulty)

4. Avoid such "I" expressions as "this is only my opinion" and "I hope I will be able to show." These statements sound uncertain and apologetic and weaken your statement.

Using First-Person Pronouns: "We" and "One"

1. Use "we" sparingly to include readers in your discussion. Make "we" references unobtrusive or revise the sentence to omit "we."

   NOT   We have seen that water will be a major factor in the politics of the Middle East.

   BUT   Water, as we have seen, will be a major factor in the politics of the Middle East.

   OR   Water will thus be a major factor in the politics of the Middle East.

2. Use "we" sparingly to refer to people in general. Be careful not to overgeneralize.

   We all remember our high school principals with affection.

   Many of us remember our high school principals with affection.

3. "One" is sometimes used in formal speech and writing to mean "people in general, including the writer," as in "One might wish for better weather." Because "one" sounds stilted when used extensively, try to eliminate it, either by using "I" (if that is what you mean) or by using a noun.

   NOT   When one watches television, one is dismayed by the scarcity of good programs.

   BUT   When I watch television, I am dismayed by the scarcity of good programs.

   OR   Many television viewers are dismayed by the scarcity of good programs.

Using Second-Person Pronouns: "You"

Second-person pronouns are appropriate when you want to speak directly to your reader, for example when you give instructions.

   You will need to wear gloves when you give your cat a bath.

Avoid using "you" to refer to people in general.

   NOT   By the end of the play, you can see that Macbeth is desperate.

   BUT   By the end of the play, Macbeth's desperation is obvious.

PRONOUNS

Using Third-Person Pronouns: "He," "She," "They"

Most often in college and university essays, you will use third-person pronouns to keep your reader's attention focused on your subject. When you use these pronouns, be careful to avoid sexist language and pronoun agreement errors.

Although *he* and other masculine singular pronouns have traditionally been used to refer to both men and women, as in the example, "The driver is responsible for the safety of all passengers in *his* vehicle," many people feel that this usage contributes to gender stereotyping. To avoid alienating your reader, try to use more inclusive language, but be careful not to introduce errors in pronoun agreement, as in "The driver is responsible for the safety of all passengers in *their* vehicle." Here are some suggestions for avoiding both sexist language and pronoun agreement errors. For more on the latter, see Pronoun Agreement.

1. Reword the sentence to eliminate unnecessary gender pronouns.

   NOT   The average commuter drives his car fifty kilometres a day.

   BUT   The average commuter drives fifty kilometres a day.

2. Make the noun and pronouns plural.

   NOT   The enterprising executive sends his managers to study foreign business practices.

   BUT   Enterprising executives send their managers to study foreign business practices.

3. Alternate references to boys and girls, men and women in examples.

   NOT   Teachers sometimes complain about their students: "He never does his homework," "He constantly disrupts the class," "He never listens."

   BUT   Teachers sometimes complain about their students: "She never does her homework," "He constantly disrupts the class," "She never listens."

EXERCISE I

Revise each of the following sentences to eliminate errors in the use of pronouns of address. Put C beside a correct sentence.

1. In this essay I hope to show that poison imagery pervades *Hamlet*.

2. We all remember junior high school dances with warm nostalgia.

3. To train a dog effectively, you should avoid games that involve pitting the dog's strength and agility against yours.

4. By the end of the novel, you can see that the protagonist is doomed.

5. The average student finds that working ten hours a week is about all he can handle in addition to his school work.

Avoiding Shifts in Pronouns of Address

Once you have decided on first-, second-, or third-person pronouns as your basic mode, be consistent in using them. If you shift pronouns without good reason, you will confuse or jar your reader.

In the example below, the writer begins with "you," shifts to "one" in the second sentence, and then shifts to a third-person reference ("a student's marks") in the last sentence.

> Are you too tense to concentrate during exams? One finds that one is concentrating on the clock instead of on the exam. Inability to concentrate can lower a student's marks.

Depending on your audience and purpose, you could correct these unnecessary pronoun shifts by using either second- or third-person pronouns consistently.

> Are you too tense to concentrate during exams? Are you concentrating on the clock instead of on the exam? This inability to concentrate can lower your marks.

> Some students are too tense to concentrate during exams. They find that they are concentrating on the clock instead of on the exam. This inability to concentrate can lower their marks.

A more common problem is the inappropriate use of first- or second-person pronouns in a piece of writing that is primarily in the third person, as in the following example:

> The student board governing the residence hall recently approved the installation of a security system designed to curb theft and vandalism by outsiders. With this system, you have locked doors, identification cards, security guards, and an obligatory sign-in procedure for visitors. Unfortunately, the system is ineffective because most of the damage is done by students who live in the residence.

You could eliminate the inappropriate shift to "you" in this paragraph by beginning the second sentence with "this system includes."

EXERCISE 2

Revise the following paragraph to eliminate all pronoun shifts.

By taking control over when and where your dog eats, the dog owner can establish dominance. When we come home from school or work, your first impulse may be to feed the dog as a way of showing care and affection. Dogs, on the other hand, interpret the right to eat first as an indication that they are the leaders. The dog owner should make the dog obey a command (such as "sit") first. Then you should eat something, even a snack, before your dog eats. Dogs often resist new feeding procedures, but if the dog owner can stick with it, your dog will see you as the leader. We will then be able to gain more control of other aspects of our relationship with our dogs.

Pronoun Agreement

A singular noun must be matched with a singular pronoun, a plural noun with a plural pronoun. Most pronoun agreement errors occur in these contexts:

1. When the noun refers to a type of person: the patient, the student, the player. You can correct this error by making the subject plural.

   NOT   The first-year student may have problems adjusting to their new freedom.

   BUT   First-year students may have problems adjusting to their new freedom.

2. When a singular noun is followed by a prepositional phrase ending with a plural noun (*of the workers, of the children*).

   NOT   One of the children left their lunch on the kitchen table.

   BUT   One of the children left his lunch on the kitchen table.

   OR   One of the children left her lunch on the kitchen table.

3. When the writer is trying to avoid gender bias. If you don't want to imply that a singular subject (the single parent, the nurse, the engineer) is always male or female, you may make errors in pronoun agreement.

   Every doctor these days complains that paper work encroaches on the time *they* can spend with their patients.

Although this error in pronoun agreement is gradually becoming more acceptable, you may want to avoid it with these strategies.

PRONOUNS

a. Make the subject plural (single parents, nurses, engineers).

b. Use *him or her, he or she* (never *he/she* or *s/he*) to refer to a singular subject.

> Typically, a two-year-old will insist that he or she be the focus of all attention.

This strategy works well in a single sentence but becomes cumbersome in a longer piece of writing.

c. Rewrite the sentence to avoid pronouns.

> Typically, a two-year-old insists on being the focus of all attention.

d. Refer to the subject with masculine pronouns in one paragraph and feminine pronouns in the next.

4. When the subject is an indefinite pronoun. In formal writing, use singular pronouns to refer to *each* and to words that end with *-body, -one*, and *-thing*: *anybody, everybody, nobody; anyone, everyone, no one; anything, everything, nothing.*

> INFORMAL SPOKEN Everyone wanted to have their picture taken.

> FORMAL WRITTEN Everyone at the convention wanted his or her vote on this issue recorded.

5. When the subject is a collective noun and the sentence indicates unanimous action. Some of the common collective nouns are *family, school, community, band, group, committee, flock, herd.*

> The committee circulated the minutes of its [not *their*] last meeting.

> The band has made its [not *their*] last public appearance.

EXERCISE 3

Correct all the errors in pronoun agreement in the following sentences.

1. When a firm meets government pollution emission standards, their expenses increase.

2. The steel worker wants to have some control over their working conditions.

3. A cancer patient may be misled by quack cures that seem to promise them miraculous results.

4. The House of Commons said that they will enforce new security measures. Everyone entering the building will be searched to determine whether they are carrying firearms.

5. Because it loses less energy than copper wire, fibres are used to transmit thousands of signals simultaneously in enormous bandwidths.

Pronoun Case

Subject and Object Pronouns

Subject pronouns, as their name implies, are most commonly used in the subject position in the sentence: *He* and *I* went to a movie. Object pronouns are used as the object of a verb or preposition: Gabriella and Simon met *him* and *me* at the concession.

SUBJECT PRONOUNS		OBJECT PRONOUNS	
Singular	Plural	Singular	Plural
I	we	me	us
you	you	you	you
he/she/it	they	him/her/it	them
who	who	whom	whom

If you use a subject pronoun where you should use an object pronoun, or vice-versa, you have made an error in pronoun case.

Use Subject Pronouns

1. In the subject position in the sentence. Be sure to use a subject pronoun when there are two subjects in the sentence.

   NOT   My brother and me bought a car together.

   BUT   My brother and I bought a car together.

2. When the subject pronoun is followed by an explanatory noun.

   NOT   Us students were enraged by the exam.

   BUT   We students were enraged by the exam.

3. After comparisons using *than* and *as*.

   NOT   The other team is weaker than us.

   BUT   The other team is weaker than we.

4. As the subject of a subordinate clause beginning with *that*.

   NOT   Mr. Ramsay said that him and his sister had rented the house on the corner.

   BUT   Mr. Ramsay said that he and his sister had rented the house on the corner.

Use Object Pronouns

1. As the object of a verb.

   NOT   The coach told Rajiv and he to come early.

   BUT   The coach told Rajiv and him to come early.

2. After a preposition.

NOT   The manager left a message for my roommate and I.

BUT   The manager left a message for my roommate and me.

Note: *Me* is not an informal form of *I*. *Me* is a perfectly acceptable object pronoun. Don't substitute *myself* for *me* when you need an object pronoun.

NOT   Please contact either the supervisor or myself if you have problems.

BUT   Please contact either the supervisor or me if you have problems.

Who and *Whom*

1. *Who* is a subject pronoun. Use *who* to refer to a subject noun.

Dr. Wong is the distinguished biologist. She will give the opening address.

Dr. Wong is the distinguished biologist who will give the opening address.

2. *Whom* is an object pronoun. Use *whom* after prepositions and to refer to an object noun.

Claudius is a smooth politician. Hamlet distrusts him.

Claudius is a smooth politician whom Hamlet distrusts.

EXERCISE 4

Revise the following sentences to correct all errors in pronoun case. Put C beside a correct sentence.

1. For now, let's keep this plan a secret between you and I.
2. Caterina said that her and Bill might get married this summer.
3. Give the money to whoever you like.
4. Us residents strongly oppose the increase in property taxes.
5. Luis has consistently put more effort into this project than she.
6. Direct all complaints to the caretaker or myself.

Possessive Pronouns

When you want to show ownership, use these possessive pronouns: *my/mine*, *his*, *her/hers*, *their/theirs*, *your/yours*, *whose*. Remember that possessive pronouns do not take apostrophes.

1. Don't confuse the possessive pronoun *its* with the contraction *it's* (it is).

   POSSESSIVE The board has made its ruling.

   CONTRACTION It's obvious that no one was listening.

2. Don't confuse the possessive pronoun *whose* with the contraction *who's* (who is).

   POSSESSIVE We must decide whose responsibility this is.

   CONTRACTION Who's responsible for this?

3. Don't confuse the possessive pronoun *their* with the dummy subject *there*.

   POSSESSIVE The Inuit in the region are close to settling their land claim.

   DUMMY SUBJECT There are still a few issues to be resolved.

4. Don't confuse the possessive pronoun *your* with the contraction *you're*.

   POSSESSIVE Don't forget to put your signature on the expense claim.

   CONTRACTION If you don't hurry, you're going to be late.

EXERCISE 5

Revise the following sentences to eliminate all errors in the use of possessive pronouns.

1. The company management has stated it's final position on the union's proposal.

2. If your satisfied with this offer, then we will accept it.

3. We still don't know whose going to teach this class.

4. Luigi and Caterina devoted all of there attention to running the pet store.

5. That beautiful cottage on the shore of the lake is their's.

Pronoun Reference

Errors in pronoun reference occur whenever a pronoun does not clearly refer to a specific noun. Here are some ways to correct ambiguous pronouns.

1. Keep the pronoun close to the noun to which it refers.

   NOT Luigi told George that he was a terrible baseball player. He was furious.

   BUT George was furious because Luigi called him a terrible baseball player.

PRONOUNS

OR   Because Luigi was furious, he called George a terrible
     baseball player.

2. Use pronouns to refer only to nouns or pronouns, not to possessive adjectives such as *his*, *her*, *Shakespeare's*.

   James snapped the guitar's neck that belonged to his mother.

   In this sentence, *that* refers to the guitar's neck, an error suggesting that only the guitar's neck belonged to James's mother.
   You could make clear that the whole guitar belonged to James's
   mother like this:

   James snapped the neck of the guitar that belonged to his
   mother.

3. Make sure *that*, *this*, and *which* refer to a specific noun or pronoun, not to the idea in the preceding sentence or clause.
   Clarify vague pronoun references by rewriting the sentence or
   supplying the missing noun or pronoun.

   NOT   He did not know whether she would leave or wait for
         him. This made him anxious.

   BUT   He did not know whether she would leave or wait for
         him. This uncertainty made him anxious.

   OR   He was anxious because he did not know whether she
         would leave or wait for him.

4. Do not use *they* to refer to people in general or to the author of a
   text.

   NOT   They said hurricanes are affected by the rain cycles in
         Africa.

   BUT   Meteorologists say hurricanes are affected by the rain
         cycles in Africa.

   NOT   They say in Shaw's play *Major Barbara* that the only
         crime is poverty.

   BUT   In Shaw's play *Major Barbara,* Undershaft says that
         the only crime is poverty.

5. Do not use *it* or *they* to refer to an implied subject. Supply the
   missing noun or rewrite the sentence.

   NOT   I spent two weeks studying for the exam, but it didn't
         improve my grade.

   BUT   I spent two weeks studying for the exam, but this ef-
         fort did not improve my grade.

   OR   Two weeks of studying for the exam did not improve
         my grade.

   NOT   I wrote to Revenue Canada about my income tax as-
         sessment, but they have not yet replied.

PRONOUNS

BUT   I wrote to Revenue Canada about my income tax assessment, but the taxation officials have not yet
replied.

OR   I have not yet received a reply to my letter to Revenue
Canada about my income tax assessment.

EXERCISE 6

Revise the following sentences to eliminate ambiguous pronoun references.

1. An important part of being a successful goalie is building up a determination to defend the net. It must occupy his or her complete attention.

2. Many people who renovate to make their houses more energy efficient are unaware that it will increase their property value and are surprised when they assess
their property for increased taxes.

3. Gradually the public began to accept the theory of evolution, which forced the
clergy into less vocal opposition.

4. She left flowers in the teacher's office who had been such a help to her.

5. The two children hid their margarine sandwiches from their classmates because
they were ashamed to let them see how poor they were.

REVIEW EXERCISE 1

Revise this paragraph to eliminate errors in pronoun agreement and ambiguous pronoun references.

In Shakespeare's *King Lear*, they show that lack of
self-knowledge has disastrous consequences for a person because without self-knowledge they are unable to judge the
motives and actions of others. Lear accepts the extreme flat-
tery of his daughters Goneril and Regan as sincere and appropriate to his dignity, which is obviously exaggerated.
When his youngest daughter, Cordelia, refuses to compete
with her sisters, she wounds Lear's vanity. This is the reason
he banishes her. When his loyal servant Kent tries to inter-
vene, he banishes him because he refuses to admit that he
might have been unjust. Lear's inability to see the truth
about himself thus initiates the tragedy, for in his blindness
he deprives himself of everyone most loyal to their king.

REVIEW EXERCISE 2

Check your own writing for problems with pronoun agreement, pronoun case, and
pronoun reference. Bring examples to class for discussion.

10 Solving Punctuation Problems

Apostrophe

The apostrophe is used to indicate missing letters in *contractions* and to show *possession*.

Recognizing Plurals, Contractions, and Possessives

Because plurals sound the same as contractions and possessives, you need to understand when and how to use an apostrophe in order to avoid confusion among the three.

> PLURAL Three bikes have been stolen in the last week.
>
> CONTRACTION This bike's for sale. (*bike's* = bike is)
>
> POSSESSIVE The bike's front wheel is warped. (front wheel belonging to the bike)

The following points will help you to distinguish among the three categories.

1. Only nouns and indefinite pronouns (such as *everybody, someone, anything*) take an apostrophe to show possession.

2. Be careful, especially with proper nouns, not to add an apostrophe when you want to indicate a plural.

> PLURAL All the Lees [plural of *Lee*] want to invite you to their reunion.
>
> POSSESSIVE The Lees' garage burned down last year. (The apostrophe shows that the garage belongs to the Lees.)

3. Do not use an apostrophe with possessive pronouns (*yours,
   hers*, *its*, *ours*, *theirs*).

   NOT   This problem is your's to solve.

   BUT   This problem is yours to solve.

   NOT   The dog pressed it's nose against the window.

   BUT   The dog pressed its nose against the window.

Using Apostrophes to Show Possession

How to Make Indefinite Pronouns and Singular Nouns Possessive

1. To make an indefinite pronoun possessive, add *'s*.

   Everybody's salary will be affected by the budget cutbacks.

2. To make a singular noun that does not end with *s* possessive,
   add *'s*.

   This little boy's epilepsy is getting worse.

3. To make a singular noun that ends with *s* or *ss* possessive, add
   's if the word is one syllable. Add only an apostrophe if the word
   is more than one syllable.

   Charles's car is in the shop again.

   The albatross' death haunted the Ancient Mariner.

How to Make Plural Nouns Possessive

1. If the plural noun ends in *s*, add only an apostrophe.

   Both boys' bathing suits were lost.

   All the students' marks were excellent.

2. If the plural noun does not end in *s*, add *'s*.

   All children's toys, men's coats, and women's shoes are on
   sale.

Joint Possession and Separate Possession

1. Joint Possession: To indicate that two or more people possess
   something together, add *'s* to the last name.

   Tom and Brenda's house is for sale.

2. Separate Possession: To indicate that two or more people possess things separately, add *'s* to each name.

   Tom's and Brenda's cars are for sale.

EXERCISE 1

Add an apostrophe or 's where necessary in the following sentences.

1. Cathy and Janis' friendship began to fall apart.
2. The boss' best workers resigned in disgust.
3. The children's destructive behaviour alarmed the staff.
4. This problem is nobody's fault but yours.
5. The Wongs' trailer was broken into.

Other Uses of the Apostrophe

1. Expressions of time can be used as possessives. Be sure that the placement of the apostrophe indicates whether the noun naming the time period is singular or plural.

   I'll contact you in a month's time (one month)

   We wasted two weeks' work.

2. To make letters plural, italicize the letter and add 's.

   Her final grades were three A's and two B's.

3. To put a word referred to as a word in the plural, italicize the word and add 's.

   There are too many *however*'s in this sentence.

4. To make an abbreviation plural, you can either add 's *or* s.

   All the SPCA's in this province are running out of money.

5. To make a date plural, add s or 's.

   Throughout most of the 1980s Canada faced a constitutional crisis.

Note that forming plurals without the apostrophe is becoming the preferred usage for both abbreviations and dates.

EXERCISE 2

Add or remove apostrophes as necessary in the following sentences.

1. Throughout most of the 1930s prairie farmers' watched in dismay as their crops shrivelled in the sun.
2. Katia took a year's leave of absence to do research in Women's Studies.
3. As I listened to the president's address, I noticed several *hopefully*'s, all of them used incorrectly.
4. Our society's obsession with thinness is affecting young girls' eating habits.
5. It's not surprising that the RCMP's latest announcement has aroused so much anger.

COMMA

EXERCISE 3

Make a list of words with missing or misused apostrophes in signs, advertisements, and similar material. Bring your list to class for discussion.

Comma

Main Clauses

Use a comma to separate main clauses joined by a coordinate conjunction (*and, but, or, nor, for, yet, so*).

> Inflation is under control, but unemployment is still a problem.
>
> No one has succeeded in proving the existence of UFOs, yet many have tried.

Subordinate Clauses

Use a comma to set off a subordinate clause at the beginning of a sentence.

> When economic conditions are poor, the incidence of family violence increases.
>
> Because the highways were icy, we postponed our trip.

Introductory Phrases

Use a comma to set off long (more than five words) or potentially confusing phrases at the beginning of a sentence.

> In his search for the meaning of life, he examined many religions. (long phrase)
>
> In winter, darkness comes early. (could be misread)

Items in a Series

Use a comma to separate more than two items joined by *and* or *or*. Include a comma before the conjunction so that the last two items are not read as a unit.

> We watched the children slide, swing, and climb.
>
> The horses galloped over the field, across the stream, and down the road.
>
> He ordered toast, eggs, coffee, and milk for breakfast. (comma indicates that four items were ordered)

Non-Restrictive Modifiers

Use a pair of commas to enclose non-restrictive modifiers (words, phrases, and clauses that add information but are not necessary to identify the noun they describe).

a. Adjectives and participial phrases following nouns.

The play, witty and well-acted, delighted the audience.

The actors, after removing their greasepaint, celebrated their success.

b. Appositives (nouns or noun phrases that rename the preceding noun).

The Beatles, the most popular rock group of the sixties, sold millions of records.

Note: Do *not* set off an appositive that is necessary to identify the noun it describes (restrictive).

The film *The Compleat Beatles* is a history of the group's rise and fall. (restrictive)

c. Non-restrictive clauses beginning with *which*, *who*, *whom*, or *whose*.

The development of fibre optics, which revolutionized communications, also had a great impact on medicine.

Orthopaedic surgeons, who often treat athletic injuries, use fibre optic instruments to assess knee damage.

Note: Do *not* set off restrictive clauses. Clauses beginning with *that* are almost always restrictive.

Tom Smith, whose knees were badly injured in a skiing accident, is slowly recovering. (non-restrictive clause)

Athletes who injure their knees often recover slowly. (restrictive clause)

The hand that rocks the cradle rules the world. (restrictive clause)

Parenthetical Expressions

Use commas to set off transitional words and phrases and other expressions that break the flow of the sentence.

Developing countries, in contrast, may be resource-rich but capital-poor.

This situation, I believe, leads to economic instability.

Well, I'd better be going.

> There were, amazingly enough, thirty thousand people at
> the demonstration.

Dates and Place Names

Use a comma with dates and place names when more than one item of information is given.

> The centre of the Canadian automobile industry is Windsor,
> Ontario.
>
> Canada officially entered the Second World War on
> September 10, 1939.

Quotations

Use a comma to set off brief quotations from introductory material.

> One minister said, "This policy should never have been
> adopted."
>
> "This policy," said one minister, "should never have been
> adopted."

EXERCISE 4

Use a pair of commas to set off non-restrictive modifiers in the following sentences. Do not enclose restrictive modifiers with commas.

1. Children who are emotionally neglected by their parents will seek attention from other adults.

2. My car, which had ~~been~~ not been plugged in for three days in -30°C weather, miraculously started.

3. John Cheever, the American short story writer, chronicled life in suburbia.

4. The actress starring in tonight's miniseries made her debut in the soaps.

5. The book that I lent you is now three weeks overdue at the library.

6. Each of these companies now facing bankruptcy once employed more than a thousand workers.

7. *Hearts of Darkness*, a film about the making of *Apocalypse Now*, provides fascinating insights into the difficulties faced by a film director.

8. An employee who suggests possible improvements in working conditions should be rewarded.

9. The Canadian champions, elated after winning the gold medal for ice-dancing, were surrounded by adoring fans.

10. The Acadians, descendants of early French settlers in the Maritimes, were pawns in the struggle between the French and the British for control of North America.

EXERCISE 5

Add commas, where appropriate, to the following sentences.

1. Because he could find no way to avoid the task, he got to work.

2. In the morning, light shone through the cracks in the roof.

3. Marvin, on the other hand, is steady, hard-working, and rather unimaginative.

4. Indeed, some of these arguments deserve closer attention.

5. The negotiators were tired and hungry, so they made little progress.

6. According to William Blake, "Imagination has nothing to do with Memory."

7. In 1842 the Webster–Ashburton Treaty between Canada and Great Britain defined the Canadian frontier.

8. The United States and Britain declared war on Japan on December 8, 1941, the day after the bombing of Pearl Harbor, Hawaii.

9. Returning home after a strenuous workout, Julia showered, reached for a cold drink, and collapsed on the sofa.

10. First Night festivities offer participants musical performances, street theatre, plays readings, and a spectacular finale complete with fireworks.

EXERCISE 6

If you have problems with commas, decide which three uses of the comma you most need to focus on to increase the clarity and effectiveness of your writing. Make a list with examples of each of the three types of comma problems and bring your list to class for discussion.

Semicolon

The semicolon is used in two ways: to join main clauses and to join a series of phrases or clauses that is too complicated for commas alone to clarify.

When to Use a Semicolon

1. Use a semicolon to join main clauses.

   a. When the ideas are closely related and there is no coordinate conjunction (*and, but, or, nor, for, so, yet*) to join the clauses.

   Mary was an idealist; Martha was a pragmatist.

   b. With a coordinate conjunction when the clauses are long or contain commas.

The hard-boiled detective, as we have seen in the works of Dashiell Hammett, Raymond Chandler, and Ross MacDonald, is a distinctively American creation; but the amateur sleuth, popularized by British writers such as Dorothy Sayers, Agatha Christie, and Michael Innis, also appears in American fiction.

c. When the second clause begins with a conjunctive adverb (*accordingly, consequently, therefore, thus, hence, furthermore, moreover, besides, likewise, nevertheless, however, otherwise, still*). Put a comma after a conjunctive adverb of more than one syllable.

Byron's poetry soon eclipsed Scott's; therefore, Scott turned to writing novels.

Few members of the legislature thought an election was necessary; nevertheless, the premier called one.

2. Use a semicolon to separate items within a series that contains commas.

The defence attorney called three witnesses: her client's brother, who testified that his sister was with him the night of the crime; the brother's caretaker, who testified that he saw the defendant arrive at 10:15 p.m.; and the brother's neighbour, who glimpsed the sister as she left at 11:30 p.m.

When Not to Use a Semicolon

1. Do not use a semicolon to join a main clause and a subordinate clause.

NOT   Helwig argues that anorectics starve themselves to protest against materialism; not because they want to look fashionably thin.

BUT   Helwig argues that anorectics starve themselves as a protest against materialism, not because they want to look fashionably thin.

Note: If you are not sure whether a clause begins with a subordinate conjunction or a conjunctive adverb, remember that coordinate and subordinate conjunctions must appear at the beginning of a clause, but conjunctive adverbs can be moved to other positions.

Few members of the legislature thought an election was necessary; the premier, nevertheless, called one.

Few members of the legislature thought an election was necessary; the premier called one, nevertheless.

2. Do not use semicolons too often. Too many semicolons will make your writing seem ponderous and stuffy. If you tend to overuse the semicolon, you are likely relying too heavily on co-ordination to join your ideas. Notice how the following passage is improved with more subordination.

> ORIGINAL PASSAGE According to Maggie Helwig, the cause of anorexia is often misunderstood; many people see anorexia as caused by women's willingness to conform to the fashion industry's definition of beauty. The desire to be thin is thought to be quite normal; anorectics have merely starved themselves too much. Helwig argues that anorexia should be seen differently; it should be seen as a statement about spiritual starvation.

> REVISED PASSAGE According to Maggie Helwig, we misunderstand anorexia if we consider the disorder to be caused by women's willingness to conform to the fashion industry's definition of beauty. We should not consider the desire to be thin as normal and anorectics as having merely starved themselves too much; instead, we should see anorexia as a statement about spiritual starvation.

EXERCISE 7

Add semicolons where appropriate to the following sentences.

1. Early in the play, Macbeth seems to recognize the futility of his ambition to remain king;nevertsheless,he pursues his bloody ambitions.

2. Lady Macbeth has been described as fiendish;however,some critics argue that she is the ideal wife.

3. Macbeth believes the witches' prophecy that he will be killed by no man born of a woman;he therefore feels invincible.

4. After the murder, Lady Macbeth, partly because she lacks Macbeth's vivid imagination, focuses on the immediate need to hide incriminating evidence;but this strategy, which ignores Macbeth's susceptibility to supernatural fears, sets in motion the chain of events that dooms them both.

5. When Macbeth is terrified by his imagination, he arouses sympathy;when he acts, he arouses contempt and hatred.

EXERCISE 8

What do Pico Iyer ("In Praise of the Humble Comma") and Lewis Thomas ("Notes on Punctuation") have to say about semicolons? Which uses of the semicolon do they illustrate in their essays?

Colon

Usually the colon indicates that what follows is an expansion of what has already been said. Use a colon for the following purposes:

1. To introduce a list that follows a complete clause. The items following the colon should be grammatically parallel.

   > Car manufacturers have introduced several improvements: better restraint systems, better pollution control devices, and better rust-proofing.

Note: Do not use a colon when the list begins with *such as* or *for example.*

   > Car manufacturers have introduced several improvements, such as better restraint systems, better pollution control devices, and better rust-proofing.

2. To introduce a phrase or clause that explains the preceding statement.

   > He wanted only one thing out of life: to make money. (explanatory phrase)

   > My new car is a real lemon: it has broken down for the third time this month. (explanatory clause)

3. To introduce a quotation. Both the quotation and the sentence that introduces it must be grammatically complete.

   > Goldberg dismissed the arguments against changes in the Fisheries Act: "Contrary to the opinions expressed by packers and the fisheries unions, the proposed changes are not designed to increase federal control over the fishing industry."

Note: Do not use a colon when the sentence introducing the quotation ends with *that.*

   > In her essay "Shakespeare in the Bush," Laura Bohannan describes her attempt to persuade her audience that "Hamlet was old enough to hoe his mother's farms himself. There was no need for her to remarry."

EXERCISE 9

Add colons, where appropriate, in the following sentences.

1. The setting was perfect for a horror movie: a dark, foggy night, an isolated, dilapidated house, shrieks and groans coming from unseen sources.

2. When Marc finished high school, he wanted only one thing: never to set foot in a classroom again.

3. When you are preparing for a long winter drive, be sure to bring some emergency equipment such as a sleeping bag, a candle, and several chocolate bars.

4. Macbeth clings to the witches' prophecies, saying that "I will not be afraid of death and bane, / Till Birnam forest come to Dunsinane."

5. Adrienne Rich says that Bach's music displays the self-control that makes a love of life possible. "This antique discipline, tenderly severe, / Renews belief in love yet masters feeling, / Asking of us a grace in what we bear."

EXERCISE 10

Write a paragraph in which you use colons in each of the three ways described above. Then replace the colons with dashes or other types of punctuation. Discuss with your classmates how these changes affect the tone of the paragraph.

Dash

A dash (or pair of dashes) indicates an interruption in a train of thought or in the structure of the sentence. It creates an air of informality and so should be used sparingly in formal writing. Use the dash for the following purposes:

1. To set off abrupt shifts in thought.

   My Aunt Sadie—you remember her, don't you?—lived to be a hundred.

2. To set off a list when it comes in the middle of a sentence.

   She had established her goals in life—to travel, to have an interesting career, to develop close relationships—before she was sixteen.

Note: When the list comes at the end of the sentence, use a colon unless you want to indicate special emphasis.

COLON Before she was sixteen, she had established her goals in life: to travel, to have an interesting career, to develop close relationships.

DASH At fourteen, Beth had only one ambition—to win a place on the Junior Olympic Wrestling Team.

EXERCISE 11

Write a paragraph using dashes for the purposes described. Then replace the dashes with colons or other punctuation. Discuss with your classmates how the punctuation affects the tone.

Parentheses

Use **parentheses** in these ways:

1. To enclose bibliographical information in the body of your essay.

   Alice Harwood's *The End of the Game* (Toronto: Dominion Press, 1984) is a study of the decline of amateur sports.

2. To enclose explanatory material, such as brief definitions and historical information.

   British drivers open the bonnet (hood), put luggage in the boot (trunk), and fill their tank with petrol (gas).

   Mozart (1756–1791) was an accomplished musician by the time he was six.

3. To indicate that explanatory material is relatively unimportant.

   The mayor (who was re-elected by a slim majority) promised to improve transportation in the city.

If you want to emphasize explanatory material, set it off with dashes. If you don't want either to emphasize or to minimize its importance, set if off with commas.

Note: Don't use parentheses to enclose essential information.

NOT   At a council meeting this morning, the mayor (who holds stock in several land development companies) disqualified herself from voting on the proposal to annex areas north and west of the city.

BUT   At a council meeting this morning, the mayor—who holds stock in several land development companies—disqualified herself from voting on the proposal to annex areas north and west of the city.

Punctuating Material in Parentheses

1. If a complete sentence in parentheses is contained within another sentence, do not begin the parenthetical sentence with a capital letter or end it with a period.

   When spring finally arrived (winter had seemed endless), children suddenly appeared on the street.

2. If the phrase, clause, or sentence within parentheses requires a question mark or an exclamation mark, put the appropriate punctuation mark inside the closing parenthesis.

Although credit cards sometimes lead people disastrously into debt (and who hasn't been appalled by a monthly statement?), they are essential for many business transactions.

REVIEW EXERCISE 1

Insert commas, semicolons, colons, dashes, and parentheses where appropriate in the following sentences.

1. In some societies work is divided in the following way men do the physically demanding or dangerous jobs the other jobs are left to women.

2. *Cabaret* directed by Bob Fosse and starring Liza Minnelli and Michael York adds a new dimension to the concept of the musical.

3. There are two types of crimes in which the perpetrator deliberately chooses to break the law crimes of desperation and crimes of defiance.

4. A woman with a limited income perhaps a single parent might steal food for example to feed her family.

5. Dickens vividly portrays the monotonous mechanical lives of factory workers in his description of Coketown "It contained several large streets all very like one another...." p. 213.

6. The goal of modern correctional institutions should not be punishment or revenge it should be the rehabilitation of the whole person.

7. *The Stone Angel* Macmillan 1964 established Margaret Laurence as an important Canadian novelist.

8. The Pope needed only to show Galileo the instruments of torture Galileo's medical knowledge of what those instruments would do accomplished the rest.

9. When I returned home most unexpectedly I might add I was astounded at the changes that had occurred during my absence.

10. Ancient Chinese and Hindu societies had much in common both were unified through stable religious and cultural patterns both had little curiosity about foreign lands both were exploited by the West.

REVIEW EXERCISE 2

Find sentences in your own writing where you could use semicolons, colons, dashes, and parentheses more effectively. Bring these examples to class for discussion.

Quotation Marks

This section covers the appropriate use of quotation marks as punctuation. For information on the format of quotations, the use of ellipses, and the integration of quotations into your writing, see Quotations.

Use quotation marks to indicate direct speech, quotations from other writers, and titles of short works.

1. Put quotation marks around direct speech.

   DIRECT SPEECH Marie said, "I should get more exercise."

   INDIRECT SPEECH Marie said that she should get more
   exercise.

2. Put quotation marks around three or more consecutive words from any printed material.

   In her comments on Faulkner's "A Rose for Emily," Judith
   Fetterley says that "the grotesque aspects of the story are a
   result of its violation of the expectations generated by the
   conventions of sexual politics" (317).

3. Use single quotation marks for quotations within quotations.

   In her interpretation of *Macbeth,* Carlyle argues that "the audience's sense of the futility of Macbeth's actions is confirmed in the 'She should have died hereafter' speech."

4. Use quotation marks to enclose titles of brief works (essays, magazine and newspaper articles, poems, short stories, songs, single episodes of a television series) that are part of larger works.

   In his article "The Influence of Popular Culture on the
   Poetry of John Doak," Martin Sommers points out that
   Doak's poem "Coming on Down" contains echoes of the
   Rolling Stones' song "Jumping Jack Flash."

5. You can put quotation marks around words referred to as words, but it's often clearer to italicize them. (See below, Italics.)

   You use "because" three times in this sentence.

Do not put quotation marks around slightly informal expressions.

   NOT   Michaela needs to learn to "stand up" for herself.

Using Other Punctuation with Quotation Marks

1. Place commas and periods inside quotation marks.

   "Many plant species," he said, "are in danger of extinction."

2. Place colons and semicolons outside quoted material.

> Fetterley argues that Emily's "status as a lady is a cage from which she cannot escape" (319); to the ever-curious towns-people, she is Miss Emily and "she is is never referred to and never thought of as otherwise."

3. a. Place other punctuation marks (question marks, exclamation marks, semicolons, colons, dashes) inside the quotation marks if they punctuate only the quoted words.

> The first lines of Keats's poem "La Belle Dame sans Merci" are "O, what can ail thee, knight-at-arms, / Alone and palely loitering?"

Refer to 204

  b. Place these punctuation marks outside the quotation marks if they punctuate the sentence containing the quotation.

> Do you agree with Keats's statement that "Beauty is truth, truth beauty"?

EXERCISE 12

Write a dialogue in which you incorporate as many different ways of using quotation marks as possible. Remember to use single quotation marks for quotations inside quotations.

Italics

Slanted writing indicates italics in typeset and word-processed material. In typed and handwritten work, italics are indicated by underlining. Use italics in the following ways.

1. For the titles of works published separately (books, magazines, newspapers, record albums, films, television series). Titles of works that have been published separately, such as novels or plays, are italicized even when these works are included in an-thologies. The names of ships and airplanes, works of art, and long musical compositions are also italicized.

> The book *False Economies* consists of a series of articles first published in *The Journal of Economic Analysis*.

2. For words and letters referred to as words or letters.

> The word *truly* does not contain an *e*.

3. For foreign words and phrases that have not been incorporated into English.

> The setting epitomized what the Germans would call *Gemütlichkeit*.

4. For emphasis.

> Library materials *must* be returned by the end of term.

Be careful not to overuse italics for emphasis, especially in formal academic writing.

EXERCISE 13

Insert quotation marks or underline to indicate italics as necessary in the following sentences. Together these sentences form a paragraph on the theme of exile in V. S. Naipaul's collection of stories *In a Free State* (Harmondsworth: Penguin, 1971).

1. The most interesting aspect of the treatment of exile is the complex relationship Naipaul creates between the concept of freedom and the movement from order to disorder.

2. For all of Naipaul's major characters, whether they are in the burning streets of Washington, the alien environment of England, or the war-torn deserts of Africa, the word freedom is highly ambiguous.

3. In the first story, One Out of Many, Santosh reflects on the freedom of the exile: I was a free man; I could do anything I wanted. I could go to the police...and say, I am an illegal immigrant here. Please deport me to Bombay.... It didn't matter what I did because I was alone. And I didn't know what to do (54–55).

4. The only way for Santosh to become an American citizen, and thus to free himself from the threat of deportation, is to give up his freedom by marrying a hubshi, an American black.

5. The first-person narrator of the story Tell Me Who to Kill and the main character of the title story, In a Free State, have also left their homeland and its restricting order to enter a state of disorder where the freedom that surrounds them becomes the one aspect of life they cannot deal with.

6. Thus for the main characters of the book In a Free State, the absence of restrictions does not bring freedom but rather an aimless drifting into exile.

REVIEW EXERCISE 3

Insert commas, parentheses, dashes, quotation marks, and italics as necessary in the paragraph below. Do not make any other changes. This paragraph is from a student essay on the character of the Duke in Browning's poem "My Last Duchess."

> Once we understand the dramatic situation in Browning's poem My Last Duchess we can see how calculating the Duke's treatment of the envoy is.

Throughout his speech the Duke addresses his listener as Sir so that even though he is not allowed to reply we are reminded of the envoy's presence. The apparent candour with which the Duke confesses his pride I choose / Never to stoop 42–43 is designed to disarm the envoy just as the Duke's passing reminders of his wealth and power are designed to intimidate him. Yet the Duke stoops to treat the envoy as an equal by suggesting that they descend the stairs together. The aim of this gesture is to ensure the envoy's goodwill in the delicate negotiations over the dowry, an intention that the Duke's flattering comment about the Count's generosity The Count your master's known munificence 49 makes clear. The silent presence of the envoy thus reveals the means the Duke is willing to employ to achieve his ends.

REVIEW EXERCISE 4

Bring to class an advertisement that uses a variety of punctuation. What is the effect of the punctuation? What tone does it create?

Hyphen

Use a **hyphen** in these ways:

1. With some compound words: *brother-in-law, major-general, buy-in.*

Note: Other compound words are written as one word (*textbook, step-mother, railway*) or as two words (*income tax, down payment, gallows humour*). There is no set pattern for forming compound words, so check your dictionary.

2. With two-word numbers (from twenty-one to ninety-nine) and with fractions used as adjectives. Do *not* hyphenate when the fraction functions as a noun.

   The gas tank was one-third full. (*one-third* as adjective)

   One third of the students withdrew from the course. (*one third* as noun)

3. To join two words that function as a single adjective and convey a single idea. If this construction comes after the noun, do *not* hyphenate unless the construction is conventionally spelled with a hyphen. Do *not* hyphenate if the construction contains an *ly* adjective.

   a well-organized essay

   The essay is well organized.

   a poorly organized essay

4. With the prefixes *self* (*self-sufficient*), *ex* (*ex-wife*); with prefixes that come before proper nouns (*anti-Catholic*); with the suffix *elect* (*president-elect*).

5. To prevent confusion: re-mark (mark again), ten-year-old children/ten year-old children.

6. To show that two or more prefixes share a common root.

   The results of both the pre- and the post-test were excellent.

How to Hyphenate Words at the End of a Line

Avoid dividing a word at the end of a line whenever possible.

Do Not Hyphenate

1. One-syllable words. (*Dragged*, for example, should not be hyphenated.)

2. Words of six or fewer letters even if they contain two or more syllables. (Do not hyphenate *diet*, *beauty*, *elegy*)

3. Words in more than two consecutive lines in a paragraph, the last word in a paragraph, or the last word on a page.

To Hyphenate a Word

If you occasionally need to hyphenate a word, follow these rules:

1. Try to divide it into two approximately equal parts that convey the sense of the whole word.

2. Divide the word between syllables, making sure that the first part of the word contains at least three letters: *com-fort*, *import-ance*.

3. If a double consonant appears at the end of a word because you have added a suffix (*running*, *committed*), divide the word between the double consonants (*run-ning*, *commit-ted*). If the double consonant is part of the root word, divide between the root word and the suffix (*drill-ing*).

4. Include a one-letter syllable with the first part of the word (*tabu-late* not *tab-ulate*).

EXERCISE 14

Hyphenate each of the following words as if it appeared at the end of a line. Put C beside a word that should not be hyphenated.

1. conferred

2. usable

3. heroes

4. recommend

5. stipulate

6. butterfly

7. begged

8. spilling

9. definitely

10. language

11 Numbers, Capitalization, and Abbreviations

Numbers

Use numerals (1, 2, 3,...):

1. To express numbers in scientific and technical writing.
2. For a series of numbers.
3. For numbers that cannot be expressed in two words.
4. For dates.
5. For page, verse, act, scene, and line numbers.

Use words:

1. For numbers that can be expressed in one or two words.
2. When you begin a sentence with a number.

Capitalization

All proper nouns are capitalized. A proper noun names a specific person, place, or thing.

> We'll meet this afternoon for a picnic in the **park**. (common noun)

> We'll meet this afternoon for a picnic in **Central Park**. (proper noun)

Use capitalization in the following ways.

1. Capitalize titles of family members when the title substitutes for a name.

   I asked Mother for a ride downtown.

   Do *not* capitalize titles of family members if they are preceded by a possessive pronoun: my father, your aunt, their brother.

2. Capitalize the names of languages, nationalities, and religions: English, Canadian, Buddhism.

3. Do *not* capitalize the name of an academic discipline unless it's the name of a language: chemistry, psychology, French.

4. Capitalize the names of specific courses: Chemistry 101, Psychology 260.

5. Capitalize the names of faculties: the Arts Faculty, the Faculty of Education.

6. Capitalize the words *college* and *university* if they are part of the name of an institution (Camrose Lutheran College) or used as a short form of the name: "Today the College announced a $500,000 budget deficit."

7. Capitalize the days of the week and the months, but not the seasons:

   Tuesday, January, spring

8. Capitalize Native and First Nations when referring to Aboriginal peoples. Do not capitalize colour words used to refer to ethnic groups:

   black, white

9. Do not capitalize the names of directions unless they are used as place names:

   Turn north after you cross the bridge.

   The old priest had lived in the North for twenty years.

10. Do not capitalize to create emphasis.

Abbreviations

1. Use abbreviations sparingly in most essays. If it's desirable to abbreviate a term you repeat frequently, give the term in full the first time; then give the abbreviation.

Sudden Infant Death Syndrome (SIDS) is not fully understood. It seems, however, that SIDS occurs more frequently in the winter months.

2. Use B.C. (before Christ) to refer to dates before the birth of Christ. Put B.C. after the date: Socrates committed suicide in 399 B.C.

3. Use A.D. (*Anno Domini*, "in the year of our Lord") to refer to dates after the birth of Christ. Put A.D. before the date. Stop using A.D. when this information is unnecessary, usually after A.D. 500.

    Venice was founded by refugees from Attila's Huns in A.D. 452.

    Johann Gutenberg, the inventor of printing in Europe, was born in 1396.

4. Do *not* abbreviate *and* with an ampersand (&). Use the ampersand only when you are copying the name of an organization, such as a publisher for a bibliographical entry: McClelland & Stewart.

5. Avoid abbreviations for Latin terms, such as e.g. (*exempli gratia*) or i.e. (*id est*). Instead, write out their English equivalents.

    NOT   From then on he was considered a coward; e.g., no one forgot that he had saved himself first when the hotel caught fire.

    BUT   From then on he was considered a coward; for example, no one forgot that he had saved himself first when the hotel caught fire.

    NOT   Susan gradually came to understand the erosion of self-esteem caused by racism: i.e., the assumption that a person's worth could be reliably assessed by the colour of his or her skin.

    BUT   Susan gradually came to understand the erosion of self-esteem caused by racism: that is, the assumption that a person's worth could be reliably assessed by the colour of his or her skin.

6. Avoid using *etc.* (especially at the end of a list). Instead use "such as" at the beginning of the list.

    NOT   Unemployment in this region has increased because of plant closures, the decline in tourism, the decreased demand for agricultural produce, etc.

    BUT   Unemployment in this region has increased because of factors such as plant closures, the decline in tourism, and the decreased demand for agricultural produce.

EXERCISE

Correct all errors in the use of numbers, capitalization, and abbreviations in the sentences below.

1. On October thirtieth, the V.P. announced that the Northern end of the railway line had finally been completed.

2. My brother & I like to go camping for 2 weeks every Summer.

3. The native friendship centre in our area hosts an annual barbecue to which everyone in the neighbourhood is invited. 151 people attended last year.

4. On our trip to the middle east last december, we noticed considerable tension between fundamentalist christians and muslims.

5. When Susan and her husband were robbed in an outdoor café in Rome, they lost most of their valuables: their passports, wallets, traveller's cheques, cameras, etc.

12 Spelling

Here are some tips that will help you to proofread for spelling errors more efficiently.

1. Check the spelling of the subjects you are writing about, including titles, authors' names, place names, technical terms, and so on. If you put your instructor's name on your title page, check the spelling of that too.

2. Make a list of the words you often misspell and check your work for them. Headliners on the list of commonly misspelled words include the following. It's worthwhile to memorize them:

   a lot, acquire, among, argument, conscience, conscious, definitely, dependent, develop, embarrass, environment, even though, existence, interest, occurred, occurrence, prejudiced, privilege, rhyme, rhythm, separate, similar, subtly, tragedy, unnecessary, weird.

3. Some instructors regard errors in the use of apostrophes as spelling mistakes, whereas others see them as punctuation errors. Either way, apostrophe errors can significantly undermine the quality and the credibility of your writing. If you are not sure how to use apostrophes, don't guess. Check the section on apostrophes and try to memorize the rules.

4. Use the spelling checker on your word processor. If you are a weak speller and your word processor lacks this feature, consider buying one. You might also consider buying a hand-held spelling checker/thesaurus. Spelling checkers will pick up most typos and commonly misspelled words. They will not, however, pick up homonyms: *to/too, there/their/they're, your/you're, it's/its, compliment/complement.*

5. Spelling checkers may show Canadian spellings (*labour/defence/centre*) as errors. If you find this irritating, you can add Canadian spellings to the spelling checker.

6. Be consistent in your use of either Canadian or American spellings. Don't write *theatre* in one sentence and *theater* in the next.

7. Don't rely on spelling checkers to find all your spelling errors. Print out a hard copy and read it carefully, sentence by sentence.

8. If you are not sure how to spell a word, don't guess. Consult a dictionary.

A Few Spelling Rules

Plurals

1. You can form most plurals by adding *s*: *rock/rocks, tower/towers*.

2. If the word ends in *s, x, sh,* or *ch,* form the plural by adding *es*: *boss/bosses, tax/taxes, bush/bushes, scratch/scratches*.

3. If the word ends in *y* preceded by a consonant, change the *y* to *i* and add *es*: *buddy/buddies*. If the word ends in *y* preceded by a vowel, add *s*: *valley/valleys*.

4. Watch for irregular plurals, especially *woman/women*.

5. ie or ei

   Memorize this little jingle:

   Put *i* before *e*

   Except after *c*

   Or when sounded like *a*

   As in n*ei*ghbour and w*ei*gh

The common exceptions to this rule are *weird, leisure, seize, height, foreign*.

Doubling the Final Consonant When You Add a Suffix

You double the final consonant under the following conditions.

1. The word must be one syllable (*drag/dragged*) or accented on the last syllable (*begin/beginning*).

2. The root word must end in a single consonant preceded by a single vowel: *regret/regrettable*

Adding Other Suffixes

1. Keep the final *e* if the suffix begins with a consonant: *lone/lonely, manage/management*.

   Exceptions: *argument, truly*

2. Drop the final *e* if the suffix begins with a vowel: *close/closing, ice/icy*.

   Exceptions: most words that end in a soft *g* or *c* keep the *e*: *noticeable, courageous*.

EXERCISE

Correct all the spelling errors in the following sentences. Most sentences include more than one error. Errors in the use of apostrophes may also be present.

1. Tanis intrest in school has increased noticably since she seperated from her husband.

2. At the begining of the term, Tanis draged herself to all her class, but her heart was definately not in her studys.

3. Like most people, Tanis was embarassed by her marriage problems and rather lonly as well, but now she is enjoying her independance.

4. She is also acheiving better grades, especially in her childrens' literature and micro computer managment courses.

5. Eventhough Tanis worrys that people might be prejudice against a women who has decided to abandon the priviledges of the affluent middle class, she has decided to devote her summer to an enviromental protection project on Bafin Island.

13 Quotations

When you are analyzing texts or writing research papers, you will often need to include direct quotations. Used effectively, quotations can provide convincing evidence to support and illustrate your points. Used awkwardly or excessively, quotations can detract from the clear, orderly presentation of your ideas.

When to Quote

1. When the precise wording of a short passage of prose, such as a definition of a key term, is the starting point for your analysis or evaluation of a concept, theory, proposal, or text.

2. When you can use a particularly well-expressed opinion by an authority on your topic to support your position, such as a statement by a respected scientist on the depletion of the ozone layer, or a literary critic's interpretation of an image in a poem.

3. When you need to give an example to illustrate a point you are making about a text. You don't need to use a quotation to support a factual point, but you should include a quotation to support every major interpretative point. If you were analyzing the character of the Duke in Browning's poem "My Last Duchess," for example, you would use a quotation to illustrate the point below.

   The Duke inadvertently reveals his arrogance when he suggests that his wife's courtesy to other men indicates her lack of respect for his name and position:

   > She thanked men,—good! but thanked
   > Somehow—I know not how—as if she ranked
   > My gift of a nine-hundred-years-old name
   > With anybody's gift (31–34).

When Not to Quote

1. When you can paraphrase someone's words or ideas without loss of meaning or impact.

Note: When you paraphrase, you must still document the source of your information. For more on this, see Chapter 13, Writing Research Papers, and Handbook, Documentation.

2. When you are summarizing factual information.

3. When the quotation merely repeats your point.

4. When you have used the quotation elsewhere in your essay. Find another passage to illustrate your point.

How to Use Quotations Effectively

1. Make all the major points in your own words and use quotations to support them. Don't rely on the quotation to make the point for you.

NOT   Hamlet says, "I am but mad north-northwest: when the wind is southerly, I know a hawk from a handsaw" (II.ii. 387–388).

Introduce the quotation through this quotation discovered...

BUT   In a conversation with his school friends Rosencrantz and Guildenstern, Hamlet reveals that he is merely feigning madness when he confides, "I am but mad north-northwest: when the wind is southerly, I know a hawk from a handsaw" (II.ii. 387–388). *(Act.scene.line)*

2. When you are using a quotation to support a point, make the point first, then give the quotation. In this way, you let your reader know what to look for in the quotation.

NOT   "I was annoyed at first, for I thought that someone was blackberrying, and depreciating the value of the undergrowth" (328). Here Forster ironically comments that owning something arouses the selfish desire to keep everyone else away from it.

BUT   By ironically commenting on his own desire to defend even his blackberries, Forster makes the point that owning something arouses the selfish desire to keep everyone else from using it: "I was annoyed at first, for I thought that someone was blackberrying, and depreciating the value of the undergrowth" (328).

3. Make the context of the quotation clear to your reader by identifying the speaker and the circumstances of the quotation.

NOT   Although anorexia was accepted as an exaggerated response to the demands of fashion, the real causes of this eating disorder are related to the ways women respond to stress. "Women are taught to take guilt, concern, problems, onto themselves personally; and especially onto their bodies" (343).

BUT   Although anorexia was accepted as an exaggerated response to the demands of fashion, the real causes of this eating disorder are related to the ways women respond to stress. As Maggie Helwig, who was anorectic for eight years, writes, "Women are taught to take guilt, concern, problems, onto themselves personally; and especially onto their bodies" (343).

[handwritten note: always needs to introduce who writes / says]

4. Make your quotations as short as possible. You can often quote only part of the sentence or line of poetry and paraphrase the rest, as in these examples.

PROSE

"A Modest Proposal" concludes with the narrator's earnest assertions that his sole motive is "the publick Good" (419) and that he himself would receive not even the profit of "a single Penny" (419).

POETRY

Apparently there are those who still believe that war will accomplish what the narrator of Tennyson's *Maud* thought it would do: unify a nation in a purpose higher than the material concerns of peacetime; wreak "God's just wrath...on a giant liar" (III. 45); and bring glory to those who would otherwise live in obscurity.

5. Do not string quotations together to make a series of points. Separate quotations with paraphrased material and explanations.

NOT   In "An Image of Africa," an essay on Conrad's *Heart of Darkness*, Chinua Achebe says that "Indeed the time is long overdue for a hard look at things" (292). "I am talking about a book which parades in the most vulgar fashion prejudices and insults from which a section of mankind has suffered untold agonies and atrocities in the past and continues to do so in many ways and many places today" (292). "The point of my observations should be quite clear by now, namely, that Conrad was a bloody racist" (289).

BUT In his essay "An Image of Africa," Chinua Achebe says that it's now time "for a hard look" (292) at Conrad's portrayal of blacks in *Heart of Darkness*. Achebe argues that Conrad is a "bloody racist" (289) and that this novella perpetuates the "prejudices and insults" (292) from which a "section of mankind" (292) continues to endure "untold agonies and atrocities" (292).

6. Do not take quotations out of context and use them in a way that is misleading, as in the following example.

The Bible says, "Cain rose up and slew his brother Abel." In another place it says, "Go thou and do likewise." Therefore we should kill our brothers.

7. Make sure the quotation fits grammatically with the sentence or phrase that introduces it.

NOT The Raven reveals his reason for planting the acorn when he returns and discovers that
> At length he returned, and with him a She,
> And the acorn was grown to a tall oak tree.
> They built them a nest in the topmost bough,
> And young ones they had, and were happy enow.
> (20–23)

BUT The Raven reveals his reason for planting the acorn when
> At length he came back, and with him a She,
> And the acorn was grown to a tall oak tree.
> They built them a nest in the topmost bough,
> And young ones they had, and were happy enow.
> (20-23)

Quotation Format

Indicating Changes in Quotations

1. **Deletions:** Use an ellipsis (…) to indicate that you have left out part of a quotation. Be sure that what remains is grammatically complete.

NOT According to Forster, property gives the owner "a vague sense...leads the artist to an act of creation" (328).

BUT   According to Forster, property gives the owner "a vague sense that he has a personality to express—the same sense which...leads the artist to an act of creation" (328).

Note: Do not use an ellipsis before or after a quotation that is obviously incomplete.

NOT   Polonius tells his daughter that Hamlet's protestations of love are mere "...springes to catch woodcocks" (I.iii. 115).

BUT   Polonius tells his daughter that Hamlet's protestations of love are mere "springes to catch woodcocks" (I. iii. 115).

2. **Insertions:** Put brackets around words added to clarify something in the quotation or to make the quotation fit into the grammatical structure of your sentence.

INSERTION "Unlike the warriors of older tribes, however," Sanders points out, "they [the soldiers of his youth] would have no say about when the battle would start or how it would be waged" (404).

CHANGE Sanders points out that modern soldiers "have no say about when the battle [will] start or how it [will] be waged" (404).

3. **Error in the text:** Put [sic] (Latin for "so," "thus") after the error to indicate typographical errors, deviant spellings, grammatical mistakes, or confused wording in the original.

According to one study, "Each of the provinces are [sic] contributing to the problem of acid rain."

Quoting Prose

Short Quotations

1. Prose quotations shorter than four lines may be indented for emphasis, but they are usually included in quotation marks within the body of your essay. Put the page reference in parentheses after the final quotation mark. Put a period **after the page reference**, not inside the quotation marks.

Suzuki points out that for decades people believed that "by carefully weighing the benefits and the bad side effects, we could make a more informed decision on whether to allow a new technology to be used" (408).

2. Use single quotation marks to indicate a quotation within a quotation. Do not use single quotation marks elsewhere in your essay.

> Achebe scrutinizes *Heart of Darkness* closely and finds that Conrad makes a "judicious change of adjective from time to time so that instead of 'inscrutable,' for example, you might have 'unspeakable,' etc., etc." (285).

Long Quotations If you are quoting more than four lines of prose, set off the quotation from the body of your essay. Triple-space before and after the quotation. Double-space the quotation. Indent ten spaces from the left-hand margin. Do not indent a paragraph within the quotation unless you quote more than one. If you need to indicate a new paragraph, indent three additional spaces. Do not put quotation marks around the passage unless they appear in the original to indicate direct speech. Remember to introduce the quotation. Put the page references, in parentheses, *after* the final punctuation.

> In "Sensual Education" Root-Bernstein argues that a curriculum integrating arts and sciences will produce more creative scientists:
>
> > The act of understanding, whether it concerns art, history, music, or science, is not purely an intellectual experience but a sensual one as well. Insight in any discipline is usually accompanied by intense physical and emotional feelings, often expressed in aural, kinesthetic or visual terms. Such feelings cannot be separated from the act of discovery itself. The intellect does not operate without the commitment of the individual as a whole, and so science will flourish only in the minds of sensitive and emotional people (395).

Quoting Poetry

Short Quotations If you are quoting no more than three lines of poetry, include the quotation in the body of your essay. Use a slash, with a space before and after it, to indicate divisions between lines. Retain the capitalization and punctuation in the original. Put the line reference in parentheses after the quotation, followed by a period.

> After he planted the acorn, "high and low, / Over hill, over dale, did the black Raven go" (14–15).

Long Quotations If you are quoting more than three lines of poetry, set them off as you would a long quotation of prose. Be sure to give the lines exactly as they are in the original, followed by the line reference.

> In "Of Silken Speech and Specious Shoe," Emily Dickinson parallels the fickle attentions of the lover and the bumblebee:
>
> > His Suit a chance
> > His Troth a Term
> > Protracted as the Breeze
> > Continual Ban propoundeth He
> > Continual divorce. (5–9)

Quoting Plays

Depending on the play, you may be quoting prose or poetry. Follow the guidelines above as appropriate. For verse plays divided into acts and scenes, give the act, scene, and line numbers in parentheses after the quotation, rather than the page number. If the play is not divided into acts, scenes, and lines, give the page number on which the quotation appears in parentheses after the quotation.

EXERCISE I

This exercise is designed to give you practice in integrating quotations. Introduce the quotation appropriately, quote only the most relevant material, and punctuate the quotations correctly.

1. "It is the women sticking their fingers down their throats who act out the equation of food and sin, who deny hunger and yet embody endless, unfulfilled appetite" (342). Helwig connects the fact that most anorectics are women with her point that women physically manifest the fears of the societies in which they live.

2. Vivian Gornick notes that George and Steiner are successful because they adhere to a fundamental scientific principle: "One must have the patience to perform the experiments meticulously (if the experiments are not absolutely clean and precise they are useless; above all, a scientist's experiments must be such that they can be replicated). Then one must do many, many, many experiments, over and over and over again, so that a legitimate data base is accumulated" (336).

3. The idea that blindness is a mental rather than a physical condition is clear when Gloucester perceives in Act Four, Scene Two, lines 21–26 of *King Lear* that he:

> I stumbled when I saw. Full oft 'tis seen,
> Our means secure us, and our mere defects
> Prove our commodities. O dear son Edgar
> The food of thy abused father's wrath!
> Might I but live to see thee in my touch
> I'd say I had eyes again!

4. An added benefit, Swift's narrator notes, is that this proposal will decrease the number of Roman Catholics in Ireland.

> For First, as I have already observed, it would greatly lessen the Number of Papists, with whom we are yearly over-run, being the principal Breeders of the Nation, as well as our most dangerous Enemies, and who stay at home on purpose with a design to deliver the Kingdom to the Pretender, hoping to take their advantage by the absence of so many good Protestants, who have chosen rather to leave their Country, than stay at home, and pay Tithes against their Conscience, to an Episcopal Curate. (416)

5. Laura Robinson believes that female athletes become anorectic not only because they are striving for a flawed ideal of the human form but also because they are responding to male chauvinist attitudes. On page 390 she writes that "If a coach's first reaction to every woman who passes by is 'What a lardass,' the message sinks in."

EXERCISE 2

Find examples from your own writing of passages in which you could have used quotations more effectively (or ones in which you used quotations particularly well). Bring examples to class for discussion.

QUOTATIONS

14 Documentation

Whenever you write a research paper, you need to acknowledge the sources of ideas and information you use. To present an idea without acknowledgement implies that it is your own. If it is not, you have committed plagiarism. Since even inadvertent plagiarism may result in severe penalties, you must protect yourself by making sure that your citations are both accurate and complete.

There are more positive reasons for documenting your sources. Using references is a vital part of learning to write like a specialist in your field. Citing the work of experts lends weight and depth to your paper and allows readers to follow up interesting ideas.

Various disciplines have their own standard format for references. We will discuss two of the most widely accepted: the in-text citation system of the Modern Languages Association (MLA), used primarily in the humanities; and the author-date system of the American Psychological Association (APA), used in the sciences and social sciences.

What to Document

1. All quotations of three consecutive words or more from primary or secondary sources. You will find examples below for both the MLA and APA systems of documentation. You do not need to document familiar quotations unless they are part of the subject of your essay. For example, if you used the line "yon Cassius has a lean and hungry look" as an allusion, you would not document the quotation; however, if you were writing an essay on *Julius Caesar*, you would.

2. Ideas and opinions you have paraphrased from any source.

3. Factual information that is not readily verifiable or that may differ according to the source you consult. You would cite the

source of unemployment figures, for example, since those figures not only change over time but also vary according to the criteria used to compile them. You do not need to document factual information that is considered "common knowledge" (the kind of information you might find in an encyclopaedia).

Most of your material is likely to come from published or electronic sources; you should also credit information and ideas that come from other sources, such as films and interviews. You will find detailed guidelines below.

Systems of Reference

MLA System

The footnote system once favoured in the humanities has largely been replaced by the much easier system of in-text citations. In this system, you place the name of the author and page number(s) of the source in parentheses immediately after the quotation or reference. Omit the author's name if you give it in introducing the material. If you refer to more than one work by the same author in your paper, include a shortened version of the title. Complete bibliographical information about the source (such as title, place, publisher, and date of publication) appears in a "Works Cited" list at the end of your paper.

In-Text Citations The following examples illustrate the use of in-text citations for particular references.

Quotation from primary text (author not previously identified)

In many affluent households, cars have been replaced by "gas-guzzling, wilderness-conquering sport utility vehicles that in the hands of most owners never venture farther off-road than the local car wash" (Laver 360).

Quotation from primary text (author previously identified)

Hamlet's next remark is an assertion that those of higher status have finer feelings: "The hand of little employment hath the daintier sense" (V.i.66).

Short titles to identify works (more than one work by same author)

In loving someone above her station, Ophelia is similar to Helena, who laments her ambition: "The hind that would be mated by the lion / Must die for love" (*All's Well* I.i.103).

Quotation from research material

> As Michael MacDonald points out, "It would be hard to think of a case better suited to illuminating the problems that identifying suicides and burying their bodies presented than the passive drowning of a madwoman of high birth" (316).

Paraphrased research material

> The death and burial of Ophelia reveal all the ambiguities surrounding cases of suicide (MacDonald 316).

Works Cited On a separate page entitled "Works Cited" (centred, without quotation marks or any other punctuation), list all the sources from which you have quoted or from which you have taken information or ideas. These entries should match the citations in your essay: every source that you refer to in your essay should appear in the Works Cited, including your primary text(s); no work should appear in the Works Cited that you do not refer to in your essay. Remember to include films, videos, interviews, and electronic sources as well as printed materials.

Format Entries begin flush with the left margin, with any lines after the first indented five spaces. Double space within and between entries. Do not number them. For punctuation, see the examples below.

Order of entries List sources alphabetically by author's surname. If an entry has no author (an encyclopaedia entry, for example), include it alphabetically by its title. Give names exactly as they appear in the source. If an author's full name is given—for instance, Frederic Raphael—do not abbreviate it in your entry to Raphael, F. For works with more than one author, give the names in the order they appear on the title page of the work; do not rearrange them into alphabetical order.

Information required

Books After the author's name, put the title of the work or the part of the work you have used. The title is followed by the name of the editor or translator, the edition, and number of volumes, if pertinent. Next comes the following publication information: the city where the work was published, the name of the publisher, and the year of publication, in that order. (If the city is not well known or could be confused with another place, include the province, state, or country, as appropriate.)

1. Book with a single author

   Didion, Joan. *Run River.* New York: Washington Square, 1963.

2. Subsequent works by the same author. Arrange titles alphabetically. Instead of repeating the author's name, type three hyphens

followed by a period. Leave two spaces and type the title and other information.

> Raphael, Frederic. *The Graduate Wife*. London: Cassell, 1962.
>
> —. *Orchestras & Beginners*. London: Cape, 1967.

3. Book with two or more authors or editors. Invert the first name only.

> Otokunefor, Henrietta C., and Obiageli C. Nwodo, eds. *Nigerian Female Writers: A Critical Perspective*. Lagos, Nigeria: Malthouse, 1989.

4. Part of a book

> Mojola, Yemi I. "The Novels of Adaora Wasi." *Nigerian Female Writers: A Critical Perspective*. Eds. Henrietta C. Otokunefor and Obiageli C. Nwodo. Lagos, Nigeria: Malthouse, 1989. 37–46.

5. Work in an anthology

> Penfield, Wendy. "African Deliverance." *Best Canadian Essays 1990*. Ed. Douglas Fetherling. Saskatoon, SK: Fifth House, 1990. 139–153.

Articles The author's name is followed by the title of the article, the title of the periodical, the volume, number, and year of publication, and the page numbers.

1. Article in a scholarly journal

> Singh, Raman. "No Longer at Ease: Traditional and Western Values in the Fiction of Chinua Achebe." *Neohelicon* 16.2 (1989): 159–167.

2. Article in a magazine. No volume or number is necessary for weekly or monthly magazines, just the date and page numbers.

> Maier, Karl. "The Flawed Finale." *Africa Report* July–August 1992: 46–48.

3. Article in an encyclopaedia. Page references are not necessary for encyclopaedia entries or for other works arranged alphabetically. If the entry is signed, put the author's name first in the note. If it is unsigned, start with the title of the entry. You do not need to give full publication data, just the year of the edition.

> "Chinua Achebe." *New Encyclopaedia Britannica*, 1974 ed.

Electronic Sources

1. CD-ROM

    a. Material with a print version. Give the name of the author (if known), publication information for the print source (as in the case of a book or article), the title of the database, publication medium (CD-ROM), name of the vendor, and electronic publication date.

Gibson, James. "The Truth About Cholesterol." *New York Times* 22 Aug. 1994, early ed.: D2, *New York Times Ondisc*. CD-ROM. UMI-Proquest. Oct. 1997.

b. Material without a print version. Give the name of the author (if known), the title of the part of the work cited (if relevant), the title of the product, edition or version, publication medium (CD-ROM), city of publication, publisher, and year of publication.

"Saskatchewan." *Encarta* 1994. CD-ROM. Redmond, WA: Microsoft, 1993.

2. The Internet

a. Article in an electronic journal. Give the name of the author (if known), the title of the article or document, the title of the journal, volume and/or issue number, date of electronic publication (in parentheses), URL (or "uniform resource locator"—the site's electronic address) in angle brackets, and date of access (in parentheses).

McNeilly, Kevin. "Ugly Beauty: John Zorn and the Politics of Postmodern Music." *Postmodern Culture* 5.2 (Jan. 1995) <http://muse.jhu.edu/journals/postmodern_culture/v005/ 5.2mcneilly.html> (7 Feb. 1997).

b. World Wide Web site. Give the author's name (if known), the title of the document (in quotation marks), the title of the complete work (italicized or underlined), date of publication or last revision (if known), URL (in angle brackets), and date of access (in parentheses).

Beck, Rowan. "A Biography." *The Edward Albee Home Page*. 9 May 1995. <http://www.en.utexas.edu/~rbeck/314fall/ drama/biography.html> (24 Jan. 1997).

c. Newsgroup message. Give the author's name (if known), author's e-mail address (in angle brackets), subject line from posting (in quotation marks), date of publication, name of newsgroup (in angle brackets), and date of access (in parentheses). If you cannot determine the author's name, use his or her e-mail address as the main entry.

Sadowy, Grace. <grace@memco.co.il> "Polonius." 2 Feb. 1997. <humanities.lit.authors.shakespeare> (10 Feb. 1997).

d. Listserv message. Give the author's name (if known), author's e-mail address (in angle brackets), subject line from posting (in quotation marks), date of publication, address of listserv (in angle brackets), and date of access (in parentheses). As in the case of a newsgroup message, use the author's e-mail address as the main entry if you cannot determine his or her name.

Levinson, Jane L. <jane_l_levinson@umail.umd.edu>
"Re: Women Printers." 13 Feb. 1997.
<wwp-l@brownvm.brown.edu> (14 Feb. 1997)

Other Types of Material

1. Film. Give the title of the film, the director, principal actors, distributor, and date.

   The Dead. Dir. John Huston. With Anjelica Huston and
   Donal McCann. Vestron, 1987.

Note: If, instead of the film itself, you are citing the work of the director, an actor, or a screenwriter, you would begin the entry with that person's name. Add any other information pertinent to your discussion, such as the name of the choreographer of a musical, before the distributor and date.

2. Interview. Give the name of the person interviewed, his or her position (if not mentioned in the essay), the type of interview (personal interview, e-mail interview), and the date.

   Edwards, Caterina. Personal interview. February 3, 1998.

You will find an example of MLA in-text citations and a list of works cited with the sample research paper "The Making of the Tragic Hero: The Graveyard Scene in *Hamlet*" in Part 3, Readings. For further information, refer to Joseph Gibaldi, ed. *MLA Handbook for Writers of Research Papers*, 4th ed. New York: Modern Languages Association, 1995. A particularly helpful source for documenting Internet sources is Andrew Harnack and Eugene Kleppinger's *Online!: A Reference Guide to Using Internet Sources*, New York: St. Martin's Press, 1997. Harnack and Kleppinger also provide through their Web site the latest information on documenting Internet materials. The Web site can be visited at <http.www.smpcollege.com/online-4styles~help>.

APA System

The American Psychological Association employs a system of documentation similar to the MLA system of in-text citations. The chief difference is that sources are cited by name and date rather than name and page number. Like the MLA system, it employs a list of works cited to document sources. This list, however, is called "References."

Full bibliographical information is included in the list of references. The format for entries differs from the MLA format, especially in punctuation. The APA system is widely accepted as the standard for papers in the sciences and social sciences.

In-Text Citations Within the text of your essay, place parenthetical citations immediately after a quotation or reference. Unless you are quoting, give only the author's surname and the year of publication. If you are quoting directly, include the page number after the year. If you are not quoting directly but wish to direct the reader to a part of a source, such as a page number, chart, table, or appendix, include the appropriate reference. Omit the author's name if it appears in your text.

> In his analysis, Suzuki (1989) concludes that empirical testing of new technology simply cannot guarantee knowledge of its final environmental impact.

> To compete professionally, female athletes must have bodies that conform to an an ideal that, unfortunately, is determined by a predominantly male coaching elite (Robinson, 1992).

> In many affluent households, cars have been replaced by "gas-guzzling, wilderness-conquering sport utility vehicles that in the hands of most owners never venture farther off-road than the local car wash" (Laver, 1997, p. 360).

For sources that have two or more authors, give both (or all) surnames, in the order in which they appear in the source, and the year of publication.

> (Hunt, Kyoto, and Kellogg, 1991)

Thereafter, use only the first surname and et al., with the year.

> (Hunt et al., 1991)

Where no author is given, use the first two or three words of the title as it appears in the list of references.

References Include full bibliographical information about your sources in an appended list entitled "References" (without the quotation marks). The purpose of the reference list is to identify your sources in such a way that your reader can find them quickly. Include *only* the sources you cite in your paper, and include *all* the sources you cite.

The entries in the list of references appear in alphabetical order arranged by surname. A source reference with two or more authors includes all the names in the order in which they appear in the source. If there are six or more authors, only the first three are listed, followed by "et al." The final two authors' names are joined with a comma followed by an ampersand (&). When you have used more than one source by an author, arrange them by year of publication, starting with the earliest. Two or more works by the same author in the same year are arranged alphabetically by the title of the work.

Each element of a bibliographical entry is followed with a period. The titles of articles in journals or periodicals are not placed in quotation marks and only the first word of the title is capitalized. Any other material necessary to identify the piece (such as editor, translator) is placed in brackets after the title.

Articles The author's name, surname first, as it appears in the article, followed by a period. The date of the publication, in parentheses, followed by a period. The title of the article, without quotation marks, only the first word and any proper names capitalized, followed by a period. The name of the journal/periodical and volume number (without a "v"), both underlined, followed by an issue number, if necessary, a comma, and the inclusive page numbers of the article, followed by a period. Do not use p. or pp. for the page numbers of journal articles, but do use them for magazine and newspaper articles.

> Vincent, J. R. (1992). The tropical timber trade and sustainable development. *Science, 256*, 1651–1655.

Books After the author, date, and title, put the place of publication and the publisher.

> Epling, W. Frank. (1991). *Solving the anorexia puzzle: a scientific approach*. Toronto: Hogrefe & Huber.

If you need to include other information, put it where it will best clarify any misunderstanding that might arise. For example, to indicate that the name beginning an entry is that of the editor, place Ed(s). in parentheses immediately after the name(s). If a book is published in a city not generally known, include the state, province, or country, usually in an abbreviated form. If a work is a translation or a revised edition or one of a multivolume set, such additional information would be noted after the title, in parentheses.

Electronic Sources

1. CD-ROM

   Give the name of the author (if known), date of electronic publication, the title of the article or part of the work cited, publication medium (CD-ROM), the title of the database or product (including edition or version), the name of the vendor (if relevant), or city of publication and publisher.

> Johnson, S. (1994). Sleep and psychology. [CD-ROM].
> *Psychological Review*, 143.2. SilverPlatter.

2. The Internet

   a. Article in an electronic journal. Give the name of the author (if known), date of electronic publication, the title of the article or document, title of the journal, volume and/or issue number, URL (or "uniform resource locator"—the site's electronic address) in angle brackets, and date of access (in parentheses, year followed by month and day).

Feldstein, Sarah. (1996). Expanding the capacity of the public library: Partnerships with community based environmental groups. *Electronic Green Journal*, 6 (Dec. 1996) <http://www.lib.uidaho.edu:70/docs/egj06/feld.html> (1997, Feb. 14).

   b. World Wide Web site. Give the author's name (if known), date of publication or last revision (if known), title of document, title of complete work, URL (in angle brackets), and date of access (in parentheses).

Southern California Coastal Water Research Project. (1996). Are contaminant inputs into the ocean increasing or declining? *Southern California Coastal Water Research Project Home Page*. <http://www.sccwrp.org/> (1997, Feb. 20).

   c. Newsgroup message. Give the author's name (if known), author's e-mail address (in angle brackets), date of publication, subject line from posting, name of the newsgroup (in angle brackets), and date of access (in parentheses). If you cannot determine the author's name, use his or her e-mail address as the main entry.

Imadi, A. <ftp://usman.imran.com/pub/articles/imadi> (1997, Jan. 30). Why is the MQM so popular in urban Sindh? <soc.culture.pakistan.history> (1997, Jan. 31).

   d. Listserv message. Give the author's name (if known), author's e-mail address (in angle brackets), date of publication, subject line from posting, address of the listserv (in angle brackets), and date of access (in parentheses).

LeBlanc, Karen. <leblanc@iro.umontreal.ca> (1997, Feb. 11). DSSSL and Gambit-C. <tei-l@listserv.uic.edu> (1997, Feb. 15).

For further information, see the Publication Manual of the *American Psychological Association*, 4th ed., Washington, D.C.: American Psychological Association, 1994. For help with documenting Internet sources, see Harnack and Kleppinger's *Online!*, cited above.

Readings

Sample Essays

AN IMAGE OF AFRICA

Chinua Achebe

It was a fine autumn morning at the beginning of this academic year such as encouraged friendliness to passing strangers. Brisk youngsters were hurrying in all directions, many of them obviously freshmen in their first flush of enthusiasm. An older man, going the same way as I, turned and remarked to me how very young they came these days. I agreed. Then he asked me if I was a student too. I said no, I was a teacher. What did I teach? African literature. Now that was funny, he said, because he never had thought of Africa as having that kind of stuff, you know. By this time I was walking much faster. "Oh well," I heard him say finally, behind me, "I guess I have to take your course to find out."

A few weeks later I received two very touching letters from high school children in Yonkers, New York, who—bless their teacher—had just read *Things Fall Apart*. One of them was particularly happy to learn about the customs and superstitions of an African tribe.

I propose to draw from these rather trivial encounters rather heavy conclusions which at first sight might seem somewhat out of proportion to them: But only at first sight.

The young fellow from Yonkers, perhaps partly on account of his age but I believe also for much deeper and more serious reasons, is obviously unaware that the life of his own tribesmen in Yonkers, New York, is full of odd customs and superstitions and, like every-

One of the most respected African writers in English, Chinua Achebe, born in Nigeria in 1930, is the author of *Things Fall Apart* (1958), *Arrow of God* (1964), *A Man of the People* (1966), and several other novels. The recurrent subject in Achebe's novels is the conflict between tradition and modernity in Nigeria, and in Africa in general. "An Image of Africa" was first delivered as a Chancellor's lecture at the University of Massachusetts at Amherst; the version that follows is from the *Massachusetts Review*, 18 (1977). Achebe focuses most of this essay on Joseph Conrad's novella *Heart of Darkness* (1902) in which the narrator, Marlow, tells the story of his journey up the River Congo in his search for Kurtz, a trader about whom disquieting rumours have been circulating. "An Image of Africa," *Massachusetts Review*, Vol. 18, #4, by Chinua Achebe has been reprinted with permission.

body else in his culture, imagines that he needs a trip to Africa to encounter those things.

The other person being fully my own age could not be excused on the grounds of his years. Ignorance might be a more likely reason; but here again I believe that something more willful than a mere lack of information was at work. For did not that erudite British historian and Regius Professor at Oxford, Hugh Trevor-Roper, pronounce a few years ago that African history did not exist?

If there is something in these utterances more than youthful experience, more than a lack of factual knowledge, what is it? Quite simply it is the desire—one might indeed say the need—in Western psychology to set Africa up as a foil in Europe, a place of negations at once remote and vaguely familiar in comparison with which Europe's own state of spiritual grace will be manifest.

This need is not new: which should relieve us of considerable responsibility and perhaps make us even willing to look at this phenomenon dispassionately. I have neither the desire nor, indeed, the competence to do so with the tools of the social and biological sciences. But, I can respond, as a novelist, to one famous book of European fiction, Joseph Conrad's *Heart of Darkness*, which better than any other work I know displays that Western desire and need which I have just spoken about. Of course, there are whole libraries of books devoted to the same purpose, but most of them are so obvious and so crude that few people worry about them today. Conrad, on the other hand, is undoubtedly one of the great stylists of modern fiction and a good storyteller into the bargain. His contribution therefore falls automatically into a different class—permanent literature—read and taught and constantly evaluated by serious academics. *Heart of Darkness* is indeed so secure today that a leading Conrad scholar has numbered it "among the half-dozen greatest short novels in the English language."[1] I will return to this critical opinion in due course because it may seriously modify my earlier suppositions about who may or may not be guilty in the things of which I will now speak.

Heart of Darkness projects the image of Africa as "the other world," the antithesis of Europe and therefore of civilization, a place where a man's vaunted intelligence and refinement are finally mocked by triumphant bestiality. The book opens on the River Thames, tranquil, resting peacefully "at the decline of day after ages of good service done to the race that peopled its banks." But the actual story takes place on the River Congo, the very antithesis of the Thames. The River Congo is quite decidedly not a River Emeritus. It has rendered no service and enjoys no old-age pension. We are told that "going up that river was like travelling back to the earliest beginning of the world."

Is Conrad saying then that these two rivers are very different, one good, the other bad? Yes, but that is not the real point. What actually worries Conrad is the lurking hint of kinship, of common ancestry. For the Thames, too, "has been one of the dark places of the earth." It conquered its darkness, of course, and is now at peace. But if it were to visit its primordial relative, the Congo, it would run the terrible risk of hearing grotesque, suggestive echoes of its own forgotten darkness, and of falling victim to an avenging recrudescence of the mindless frenzy of the first beginnings.

I am not going to waste your time with examples of Conrad's famed evocation of the African atmosphere. In the final consideration it amounts to no more than a steady, ponderous, fake-ritualistic repetition of two sentences, one about silence and the other about frenzy. An example of the former is "It was the stillness of an implacable force brooding over an inscrutable intention" and of the latter, "The steamer toiled along slowly on the edge of a black and incomprehensible frenzy." Of course, there is a judicious change of adjective from time to time so that instead of "inscrutable," for example, you might have "unspeakable," etc., etc.

The eagle-eyed English critic, F. R. Leavis, drew attention nearly thirty years ago to Conrad's "adjectival insistence upon inexpressible and incomprehensible mystery." That insistence must not be dismissed lightly, as many Conrad critics have tended to do, as a mere stylistic flaw. For it raises serious questions of artistic good faith. When a writer, while pretending to record scenes, incidents and their impact, is in reality engaged in inducing hypnotic stupor in his readers through a bombardment of emotive words and other forms of trickery much more has to be at stake than stylistic felicity. Generally, normal readers are well armed to detect and resist such underhand activity. But Conrad chose his subject well—one which was guaranteed not to put him in conflict with the psychological predisposition of his readers or raise the need for him to contend with their resistance. He chose the role of purveyor of comforting myths.

The most interesting and revealing passages in *Heart of Darkness* are, however, about people. I must quote a long passage from the middle of the story in which representatives of Europe in a steamer going down the Congo encounter the denizens of Africa:

> We were wanderers on a prehistoric earth, on an earth that wore the aspect of an unknown planet. We could have fancied ourselves the first of men taking possession of an accursed inheritance, to be subdued at the cost of profound anguish and of excessive toil. But suddenly, as we struggled round a bend, there would be a glimpse of rush walls, of

peaked grass-roofs, a burst of yells, a whirl of black limbs, a mass of hands clapping, of feet stamping, of bodies swaying, of eyes rolling, under the droop of heavy and motionless foliage. The steamer toiled along slowly on the edge of a black and incomprehensible frenzy. The prehistoric man was cursing us, praying to us, welcoming us—who could tell? We were cut off from the comprehension of our surroundings; we glided past like phantoms, wondering and secretly appalled, as sane men would be before an enthusiastic outbreak in a madhouse. We could not remember because we were travelling in the night of first ages, of those ages that are gone, leaving hardly a sign—and no memories.

The earth seemed unearthly. We are accustomed to look upon the shackled form of a conquered monster, but there—there you could look at a thing monstrous and free. It was unearthly, and the men were—No, they were not inhuman. Well, you know, that was the worst of it—this suspicion of their not being inhuman. It would come slowly to one. They howled and leaped, and spun, and made horrid faces; but what thrilled you was just the thought of your remote kinship with this wild and passionate uproar. Ugly. Yes, it was ugly enough; but if you were man enough you would admit to yourself that there was in you just the faintest trace of a response to the terrible frankness of that noise, a dim suspicion of there being a meaning in it which you—you so remote from the night of first ages—could comprehend.

Herein lies the meaning of *Heart of Darkness* and the fascination it holds over the Western mind: "What thrilled you was just the thought of their humanity—like yours....Ugly."

Having shown us Africa in the mass, Conrad then zeros in on a specific example, giving us one of his rare descriptions of an African who is not just limbs or rolling eyes:

And between whiles I had to look after the savage who was fireman. He was an improved specimen; he could fire up a vertical boiler. He was there below me, and, upon my word, to look at him was as edifying as seeing a dog in a parody of breeches and a feather hat, walking on his hind legs. A few months of training had done for that really fine chap. He squinted at the steam gauge and at the water gauge with an evident effort of intrepidity—and he had filed his teeth, too, the poor devil, and the wool of his pate shaved into queer patterns, and three ornamental scars on each of his cheeks.

He ought to have been clapping his hands and stamping his
feet on the bank, instead of which he was hard at work, a
thrall to strange witchcraft, full of improving knowledge.

As everybody knows, Conrad is a romantic on the side. He might
not exactly admire savages clapping their hands and stamping their
feet but they have at least the merit of being in their place, unlike this
dog in a parody of breeches. For Conrad, things (and persons) being in
their place is of the utmost importance.

Towards the end of the story, Conrad lavishes great attention quite
unexpectedly on an African woman who has obviously been some kind
of mistress to Mr. Kurtz and now presides (if I may be permitted a little
imitation of Conrad) like a formidable mystery over the inexorable im-
minence of his departure:

She was savage and superb, wild-eyed and magnificent...She
stood looking at us without a stir and like the wilderness itself, with an air of brooding over an inscrutable purpose.

This Amazon is drawn in considerable detail, albeit of a predictable
nature, for two reasons. First, she is in her place and so can win
Conrad's special brand of approval; and second, she fulfills a structural
requirement of the story; she is a savage counterpart to the refined,
European woman with whom the story will end:

She came forward, all in black with a pale head, floating towards me in the dusk. She was in mourning...She took both
my hands in hers and murmured, "I had heard you were
coming"... She had a mature capacity for fidelity, for belief,
for suffering.

The difference in the attitude of the novelist to these two women is
conveyed in too many direct and subtle ways to need elaboration. But ·
perhaps the most significant difference is the one implied in the author's bestowal of human expression to the one and the withholding of
it from the other. It is clearly not part of Conrad's purpose to confer
language on the "rudimentary souls" of Africa. They only "exchanged
short grunting phrases" even among themselves but mostly they were
too busy with their frenzy. There are two occasions in the book, however, when Conrad departs somewhat from his practice and confers
speech, even English speech, on the savages. The first occurs when
cannibalism gets the better of them:

"Catch 'im," he snapped, with a bloodshot widening of his
eyes and a flash of sharp white teeth—"catch 'im. Give 'im to

us." "To you, eh?" I asked; "what would you do with them?"
"Eat 'im!" he said curtly...

The other occasion is the famous announcement:

Mistah Kurtz—he dead.

At first sight, these instances might be mistaken for unexpected acts of generosity from Conrad. In reality, they constitute some of his best assaults. In the case of the cannibals, the incomprehensible grunts that had thus far served them for speech suddenly proved inadequate for Conrad's purpose of letting the European glimpse the unspeakable craving in their hearts. Weighing the necessity for consistency in the portrayal of the dumb brutes against the sensational advantages of securing their conviction by clear, unambiguous evidence issuing out of their own mouths, Conrad chose the latter. As for the announcement of Mr. Kurtz's death by the "insolent black head of the doorway," what better or more appropriate *finis* could be written to the horror story of that wayward child of civilization who willfully had given his soul to the powers of darkness and "taken a high seat amongst the devils of the land" than the proclamation of his physical death by the forces he had joined?

It might be contended, of course, that the attitude to the African in *Heart of Darkness* is not Conrad's but that of his fictional narrator, Marlow, and that far from endorsing it Conrad might indeed be holding it up to irony and criticism. Certainly, Conrad appears to go to considerable pains to set up layers of insulation between himself and the moral universe of his story. He has, for example, a narrator behind a narrator. The primary narrator is Marlow but his account is given to us through the filter of a second, shadowy person. But if Conrad's intention is to draw a *cordon sanitaire* between himself and the moral and psychological malaise of his narrator, his care seems to me totally wasted because he neglects to hint however subtly or tentatively at an alternative frame of reference by which we may judge the actions and opinions of his characters. It would not have been beyond Conrad's power to make that provision if he had thought it necessary. Marlow seems to me to enjoy Conrad's complete confidence—a feeling reinforced by the close similarities between their careers.

Marlow comes through to us not only as a witness of truth, but one holding those advanced and humane views appropriate to the English liberal tradition which required all Englishmen of decency to be deeply shocked by atrocities in Bulgaria or the Congo of King Leopold of the Belgians or wherever. Thus Marlow is able to toss out such bleeding-heart sentiments as these:

> They were all dying slowly—it was very clear. They were not enemies, they were not criminals, they were nothing earthly now—nothing but black shadows of disease and starvation, lying confusedly in the greenish gloom. Brought from all the recesses of the coast in all the legality of time contracts, lost in uncongenial surroundings, fed on unfamiliar food, they sickened, became inefficient, and were then allowed to crawl away and rest.

The kind of liberalism espoused here by Marlow/Conrad touched all the best minds of the age in England, Europe, and America. It took different forms in the minds of different people but almost always managed to sidestep the ultimate question of equality between white people and black people. That extraordinary missionary, Albert Schweitzer, who sacrificed brilliant careers in music and theology in Europe for a life of service to Africans in much the same areas as Conrad writes about, epitomized the ambivalence. In a comment which I have often quoted but must quote one last time Schweitzer says: "The African is indeed my brother but my junior brother." And so he proceeded to build a hospital appropriate to the needs of junior brothers with standards of hygiene reminiscent of medical practice in the days before the germ theory of disease came into being. Naturally, he became a sensation in Europe and America. Pilgrims flocked, and I believe still flock even after he has passed on, to witness the prodigious miracle in Lamberene, on the edge of the primeval forest.

Conrad's liberalism would not take him quite as far as Schweitzer's, though. He would not use the word "brother" however qualified; the farthest he would go was "kinship." When Marlow's African helmsman falls down with a spear in his heart he gives his white master one final disquieting look:

> And the intimate profundity of that look he gave me when he received his hurt remains to this day in my memory—like a claim of distant kinship affirmed in a supreme moment.

It is important to note that Conrad, careful as ever with his words, is not talking so much about *distant kinship* as about someone *laying a claim* on it. The black man lays a claim on the white man which is well-nigh intolerable. It is the laying of this claim which frightens and at the same time fascinates Conrad, "...the thought of their humanity—like yours...Ugly."

The point of my observations should be quite clear by now, namely, that Conrad was a bloody racist. That this simple truth is glossed over in criticism of his work is due to the fact that white racism against Africa is such a normal way of thinking that its manifestations go completely undetected. Students of *Heart of Darkness* will often tell you that Conrad is concerned not so much with Africa as with the deterioration of one European mind caused by solitude and sickness. They will point out to you that Conrad is, if anything, less charitable to the Europeans in the story than he is to the natives. A Conrad student told me in Scotland last year that Africa is merely a setting for the disintegration of the mind of Mr. Kurtz.

Which is partly the point: Africa as setting and backdrop which eliminates the African as human factor. Africa as a metaphysical battlefield devoid of all recognizable humanity, into which the wandering European enters at his peril. Of course, there is a preposterous and perverse kind of arrogance in thus reducing Africa to the role of props for the breakup of one petty European mind. But that is not even the point. The real question is whether the dehumanization of Africa and Africans which this age-long attitude has fostered and which celebrates this dehumanization, which depersonalizes a portion of the human race, can be called a great work of art. My answer is: No, it cannot. I would not call that man an artist, for example, who composes an eloquent instigation to one people to fall upon another and destroy them. No matter how striking his imagery or how beautifully his cadences fall such a man is no more a great artist than another may be called a priest who reads the mass backwards or a physician who poisons his patients. All those men in Nazi Germany who lent their talent to the service of virulent racism whether in science, philosophy or the arts have generally and rightly been condemned for their perversions. The time is long overdue for taking a hard look at the work of creative artists who apply their talents, alas often considerable as in the case of Conrad, to set people against people. This, I take it, is what Yevtushenko is after when he tells us that a poet cannot be a slave trader at the same time, and gives the striking example of Arthur Rimbaud who was fortunately honest enough to give up any pretenses to poetry when he opted for slave trading. For poetry surely can only be on the side of man's deliverance and not his enslavement; for the brotherhood and unity of all mankind and against the doctrines of Hitler's master races or Conrad's "rudimentary souls."

Last year was the 50th anniversary of Conrad's death. He was born in 1857, the very year in which the first Anglican missionaries were arriving among my own people in Nigeria. It was certainly not his fault that he lived his life at a time when the reputation of the black man was at a particularly low level. But even after due allowances have been made for all the influences of contemporary prejudice on his sensibility, there remains still in Conrad's attitude a residue of antipathy to black people which his peculiar psychology alone can explain. His own account of his first encounter with a black man is very revealing:

> A certain enormous buck nigger encountered in Haiti fixed my conception of blind, furious, unreasoning rage, as manifested in the human animal to the end of my days. Of the nigger I used to dream for years afterwards.

Certainly, Conrad had a problem with niggers. His inordinate love of that word itself should be of interest to psychoanalysts. Sometimes his fixation on blackness is equally interesting as when he gives us this brief description:

> A black figure stood up, strode on long black legs, waving long black arms.[2]

As though we might expect a black figure striding along on black legs to have *white* arms! But so unrelenting is Conrad's obsession.

As a matter of interest Conrad gives us in *A Personal Record* what amounts to a companion piece to the buck nigger of Haiti. At the age of sixteen Conrad encountered his first Englishman in Europe. He calls him "my unforgettable Englishman" and describes him in the following manner:

> [his] calves exposed to the public gaze...dazzled the beholder by the splendor of their marble-like condition and their rich tone of young ivory...The light of a headlong, exalted satisfaction with the world of men...illumined his face...and triumphant eyes. In passing he cast a glance of kindly curiosity and a friendly gleam of big, sound, shiny teeth...his white calves twinkled sturdily.[3]

Irrational love and irrational hate jostling together in the heart of that tormented man. But whereas irrational love may at worst engender foolish acts of indiscretion, irrational hate can endanger the life of the community. Naturally, Conrad is a dream for psychoanalytic critics. Perhaps the most detailed study of him in this direction is by Bernard C. Meyer, M.D. In this lengthy book, Dr. Meyer follows every conceivable lead (and sometimes inconceivable ones) to explain Conrad. As an example, he gives us long disquisitions on the significance of hair and hair-cutting in Conrad. And yet not even one word is spared for his attitude to black people. Not even the discussion of Conrad's antisemitism was enough to spark off in Dr. Meyer's mind those other dark and explosive thoughts. Which only leads one to surmise that Western psychoanalysts must regard the kind of racism displayed by Conrad as absolutely normal despite the profoundly important work done by Frantz Fanon in the psychiatric hospitals of French Algeria.

Whatever Conrad's problems were, you might say he is now safely dead. Quite true. Unfortunately, his heart of darkness plagues us still. Which is why an offensive and totally deplorable book can be described by a serious scholar as "among the half-dozen greatest short novels in the English language," and why it is today perhaps the most commonly prescribed novel in the twentieth-century literature courses in our own English Department here. Indeed the time is long overdue for a hard look at things.

There are two probable grounds on which what I have said so far may be contested. The first is that it is no concern of fiction to please people about whom it is written. I will go along with that. But I am not talking about pleasing people. I am talking about a book which parades in the most vulgar fashion prejudices and insults from which a section of mankind has suffered untold agonies and atrocities in the past and continues to do so in many ways and many places today. I am talking about a story in which the very humanity of black people is called in question. It seems to me totally inconceivable that great art or even good art could possibly reside in such unwholesome surroundings.

Secondly, I may be challenged on the grounds of actuality. Conrad, after all, sailed down the Congo in 1890 when my own father was still a babe in arms, and recorded what he saw. How could I stand up in 1975, fifty years after his death and purport to contradict him? My answer is that as a sensible man I will not accept just any traveller's tales solely on the grounds that I have not made the journey myself. I will not trust the evidence even of a man's very eyes when I suspect them to be as jaundiced as Conrad's. And we also happen to know that Conrad was, in the words of his biographer, Bernard C. Meyer, "notoriously inaccurate in the rendering of his own history."[4]

But more important by far is the abundant testimony about Conrad's savages which we could gather if we were so inclined from other sources and which might lead us to think that these people must have had other occupations besides merging into the evil forest or materializing out of it simply to plague Marlow and his dispirited band. For as it happened, soon after Conrad had written his book an event of far greater consequence was taking place in the art world of Europe. This is how Frank Willett, a British art historian, describes it:

> Gauguin had gone to Tahiti, the most extravagant individual act of turning to a non-European culture in the decades immediately before and after 1900, when European artists were avid for new artistic experiences, but it was only about 1904–5 that African art began to make its distinctive impact. One piece is still identifiable; it is a mask that had been

given to Maurice Vlaminck in 1905. He records that Derain was "speechless" and "stunned" when he saw it, bought it from Vlaminck and in turn showed it to Picasso and Matisse, who were also greatly affected by it. Ambroise Vollard then borrowed it and had it cast in bronze...The revolution of twentieth century art was under way![5]

The mask in question was made by other savages living just north of Conrad's River Congo. They have a name, the Fang people, and are without a doubt among the world's greatest masters of the sculptured form. As you might have guessed, the event to which Frank Willett refers marked the beginning of cubism and the infusion of new life into European art that had run completely out of strength.

The point of all this is to suggest that Conrad's picture of the people of the Congo seems grossly inadequate even at the height of their subjection to the ravages of King Leopold's International Association for the Civilization of Central Africa. Travellers with closed minds can tell us little except about themselves. But even those not blinkered, like Conrad, with xenophobia, can be astonishingly blind.

Let me digress a little here. One of the greatest and most intrepid travellers of all time, Marco Polo, journeyed to the Far East from the Mediterranean in the thirteenth century and spent twenty years in the court of Kublai Khan in China. On his return to Venice he set down in his book entitled *Description of the World* his impressions of the peoples and places and customs he had seen. There are at least two extraordinary omissions in his account. He says nothing about the art of printing unknown as yet in Europe but in full flower in China. He either did not notice it at all or if he did, failed to see what use Europe could possibly have for it. Whatever reason, Europe had to wait another hundred years for Gutenberg. But even more spectacular was Marco Polo's omission of any reference to the Great Wall of China nearly 4000 miles long and already more than 1000 years old at the time of his visit. Again, he may not have seen it; but the Great Wall of China is the only structure built by man which is visible from the moon![6] Indeed, travellers can be blind.

As I said earlier, Conrad did not originate the image of Africa which we find in his book. It was and is the dominant image of Africa in the Western imagination and Conrad merely brought the peculiar gifts of his own mind to bear on it. For reasons which can certainly use close psychological inquiry, the West seems to suffer deep anxieties about the precariousness of its civilization and to have a need for constant reassurance by comparing it with Africa. If Europe, advancing in civilization, could cast a backward glance periodically at Africa trapped in primordial barbarity, it could say with faith and feeling: There go I but for the grace of God. Africa is to Europe as the picture is to Dorian Gray—a carrier onto whom the master unloads his physical and moral deformities so that he may go forward, erect and immaculate. Consequently, Africa is something to be avoided just as the picture has to be hidden away to safeguard the man's jeopardous integrity. Keep away from Africa, or else! Mr. Kurtz of *Heart of Darkness* should have heeded that warning and the prowling horror in his heart would have kept its place, chained to its lair. But he foolishly exposed himself to the wild irresistible allure of the jungle and lo! the darkness found him out.

In my original conception of this talk I had thought to conclude it nicely on an appropriately positive note in which I would suggest from my privileged position in African and Western culture some advantages the West might derive from Africa once it rid its mind of old prejudices and began to look at Africa not through a haze of distortions and cheap mystification but quite simply as a continent of people—not angels, but not rudimentary souls either—just people, often highly gifted people and often strikingly successful in their enterprise with life and society. But as I thought more about the stereotype image, about its grip and pervasiveness, about the willful tenacity with which the West holds it to its heart; when I thought of your television and the cinema and newspapers, about books read in schools and out of school, of churches preaching to empty pews about the need to send help to the heathen in Africa, I realized that no easy optimism was possible. And there is something totally wrong in offering bribes to the West in return for its good opinion of Africa. Ultimately, the abandonment of unwholesome thoughts must be its own and only reward. Although I have used the word *willful* a few times in this talk to characterize the West's view of Africa it may well be that what is happening at this stage is more akin to reflex action than calculated malice. Which does not make the situation more, but less, hopeful. Let me give you one last and really minor example of what I mean.

Last November the *Christian Science Monitor* carried an interesting article written by its Education Editor on the serious psychological and learning problems faced by little children who speak one language at home and then go to school where something else is spoken. It was a wide-ranging article taking in Spanish-speaking children in this country, the children of migrant Italian workers in Germany, the quadrilingual phenomenon in Malaysia and so on. And all this while the article speaks unequivocally about *language*. But then out of the blue sky comes this:

> In London there is an enormous immigration of children who speak Indian or Nigerian dialects, or some other native language.[7]

I believe that the introduction of *dialects*, which is technically erroneous in the context, is almost a reflex action caused by an instinctive desire of the writer to downgrade the discussion to the level of Africa and India. And this is quite comparable to Conrad's withholding of language from his rudimentary souls. Language is too grand for these chaps; let's give them dialects. In all this business a lot of violence is inevitably done to words and their meaning. Look at the phrase "native language" in the above excerpt. Surely the only native language possible in London is Cockney English. But our writer obviously means something else—something Indians and Africans speak.

Perhaps a change will come. Perhaps this is the time when it can begin, when the high optimism engendered by the breathtaking achievements of Western science and industry is giving way to doubt and even confusion. There is just the possibility that Western man may begin to look seriously at the achievements of other people. I read in the papers the other day a suggestion that what America needs at this time is somehow to bring back the extended family. And I saw in my mind's eye future African Peace Corps Volunteers coming to help you set up the system.

Seriously, although the work which needs to be done may appear too daunting, I believe that it is not one day too soon to begin. And where better than at a University?

NOTES (AUTHOR'S)

[1] Albert J. Guerard, Introduction to *Heart of Darkness* (New York: New American Library, 1950), p. 9.

[2] Jonah Raskin, *The Mythology of Imperialism* (New York: Random House, 1971), p. 143.

[3] Bernard C. Meyer, M.D., *Joseph Conrad: A Psychoanalytic Biography* (Princeton, N.J.: Princeton University Press, 1967), p. 30.

[4] *Ibid,* p. 30.

[5] Frank Willett, *African Art* (New York: Praeger, 1971), pp. 35–36.

[6] About the omission of the Great Wall of China I am indebted to *The Journey of Marco Polo* as recreated by artist Michael Foreman, published by *Pegasus* Magazine, 1974.

[7] *Christian Science Monitor*, Nov. 25, 1974, p. 11.

VOCABULARY

cordon sanitaire—a guarded boundary around an area set apart because of disease

disquisition—a formal discourse in which every aspect of a subject is treated

erudite—very learned or scholarly

recrudescence—a fresh outbreak of a disease or an undesirable activity

rudimentary—incompletely developed, crude

virulent—actively poisonous, deadly

xenophobia—an unreasonable fear of foreigners and foreign customs

QUESTIONS

1. Do the quotations from *Heart of Darkness* convince you that Conrad is racist? Explain why or why not.

2. What aspects of Conrad's style does Achebe focus on? What message does Achebe think Conrad conveys through his style?

3. Achebe dismisses the claim that Conrad should not be identified with either Marlow or the unnamed narrator in *Heart of Darkness*. Do you agree? Why or why not?

4. What relationship with his readers and his subject is Achebe trying to create by beginning his essay with personal anecdotes about his encounter with an older student and the letters from high school students? Do you think this introduction provides an effective orientation to Achebe's criticism in *Heart of Darkness*?

5. How would you describe Achebe's tone in this essay? In what places are his attitudes to himself, his reader, and his subject most obvious? Are there shifts of tone during the essay?

SUGGESTION FOR WRITING

Achebe argues that a piece of literature which, in his view, "depersonalizes a portion of the human race" cannot "be called a great work of art." Do you agree that a moral standard of evaluation ought to take precedence over an aesthetic standard? What are the implications of Achebe's position? Is a painting depicting the heroic farmer feeding the nation superior to a Picasso? If this issue interests you, write a letter to Achebe expressing your opinions.

HOW TO PRESERVE THE HEALTH-CARE SAFETY NET (1996)

Barbara Amiel

Like all pundits, I've made some significant miscalculations. Here's one prediction, though, written in 1979, that holds up. I was writing in my book *Confessions*[1] about the future of health care if Ottawa abolished private insurance and private medicine:

"When health care becomes a free commodity like air and water, it is treated less seriously. It is abused in major or minor ways. People go to see doctors for colds. My middle-class girlfriends go to see psychiatrists at public expense to cope with the problems of their love lives. Administrative costs soar as they do in any state enterprise.

"Reducing administrative costs is hopeless. However, coercion not only is possible, but becomes natural and the only way out of the government's dilemma. Gradually, the freedom of doctors to opt in or out of the health-care scheme is replaced by a coercive condition of some kind. Then, the patients' freedom to select their own doctors is limited by requirements of residence or workplace."

I wrote that about the time Minister of Health Monique Bégin and Prime Minister Pierre Trudeau turned up the heat to abolish private medicine in Canada by withdrawing federal funds to any province that allowed extra billing. The story of how doctors responded to attacks on their independence is not impressive. The very few of us who were on their side, fighting for a health-care system that allowed private medicine to co-exist with a public safety net, simply gave up as the doctors started behaving just like unionized workers. They did not resist socialized medicine on principle and say this will ruin health care. By fighting only over the salaries and fees they would get in return for giving up their independent status, they proved that all the people who claimed the issue for doctors was just a matter of money were correct.

Now, we have Ontario's Mike Harris faced with stratospheric health-care costs and plan-

Barbara Amiel (1940–) has been a columnist for *Maclean's* since 1976. Born in England, she came to Canada in 1952. In 1981 she became a columnist, then editor, at the *Toronto Sun*. Moving back to England in 1985, she wrote for *The Times*, and in 1991 became the leading political columnist for *The Sunday Times*. She married newspaper magnate Conrad Black in 1992. Her autobiography, *Confessions*, was published in 1980. "How to Preserve the Health-Care Safety Net" is reprinted with permission of Maclean's Magazine.

ning coercive measures against doctors, such as denying them the right to practise in some urban centres. Harris and his government face problems inherited by the combined mismanagement of every Ontario premier from Bill Davis to Bob Rae, but more coercion is not the answer. The only solution is to tell people the truth about their cherished "free" health care.

There are two main problems with modern medicine. One, actually a series, has absolutely nothing to do with socialized medicine and would have existed in 1996 no matter what. Simply put, medical advances cost a fortune. It is marvellous that we can transplant organs and, instead of cutting off limbs, we can sew them back on. But an amputated limb is infinitely cheaper than the cost of all the hospital facilities required to sew it back. No one wants to forgo multi-million-dollar diagnostic machines, new drugs and technology, but this also increases costs by incalculable amounts. Then there are the increased costs of hospital workers, not including doctors, from nurses and orderlies down. Finally, we are able to extend the human lifespan in terms of economically useful life but also for economically useless lives at exactly the time our population bulge is in its 50s. This raises both cost and ethical problems. Who will fund care for these older people? Who will get the limited number of organs available for transplant? Who will get access to dialysis machines[2] or CAT[3] scans? First come, first served? Highest bidder? The person most economically useful to society?

What makes the current situation so difficult, however, is the second problem: socialized medicine itself. I arrived in Canada in the 1950s after experiencing the horrors of British socialized medicine with its lengthy waiting lists and run-down hospitals. Canada was a dream. At that time, Canada had private insurance plans that actually made a profit and gave fantastic benefits. When, as a university student, I couldn't afford my insurance and happened to end up in Toronto General Hospital, I was amazed to find that I was on a "public ward" that had only six beds and my doctor was the most renowned internal specialist in the city. All the nightmarish preconceptions that the British held about North American health care were a lie. Today, the nightmarish conceptions that Canadians hold about the notion of "two-tier" medicine are equally a lie.

Socialized medicine raises problems that occur when any endeavor is shifted from private business between a customer and a service provider to a government bureaucracy. Bureaucratic considerations immediately take priority over service considerations. Neither customer nor provider (the doctor) will be in charge, but rather some government clerk. Patients will be reduced to petitioners. Inevitably, patients and doctors will find a backdoor such as under-the-table payments and personal connections. Two-tier medicine, whether official or unofficial, is re-established.

The bureaucracy will run out of money and will never cut itself deeply, only the services it provides. The first things to go are the hotel services health care gives: the little comforts for people when they are at their most vulnerable and needy. Hospital patients are de-humanized by humiliations: they need a bedpan or an understanding nurse. What they get is endless waiting, harassed staff and often lower quality personnel. Waiting lists get longer. The state makes all sorts of medical decisions based on non-medical criteria. The brain drain of doctors speeds up. The wealthy go out of the country for their heart surgery.

The public debate about this should be widespread and informed. Governments have to realize that insurance companies must be allowed to make money. If you don't want a medical health-care system that functions like the post office, then return doctors to their role as independent professionals and not de facto[4] members of CUPE.[5] Cut the bureaucracy, make the so-called two-tier system official rather than unofficial and that way every indigent[6] person in Canada will be assured of medical care. None of us want to have anything to do with a country that turns people away from necessary medical care for lack of funds. But today, that is what we have. It will take political guts of steel to undo it.

NOTES

[1] *Confessions* is Barbara Amiel's autobiography, published in 1980.

[2] A dialysis machine is a machine that functions as an artificial kidney, removing blood from a person, purifying it, and returning it to the bloodstream.

[3] CAT: Computerized Axial Tomography. A machine that, through the use of X-rays, "reads" deep internal structures of the body, "seeing" parts of the body otherwise obscured by other organs.

[4] *de facto*: existing/in fact/actual

[5] CUPE: Canadian Union of Public Employees

[6] indigent: needy, poor

SHAKESPEARE (1966)
IN THE BUSH

Laura Bohannan

Just before I left Oxford for the Tiv[1] in West Africa, conversation turned to the season at Stratford. "You Americans," said a friend, "often have difficulty with Shakespeare. He was, after all, a very English poet, and one can easily misinterpret the universal by misunderstanding the particular."

I protested that human nature is pretty much the same the whole world over; at least the general plot and motivation of the greater tragedies would always be clear—everywhere—although some details of custom might have to be explained and difficulties of translation might produce other slight changes. To end an argument we could not conclude, my friend gave me a copy of *Hamlet* to study in the African bush: it would, he hoped, lift my mind above its primitive surroundings, and possibly I might, by prolonged meditation, achieve the grace of correct interpretation.

It was my second field trip to that African tribe, and I thought myself ready to live in one of its remote sections—an area difficult to cross even on foot. I eventually settled on the hillock of a very knowledgeable old man, the head of a homestead of some hundred and forty people, all of whom were either his close relatives or their wives and children. Like the other elders of the vicinity, the old man spent most of his time performing ceremonies seldom seen these days in the more accessible parts of the tribe. I was delighted. Soon there would be three months of enforced isolation and leisure, between the harvest that takes place just before the rising of the swamps and the clearing of new farms when the water goes down. Then, I thought, they would have even more time to perform ceremonies and explain them to me.

I was quite mistaken. Most of the ceremonies demanded the presence of elders from several homesteads. As the swamps rose even higher, all activities but one came to an end. The women brewed beer from maize and millet. Men, women, and children sat on their hillocks and drank it.

Dr. Laura Bohannan (1922–), a former lecturer in anthropology at the University of Chicago, was in 1992 a professor at the University of Illinois in Chicago. With her husband, Paul Bohannan, she co-authored many works on the Tiv. She is best known for *Return to Laughter* (1954), written under the pseudonym Elenore Smith Bowen. "Shakespeare in the Bush" (1966) was written for BBC radio's "Third Programme." "Shakespeare in the Bush" is from *Introduction to Literature: British, American, Canadian,* 1981. Reprinted with permission of Laura Bohannon.

People began to drink at dawn. By midmorning the whole homestead was singing, dancing, and drumming. When it rained, people had to sit inside their huts: there they drank and sang or they drank and told stories. In any case, by noon or before, I either had to join the party or retire to my own hut and my books. "One does not discuss serious matters when there is beer. Come, drink with us." Since I lacked their capacity for the thick native beer, I spent more and more time with *Hamlet*. Before the end of the second month, grace descended on me. I was quite sure that *Hamlet* had only one possible interpretation, and that one universally obvious.

Early every morning, in the hope of having some serious talk before the beer party, I used to call on the old man at his reception hut—a circle of posts supporting a thatched roof above a low mud wall to keep out wind and rain. One day I crawled through the low doorway and found most of the men of the homestead sitting huddled in their ragged cloths on stools, low plank beds, and reclining chairs, warming themselves against the chill of the rain around a smoky fire. In the center were three pots of beer. The party had started.

The old man greeted me cordially. "Sit down and drink." I accepted a large calabash full of beer, poured some into a small drinking gourd, and tossed it down. Then I poured some more into the same gourd for the man second in seniority to my host before I handed my calabash over to a young man for further distribution. Important people shouldn't ladle beer themselves.

"It is better like this," the old man said, looking at me approvingly and plucking at the thatch that had caught in my hair. "You should sit and drink with us more often. Your servants tell me that when you are not with us, you sit inside your hut looking at a paper."

The old man was acquainted with four kinds of "papers": tax receipts, bride price receipts,[2] court receipts, and letters. The messenger who brought him letters from the chief used them mainly as a badge of office, for he always knew what was in them and told the old man. Personal letters for the few who had relatives in the government or mission stations were kept until someone went to a large market where there was a letter writer and reader. Since my arrival, letters were brought to me to be read. A few men also brought me bride price receipts, privately, with requests to change the figures to a higher sum. I found moral arguments were of no avail, since in-laws are fair game, and the technical hazards of forgery difficult to explain to an illiterate people. I did not wish them to think me silly enough to look at any such papers for days on end, and I hastily explained that my "paper" was one of the "things of long ago" of my country.

"Ah," said the old man. "Tell us."

I protested that I was not a storyteller. Storytelling is a skilled art among them; their standards are high, and the audiences critical—and vocal in their criticism. I protested in vain. This morning they wanted to hear a story while they drank. They threatened to tell me no more stories until I told them one of mine. Finally, the old man promised that no one would criticize my style "for we know you are struggling with our language." "But," put in one of the elders, "you must explain what we do not understand, as we do when we tell you our stories." Realizing that here was my chance to prove *Hamlet* universally intelligible, I agreed.

The old man handed me some more beer to help me on with my storytelling. Men filled their long wooden pipes and knocked coals from the fire to place in the pipe bowls; then, puffing contentedly, they sat back to listen. I began in the proper style, "Not yesterday, not yesterday, but long ago, a thing occurred. One night three men were keeping watch outside the homestead of the great chief, when suddenly they saw the former chief approach them."

"Why was he no longer their chief?"

"He was dead," I explained. "That is why they were troubled and afraid when they saw him."

"Impossible," began one of the elders, handing his pipe on to his neighbor, who interrupted, "Of course it wasn't the dead chief. It was an omen sent by a witch. Go on."

Slightly shaken, I continued. "One of these three was a man who knew things"—the closest translation for scholar, but unfortunately it also meant witch. The second elder looked triumphantly at the first. "So he spoke to the dead chief saying, 'Tell us what we must do so you may rest in your grave,' but the dead chief did not answer. He vanished, and they could see him no more. Then the man who knew things—his name was Horatio—said this event was the affair of the dead chief's son, Hamlet."

There was a general shaking of heads around the circle. "Had the dead chief no living brothers? Or was this son the chief?"

"No," I replied. "That is, he had one living brother who became the chief when the elder brother died."

The old men muttered: such omens were matters for chiefs and elders, not for youngsters; no good could come of going behind a chief's back; clearly Horatio was not a man who knew things.

"Yes, he was," I insisted, shooing a chicken away from my beer. "In our country the son is next to the father. The dead chief's younger brother had become the great chief. He had also married his elder brother's widow only about a month after the funeral."

"He did well," the old man beamed and announced to the others, "I told you that if we knew more about Europeans, we would find they really were very like us. In our country also," he added to me, "the younger brother marries the elder brother's widow and becomes the father of his children. Now, if your uncle, who married your widowed mother, is your father's full brother, then he will be a real father to you. Did Hamlet's father and uncle have one mother?"

His question barely penetrated my mind; I was too upset and thrown too far off balance by having one of the most important elements of *Hamlet* knocked straight out of the picture. Rather uncertainly I said that I thought they had the same mother, but I wasn't sure—the story didn't say. The old man told me severely that these genealogical details made all the difference and that when I got home I must ask the elders about it. He shouted out the door to one of his younger wives to bring his goatskin bag.

Determined to save what I could of the mother motif, I took a deep breath and began again. "The son Hamlet was very sad because his mother had married again so quickly. There was no need for her to do so, and it is our custom for a widow not to go to her next husband until she has mourned for two years."

"Two years is too long," objected the wife, who had appeared with the old man's battered goatskin bag. "Who will hoe your farms for you while you have no husband?"

"Hamlet," I retorted without thinking, "was old enough to hoe his mother's farms himself. There was no need for her to remarry." No one looked convinced. I gave up. "His mother and the great chief told Hamlet not to be sad, for the great chief himself would be a father to Hamlet. Furthermore, Hamlet would be the next chief: therefore he must stay to learn the things of a chief. Hamlet agreed to remain, and all the rest went off to drink beer."

While I paused, perplexed at how to render Hamlet's disgusted soliloquy to an audience convinced that Claudius and Gertrude had behaved in the best possible manner, one of the younger men asked me who had married the other wives of the dead chief.

"He had no other wives," I told him.

"But a chief must have many wives! How else can he brew beer and prepare food for all his guests?"

I said firmly that in our country even chiefs had only one wife, that they had servants to do their work, and that they paid them from tax money.

It was better, they returned, for a chief to have many wives and sons who would help him hoe his farms and feed his people; then everyone loved the chief who gave much and took nothing—taxes were a bad thing.

I agreed with the last comment, but for the rest fell back on their favorite way of fobbing off my questions: "That is the way it is done, so that is how we do it."

I decided to skip the soliloquy: Even if Claudius was here thought quite right to marry his brother's widow, there remained the poison motif, and I knew they would disapprove of fratricide. More hopefully I resumed, "That night Hamlet kept watch with the three who had seen his dead father. The dead chief again appeared, and although the others were afraid, Hamlet followed his dead father off to one side. When they were alone, Hamlet's dead father spoke."

"Omens can't talk!" The old man was emphatic.

"Hamlet's dead father wasn't an omen. Seeing him might have been an omen, but he was not." My audience looked as confused as I sounded. "It *was* Hamlet's dead father. It was a thing we call a 'ghost.'" I had to use the English word, for unlike many of the neighboring tribes, these people didn't believe in the survival after death of any individuating part of the personality.

"What is a 'ghost'? An omen?"

"No, a 'ghost' is someone who is dead but who walks around and can talk, and people can hear him and see him but not touch him."

They objected. "One can touch zombis."

"No, no! It was not a dead body the witches had animated to sacrifice and eat. No one else made Hamlet's dead father walk. He did it himself."

"Dead men can't walk," protested my audience as one man.

I was quite willing to compromise. "A 'ghost' is the dead man's shadow."

But again they objected. "Dead men cast no shadows."

"They do in my country," I snapped.

The old man quelled the babble of disbelief that arose immediately and told me with that insincere, but courteous, agreement one extends to the fancies of the young, ignorant, and superstitious, "No doubt in your country the dead can also walk without being zombis." From the depths of his bag he produced a withered fragment of kola nut, bit off one end to show it wasn't poisoned, and handed me the rest as a peace offering.

"Anyhow," I resumed, "Hamlet's dead father said that his own brother, the one who became chief, had poisoned him. He wanted Hamlet to avenge him. Hamlet believed this in his heart, for he did not like his father's brother." I took another swallow of beer. "In the country of the great chief, living in the same homestead, for it was a very large one, was an important elder who was often with the chief to advise and help him. His name was Polonius. Hamlet was courting his daughter, but her father and her brother ... [I cast hastily about for some tribal analogy] warned her not to let Hamlet visit her when she was alone on her farm, for he would be a great chief and so could not marry her."

"Why not?" asked the wife, who had settled down on the edge of the old man's chair. He frowned at her for asking stupid questions and growled, "They lived in the same homestead."

"That was not the reason," I informed them. "Polonius didn't think he would. After all, Hamlet was a man of great importance who ought to marry a chief's daughter, for in his country a man could have only one wife. Polonius was afraid that if Hamlet made love to his daughter, then no one else would give a high price for her."

"That might be true," remarked one of the shrewder elders, "but a chief's son would give his mistress's father enough presents and patronage to more than make up the difference. Polonius sounds like a fool to me."

"Many people think he was," I agreed. "Meanwhile Polonius sent his son Laertes off to Paris to learn the things of that country, for it was the homestead of a very great chief indeed. Because he was afraid that Laertes might waste a lot of money on beer and women and gambling, or get into trouble by fighting, he sent one of his servants to Paris secretly, to spy out what Laertes was doing. One day Hamlet came upon Polonius's daughter Ophelia. He behaved so oddly he frightened her. Indeed"—I was fumbling for words to express the dubious quality of Hamlet's madness—"the chief and many others had also noticed that when Hamlet talked one could understand the words but not what they meant. Many people thought that he had become mad." My audience suddenly became much more attentive. "The great chief wanted to know what was wrong with Hamlet, so he sent for two of Hamlet's age mates [school friends would have taken long explanation] to talk to Hamlet and find out what troubled his heart. Hamlet, seeing that they had been bribed by the chief to betray him, told them nothing. Polonius, however, insisted that Hamlet was mad because he had been forbidden to see Ophelia, whom he loved."

"Why," inquired a bewildered voice, "should anyone bewitch Hamlet on that account?"

"Bewitch him?"

"Yes, only witchcraft can make anyone mad, unless, of course, one sees the beings that lurk in the forest."

I stopped being a storyteller, took out my notebook and demanded to be told more about these two causes of madness. Even while they spoke and I jotted notes, I tried to calculate the effect of this new factor on the plot. Hamlet had not been exposed to the beings that lurk in the forest. Only his relatives in the male line could bewitch him. Barring relatives not mentioned by Shakespeare, it had to be Claudius who was attempting to harm him. And, of course, it was.

For the moment I staved off questions by saying that the great chief also refused to believe that Hamlet was mad for the love of

Ophelia and nothing else. "He was sure that something much more important was troubling Hamlet's heart."

"Now Hamlet's age mates," I continued, "had brought with them a famous storyteller. Hamlet decided to have this man tell the chief and all his homestead a story about a man who had poisoned his brother because he desired his brother's wife and wished to be chief himself. Hamlet was sure the great chief could not hear the story without making a sign if he was indeed guilty, and then he would discover whether his dead father had told him the truth."

The old man interrupted, with deep cunning, "Why should a father lie to his son?" he asked.

I hedged: "Hamlet wasn't sure that it really was his dead father." It was impossible to say anything, in that language, about devil-inspired visions.

"You mean," he said, "it actually was an omen, and he knew witches sometimes send false ones. Hamlet was a fool not to go to one skilled in reading omens and divining the truth in the first place. A man-who-sees-the-truth could have told him how his father died, if he really had been poisoned, and if there was witchcraft in it; then Hamlet could have called the elders to settle the matter."

The shrewd elder ventured to disagree. "Because his father's brother was a great chief, one-who-sees-the-truth might therefore have been afraid to tell it. I think it was for that reason that a friend of Hamlet's father—a witch and an elder—sent an omen so his friend's son would know. Was the omen true?"

"Yes," I said, abandoning ghosts and the devil; a witch-sent omen it would have to be. "It was true, for when the storyteller was telling his tale before all the homestead, the great chief rose in fear. Afraid that Hamlet knew his secret, he planned to have him killed."

The stage set of the next bit presented some difficulties of translation. I began cautiously. "The great chief told Hamlet's mother to find out from her son what he knew. But because a woman's children are always first in her heart, he had the important elder Polonius hide behind a cloth that hung against the wall of Hamlet's mother's sleeping hut. Hamlet started to scold his mother for what she had done."

There was a shocked murmur from everyone. A man should never scold his mother.

"She called out in fear, and Polonius moved behind the cloth. Shouting, 'A rat!' Hamlet took his machete and slashed through the cloth." I paused for dramatic effect. "He had killed Polonius!"

The old men looked at each other in supreme disgust. "That Polonius truly was a fool and a man who knew nothing! What child would not know enough to shout, 'It's me!'" With a pang, I remembered that these people are ardent hunters, always armed with bow, arrow, and machete; at the first rustle in the grass an arrow is aimed and ready, and the hunter shouts "Game!" If no human voice answers immediately, the arrow speeds on its way. Like a good hunter Hamlet had shouted, "A rat!"

I rushed in to save Polonius's reputation. "Polonius did speak. Hamlet heard him. But he thought it was the chief and wished to kill him to avenge his father. He had meant to kill him earlier that evening..." I broke down, unable to describe to these pagans, who had no belief in individual afterlife, the difference between dying at one's prayers and dying "unhousell'd, disappointed, unaneled."

This time I had shocked my audience seriously. "For a man to raise his hand against his father's brother and the one who has become his father—that is a terrible thing. The elders ought to let such a man be bewitched."

I nibbled at my kola nut in some perplexity, then pointed out that after all the man had killed Hamlet's father.

"No," pronounced the old man, speaking less to me than to the young men sitting behind the elders. "If your father's brother has killed your father, you must appeal to your father's age mates; *they* may avenge him. No man may use violence against his senior relatives." Another thought struck him. "But if his father's brother had indeed been wicked enough to bewitch Hamlet and make him mad that would be a good story indeed, for it would be his fault that Hamlet, being mad, no longer had any sense and thus was ready to kill his father's brother."

There was a murmur of applause. *Hamlet* was again a good story to them, but it no longer seemed quite the same story to me. As I thought over the coming complications of plot and motive, I lost courage and decided to skim over dangerous ground quickly.

"The great chief," I went on, "was not sorry that Hamlet had killed Polonius. It gave him a reason to send Hamlet away, with his two treacherous age mates, with letters to a chief of a far country, saying that Hamlet should be killed. But Hamlet changed the writing on their papers, so that the chief killed his age mates instead." I encountered a reproachful glare from one of the men whom I had told undetectable forgery was not merely immoral but beyond human skill. I looked the other way.

"Before Hamlet could return, Laertes came back for his father's funeral. The great chief told him Hamlet had killed Polonius. Laertes swore to kill Hamlet because of this, and because his sister Ophelia, hearing her father had been killed by the man she loved, went mad and drowned in the river."

"Have you already forgotten what we told you?" The old man was reproachful. "One cannot take vengeance on a madman; Hamlet killed Polonius in his madness. As for the girl, she not only went mad, she was drowned. Only witches can make people drown. Water itself can't hurt anything. It is merely something one drinks and bathes in."

I began to get cross. "If you don't like the story, I'll stop."

The old man made soothing noises and himself poured me some more beer. "You tell the story well, and we are listening. But it is clear that the elders of your country have never told you what the story really means. No, don't interrupt! We believe you when you say your marriage customs are different, or your clothes and weapons. But people are the same everywhere; therefore, there are always witches and it is we, the elders, who know how witches work. We told you it was the great chief who wished to kill Hamlet, and now your own words have proved us right. Who were Ophelia's male relatives?"

"There were only her father and her brother." Hamlet was clearly out of my hands.

"There must have been many more; this also you must ask of your elders when you get back to your country. From what you tell us, since Polonius was dead, it must have been Laertes who killed Ophelia, although I do not see the reason for it."

We had emptied one pot of beer, and the old men argued the point with slightly tipsy interest. Finally one of them demanded of me, "What did the servant of Polonius say on his return?"

With difficulty I recollected Reynaldo and his mission. "I don't think he did return before Polonius was killed."

"Listen," said the elder, "and I will tell you how it was and how your story will go, then you may tell me if I am right. Polonius knew his son would get into trouble, and so he did. He had many fines to pay for fighting, and debts from gambling. But he had only two ways of getting money quickly. One was to marry off his sister at once, but it is difficult to find a man who will marry a woman desired by the son of a chief. For if the chief's heir commits adultery with your wife, what can you do? Only a fool calls a case against a man who will someday be his judge. Therefore Laertes had to take the second way: he killed his sister by witchcraft, drowning her so he could secretly sell her body to the witches."

I raised an objection. "They found her body and buried it. Indeed Laertes jumped into the grave to see his sister once more—so, you see, the body was truly there. Hamlet, who had just come back, jumped in after him."

"What did I tell you?" The elder appealed to the others. "Laertes was up to no good with his sister's body. Hamlet prevented him, because the chief's heir, like a chief, does not wish any other man to grow rich and powerful. Laertes would be angry, because he would have killed his sister without benefit to himself. In our country he would try to kill Hamlet for that reason. Is this not what happened?"

"More or less," I admitted. "When the great chief found Hamlet was still alive, he encouraged Laertes to try to kill Hamlet and arranged a fight with machetes between them. In the fight both the young men were wounded to death. Hamlet's mother drank the poisoned beer that the chief meant for Hamlet in case he won the fight. When he saw his mother die of poison, Hamlet, dying, managed to kill his father's brother with his machete."

"You see, I was right!" exclaimed the elder.

"That was a very good story," added the old man, "and you told it with very few mistakes. There was just one more error, at the very end. The poison Hamlet's mother drank was obviously meant for the survivor of the fight, whichever it was. If Laertes had won, the great chief would have poisoned him, for no one would know that he arranged Hamlet's death. Then, too, he need not fear Laertes' witchcraft; it takes a strong heart to kill one's only sister by witchcraft.

"Sometime," concluded the old man, gathering his ragged toga about him, "you must tell us some more stories of your country. We, who are elders, will instruct you in their true meaning, so that when you return to your own land your elders will see that you have not been sitting in the bush, but among those who know things and who have taught you wisdom."

NOTES

[1] The Tiv are a tribe of people who live on the banks of the river Benue in central Nigeria.

[2] A bride price receipt is given by a Native Court to a suitor indicating the price he must pay to the parents of his intended bride.

QUESTIONS

1. Bohannan organizes her account of telling the story of *Hamlet* as a narrative, an account of a series of events. Is this an effective way to present the material to support her thesis? What is her thesis?

2. Suppose Bohannan had organized her material as an analysis of the causes of misreadings between cultures. Would she be able to make the same point?

3. Now that you have read this essay, do you think great art can transcend the "details of custom"? Why or why not?

4. Did Bohannan's essay give you any new insights into Shakespeare's play?

5. How would you describe Bohannan's attitudes to herself, her subject, and her double audience (the Tiv and the reader)? What tone does she create in this essay?

6. How does the tone in this essay differ from the tone of Achebe's essay? Do you think Achebe would call Bohannan a racist?

7. What are some of the instances of irony in Bohannan's essay? At whom and what is the irony directed? How does the irony in "Shakespeare in the Bush" compare with the irony in "Unchopping a Tree" and "A Modest Proposal"?

THE NURSES

THE FRONT-LINE CARE-GIVERS ARE BURNED OUT. IS IT ANY WONDER?

Sharon Doyle Driedger

It is the worst possible time for the cell phone batteries to die. The messages blaring out of the emergency room intercom demand a response: "Ambulance on the way—traffic accident victim. Charge nurse call triage re incoming car accident." Janet Spence, the registered nurse running the emergency room at the new Halifax Infirmary, presses and re-presses the buttons on her cell phone. Dead. A paramedic steps forward to help, and in the half-minute it takes him to fix her phone, Spence surveys the hectic scene, assessing the priority of cases in the 28 beds and the pressures facing the 10 bustling nurses. "Over there we have three sick cardiac patients—they all need to be seen as soon as possible," she says, a stethoscope dangling over the white jacket that only partly covers her pink sweat suit. "And there's an overdose here. We are full and about to overflow."

Twenty minutes later, Spence receives another alert. "The police just brought in somebody with sexual assault, which means tying up a nurse and a doctor with double evidence," she groans. "It could take two hours—we can't take a nurse and a doctor out of this mess now." When Spence discovers that a physician has cleared a patient for discharge, she pushes an incoming patient—slumped in a wheelchair—towards the bed. There is a moment of confusion when the pink curtain is drawn back to reveal a grey-haired woman, surprised to hear about the doctor's decision. "I thought she was being admitted," says her young companion. But nurse Glenda Keys—who has been busy with three critically ill patients—confirms she is to go home. "Sixteen years ago, when I started, nurses had time to spend at the bedside," she says wearily as she changes the sheets. "Now, they just get basic care. We're running all the time—nursing has gone to hell."

That was the frantic scene one recent night at the Halifax Infirmary, part of the huge Queen Elizabeth II Health Sciences Centre complex. Versions of it are played out at hospitals across Canada every day. Nurses—the front-line care-givers in Canada's beleaguered health system—are burning out. "Nursing is in crisis," says Heather Henderson, president

Sharon Doyle Driedger has worked for *Maclean's* since 1984 as a researcher/reporter, as an assistant editor, and now as an associate editor. Her special writing interests are health, lifestyles, and art. "The Nurses," her first cover essay, is reprinted from *Maclean's* with permission.

of the Nova Scotia Nurses Union. "Workloads are increasing and patients are sicker. Nurses are starting to be very worried that they cannot provide care to all their patients in a safe way."

Frustration, fatigue and anger are common among Canada's 262,400 registered nurses. "Enough is enough," states Rachel Bard, Moncton-based president of the Canadian Nurses Association (CNA). "We've gone far enough in terms of reductions. The health of Canadians is clearly at risk and Canadians have reason to be concerned."

Nurses, and the people who train them, are watching the pressures on the profession with alarm. Thousands of full-time jobs have disappeared in the past five years as hospitals have closed beds, merged or, in some cases, shut down completely. "Patient care is suffering," says Jim Rankin, associate dean of nursing at the University of Calgary. "The grassroots-level staff nurse is getting burned out." In Ontario, as many as 15,000 nurses could lose their jobs over the next three years. In some hospitals in New Brunswick, Quebec and Nova Scotia, RN staff has even slipped below agreed-upon essential service levels during a strike.

At the same time, pressures to send patients home earlier mean that those who remain in hospital are in greater need of care. Henderson, 42, an obstetrics nurse at Halifax's Isaac Walton Killam Grace Health Centre, recalls "the good old days" at the start of her career. "If you had eight patients, four may have been there for over a week and on the road to recovery, and another four on the first day of post-op," she says. "Now, all your patients are very sick—and you may have 10." Many doctors express sympathy. "There is so much stress on nurses," says Halifax surgeon Vivian McAlister. "They are working longer hours under less than fair conditions, many of them casual and part time." Life in hospitals, he adds, "isn't as fun or as happy" as it used to be.

* * *

To take a close look at the pressures besetting nursing, *Maclean's* spent a week observing conditions at two respected Halifax hospitals—the 1,100-bed QE II complex and the 377-bed IWK Grace. Nurses are feeling the crunch of four successive years of staff and funding cutbacks at the QE II, which has merged six facilities into five, including the new infirmary. At the complex's Camphill Veterans' Memorial building, Helen Gillis's voice falters as she recalls the early days of her 37-year nursing career. "It was a little romantic," she says, with a hint of a Cape Breton lilt. "When I started here, the nurses wore veils and they were called sisters." Gillis—who only recently stopped wearing a traditional white nurse's cap, feeling subtle pressure from the capless majority—thinks the profession has lost some of its pride. "Years ago, a nurse wore a cap and a white uniform and patients knew who you were," she says. "Now, they even wear jeans—white jeans, but they are jeans," she adds disapprovingly. Gillis, who plans to retire in May, also feels nursing being drawn away from the bedside. "Thank goodness my time as a nurse is behind me, not ahead of me," she says.

Nurses just beginning their careers face enormous changes. Medical technology, health reform, research developments, the Internet, preventive and alternative medicine, a more informed public, feminism, increased education—those are just some of the factors transforming the profession's traditional roles. Today, most nurses—62 per cent—work in hospitals. But hospital jobs are disappearing, and new needs are developing in community health care. Helen Mussallem, 77, a widely respected former executive director of the CNA, predicts that hospital nurses will become fewer in number and more highly specialized. She also envisions "neighborhood nurses" running 24-hour clinics offering a range of services from the diagnosis of simple ailments to medical testing and the promotion of health. "I see nurses as the leaders of health services in the community," says Mussallem.

Anna Svendsen has seen the future—and she is already there. "I was the first one," says the tall redhead, pointing to the "ERN"—for Extended-Role Nurse—on her nameplate. Svendsen, who has a master of science degree in nursing, is one of a new breed of nurse practitioner, with an expanded role that occasionally overlaps the once-exclusive territory of the doctor. Working in admissions in the Halifax Infirmary's cardiology department, Svendsen takes detailed medical histories of patients and performs "head to toe" physicals as well as a number of procedures, including cardiac catheterization. A large part of her job is patient education and follow-up, to encourage a healthy lifestyle. "It is well documented in the literature that patients are more comfortable talking to a nurse," says Svendsen. "They feel like they are wasting a doctor's time or the doctor talks over their head."

Institutions in several provinces have informally enhanced the roles of nurses in some specialities through pilot projects, without waiting for new licensing guidelines. Nova Scotia formalized its licensing only this month. Marilyn Bacon, vice-president of nursing at IWK Grace, waves the newly received announcement from the Registered Nurses Association of Nova Scotia like a victory flag. "This represents three years of work," she says.

But even RNs who do not take the practitioner route are finding themselves doing jobs they never dreamed of. "Technology has changed my life as a nurse," says Philip MacDougall, squatting to adjust one of a dozen electronic pumps at the bedside of an elderly patient undergoing a bone marrow transplant for advanced cancer. That patient, he explains later, is on a continuous morphine drip for sores in his mouth. "It's excruciating pain," he adds. "It's serious stuff—the patients know if it doesn't succeed, they will die." MacDougall is a technical whiz, handling intricate computerized instruments. He also provides information and counselling to seriously ill patients and their worried families—in a ward where death is almost a daily event. And he empties urinals, mops the floor and bathes patients—traditional nursing tasks that are now a source of conflict and controversy. Increasingly, hospital administrators are hiring not just less fully trained Certified Nursing Assistants (CNAs) and Licensed Practical Nurses (LPNs) but also unregulated, less-skilled and considerably lower-paid personal-care workers to carry out "non-nursing" duties.

What, then, is the role of the nurse? Few would disagree with Ann Miller, a nursing director at IWK Grace who says that "mopping a floor is definitely not nursing." Still, some "menial" tasks are important in the "art" of nursing, she adds. "You can learn a lot about a patient and their situation when you are taking away a bedpan or doing a bath," Miller says. Others are happy to be relieved of the basic tasks. "I am a degree-educated nurse," says Jill Yates, a cardiology nurse at the Halifax Infirmary. "I don't need a degree to put a patient in a clinic room, carry the chart around or clean up." Chris Power, vice-president of nursing at the QE II, says the hospital is considering hiring people to do some non-nursing chores. While acknowledging that basic tasks may provide insight into a patient's health, she asks: "Can't we find a way to do that assessment in five minutes, instead of the 25 minutes it takes to do a bed bath?"

In fact, nurses interact with patients in many ways. During a busy shift at the infirmary, emergency nurse Carole Daulton prays with a critically ill patient. "She insisted," Daulton says later with a broad grin. "I said the Our Father, the whole thing." On the same day, in an operating room on the eleventh floor of the Victoria General—another part of the QE II complex—nurse Michele Singer takes time out from setting up the instruments for an operation to comfort a frightened patient until the anesthetic takes effect. "The bottom line is, the patient is scared and they need you," says Singer. "The day this job becomes all technique is the day I have to stop."

Time of any kind is at a premium. In the post-partum unit at IWK Grace, the alarm sounds at the nursing station shortly after 10 a.m. Nurse Debbie Trimper races down the hall towards the door with the flashing red light, joining a nurse who arrived seconds earlier. A pale young mother looks relieved—her infant, born only a few hours earlier, is fine. "Choking baby," explains Trimper, who has seen it all—and seen it all change—in her 23 years as a maternity nurse. Now, mothers and babies room together for their short hospital stays—generally only 24 hours, compared with nearly a week just a decade ago.

And while Trimper cares for fewer mothers, their needs, in the immediate aftermath of childbirth, are great. "The frustrating part is that sometimes two moms need you at once," she says. "It's a question of who needs you the most." For one mother, leaning against a corridor wall clutching her hungry baby, it means waiting a little longer for help with breastfeeding. "I'll be there as soon as I can," Trimper assures her. "Oh, I know, you're busy with patients," the tired mother says.

Some of the stresses of nursing are unavoidable. Paula Ernst remembers her first week in the bone marrow transplant unit of QE II's Victoria General building six years ago. "When I came out of nursing school, I was going to save everybody," she says. "I started at a time when everyone was dying, two one day, three the next. I had a couple of drinks at a party that weekend and I burst into tears. It all came out. Nearly everybody dies on BMT. Then I learned that part of the job is to help people die."

Another part is the role of patient advocate. In what many perceive as a disintegrating health-care system, nurses are convinced it is a more important function than ever. "It's up to the nurse to speak up," says operation room nurse Carol St. Clair, an outspoken 60-year-old who believes it is her duty to act as a role model. "Junior nurses are timid about asserting themselves—the doctors are the age of their fathers. But in OR,[5] we watch their competence." All hospitals have problems and St. Clair says it is important to deal with them. "Doctors are not gods," she says firmly. "Some have their addictions and their weaknesses."

IWK Grace's Miller believes that, for the most part, the relationship between nurses and physicians has improved since she began her career nearly 30 years ago. "In the early days, there was a lot of respect between doctors and nurses," says Miller. "But there was a very clear understanding of what their roles were—the doctor was at the top of the heap and the nurses' role was largely what the doctors left for them to do." Now, nurses are more aware of their responsibilities as licensed practitioners. "We don't always agree with a doctor," notes Daulton, who says that if she suspects an error, she will "check it out" and ask the physician to "clarify" an order. "I'm not a chattel," she adds. "I'm a nurse, God help me."

People take up the calling for a variety of reasons. MacDougall did it because he wanted to travel. "It was the '80s, you could go anywhere and immediately get a job," he recalls. But now, MacDougall plans to stay put, because "you just don't get permanent jobs any more." Job security has become a major concern. "If you have a specialty like this under your belt," says Singer, an experienced operating room nurse, "you have a much better chance of getting a job." But even then, possibly not a full-time job with benefits. "In many hospitals across Canada, the trend is to hire casual nurses," says union leader Henderson. Some nurses say they like the flexibility of casual work. "It suits me just fine," says operating room specialist Merete Hansen, who plans to return to university part time next fall.

While jobs disappear, many nurses, lured by active recruiting, are leaving Canada for full-time positions with higher pay and better benefits in the United States and abroad. Joanne Moser leaves next month for Saudi Arabia on a five-year contract that will net her more than $50,000 a year—more than an experienced general duty nurse might expect to earn before taxes in Nova Scotia. "I love my job," says Moser, an operating room nurse at the Victoria. "But the salary is only enough to go paycheque to paycheque." Meanwhile, Donna Miller has just spent eight years working as a travelling nurse in the United States, where she enjoyed good money and benefits. But she returned to Canada because U.S. patient care was not as good, she says. "Bed sores are common there," Miller recounts. "Patients may have to wait up to two days in emergency wards. They bring in food, blankets."

While job prospects dwindle, RNs will soon require more extensive training. More than 80 per cent of nurses currently practising in Canada are "diploma-prepared"—that is, they trained in one- or two-year hospital or community college programs. But starting in 2000, RN candidates in Canada will have to have a BA or BSc degree. Many working nurses feel a degree is unnecessary for bedside work—and may be an expensive deterrent for some candidates. Dalhousie University nursing professor Gail Tomblin-Murphy says she has even heard criticism from physicians. "The cry is, 'Oh my God, those university people are not going to be happy at the bedside.'" But she and others argue that a degree will provide "the independent thought, the critical decision-making" that nurses need to take an active role in the formation of health-care policy.

Thousands of hospital-trained nurses are upgrading their education. Trimper—who trained in a hospital 25 years ago and is now studying part time for a BSc—feels that she has no hope of advancement without a degree. "Nursing is a dead-end job if you work in an institution," says Trimper. But others, like Barb Egan, who works with MacDougall in the bone marrow unit, see little point in taking nursing courses. "I can't advance anyway," she argues. "There are no jobs." And the financial reward is slim. In Nova Scotia, nurses with degrees earn a premium of just $25 a month.

Nurses acknowledge—in fact, they boast about—the "sick sense of humor" that helps them deal with trauma. It may amuse them, then, in the midst of job shortages, to see that some planners are predicting a shortage of nurses in just five years. That is because high unemployment, low salaries and higher educational requirements are discouraging young people from entering the profession. Governments, in turn, are planning to reduce class sizes in nursing schools. As Nova Scotia health department official Mary Jane Hampton puts it: "Why glut the market when you have people already trained who are unemployed?"

Meanwhile, as the number of nurses needed in hospitals shrinks, long-promised community and home-care nursing jobs have not—and may never—materialize. "One of the greatest myths in health care," says Hampton, "is that jobs lost in hospitals will be picked up in the community." Still, many nurses argue that although their profession is ailing, it is far from dead. There is in fact a growing emphasis on health promotion and community-based nursing, notes Dalhousie's Tomblin-Murphy—"what nurses have been advocating for 20 years." And it is a challenge that many of her young students are willing to embrace. Tanya Brown, in her fourth year, is forming a company to offer first-aid courses to parents and day-care workers. She calls herself a "nurse entrepreneur," and she may be helping to define the nurse of the 21st century.

VOCABULARY

triage—assigning degrees of urgency to medical cases in order to determine treatment priority

double evidence——confirming evidence

cardiac catheterization—use of a catheter (hollow tube) in the treatment of heart conditions

post-partum—after childbirth

OR—operating room

chattel—an item of property

QUESTIONS

1. Is "burnout" a good word to describe the way nurses are feeling about their jobs? What is the dictionary definition of this word? How would you define it?

2. Reread the first three paragraphs of this article. How does Driedger use descriptive details to make a persuasive point?

3. As Driedger makes clear, nursing is going through a period of profound changes. Which of these changes are positive? Which are negative?

4. What makes Driedger's use of examples effective? What other kinds of evidence does she use?

5. Do you think the title of this essay is effective? Is it too general? Could you suggest an alternative title that would still fit with the overall content of the article?

6. Driedger does not state her thesis explicitly. Is this a strength or a weakness in the essay? What is her thesis?

SUGGESTION FOR WRITING

If you are like most people, you have experienced "burnout" from time to time. Write a paragraph describing this feeling. Then write a paragraph suggesting creative ways to prevent burnout or to cope with it.

A ROSE FOR
"A ROSE FOR EMILY"[1]

Judith Fetterley

In "A Rose for Emily" the grotesque reality implicit in Aylmer's ideal-ization of Georgiana[2] becomes explicit. Justifying Faulkner's use of the grotesque[3] has been a major concern of critics who have written on the story. If, however, one approaches "A Rose for Emily" from a feminist perspective, one notices that the grotesque aspects of the story are a result of its violation of the expectations generated by the conventions of sexual politics. The ending shocks us not simply by its hint of necrophilia; more shocking is the fact that it is a woman who provides the hint. It is one thing for Poe to spend his nights in the tomb of Annabel Lee[4] and another thing for Miss Emily Grierson to de-posit a strand of iron-gray hair on the pillow beside the rotted corpse of Homer Barron. Further, we do not expect to discover that a woman has murdered a man. The conventions of sexual politics have familiarized us with the image of Georgiana nobly accepting death at her husband's hand. To reverse this "natural" pattern inevitably produces the grotesque.

Faulkner, however, is not interested in invoking the kind of grotesque which is the consequence of reversing the clichés of sexism for the sake of a cheap thrill; that is left to writers like Mickey Spillane.[5] (Indeed, Spillane's ready willingness to capitalize on the shock value provided by the image of woman as killer in *I, the Jury* suggests, by contrast, how little such a sexist gambit is Faulkner's intent.) Rather, Faulkner invokes the grotesque in order to illuminate and de-fine the true nature of the conventions on which it depends. "A Rose for Emily" is a story not of a conflict between the South and the North or between the old order and the new; it is a story of the patriarchy North and South, new and old, and of the sexual conflict within it. As Faulkner himself has implied, it is a story of a woman victimized and betrayed by the system of sexual politics, who never-

Judith Fetterley is a professor of English at the State University of New York, Albany. She has published *The Resisting Reader: A Feminist Approach to American Fiction* (1978); *Provisions: A Reader From 19th-Century American Women* (1985); and *Alice Cary 1820–1871: Clovernook Sketches and Other Stories* (1987). The following essay is from *The Resisting Reader*. In the previous chapter Fetterley has discussed Hawthorne's "The Birthmark." She now moves on to Faulkner's "A Rose for Emily." If you have read neither story, see the first two endnotes. *The Resisting Reader: A Feminist Approach to American Fiction*, Bloomington/Indiana University Press, 1978. Reprinted with the permis-sion of Judith Fetterley.

theless has discovered, within the structures that victimize her, sources of power for herself. If "The Birthmark" is the story of how to murder your wife and get away with it, "A Rose for Emily" is the story of how to murder your gentleman caller and get away with it. Faulkner's story is an analysis of how men's attitudes toward women turn back upon themselves; it is a demonstration of the thesis that it is impossible to kill without creating the conditions for your own murder. "A Rose for Emily" is the story of a *lady* and her revenge for that grotesque identity.

"When Miss Emily Grierson died, our whole town went to her funeral." The public and communal nature of Emily's funeral, a festival that brings the town together, clarifying its social relationships and revitalizing its sense of the past, indicates her central role in Jefferson. Alive, Emily is town property and the subject of shared speculation; dead, she is town history and the subject of legend. It is her value as a symbol, however obscure and however ambivalent, for something that is of central significance to the identity of Jefferson and to the meaning of its history, that compels the narrator to assume a communal voice to tell her story. For Emily, like Georgiana, is a man-made object, a cultural artifact, and what she is reflects and defines the culture that has produced her.

The history the narrator relates to us reveals Jefferson's continuous emotional involvement with Emily. Indeed, though she shuts herself up in a house which she rarely leaves and which no one enters, her furious isolation is in direct proportion to the town's obsession with her. Like Georgiana, she is the object of incessant attention; her every act is immediately consumed by the town for gossip and seized on to justify their interference in her affairs. Her private life becomes a public document that the town folk feel free to interpret at will, and they are alternately curious, jealous, spiteful, pitying, partisan, proud, disapproving, admiring, and vindicated. Her funeral is not simply a communal ceremony; it is also the climax of their invasion of her private life and the logical extension of their voyeuristic attitude toward her. Despite the narrator's demurral, getting inside Emily's house is the all-consuming desire of the town's population, both male and female; while the men may wait a little longer, their motive is still prurient curiosity: "Already we knew that there was one room in that region above stairs which no one had seen in forty years, and which would have to be forced. They waited until Miss Emily was decently in the ground before they opened it."

In a context in which the overtones of violation and invasion are so palpable, the word "decently" has that ironic ring which gives the game away. When the men finally do break down the door, they find that Emily has satisfied their prurience with a vengeance and in doing so has created for them a mirror image of themselves. The true nature of Emily's relation to Jefferson is contained in the analogies between what those who break open that room see in it and what has brought them there to see it. The perverse, violent, and grotesque aspects of the sight of Homer Barron's rotted corpse in a room decked out for a bridal and now faded and covered in dust reflects back to them the perverseness of their own prurient interest in Emily, the violence implicit in their continued invasions of her life, and the grotesqueness of the symbolic artifact they have made of her—their monument, their idol, their lady. Thus, the figure that Jefferson places at the center of its legendary history does indeed contain the clue to the meaning of that history—a history which began long before Emily's funeral and long before Homer Barron's disappearance or appearance and long before Colonel Sartoris' fathering of edicts and remittances. It is recorded in that emblem which lies at the heart of the town's memory and at the heart of patriarchal culture: "We had long thought of them as a tableau, Miss Emily a slender figure in white in the background, her father a spraddled silhouette in the foreground, his back to her and clutching a horsewhip, the two of them framed by the back-flung front door."

The importance of Emily's father in shaping the quality of her life is insistent throughout the story. Even in her death the force of his presence is felt; above her dead body sits "the crayon face of her father musing profoundly," symbolic of the degree to which he has dominated and shadowed her life, "as if that quality of her father which had thwarted her woman's life so many times had been too virulent and too furious to die." The violence of this consuming relationship is made explicit in the imagery of the tableau. Although the violence is apparently directed outward—the upraised horsewhip against the would-be suitor—the real object of it is the woman-daughter, forced into the background and dominated by the phallic figure of the spraddled father whose back is turned on her and who prevents her from getting out at the same time that he prevents them from getting in. Like Georgiana's spatial confinement in "The Birthmark," Emily's is a metaphor for her psychic confinement: her identity is determined by the constructs of her father's mind, and she can no more escape from his creation of her as "a slender figure in white" than she can escape his house.

What is true for Emily in relation to her father is equally true for her in relation to Jefferson: her status as a lady is a cage from which she cannot escape. To them she is always *Miss* Emily; she is never referred to and never thought of as otherwise. In omitting her title from his, Faulkner emphasizes the point that the real violence done to Emily is in making her a "Miss"; the omission is one of his roses for her. Because she is *Miss* Emily *Grierson*, Emily's father dresses her in white, places her in the background, and drives away her suitors.

Because she is *Miss* Emily *Grierson*, the town invests her with that communal significance which makes her the object of their obsession and the subject of their incessant scrutiny. And because she is a lady, the town is able to impose a particular code of behavior on her ("But there were still others, older people, who said that even grief could not cause a real lady to forget *noblesse oblige*") and to see in her failure to live up to that code an excuse for interfering in her life. As a lady, Emily is venerated, but veneration results in the more telling emotions of envy and spite: "it was another link between the gross, teeming world and the high and mighty Griersons"; "People ... believed that the Griersons held themselves a little too high for what they really were." The violence implicit in the desire to see the monument fall and reveal itself for clay suggests the violence inherent in the original impulse to venerate.

The violence behind veneration is emphasized through another telling emblem in the story. Emily's position as an hereditary obligation upon the town dates from "that day in 1894 when Colonel Sartoris, the mayor—he who fathered the edict that no Negro woman should appear on the streets without an apron on—remitted her taxes, the dispensation dating from the death of her father on into perpetuity." The conjunction of these two actions in the same syntactic unit is crucial, for it insists on their essential similarity. It indicates that the impulse to exempt is analogous to the desire to restrict, and that what appears to be a kindness or an act of veneration is in fact an insult. Sartoris' remission of Emily's taxes is a public declaration of the fact that a lady is not considered to be, and hence not allowed or enabled to be, economically independent (consider, in this connection, Emily's lessons in china painting; they are a latter-day version of Sartoris' "charity" and a brilliant image of Emily's economic uselessness). His act is a public statement of the fact that a lady, if she is to survive, must have either husband or father, and that, because Emily has neither, the town must assume responsibility for her. The remission of taxes that defines Emily's status dates from the death of her father, and she is handed over from one patron to the next, the town instead of husband taking on the role of father. Indeed, the use of the word "fathered" in describing Sartoris' behavior as mayor underlines the fact that his chivalric attitude toward Emily is simply a subtler and more dishonest version of her father's horsewhip.

The narrator is the last of the patriarchs who take upon themselves the burden of defining Emily's life, and his violence toward her is the most subtle of all. His tone of incantatory reminiscence and nostalgic veneration seems free of the taint of horsewhip and edict. Yet a thoroughgoing contempt for the "ladies" who spy and pry and gossip out of their petty jealousy and curiosity is one of the clearest strands in the narrator's consciousness. Emily is exempted from the general indictment because she is a *real* lady—that is, eccentric, slightly crazy, obsolete, a "stubborn and coquettish decay," absurd but indulged; "dear, inescapable, impervious, tranquil, and perverse"; indeed, anything and everything but human.

Not only does "A Rose for Emily" expose the violence done to a woman by making her a lady; it also explores the particular form of power the victim gains from this position and can use on those who enact this violence. "A Rose for Emily" is concerned with the consequences of violence for both the violated and the violators. One of the most striking aspects of the story is the disparity between Miss Emily Grierson and the Emily to whom Faulkner gives his rose in ironic imitation of the chivalric behavior the story exposes. The form of Faulkner's title establishes a camaraderie between author and protagonist and signals that a distinction must be made between the story Faulkner is telling and the story the narrator is telling. This distinction is of major importance because it suggests, of course, that the narrator, looking through a patriarchal lens, does not see Emily at all but rather a figment of his own imagination created in conjunction with the cumulative imagination of the town. Like Ellison's invisible man,[6] nobody sees *Emily*. And because nobody sees *her*, she can literally get away with murder. Emily is characterized by her ability to understand and utilize the power that accrues to her from the fact that men do not see her but rather their concept of her: " 'I have no taxes in Jefferson. Colonel Sartoris explained it to me ... Tobe! ... show these gentlemen out.' " Relying on the conventional assumptions about ladies who are expected to be neither reasonable nor in touch with reality, Emily presents an impregnable front that vanquishes the men "horse and foot, just as she had vanquished their fathers thirty years before." In spite of their "modern" ideas, this new generation, when faced with Miss Emily, are as much bound by the code of gentlemanly behavior as their fathers were ("They rose when she entered"). This code gives Emily a power that renders the gentlemen unable to function in a situation in which a lady neither sits down herself nor asks them to. They are brought to a "stumbling halt" and can do nothing when confronted with her refusal to engage in rational discourse. Their only recourse in the face of such eccentricity is to engage in behavior unbecoming to gentlemen, and Emily can count on their continuing to see themselves as gentlemen and her as a lady and on their returning a verdict of helpless noninterference.

It is in relation to Emily's disposal of Homer Barron, however, that Faulkner demonstrates most clearly the power of conventional assumptions about the nature of ladies to blind the town to what is going on and to allow Emily to murder with impunity. When Emily buys the poison, it never occurs to anyone that she intends to use it on Homer, so strong is the presumption that ladies when jilted commit suicide, not murder. And when her house begins to smell, the women blame it on the eccentricity of having a man servant rather than a woman, "as if a man—any man— could keep a kitchen properly." And then they hint that her eccentricity may have shaded over into madness, "remembering how old lady Wyatt, her great aunt, had gone completely crazy at last." The presumption of madness, that preeminently female response to bereavement, can be used to explain away much in the behavior of ladies whose activities seem a bit odd.

But even more pointed is what happens when the men try not to explain but to do something about the smell: " 'Dammit, sir,' Judge Stevens said, 'will you accuse a lady to her face of smelling bad?' " But if a lady cannot be told that she smells, then the cause of the smell cannot be discovered and so her crime is "perfect." Clearly, the assumptions behind the Judge's outraged retort go beyond the myth that ladies are out of touch with reality. His outburst insists that it is the responsibility of gentlemen to make them so. Ladies must not be confronted with facts; they must be shielded from all that is unpleasant. Thus Colonel Sartoris remits Emily's taxes with a palpably absurd story, designed to protect her from an awareness of her poverty and her dependence on charity, and to protect him from having to confront her with it. And thus Judge Stevens will not confront Emily with the fact that her house stinks, though she is living in it and can hardly be unaware of the odor. Committed as they are to the myth that ladies and bad smells cannot coexist, these gentlemen insulate themselves from reality. And by defining a lady as a subhuman and hence sublegal entity, they have created a situation their laws can't touch. They have made it possible for Emily to be extra-legal: " 'Why, of course,' the druggist said, 'If that's what you want. But the law requires you to tell what you are going to use it for.' Miss Emily just stared at him, her head tilted back in order to look him eye for eye, until he looked away and went and got the arsenic and wrapped it up." And, finally, they have created a situation in which they become the criminals: "So the next night, after midnight, four men crossed Miss Emily's lawn and slunk about the house like burglars." Above them, "her upright torso motionless as that of an idol," sits Emily, observing them act out their charade of chivalry. As they leave, she confronts them with the reality they are trying to protect her from: she turns on the light so that they may see her watching them. One can only wonder at the fact, and regret, that she didn't call the sheriff and have them arrested for trespassing.

Not only is "A Rose for Emily" a supreme analysis of what men do to women by making them ladies; it is also an exposure of how this act in turn defines and recoils upon men. This is the significance of the dynamic that Faulkner establishes between Emily and Jefferson. And it is equally the point of the dynamic implied between the tableau of Emily and her father and the tableau which greets the men who break down the door of that room in the region above the stairs. When the would-be "suitors" finally get into her father's house, they discover the consequences of his oppression of her, for the violence contained in the rotted corpse of Homer Barron is the mirror image of the violence represented in the tableau, the back-flung front door flung back with a vengeance. Having been consumed by her father, Emily in turn feeds off Homer Barron, becoming, after his death, suspiciously fat. Or, to put it another way, it is as if, after her father's death, she has reversed his act of incorporating her by incorporating and becoming him, metamorphosed from the slender figure in white to the obese figure in black whose hair is "a vigorous iron-gray, like the hair of an active man." She has taken into herself the violence in him which thwarted her and has reenacted it upon Homer Barron.

That final encounter, however, is not simply an image of the reciprocity of violence. Its power of definition also derives from its grotesqueness, which makes finally explicit the grotesqueness that has been latent in the description of Emily throughout the story: "Her skeleton was small and spare; perhaps that was why what would have been merely plumpness in another was obesity in her. She looked bloated, like a body long submerged in motionless water, and of that pallid hue. Her eyes, lost in the fatty ridges of her face, looked like two small pieces of coal pressed into a lump of dough." The impact of this description depends on the contrast it establishes between Emily's reality as a fat, bloated figure in black and the conventional image of a lady—expectations that are fostered in the town by its emblematic memory of Emily as a slender figure in white and in us by the narrator's tone of romantic invocation and by the passage itself. Were she not expected to look so different, were her skeleton not small and spare, Emily would not be so grotesque. Thus, the focus is on the grotesqueness that results when stereotypes are imposed upon reality. And the implication of this focus is that the real grotesque is the stereotype itself. If Emily is both lady and grotesque, then the syllogism must be completed thus: the idea of a lady is grotesque. So Emily is metaphor and mirror for the town of Jefferson; and when, at the end, the town folk finally discover who and what she is, they have in fact encountered who and what they are.

Despite similarities of focus and vision, "A Rose for Emily" is more implicitly feminist than "The Birthmark." For one thing, Faulkner does not have Hawthorne's compulsive ambivalence; one is not invited to misread "A Rose for Emily" as one is invited to misread "The

Birthmark." Thus, the interpretation of "The Birthmark" that sees it as a story of misguided idealism, despite its massive oversights, nevertheless *works;* while the efforts to read "A Rose for Emily" as a parable of the relations between North and South, or as a conflict between an old order and a new, or as a story about the human relation to Time, don't work because the attempt to make Emily representative of such concepts stumbles over the fact that woman's condition is not the "human" condition. To understand Emily's experience requires a primary awareness of the fact that she is a woman.

But, more important, Faulkner provides us with an image of retaliation. Unlike Georgiana, Emily does not simply acquiesce; she prefers to murder rather than to die. In this respect she is a welcome change from the image of woman as willing victim that fills the pages of our literature, and whose other face is the ineffective fulminations of Dame Van Winkle. Nevertheless, Emily's action is still reaction. "A Rose for Emily" exposes the poverty of a situation in which turnabout is the only possibility and in which one's acts are neither self-generated nor self-determined but are simply a response to and a reflection of forces outside oneself. Though Emily may be proud, strong, and indomitable, her murder of Homer Barron is finally an indication of the severely limited nature of the power women can wrest from the system that oppresses them. Aylmer's murder of Georgiana is an indication of men's absolute power over women; it is an act performed in the complete security of his ability to legitimize it as a noble and human pursuit. Emily's act has no such context. It is possible only because it can be kept secret; and it can be kept secret only at the cost of exploiting her image as a lady. Furthermore, Aylmer murders Georgiana in order to get rid of her; Emily murders Homer Barron in order to have him.

Patriarchal culture is based to a considerable extent on the argument that men and women are made for each other and on the conviction that "masculinity" and "femininity" are the natural reflection of that divinely ordained complement. Yet, if one reads "The Birthmark" and "A Rose for Emily" as analyses of the consequences of a massive differentiation of everything according to sex, one sees that in reality a sexist culture is one in which men and women are not simply incompatible but murderously so. Aylmer murders Georgiana because he must at any cost get rid of woman; Emily murders Homer Barron because she must at any cost get a man. The two stories define the disparity between cultural myth and cultural reality, and they suggest that in this disparity is the ultimate grotesque.

NOTES

1 "A Rose for Emily" by William Faulkner (1897–1962) is set in the years 1865 to 1924. It is the story of Miss Emily Grierson, a remnant of the old, aristocratic, romantic South. In 1882, Emily's father, who had always kept suitors far away, dies. The following summer, Emily, now 30, meets Homer Barron, a construction foreman. He is brash and uncouth, a man of the new order. They are seen about town, causing gossip. Two female cousins arrive in Jefferson to persuade Emily to behave in keeping with her heritage. Homer leaves town to avoid the cousins and Emily buys a suit of men's clothes and a silver toilet set, as well as rat poison. The cousins leave, and Homer returns and then disappears. The townspeople assume that Homer has left town. He is never seen again. In 1925 Miss Emily dies and a group of townspeople invade her home. Her black servant, Tobe, leaves and is never seen again, and in an upstairs bedroom, locked up, the townspeople discover the desiccated remains of Homer Barron dressed in the suit. On the pillow beside him they discover a strand of iron-grey hair, evidence that Miss Emily had lain in the bed beside him long after his death.

2 In "The Birthmark" by Nathaniel Hawthorne (American, 1804–1864), Georgiana's beauty is marred, in her scientist husband Aylmer's eyes, only by a birthmark on her cheek. In his obsessive desire to make her into a perfect object, he attempts to eradicate the birthmark. He perfects a poison that succeeds in removing the blemish but in the process kills Georgiana.

3 The grotesque in art presents an object, usually the human figure, in an exaggerated and distorted way.

4 "Annabel Lee," a lyric ballad by the nineteenth-century writer Edgar Allan Poe (1809–1849), tells of a man's loss of a beautiful and beloved woman.

5 Mickey Spillane (1918–) is the author of detective stories based on violence and a "tough guy" ethic rather than on mystery. His works include *I, the Jury* (1947) and *The Big Kill* (1951).

6 In Ralph W. Ellison's *The Invisible Man* (1952) the hero, an idealistic and ambitious young black man, wishes to become the new, improved Booker T. Washington. He is kept stumbling through society, being used by everyone around him, unable to realize his ambitions. Self-fulfillment becomes possible only when he realizes how people have used him for their own ends. The theme of the book is that everyone is invisible.

VOCABULARY

fulminations—bursts of lightning and thunder; angry outbursts

necrophilia—a morbid attraction to corpses

noblesse oblige—the notion that with privilege comes responsibility

prurient—given to impure, lewd thoughts

spraddled—with legs spread wide

QUESTIONS

1. Academic articles on literature often begin with a brief summary of the interpretations of other critics. Why does Fetterley make critical commentary on the "grotesque" in "A Rose for Emily" the starting point for her feminist interpretation of this story?

2. Is Fetterley's essay organized inductively, deductively, or in some other way? What is its thesis?

3. Fetterley reads "A Rose for Emily" as an "implicitly feminist" story. What, in her view, makes the story "implicitly feminist"? Are you convinced by the evidence she presents? Why or why not?

4. Defining Emily Grierson as a "lady," according to Fetterley, does "violence" to both men and women. Can you explain her use of this term? Is it justified?

MY WOOD

E. M. Forster

Afew years ago I wrote a book which dealt in part with the difficulties of the English in India. Feeling that they would have had no difficulties in India themselves, the Americans read the book freely. The more they read it the better it made them feel, and a cheque to the author was the result. I bought a wood with the cheque. It is not a large wood—it contains scarcely any trees, and it is intersected, blast it, by a public footpath. Still, it is the first property that I have owned, so it is right that other people should participate in my shame, and should ask themselves, in accents that will vary in horror, this very important question: What is the effect of property on the character? Don't let's touch economics; the effect of private ownership upon the community as a whole is another question—a more important question, perhaps, but another one. Let's keep to psychology. If you own things, what's their effect on you? What's the effect on me of my wood?

In the first place, it makes me feel heavy. Property does have this effect. Property produces men of weight, and it was a man of weight who failed to get into the Kingdom of Heaven. He was not wicked, that unfortunate millionaire in the parable, he was only stout; he stuck out in front, not to mention behind, and as he wedged himself this way and that in the crystalline entrance and bruised his well-fed flanks, he saw beneath him a comparatively slim camel passing through the eye of a needle and being woven into the robe of God. The Gospels all through couple stoutness and slowness. They point out what is perfectly obvious, yet seldom realized: that if you have a lot of things you cannot move about a lot, that furniture requires dusting, dusters require servants, servants require insurance stamps,[1] and the whole tangle of them makes you think twice before you accept an invitation to dinner or go for a bathe in the Jordan.[2] Sometimes the Gospels proceed further and say with Tolstoy[3] that property is sinful; they approach the difficult ground of asceticism here, where I cannot follow them. But as to the immediate effects of property on people they just show straightforward logic. It produces men of weight. Men of weight cannot, by definition, move like the lightning from the East unto the West, and

The opening sentence of "My Wood" refers to the success of Edward Morgan Forster's most famous novel, *A Passage to India* (1924). Besides novels and short stories, Forster (1879–1970) also wrote *Aspects of the Novel* (1927), a work of literary criticism, biography, travel writing, and two collections of essays: *Abinger Harvest* (1936), from which "My Wood" is taken, and *Two Cheers for Democracy* (1951). Reprinted by permission of King's College, Cambridge and The Society of Authors as the literary representatives of the E. M. Forster estate.

the ascent of a fourteen-stone[4] bishop into a pulpit is thus the exact antithesis of the coming of the Son of Man. My wood makes me feel heavy.

In the second place, it makes me feel it ought to be larger.

The other day I heard a twig snap in it. I was annoyed at first, for I thought that someone was blackberrying, and depreciating the value of the undergrowth. On coming nearer, I saw it was not a man who had trodden on the twig and snapped it, but a bird, and I felt pleased. My bird. The bird was not equally pleased. Ignoring the relation between us, it took fright as soon as it saw the shape of my face, and flew straight over the boundary hedge into a field, the property of Mrs. Henessy, where it sat down with a loud squawk. It had become Mrs. Henessy's bird. Something seemed grossly amiss here, something that would not have occurred had the wood been larger. I could not afford to buy Mrs. Henessy out, I dared not murder her, and limitations of this sort beset me on every side. Ahab[5] did not want that vineyard—he only needed it to round off his property, preparatory to plotting a new curve—and all the land around my wood has become necessary to me in order to round off the wood. A boundary protects. But—poor little thing—the boundary ought in its turn to be protected. Noises on the edge of it. Children throw stones. A little more, and then a little more, until we reach the sea. Happy Canute![6] Happier Alexander![7] And after all, why should even the world be the limit of possession? A rocket containing a Union Jack, will, it is hoped, be shortly fired at the moon. Mars. Sirius. Beyond which ... But these immensities ended by saddening me. I could not suppose that my wood was the destined nucleus of universal dominion—it is so very small and contains no mineral wealth beyond the blackberries. Nor was I comforted when Mrs. Henessy's bird took alarm for the second time and flew clean away from us all, under the belief that it belonged to itself.

In the third place, property makes its owner feel that he ought to do something to it. Yet he isn't sure what. A restlessness comes over him, a vague sense that he has a personality to express—the same sense which, without any vagueness, leads the artist to an act of creation. Sometimes I think I will cut down such trees as remain in the wood, at other times I want to fill up the gaps between them with new trees. Both impulses are pretentious and empty. They are not honest movements towards money-making or beauty. They spring from a foolish desire to express myself and from an inability to enjoy what I have got. Creation, property, enjoyment form a sinister trinity in the human mind. Creation and enjoyment are both very very good, yet they are often unattainable without a material basis, and at such moments property pushes itself in as a substitute, saying, 'Accept me instead—I'm good enough for all three.' It is not enough. It is, as Shakespeare said of lust, 'The expense of spirit in a waste of shame': it is 'Before, a joy proposed; behind, a dream.'[8] Yet we don't know how to shun it. It is forced on us by our economic system as the alternative to starvation. It is also forced on us by an internal defect in the soul, by the feeling that in property may lie the germs of self-development and of exquisite or heroic deeds. Our life on earth is, and ought to be, material and carnal.[9] But we have not yet learned to manage our materialism and carnality properly; they are still entangled with the desire for ownership, where (in the words of Dante) 'Possession is one with loss.'

And this brings us to our fourth and final point: the blackberries.

Blackberries are not plentiful in this meagre grove, but they are easily seen from the public footpath which traverses it, and all too easily gathered. Foxgloves, too—people will pull up the foxgloves, and ladies of an educational tendency even grub for toadstools to show them on the Monday in class. Other ladies, less educated, roll down the bracken in the arms of their gentlemen friends. There is paper, there are tins. Pray, does my wood belong to me or doesn't it? And, if it does, should I not own it best by allowing no one else to walk there? There is a wood near Lyme Regis,[10] also cursed by a public footpath, where the owner has not hesitated on this point. He has built high stone walls each side of the path, and has spanned it by bridges, so that the public circulate like termites while he gorges on the blackberries unseen. He really does own his wood, this able chap. Dives[11] in Hell did pretty well, but the gulf dividing him from Lazarus could be traversed by vision, and nothing traverses it here. And perhaps I shall come to this in time. I shall wall in and fence out until I really taste the sweets of property. Enormously stout, endlessly avaricious, pseudo-creative, intensely selfish, I shall weave upon my forehead the quadruple crown of possession until those nasty Bolshies[12] come and take it off again and thrust me aside into the outer darkness.

NOTES

[1] Insurance Stamps: required in the U.K. to validate health and disability insurance benefits.

[2] The Jordan River flows between the Sea of Galilee and the Dead Sea.

[3] A Russian writer, author of *War and Peace* (1869) and *Anna Karenina* (1877), Leo Tolstoy (1828–1910) believed that possession of private property was an evil and practised severe asceticism.

[4] A stone equals fourteen pounds.

[5] Ahab was the seventh king of Israel from 874 to 853 B.C. His wife, Jezebel, coveting a fine vineyard adjoining the palace grounds, arranged that its owner, Naboth, be convicted of blasphemy and executed. Ahab then became legal owner of the vineyard.

[6] Canute, or C'nut, was an ambitious conqueror of the 11th century who was simultaneously King of England (1016–1035), Denmark (1018–1035), and Norway (1028–1035).

7 Alexander the Great, King of Macedonia, sought to conquer the entire world to satisfy his desire for power and glory.

8 The phrases are from Shakespeare's Sonnet 129. The single quotation marks are British usage.

9 In Forster's day the word *carnal* referred to the body as the seat of all appetites. Also, archaically, *carnal* was used as the opposite of *spiritual*.

10 Lyme Regis. A coastal town in England chartered as a royal borough in 1284 that eventually became known, in Forster's time, as a beach resort of some notoriety.

11 Dives and Lazarus figure in a biblical story. Dives, a rich man, takes no notice of Lazarus, a beggar. Dives ends up in Hades and Lazarus in heaven (Luke 16:19–31).

12 Bolshies. The Bolsheviks were the majority group of the Russian Social Democratic Party. They favoured revolutionary tactics to achieve socialism and seized power during the Russian Revolution to set up a workers' state.

QUESTIONS

1. In the first paragraph of "My Wood," Forster announces that his essay is concerned with the effects of owning something on a person's character. What does he mean by "character"? Does Forster confine his essay to the effects of ownership on the individual?

2. Does Forster list these effects in an order of increasing importance? in some other order? Explain.

3. Forster introduces the first three effects with a topic sentence beginning "It (or property) makes me (or its owner) feel ...." Why does he abandon this formula when he introduces the fourth effect?

4. Forster's novel *A Passage to India* (1924) is about the corrupting effects of property and imperialism on the British in India. Thus it is ironic that the proceeds of this novel allowed Forster himself to buy property. Can you find other instances of irony, or an ironic tone, in the essay? Do you think irony, rather than direct statement, makes this essay more persuasive? Explain.

5. Throughout this essay, Forster makes a number of allusions to figures in religion, history, and literature. Why does Forster include these allusions? How do they affect you as a reader?

6. "My Wood" was first published in England in 1936. Does this context illuminate any of the attitudes and concerns in this essay?

SUGGESTION FOR WRITING

Using "My Wood" as a model, write an essay explaining how owning something (a house, a car, a CD collection) corrupted your character. Organize your essay in the same way Forster does, with an introduction and three or four middle paragraphs. Deal with one effect in each paragraph. Like Forster, you can add a separate conclusion. Include allusions if you think they will strengthen your rapport with your reader.

ACHIEVING VIRTUE THROUGH STINGINESS

Charles Gordon

A s Canada's neoconservatives dig in, and even flourish, it is not surprising that they would seek to develop a philosophy of sorts, something with a bit more sophistication than the Ayn Randisms[1] they learned at prep school.

The impulse behind philosophical neoconservatism, clearly, is to make neo-cons feel justified in keeping their money from being taxed. Government action is what causes money to be taxed, so the neoconservatives must attack government action; the philosophy must be, in effect, a defence of inaction, which is not exactly a concept to set the pulse racing.

In the absence of a lofty-sounding justification for keeping their money, neo-cons are vigorously attacking in the media the values and intentions of those who would spend it. You might have noticed that neo-cons, whatever their other attributes, are not likely to be drawn from among the less fortunate areas of society. In the old days, when liberals and worse were running the country and dominating its media, people who had money were made to feel guilty for that. Now, neoconservatives own the media, and every day we see attempts to make that guilt go away.

Remember the notion that homeless people actually prefer to be homeless? What a great excuse not to spend effort and money helping them. More recently, with the Liberal government gearing up for an attack on child poverty, there are attempts on the right to redraw the poverty line, so that fewer people are under it. If Statistics Canada[2] sets the urban poverty line at $32,000 and you, the neo-con economist, set it at $18,000 that's quite a few of your tax dollars that don't have to be spent helping the poor.

"If we are asking how many children are likely to be hungry or ill-housed, as opposed to lacking some social amenities, then we don't have nearly anything like the official rate," says one report published by the neo-con idea bank, the Fraser Institute.[3]

Charles Gordon (1940–) was born in New York and attended schools in the United States, Japan, Egypt, Italy, and Lebanon before enrolling at Queen's University. A columnist and editor for the *Brandon Sun* and, since 1974, for the *Ottawa Citizen*, Gordon is also a regular contributor to *Maclean's*. He has published four books. The most recent, *The Canada Trip* (1997), is an account of a cross-Canada expedition. "Achieving Virtue Through Stinginess" is reprinted with permission of Maclean's Magazine.

You recognize the key words there. "Some social amenities"—a lot of people officially classified as living in poverty are really just lacking some social amenities. Visions of social amenities dance in neo-con heads: color TVs, golf memberships, VCRs, ballet lessons. Should we call people poor, they ask, just because they can't afford golf memberships? Should we spend our tax dollars to help them? A good philosophy can make a person feel positively virtuous about refusing to help at all.

This philosophy of stinginess is most dramatically illustrated in the recent attacks on the Chrétien government's attempt to mount a mission in aid of the hundreds of thousands of refugees in Zaïre.[4] When many of the refugees returned to Rwanda before Canadian troops could be of any assistance to them, commentators, without even pausing to be happy for a peaceful resolution of the situation, gleefully declared the mission a failure. More significant, we have begun to see attacks on aid itself, with the intriguing suggestion that the blame for disease, starvation and genocide[5] should be attached to those, particularly aid organizations, who are trying to heal, feed and protect.

Following upon that logic, of course, the less we give to help the unfortunate, the greater contribution we make. What a comforting philosophy for those who don't want to help. Not only do you get to keep your dollars; you get to feel superior for doing so. The neo-con dream. In technicolor.

Those who espouse such views like to think of themselves as realistic and hard-headed, but a stunning naïveté accompanies them. Witness the horror expressed by government critics that "political motives" were behind the Chrétien rescue mission. Yes. Political motives are what politicians have. And what is behind those political motives? The desire to be elected. And how do you get elected, or re-elected? By doing things people like.

Chrétien, in his Zaïrean initiative, stands accused of trying to do something that people liked. That is the way the political system works in democracy. Politicians try to do things people will like. Is this cynical on behalf of the politicians? Well, for 129 years in this country it has got the job done. Recently, politicians have tried to do things bankers like, and economists like, and the Fraser Institute likes. We will see how that works.

It may not. In fact, it can be argued that Liberal governments always do best when an election is near and the thought of trying to do something popular intrudes. Without a looming election to concentrate the mind, they become muddled and blunder into things like trying to cut the deficit.

That is only half-flippant. In the case at hand, deficit-obsessed governments all over the developed world have been cutting back on development assistance to less fortunate countries, though such assistance could help forestall the Rwandas of the future. In the meantime, the applause of the neo-con community goes out to the aid-cutters and only scorn greets the aid-givers.

That doesn't sound like us, does it?

In Chrétien's case, he acted hastily, in the face of what appeared to be an emergency. Certainly, no one at the time was disputing the fact that it was an emergency. He wanted to do something—anything—and many people applauded him for it. It was a human impulse. When the thing derailed, people began adding up the costs, to set a dollar figure on the amount "wasted." This too is part of the neo-con approach—to measure everything in terms of what it costs. As the years go on, these people can take more and more comfort in being able to count the money we are not spending. That spirit is not what made this country great.

NOTES

[1] Ayn Randisms: ideas derived from Ayn Rand (1905–1982), a Russian-born American novelist whose work advocates the philosophy of objectivism, asserting that all achievement results from individual effort and ability, that *laissez-faire* conservatism enables the flourishing of talent, and that selfishness is a virtue. Her texts include *The Fountainhead* (1943) and *Atlas Shrugged* (1957).

[2] Statistics Canada is a federal government-linked organization that produces the official figures for the census, unemployment statistics, and so on.

[3] The Fraser Institute is a conservative Canadian economic think tank.

[4] Chrétien's attempts to help in Zaïre refers to attempts to assist in the repatriation of Rwandan refugees in November 1996.

[5] Genocide is the systematic murder of a group, normally identified by race, ethnicity or religion, with the intent of eradication.

QUESTIONS

1. What standard(s) of evaluation does Gordon use as the basis of his attack on neo-conservative philosophy?

2. Does Gordon present any clear alternative to neo-conservative philosophy?

3. What kinds of arguments and evidence does Gordon include to support his views? Would they be especially convincing to a Canadian audience?

4. How would you describe the tone of this essay? Be specific about how Gordon conveys his attitude to himself, his readers, and his subject.

SUGGESTION FOR WRITING

Is it sometimes wise to be stingy with your time, money, energy, emotions? Write an essay in which you try to persuade your reader that stinginess in one of these areas is or is not a virtue.

TWO WOMEN OF SCIENCE:

CAROL STEINER AND SHARLENE GEORGE

Vivian Gornick

Carol Steiner, a forty-year-old geneticist at a medical school outside of Philadelphia, comes up with a fine metaphor for how to make a working proposition of scientific mystery. "Imagine," she says, "that you have a jigsaw puzzle with no picture printed on it. All you have is pieces you haven't a clue how to make sense of. The pieces are your separate scientific observations. Here's an example of how you might try to get a handle on the puzzle:

"We have a microorganism with a secretory structure on one end. We know this structure is always on the same place in the cell, and that the position of this structure is inherited. The question that we want to answer is: how can inherited information be translated into positional information? Why in that one place, and no place else? Is the genetic code involved, and if so, how? The answer will tell us how the genes work in concert with the rest of the cell to put things where they belong.

Vivian Gornick wrote for *The Village Voice* (New York City) for ten years. Many of those essays are collected in *Essays In Feminism* (1978). She taught English at Hunter College of the City University of New York, and at the State University of New York. She is also the author of *In Search of Ali Mahmoud: An American Woman in Egypt* (1973) and *Fierce Attachments: A Memoir* (1988). The following is an extract from *Women in Science: Portraits from a World in Transition* (1983). The extract was first reprinted in Fred D. White's *Science and the Human Spirit* (1989).

"In order to gather pieces of the jigsaw puzzle (that is, pieces of information), we poke at the cell. We change it a little. Now, there are two ways to change the cell. One way is to mutate away the structure and then hope to find out what has changed biochemically inside this cell so that this structure is no longer made. The other way is to make mutations which affect known events occurring in the cell, defining these alterations precisely, both genetically and biochemically, and then ask how these alterations affect the formation of the structure. In my kind of genetics we do the latter.

"A specific mutation that altered the membrane structure of the cell was found to turn off the synthesis of the secretory structure. This was a piece of the jigsaw puzzle.

But just one piece. Because we hadn't a clue as to how this *had* happened or *could* happen. Then we got another piece of the jigsaw. It was found that shutting off replication of the chromosome (DNA synthesis) also shut off the formation of the structure. Then we found that mutants which shut off membrane synthesis in fact also shut off DNA synthesis, and two pieces of the puzzle were put together to form a working hypothesis: the structure synthesis of the secretory structure was shut off by mutants in membrane synthesis *because* these mutants in membrane synthesis *first* shut off DNA synthesis. This hypothesis suggests many further questions that will lead to experiments whose results will print pictures on the pieces of the jigsaw puzzle. Not put the puzzle together, mind you. But help us think about what the picture will ultimately look like."

The realized picture on Carol Steiner's jigsaw puzzle is the map of gene expression laid out clearly with all roads, pathways, connecting signal points, and railway junctions marked out so that any tourist can find his or her way in this beautiful country which is confusing only when one is wandering about in ignorance—as we all are now—with a highly incomplete map.

Steiner is a scientist for whom that flash of scientific wholeness—which came to her through genetics—is recalled regularly. When she speaks of the position of the secretory structures on the cell ("The question we want to answer is why in that one place, and no place else") her speech is repeatedly animated by the sentence "This is a question *fundamental* to developmental genetics." The single piece of information about the position of the secretory structure is what Steiner concentrates on in her daily working life, but worrying it, obsessing over it, learning everything there is to know about it, figuring out what it *really* means inevitably puts the glow back in her mind, makes her remember why she does science.

Another scientist with a strong sense of the relation between developmental genetics, moments of discovery, and the daily work in the lab is Sharlene George, a thirty-five-year-old geneticist (colleague and collaborator of Carol Steiner). With Sharlene one begins to see exactly how a scientist lives with a problem for months and years at a time.

Sharlene George works with Tetrahymena because it is an organism whose cells resemble those of humans more than do the cells of bacteria (a Tetrahymena cell, unlike a bacterial cell, has membranes, structures within the cell, lateral chromosomes). George's genetic interest became the regulatory function of the cell's outer membrane. The question she asked as a graduate student was: How does the cell elaborate and control its membrane?

An experimental approach important to biological research—and the one Sharlene George adopted—is the creation and study of mutations. Thousands of mutants are artificially bred in laboratories and studied by scientists who try to see exactly where and how they differ, and deduce what is happening biologically as a result of the departure from the normal. A cell biologist will commonly take a small "known" in the cell, mutate it, and see what can be deduced about the whole from this one specific.

This was Sharlene George's small known: The membrane is composed of an elaborate "sheet" of lipids and proteins that hang together not out of electrical impulses but out of a kind of affinity and an indissolubleness (beads that don't dissolve out). The question: How does the cell make this complex sheet of membranes? That is, how many genes in the organism have the information for telling the cell to make the different components of the membrane? How many genes encode for a particular function? How many genes regulate that function? How is regulation carried out?

It takes years for a scientist to even begin to answer such a question. Hundreds, literally hundreds of experiments are made by first growing large laboratory cultures of cells, then adding to these cells a mutagenic compound that produces hundreds of random mutations, then screening repeatedly for the mutation that will yield up useful results. After which begins the real work: observing keenly, intently, endlessly the results of these mutation experiments to make both large and small sense of them. What's alike here? What's different? How does this square with the last six papers written on this subject? Where does it fit into the theoretical picture? Does this *change* the theoretical picture?

The work is both tedious and imaginative. One must have the patience to perform the experiments meticulously (if the experiments are not absolutely clean and precise they are useless; above all, a scientist's experiments must be such that they can be replicated). Then one must do many, many, many experiments, over and over and over again, so that a legitimate data base is accumulated. Then one must sit down with the data and think hard about it, sifting through one's mind all the literature, all the conversations, all the odd thoughts one has read and had on the subject.

Sharlene George's Ph.D. dissertation established that many genes controlled the structure of the fatty acids of the membranes. This took three years of work, years in which she designed, executed, and analyzed hundreds of cell mutation experiments in the laboratory. Membrane biogenesis remained her subject. Today she is a highly granted principal investigator running a laboratory filled with technicians, graduate students, and postdoctoral fellows. On the shelf above her desk are five dissertation theses by graduate students who have worked in her laboratory, each one advancing the question, adding information to the large picture of how cell regulation of the membrane works.

Slowly, as the years have gone on, an overriding interest developed in this lab. There were four protein components which appeared to be regulated in a common manner. The people in Sharlene George's lab wanted to know: How does the cell control the relative proportions of these four components?

Hundreds of experiments with mutants have been made here over the last few years by changing the DNA which gives altered enzymes to make one or another of these compounds. The genetic structure of each of the mutants was studied and its biochemistry analyzed. A great deal of information was amassed, many speculations filled many notebooks, many conversations went on well into the night. Nothing really jelled.

"I was always thinking about the problem," says Sharlene. "When I was doing something, nothing, anything. Shopping at the supermarket, talking with my friends, cooking dinner. This question of the proportions of the components was always there, waiting for me. It's as though circuits are forged in the brain after years of work. These thoughts become an accompaniment to the day's activity. They're a comfort when I'm down, a goad when I'm lazy, a prod and a friend.

"It came to me on a Friday night in the shower, when I was getting ready to go out. I suddenly realized that a major factor in controlling the proportions of these components was the cell's response to a single precursor. I saw that the response was mediated through the membrane *itself*. The precursor caused an alteration in the activity of an enzyme in the membrane, and this alteration was transmitted to the cytoplasm and turned off the gene responsible for synthesis of the precursor.

"I ran out of the shower dripping wet and immediately put my conclusions on paper. They really *were* synthesizing! Suddenly I could account for so much that had remained puzzling. I was able to make a table of correspondences that explained a dozen different activities in the membrane and accounted better than anything else for the regulation that had been observed. It was a eureka moment.

"I got so excited I began to tell my husband about it. But I really needed to talk to another scientist. I had to call Carol and tell her. Five years of work, and it had come out so beautifully! It was one of those times you think, Jesus, I've put a tiny piece of the creation in place. I was *flying*."

Carol Steiner confirms the memory of that night. "Do you realize what she had done? She had shown that changing the consistency of the membrane affected what happened inside the cell. This revealed that there's a conversation going on between the membrane on the *outside* of the cell and the genetic machinery *inside* the cell. It's a fundamental observation on one of the ways in which the cell controls its own life processes. It was a fine piece of work, the kind of work that reminds you of what it's all about, and keeps you going for *another* five years."

"But you've got to love it all," Sharlene sighs. "The rote work in the lab, the drudgery, the disappointments, the niggling difficulties that can make you jump out of your skin with impatience. Some days you come in, nothing goes right. The petri dishes aren't clean, the water is contaminated, nothing's growing, the equipment isn't working, the results aren't coming up clean. Everything takes forever. Weeks, months. *Forever.* You gotta love it, anyway. Or else you can't get to the moment that makes it all worthwhile."

QUESTIONS

1. "Two Women. . . " is structured as a description of one scientist's work and then of another's. Do you think this block method of organizing a comparison is effective in this essay? Would there be any advantages in organizing this comparison point-by-point?

2. Steiner compares scientific investigation to both a map and a jigsaw puzzle (where you have some of the pieces but no picture to follow). What is the purpose of these analogies? Do you think analogies are useful in descriptions of scientific work?

3. What is Gornick's purpose in writing this essay? Consider the original audience for this essay in your response to this question.

4. What is Gornick's thesis? Why does she imply her thesis rather than stating it directly?

SUGGESTIONS FOR WRITING

1. In "Two Women ..." Gornick says that both Steiner and George have a "strong sense of the relation between developmental genetics, moments of discovery, and the daily work in the lab ...." Suppose you were writing an essay comparing the two scientists and their work. Make an outline for this essay, indicating the categories you would use for comparison. Then work out a thesis for this essay.

2. An analogy can be an effective method to develop an explanation, especially when you explain something unfamiliar by comparing it with something familiar. (An embolism is like a dam in a stream.) Write a paragraph explaining a concept, a condition, or a process through an analogy. Begin with a simile: X is like . . . .

A CERTAIN HUNGER:

THE BODY LANGUAGE OF ANOREXIA

Maggie Helwig

Consider that it is now normal for North American women to have eating disorders. Consider that anorexia—deliberate starvation—and bulimia—self-induced vomiting—and obsessive patterns for weight-controlling exercise are now the ordinary thing for young women, and are spreading at a frightening rate to older women, to men, to ethnic groups and social classes that were once "immune." Consider that some surveys suggest that eighty percent of the women on an average university campus have borderline-to-severe eating disorders; that it is almost impossible to get treatment unless the problem is life-threatening; that, in fact, if it is not life-threatening it is not considered a problem at all. I once sat in a seminar on nutritional aspects of anorexia, and ended up listening to people tell me how to keep my weight down. All this is happening in one of the richest countries in the world, a society devoted to consumption. Amazing as it may seem, we have normalized anorexia and bulimia, even turned them into an industry.

We've also trivialized them; made them into nothing more than an exaggerated conformity with basically acceptable standards of behaviour. Everyone wants to be thin and pretty, after all. Some people take it a little too far; you have to get them back on the right track, but it's all a question of knowing just how far is proper.

The consumer society has gone so far we can even buy into hunger.

But that is not what it's about. You do not stuff yourself with food and force yourself to vomit just because of fashion magazines. You do not reduce yourself to the condition of a skeleton in order to be attractive. This is not just a problem of proportion. This is the nightmare of consumerism acted out in women's bodies.

This is what we are saying as we starve: it is not all right. It is not all right. It is not all right.

Maggie Helwig is a writer and political activist living in Toronto. She was born in London, England, in 1961 and was raised in Kingston, Ontario. She has published six books of poetry including *Walking Through Fire* (1981); *Eden Poems* (1987); and *Talking Prophet Blues* (1989). With her father, the author David Helwig, she co-edits the series *Best Canadian Stories* and the companion series, *Coming Attractions*, which features new writers previously published only in small or private presses. "A Certain Hunger: The Body Language of Anorexia" was published in *This Magazine*, Vol. 22, No. 7, February 1989. Reprinted by permission of Maggie Helwig.

There've always been strange or disordered patterns of eating, associated mainly with religious extremism or psychological problems (which some, not myself, would say were the same thing). But the complex of ideas, fears, angers and actions that make up contemporary anorexia and bulimia seems to be of fairly recent origin. Anorexia did not exist as a recognized pattern until the sixties, and bulimia not until later than that—and at first they were deeply shocking. The idea that privileged young women (the first group to be affected) were voluntarily starving themselves, sometimes to death, or regularly sticking their fingers down their throats to make themselves throw up, shook the culture badly. It was a fad, in a sense, the illness of the month, but it was also a scandal, and a source of something like horror.

Before this, though, before anorexia had a widely recognized name, one of the first women to succumb to this had made her own scandalous stand, and left a body of writing that still has a lot to say about the real meaning of voluntary hunger.

Simone Weil[1] was a brilliant, disturbed, wildly wrong-headed and astonishingly perceptive young French-woman who died from the complications of self-starvation in America during World War II, at the age of thirty-four. She never, of course, wrote directly about her refusal to eat—typically for any anorexic, she insisted she ate perfectly adequate amounts. But throughout her philosophical and theological writing (almost all of it fragments and essays collected after her death), she examines and uses the symbolism of hunger, eating and food.

Food occupied, in fact, a rather important and valued position in her philosophy—she once referred to food as "the irrefutable proof of the reality of the universe," and at another time said that the foods served at Easter and Christmas, the turkey and *marron glacés*,[2] were "the true meaning of the feast"; although she could also take the more conventional puritan position that desire for food is a "base motive." She spoke often of eating God (acceptable enough in a Christian context) and of being eaten by God (considerably less so). The great tragedy of our lives, she said, is that we cannot really eat God; and also "it may be that vice, depravity and crime are almost always ... attempts to eat beauty."

But it is her use of the symbolism of hunger that explains her death. "We have to go down into ourselves to the abode of the desire which is not imaginary. Hunger: we imagine kinds of food, but the hunger itself is real: we have to fasten onto the hunger."

Hunger, then, was a search for reality, for the irreducible need that lies beyond all imaginary satisfactions. Weil was deeply perturbed by the "materialism" of her culture; though she probably could not have begun to imagine the number of imaginary and illusory "satisfactions" now available. Simply, she wanted truth. She wanted to reduce herself to the point where she would *know* what needs, and what foods, were real and true.

Similarly, though deeply drawn to the Catholic faith, she refused to be baptized and to take Communion (to, in fact, eat God). "I cannot help wondering whether in these days when so large a proportion of humanity is sunk in materialism, God does not want there to be some men and women who have given themselves to him and to Christ and who yet remain outside the Church." For the sake of honesty, of truth, she maintained her hunger.

Weil, a mystic and a political activist simultaneously until the end of her short life—she was one of the first French intellectuals to join the Communist party and one of the first to leave, fought in the Spanish civil war and worked in auto factories—could not bear to have life be less than a total spiritual and political statement. And her statement of protest, of dissatisfaction, her statement of hunger, finally destroyed her.

The term anorexia nervosa was coined in the nineteenth century, but it was not until sometime in the sixties that significant—and constantly increasing—numbers of well-off young women began dying of starvation, and not until the early seventies that it became public knowledge.

It is the nature of our times that the explanations proffered were psychological and individualistic; yet, even so, it was understood as being, on some level, an act of protest. And of course symbolically, it could hardly be other—it was, simply, a hunger strike. The most common interpretation, at that point, was that it was a sort of adolescent rebellion against parental control, an attempt, particularly, to escape from an over-controlling mother. It was a fairly acceptable paradigm for the period, although many mothers were justifiably disturbed; sometimes deeply and unnecessarily hurt. The theory still has some currency, and is not entirely devoid of truth.

But can it be an accident that this happened almost precisely to coincide with the growth of the consumer society, a world based on a level of material consumption that, by the end of the sixties, had become very nearly uncontrollable? Or with the strange, underground guilt that has made "conspicuous consumption" a matter of consuming vast amounts and *hiding it*, of million-dollar minimalism? With the development of what is possibly the most emotionally depleted society in history, where the only "satisfactions" seem to be the imaginary ones, the material buy-off?

To be skeletally, horribly thin makes one strong statement. It says, I am hungry. What I have been given is not sufficient, not real, not true, not acceptable. I am starving. To reject food, whether by refusing it or by vomiting it back, says simply, I will not consume. I will not participate. This is not real.

Hunger is the central nightmare image of our society. Of all the icons of horror the last few generations have offered us, we have chosen, above all, pictures of hunger—the emaciated prisoners of Auschwitz and Belsen, Ethiopian children with bloated bellies and stick-figure limbs. We carry in our heads these nightmares of the extreme edge of hunger.

And while we may not admit to guilt about our level of consumption in general, we admit freely to guilt about eating, easily equate food with "sin." We cannot accept hunger of our own, cannot afford to consider it.

It is, traditionally, women who carry our nightmares. It was women who became possessed by the Devil, women who suffered from "hysterical disorders," women who, in all popular culture, are the targets of the "monster." One of the roles women are cast in is that of those who act out the subconscious fears of their society. And it is women above all, in this time, who carry our hunger.

It is the starving women who embody the extremity of hunger that terrifies and fascinates us, and who insist that they are not hungry. It is the women sticking their fingers down their throats who act out the equation of food and sin, who deny hunger and yet embody endless, unfulfilled appetite. It is these women who live through every implication of our consumption and our hunger, our guilt and ambiguity and our awful need for something real to fill us.

We have too much; and it is poison.

It was first—in fact, almost exclusively—feminist writers who began to explore the symbolic language of anorexia and bulimia; Sheila MacLeod (*The Art of Starvation*),[3] Susie Orbach (*Hunger Strike*),[4] and others. However, as their work began to appear, a new presentation of eating disorders was entering the general consciousness, one that would no longer permit them to be understood as protest at *any* level.

For, as eating disorders became increasingly widespread, they also became increasingly trivialized, incorporated into a framework already "understood" all too well. Feminist writers had, early on, noted that anorexia had to be linked with the increasing thinness of models and other glamour icons, as part of a larger cultural trend. This is true enough as a starting point, for the symbolic struggle being waged in women's bodies happens on many levels, and is not limited to pathology cases. Unfortunately, this single starting point was seized on by "women's magazines" and popularizing accounts in general. Anorexia was now understandable, almost safe—really, it was just fashion gone out of control. Why, these women were *accepting* the culture, they just needed a sense of proportion. What a relief.

Now it could be condoned. Now it could, in fact, become the basis for an industry; could be incorporated neatly into consumer society.

According to Jane Fonda, the solution to bulimia is to remain equally unhealthily thin by buying the twenty-minute workout and becoming an obsessive fitness follower (at least for those who can afford it). The diet clinic industry, the Nutrisystem package, the aerobics boom. An advertising industry that plays equally off desire and guilt, for they now reinforce each other. Thousands upon thousands of starving, tormented women, not "sick" enough to be taken seriously, not really troubled at all.

One does not reduce oneself to the condition of a skeleton in order to be fashionable. One does not binge and vomit daily as an acceptable means of weight control. One does not even approach or imagine or dream of these things if one is not in some sort of trouble. If it were as simple as fashion, surely we would not be so ashamed to speak of these things, we would not feel that either way, whether we eat or do not eat, we are doing something wrong.

I was anorexic for eight years. I nearly died. It was certainly no help to me to be told I was taking fashion too far—I knew perfectly well that had nothing to do with it. It did not help much to be told I was trying to escape from my mother, since I lived away from home and was in only occasional contact with my family; it did not help much to be approached on an individualistic, psychological level. In fact, the first person I was able to go to for help was a charismatic Catholic, who at least understood that I was speaking in symbols of spiritual hunger.

I knew that I had something to say, that things were not all right, that I had to make that concretely, physically obvious. I did not hate or look down on my body—I spoke through it and with it.

Women are taught to take guilt, concern, problems, onto themselves personally; and especially onto their bodies. But we are trying to talk about something that is only partly personal. Until we find new ways of saying it and find the courage to talk to the world about the world, we will speak destruction to ourselves.

We must come to know what we are saying—and say it.

NOTES

[1] Simone Weil (1909–1943). Weil was a philosopher, teacher of philosophy, student of classical and modern history, science and literature. She was a member of the French Resistance in London in 1943. She died of tuberculosis and complications due to malnutrition. Her life was characterized by a thorough-minded dedication to the principles in which she believed.

[2] *Marron glacés* are preserved and glazed chestnuts.

[3] Sheila MacLeod, *The Art of Starvation: A Story of Anorexia and Survival* (1982).

[4] Susie Orbach, *Hunger Strike: The Anorectic's Struggle as a Metaphor for Our Age* (1986). Susie Orbach is a practising psychotherapist who co-founded the Women's Therapy Centre in London, England, in 1976 and the Women's Therapy Centre Institute in New York in 1981.

She is also the author of *Fat Is a Feminist Issue*, and, with Louise Eichenbaum, of *Understanding Women: A Feminist Psychoanalytic Approach* (1983), and *Between Women: Love, Envy, and Competition in Women's Friendships* (1988).

QUESTIONS

1. What, according to Helwig, is the most currently popular explanation for anorexia and bulimia? What are her reasons for rejecting this explanation?

2. Does Helwig provide convincing evidence for her explanation of anorexia and bulimia as manifestations of spiritual hunger? Do you agree with her thesis? Why or why not?

3. Helwig argues that women act out through their bodies "the subconscious fears of their society." What links does she see between voluntary starvation and our society? In what ways is anorexia a kind of body language?

4. "A Certain Hunger" does not seem to be organized as a systematic argument, with each point supported with specific evidence. Does this lack of systematic argument and evidence weaken the essay, or is Helwig using some alternative means of argumentation?

5. Examine the pronoun shifts from "we" to "you" to "one" to "I." Are these shifts justified? helpful?

SUGGESTION FOR WRITING

Write an essay comparing Helwig's ideas on voluntary starvation with Laura Robinson's in "Starving for the Gold." What common ground do they share? How do their essays differ in form and content? Can you relate any of the differences to the audiences for whom they were written?

SUGGESTION FOR RESEARCH

Do some research on Simone Weil so that you can reach your own conclusions about her life and death. Was she, as Helwig suggests, "wildly wrong-headed"? You might begin with the entry on Weil in the *Encyclopaedia Britannica*, where the first two facts suggest that she did not fight in the Spanish Civil War and that she did not die in the United States. Check the entries under Biographical Dictionaries and Bibliographies in our Annotated Survey of Reference Sources for more sources of information.

THE VOYAGERS

Linda Hogan

I remember one night, lying on the moist spring earth beside my mother. The fire of stars stretched away from us, and the mysterious darkness traveled without limit beyond where we lay on the turning earth. I could smell the damp new grass that night, but I could not touch or hold such black immensity that lived above our world, could not contain within myself even a small corner of the universe.

There seemed to be two kinds of people: earth people and those others, the sky people, who stumbled over pebbles while they walked around with their heads in clouds. Sky people loved different worlds than I loved; they looked at nests in treetops and followed the long white snake of vapor trails. But I was an earth person, and while I loved to gaze up at night and stars, I investigated the treasures at my feet, the veined wing of a dragonfly opening a delicate blue window to secrets of earth, a lusterless beetle that drank water thirstily from the tip of my finger and was transformed into sudden green and metallic brilliance. It was enough mystery for me to ponder the bones inside our human flesh, bones that through some incredible blueprint of life grow from a moment's sexual passion between a woman and a man, walk upright a short while, then walk themselves back to dust.

Years later, lost in the woods one New Year's eve, a friend found the way home by following the north star, and I began to think that learning the sky might be a practical thing. But it was the image of earth from out in space that gave me upward-gazing eyes. It was the same image that gave the sky people an anchor in the world, for it returned us to our planet in a new and loving way.

To dream of the universe is to know that we are small and brief as insects, born in a flash of rain and gone a moment later. We are delicate and our world is fragile. It was the transgression of Galileo[1] to tell us that we were not the center of the universe, and now, even in our own time, the news of our small being here is treacherous enough that early in the space program, the photographs of Earth were classified as secret documents by the government. It was thought, and rightfully so,

Linda Hogan (1947–) was born in Denver, Colorado. A Chickasaw poet, novelist and essayist, she includes in her published work two collections of poems, *Calling Myself Home* (1978), and *Seeing Through the Sun* (1985), and three novels, *Savings* (1988), *Mean Spirit* (1990), and *Solar Storms* (1995). Hogan is an associate professor of creative writing, fiction and Native American literature at the University of Colorado. "The Voyagers" from DWELLINGS: A Spiritual History of the Living World by Linda Hogan. Copyright © 1995 by Linda Hogan. Reprinted by permission of W.W. Norton & Company, Inc.

that the image of our small blue Earth would forever change how we see ourselves in context with the world we inhabit.

When we saw the deep blue and swirling white turbulence of our Earth reflected back to us, says photographer Steven Meyers,[2] we also saw "the visual evidence of creative and destructive forces moving around its surface, we saw for the first time the deep blackness of that which surrounds it, we sensed directly, and probably for the first time, our incredibly profound isolation, and the special fact of our being here." It was a world whose intricately linked-together ecosystem[3] could not survive the continuing blows of exploitation.

In 1977, when the Voyagers[4] were launched, one of these space-craft carried the Interstellar Record, a hoped-for link between earth and space that is filled with the sounds and images of the world around us. It carries parts of our lives all the way out to the great Forever. It is destined to travel out of our vast solar system, out to the far, unexplored regions of space in hopes that somewhere, millions of years from now, someone will find it like a note sealed in a bottle carrying our history across the black ocean of space. This message is intended for the year 8,000,000.

One greeting onboard from Western India says: "Greetings from a human being of the Earth. Please contact." Another, from Eastern China, but resembling one that could have been sent by my own Chickasaw[5] people, says: "Friends of space, how are you all? Have you eaten yet? Come visit us if you have time."

There is so much hope in those greetings, such sweetness. If found, these messages will play our world to a world that's far away. They will sing out the strangely beautiful sounds of Earth, sounds that in all likelihood exist on no other planet in the universe. By the time the record is found, if ever, it is probable that the trumpeting bellows of elephants, the peaceful chirping of frogs and crickets, the wild dogs baying out from the golden needle and record, will be nothing more than a gone history of what once lived on this tiny planet in the curving tail of a spiral galaxy. The undeciphered language of whales will speak to a world not our own, to people who are not us. They will speak of what we value the most on our planet, things that in reality we are almost missing.

A small and perfect world is traveling there, with psalms journeying past Saturn's icy rings, all our treasured life flying through darkness, going its way alone back through the universe. There is the recorded snapping of fire, the song of a river traveling the continent, the living wind passing through dry grasses, all the world that burns and pulses around us, even the comforting sound of a heartbeat taking us back to the first red house of our mothers' bodies, all that, floating through the universe.

The Voyager carries music. A Peruvian wedding song is waiting to be heard in the far, distant regions of space. The Navajo Night Chant[6] travels through darkness like medicine for healing another broken world. Blind Willie Johnson's[7] slide guitar and deep down blues are on that record, in night's long territory.

The visual records aboard the Voyager depict a nearly perfect world, showing us our place within the whole; in the image of a snow-covered forest, trees are so large that human figures standing at their base are almost invisible. In the corner of this image is a close-up of a snow crystal's elegant architecture of ice and air. Long-necked geese fly across another picture, a soaring eagle. Three dolphins, sun bright on their silver sides, leap from a great ocean wave. Beneath them are underwater blue reefs with a shimmering school of fish. It is an abundant, peaceful world, one where a man eats from a vine heavy with grapes, an old man walks through a field of white daisies, and children lovingly touch a globe in a classroom. To think that the precious images of what lives on earth beside us, the lives we share with earth, some endangered, are now tumbling through time and space, more permanent than we are, and speaking the sacred language of life that we ourselves have only just begun to remember.

We have sent a message that states what we most value here on earth: respect for all life and ways. It is a sealed world, a seed of what we may become. What an amazing document is flying above the clouds, holding Utopia.[8] It is more magical and heavy with meaning than the cave paintings of Lascaux,[9] more wise than the language of any holy book. These are images that could sustain us through any cold season of ice or hatred or pain.

In *Murmurs of Earth*,[10] written by members of the committee who selected the images and recordings, the records themselves are described in a way that attests to their luminous quality of being: "They glisten, golden, in the sunlight,...encased in aluminum cocoons." It sounds as though, through some magical metamorphosis,[11] this chrysalis of life will emerge in another part of infinity, will grow to a wholeness of its own, and return to us alive, full-winged, red, and brilliant.

There is so much hope there that it takes us away from the dark times of horror we live in, a time when the most cruel aspects of our natures have been revealed to us in regions of earth named Auschwitz, Hiroshima, My Lai, and Rwanda,[12] a time when televised death is the primary amusement of our children, when our children are killing one another on the streets.

At second glance, this vision for a new civilization, by its very presence, shows us what is wrong with our world. Defining Utopia, we see what we could be now, on earth, at this time, and next to the images of a better world, that which is absent begins to cry out. The underside of our lives grows in proportion to what is denied. The darkness is made darker by the record of light. A screaming silence falls between the stars of space. Held inside that silence are the sounds of gunfire, the wailings of grief and hunger, the last, extinct song of a bird. The dammed river goes dry, along with its valleys. Illnesses that plague our bodies live in this crack of absence. The broken link between us and the rest of our world grows too large, and the material of nightmares grows deeper while the promises for peace and equality are empty, are merely dreams without reality.

But how we want it, how we want that half-faced, one-sided God.

In earlier American days, when Catholic missions were being erected in Indian country, a European woman, who was one of the first white contacts for a northern tribe of people, showed sacred paintings to an Indian woman. The darker woman smiled when she saw a picture of Jesus and Mary encircled in their haloes of light. A picture of the three kings with their crowns and gifts held her interest. But when she saw a picture of the crucifixion, the Indian woman hurried away to warn others that these were dangerous people, people to fear, who did horrible things to one another. This picture is not carried by the Voyager, for fear we earth people would "look" cruel. There is no image of this man nailed to a cross, no saving violence. There are no political messages, no photographs of Hiroshima. This is to say that we know our own wrongdoings.

Nor is there a true biology of our species onboard because NASA[13] officials vetoed the picture of a naked man and pregnant woman standing side by side, calling it "smut." They allowed only silhouettes to be sent, as if our own origins, the divine flux of creation that passes between a man and a woman, are unacceptable, something to hide. Even picture diagrams of the human organs, musculature,[14] and skeletal system depict no sexual organs, and a photograph showing the birth of an infant portrays only the masked, gloved physician lifting the new life from a mass of sheets, the mother's body hidden. While we might ask if they could not have sent the carved stone gods and goddesses in acts of beautiful sexual intimacy on temple walls in India, this embarrassment about our own carriage of life and act of creative generation nevertheless reveals our feelings of physical vulnerability and discomfort with our own life force.

From an American Indian perspective, there are other problems here. Even the language used in the selection process bespeaks many of the failings of an entire system of thought and education. From this record, we learn about our relationships, not only with people, but with everything on earth. For example, a small gold-eyed frog seen in a human hand might have been a photograph that bridges species, a statement of our kinship with our lives on earth, but the hand is described, almost apologetically, as having "a dirty fingernail." Even the clay of creation has ceased to be the rich element from which life grows. I recall that the Chilean poet Pablo Neruda wrote "What can I say without touching the earth with my hands?"[15] We must wonder what of value can ever be spoken from lives that are lived outside of life, without a love or respect for the land and other lives.

In *Murmurs of Earth*, one of the coauthors writes about hearing dolphins from his room, "breathing, playing with one another. Somehow," he says, "one had the feeling that they weren't just some sea creatures but some very witty and intelligent beings living in the next room." This revealing choice of words places us above and beyond the rest of the world, as though we have stepped out of our natural cycles in our very existence here on earth. And isn't our world full of those rooms? We inhabit only a small space in the house of life. In another is a field of corn. In one more is the jungle world of the macaw. Down the hall, a zebra is moving. Beneath the foundation is the world of snakes and the five beating hearts of the earthworm.

In so many ways, the underside of our lives is here. Even the metals used in the record tell a story about the spoils of inner earth, the laborers in the hot mines. Their sweat is in that record, hurtling away from our own galaxy.

What are the possibilities, we wonder, that our time capsule will be found? What is the possibility that there are lives other than our own in the universe? Our small galaxy, the way of the milk, the way of sustenance, is only one of billions of galaxies, but there is also the possibility that we are the only planet where life opens, blooms, is gone, and then turns over again. We hope this is not the case. We are so young we hardly know what it means to be a human being, to have natures that allow for war. We barely even know our human histories, so much having unraveled before our time, and while we know that our history creates us, we hope there is another place, another world we can fly to when ours is running out. We have come so far away from wisdom, a wisdom that is the heritage of all people, an old kind of knowing that respects a community of land, animals, plants, and other people as equal to ourselves. Where we know the meaning of relationship.

As individuals, we are not faring much better. We are young. We hardly know who we are. We face the search for ourselves alone. In spite of our search through the universe, we do not know our own personal journeys. We still wonder if the soul weighs half an ounce, if it goes into the sky at the time of our death, if it also reaches out, turning, through the universe.

But still, this innocent reaching out is a form of ceremony, as if the Voyager were a sacred space, a ritual enclosure that contains our dreaming the way a cathedral holds the bones of saints.

The people of earth are reaching out. We are having a collective vision. Like young women and men on a vision quest, we seek a way to live out the peace of the vision we have sent to the world of stars. We want to live as if there is no other place, as if we will always be here. We want to live with devotion to the world of waters and the universe of life that dwells above our thin roofs.

I remember that night with my mother, looking up at the black sky with its turning stars. It was a mystery, beautiful and distant. Her body I came from, but our common ancestor is the earth, and the ancestor of earth is space. That night we were small, my mother and I, and we were innocent. We were children of the universe. In the gas and dust of life, we are voyagers. Wait. Stop here a moment. Have you eaten? Come in. Eat.

NOTES

1 Galileo (1564–1642) was an Italian physicist and astronomer who supported Copernicus's theory that the earth and planets moved around the sun. He developed the astronomical telescope, which enabled him to discover craters on the moon, and showed that the Milky Way is composed of stars.

2 Steven Meyers, photographer, is the author of *On Seeing Nature* (Golden, Colorado: Fulcrum, 1987).

3 Ecosystem refers to the ecological balance of the earth's environment.

4 Voyagers: unmanned interplanetary probes designed to send information about the outer planetary system back to earth.

5 Chickasaw: a tribe now based in Oklahoma, in the United States.

6 The Navajo are located in Arizona and New Mexico, in the United States. The Night Chant is a sacred ritual.

7 Blind Willie Johnson (c. 1902–1949) was a Texas–born religious singer-songwriter and guitarist, who gave black people inspiration in difficult times.

8 Utopia, derived from the title of Thomas More's novel *Utopia* (1516), refers to an imagined ideal place or state of social or political perfection.

9 The cave paintings of Lascaux, situated in Dordogne, France, are paintings of animals believed to date from 15,000 to 13,000 B.C. They were discovered in 1940 in a cave believed to be an ancient centre for the performance of hunting and magical rites.

10 Carl Sagan, et al., *Murmurs of Earth: the Voyager Interstellar Record* (New York: Random House, 1978).

11 Metamorphosis: transformation or change of form by magic or natural development.

12 Auschwitz was a Nazi concentration camp in Poland, operational 1940–1945, where up to four million prisoners died. Hiroshima is a city in Japan, the site of the first wartime use of the atomic bomb, in August 1945, when over 160,000 people died. My Lai refers to the massacre of civilian elderly, women, and children in a village in Vietnam, by U.S. army troops

in March 1968. Rwanda is a country in east-central Africa, site of the tribal massacre of half a million Tutsis in 1994.

13 NASA: National Aeronautics and Space Administration (U.S.).

14 Musculature: the muscular system of the body.

15 The quotation is from "Party's End," section XIII of *Ceremonial Songs*, 1961, in Pablo Neruda, *A New Decade: Poems: 1958–1967* (1969).

QUESTIONS

1. How does Hogan develop her initial distinction between "earth people" and "sky people" in the course of her essay?

2. The selection of sounds and images for the Interstellar Record, as Hogan describes it, suggests both a hopeful desire to communicate with other intelligences and a desire to make ourselves look as good as possible. What, in Hogan's opinion, does the Interstellar Record suggest about what we value on our own planet?

3. What does the decision to omit some aspects of life on Earth from the space capsule reveal about us?

4. How does Hogan develop a variety of possible meanings for the term *voyager*? How, for example, is the Voyager connected with the dream vision?

5. How would you describe the tone of this essay? Try to be specific about Hogan's attitude towards herself, her readers, and her subject.

6. Do you think Hogan presents a distinctively aboriginal perspective on the issues she discusses in this essay?

SUGGESTION FOR WRITING

Do you think a space capsule should present us as we wish to be seen by strangers, or should we be more honest? If you were in charge of assembling the materials for a space capsule, what aspects of human life and earth's ecosystems would you include? What would you leave out? Write a short essay on this topic. Try to be specific.

IN PRAISE OF THE HUMBLE COMMA

Pico Iyer

The gods, they say, give breath, and they take it away. But the same could be said—could it not?—of the humble comma. Add it to the present clause, and, of a sudden, the mind is, quite literally, given pause to think; take it out if you wish or forget it and the mind is deprived of a resting place. Yet still the comma gets no respect. It seems just a slip of a thing, a pedant's tick, a blip on the edge of our consciousness, a kind of printer's smudge almost. Small, we claim, is beautiful (especially in the age of the microchip). Yet what is so often used, and so rarely recalled, as the comma—unless it be breath itself?

Punctuation, one is taught, has a point: to keep up law and order. Punctuation marks are the road signs placed along the highway of our communication—to control speeds, provide directions and prevent head-on collisions. A period has the unblinking finality of a red light; the comma is a flashing yellow light that asks us only to slow down; and the semicolon is a stop sign that tells us to ease gradually to a halt, before gradually starting up again. By establishing the relations between words, punctuation establishes the relations between the people using words. That may be one reason why schoolteachers exalt it and lovers defy it ("We love each other and belong to each other let's don't ever hurt each other Nicole let's don't ever hurt each other," wrote Gary Gilmore[1] to his girlfriend). A comma, he must have known, "separates inseparables," in the clinching words of H. W. Fowler, King of English Usage.

Punctuation, then, is a civic prop, a pillar that holds society upright. (A run-on sentence, its phrases piling up without division, is as unsightly as a sink piled high with dirty dishes.) Small wonder, then, that punctuation was one of the first proprieties of the Victorian age, the age of the corset, that the modernists threw off: the sexual revolution might be said to have begun when Joyce's Molly Bloom spilled out all her private thoughts in 36 pages of unbridled, almost unperioded and officially censored prose;

Pico Iyer is the author of two travel books: *Video Night in Kathmandu: And Other Reports from the Not-So-Far East* (1988) and *The Lady and the Monk: Four Seasons in Kyoto* (1991). The following essay appeared in *Time*, June 13, 1988. "In Praise of the Humble Comma" by Pico Iyer. Copyright 1988 TIME Inc. Reprinted by permission.

and another rebellion was surely marked when E. E. Cummings first felt free to commit "God" to the lower case.

Punctuation thus becomes the signature of cultures. The hot-blooded Spaniard seems to be revealed in the passion and urgency of his doubled exclamation points and question marks ("¡*Caramba!¿Quien sabe?*"), while the impassive Chinese traditionally added to his so-called inscrutability by omitting directions from his ideograms. The anarchy and commotion of the '60s were given voice in the exploding exclamation marks, riotous capital letters and Day-Glo italics of Tom Wolfe's spray-paint prose; and in Communist societies, where the State is absolute, the dignity—and divinity—of capital letters is reserved for Ministries, Sub-Committees and Secretariats.

Yet punctuation is something more than a culture's birthmark; it scores the music in our minds, gets our thoughts moving to the rhythm of our hearts. Punctuation is the notation in the sheet music of our words, telling us when to rest, or when to raise our voices; it acknowledges that the meaning of our discourse, as of any symphonic composition, lies not in the units but in the pauses, the pacing and the phrasing. Punctuation is the way one bats one's eyes, lowers one's voice or blushes demurely. Punctuation adjusts the tone and color and volume till the feeling comes into perfect focus: not disgust exactly, but distaste; not lust, or like, but love.

Punctuation, in short, gives us the human voice, and all the meanings that lie between the words. "You aren't young, are you?" loses its innocence when it loses the question mark. Every child knows the menace of a dropped apostrophe (the parent's "Don't do that" shifting into the more slowly enunciated "Do not do that"), and every believer, the ignominy of having his faith reduced to "faith." Add an exclamation point to "To be or not to be..." and the gloomy Dane has all the resolve he needs; add a comma, and the noble sobriety of "God save the Queen" becomes a cry of desperation bordering on double sacrilege.

Sometimes, of course, our markings may be simply a matter of aesthetics. Popping in a comma can be like slipping on the necklace that gives an outfit quiet elegance, or like catching the sound of running water that complements, as it completes, the silence of a Japanese landscape. When V. S. Naipaul, in his latest novel, writes, "He was a middle-aged man, with glasses," the first comma can seem a little precious. Yet it gives the description a spin, as well as a subtlety, that it otherwise lacks, and it shows that the glasses are not part of the middle-agedness, but something else.

Thus all these tiny scratches give us breadth and heft and depth. A world that has only periods is a world without inflections. It is a world without shade. It has a music without sharps and flats. It is a martial music. It has a jackboot rhythm. Words cannot bend and curve. A comma, by comparison, catches the gentle drift of the mind in thought, turning in on itself and back on itself, reversing, redoubling and returning along the course of its own sweet river music; while the semicolon brings clauses and thoughts together with all the silent discretion of a hostess arranging guests around her dinner table.

Punctuation, then, is a matter of care. Care for words, yes, but also, and more important, for what the words imply. Only a lover notices the small things: the way the afternoon light catches the nape of a neck, or how a strand of hair slips out from behind an ear, or the way a finger curls around a cup. And no one scans a letter so closely as a lover, searching for its small print, straining to hear its nuances, its gasps, its sighs and hesitations, poring over the secret messages that lie in every cadence. The difference between "Jane (whom I adore)" and "Jane, whom I adore—" marks all the distance between ecstasy and heartache. "No iron can pierce the heart with such force as a period put at just the right place," in Isaac Babel's lovely words; a comma can let us hear a voice break, or a heart. Punctuation, in fact, is a labor of love. Which brings us back, in a way, to gods.

NOTE

[1] Gary Gilmore, convicted of the cold-blooded murder of a Utah gas attendant and a Utah motel owner, gained notoriety partly through his repeated demands to be executed. He is the subject of Norman Mailer's *The Executioner's Song*.

QUESTIONS

1. List the various functions of punctuation that Pico Iyer discusses in this essay. Which of these functions does he finally see as most valuable, and why?

2. Iyer makes extensive use of similes, metaphors, and analogies in this essay. What does he compare punctuation to? How effective are these comparisons in explaining the nature and purpose of punctuation?

3. Where does Iyer's use of punctuation demonstrate his points? Is this method of explanation effective? clear?

4. Do you agree with Iyer's statement that punctuation is the "signature of cultures"? Do his comments on the "hot-blooded Spaniard" and the "impassive Chinese" undermine the credibility of this section of the essay?

SUGGESTION FOR WRITING

Make an outline for an essay comparing Pico Iyer's essay with Lewis Thomas' "Notes on Punctuation." What are the main differences in structure and tone? What other similarities and differences can you find?

HE WAS A BOXER WHEN I WAS SMALL

Lenore Keeshig-Tobias

His thundering rages are most vivid, his tears subtle. Watching and feeling for them, but unable to bridge the gap, I learned to love, hate him all in the same breath. No one ever knew this. They saw a kid in love with her father.

He was a boxer when I was small. People say he was good and would have made it had he started younger, but he had a wife and growing family to provide for. Amateur boxing paid nothing, but he loved it. I think he must have been about twenty-two then. He claims that we were too young to have seen him fight, but I remember.

I remember the lights, the ring, my mother shouting "Kill him, Don, kill him!" and my sister eating popcorn. I remember how he'd shadow box at home, punching, dancing lightly, swinging left—left—right, and missing because there was nothing there except air.

His prowess[1] in the ring must have cowed my mother during his drunken rages. Or maybe it was his thundering voice, or the way the furniture went flying. Yet, with all his storming and her crying, I couldn't help but think that there was something more, something he couldn't articulate. When his ferocity gave way to tears of exasperation, I would cry with him, my dad, the boxer, the young man out to beat the world.

"It's not his fault," I would argue, "It's not all his fault, it's Mom's fault too," I would tell Gramma, even if I didn't know whose fault it was. She would disdainfully look off into the tree whenever I answered with this. Mom had Gramma to stick up for her. Dad had no one, only me.

There were, of course, times when things were fine. Dad would have a good job, Mom would be fresh with child,[2] and my sisters and brothers carefree. We would spread a blanket in the front yard, or gather around the kitchen table. Dad would tell stories of Nanabush,[3] stories of long ago when only the Indians and animals lived here. Good ole Nanabush danced before our eyes. We saw his courage, his generosity and love for the animals and our people. We also saw his anger, miserly ways, and

Lenore Keeshig-Tobias (1950–) is an Ojibway poet, playwright, fiction writer, editor, filmmaker, and cultural activist. She has edited *The Ontario Indian*, *Sweetgrass*, and *The Magazine to Re-establish the Trickster*. Her children's book, *Bird Talk* (1991), is a bilingual English/Ojibway story. She recently edited *Into the Moon: Heart, Mind, Body, Soul*, a collection of writings by the Native Women's Writing Circle (1996). This essay is reprinted with permission of Lenore Keeshig-Tobias.

blundering practical jokes, but we loved him and would laugh until we cried.

At other times we would play, all of us, seven, eight, nine of us rolling and tumbling while Mom sat back beaming like a big fat sun. We'd pretend box, then race, roll, and tumble again. How I wished those times would go on and on. He would stand shoulders up to the sky, as we climbed. He could carry all of us on his back.

One summer my sides ached with laughter. Then one day, I moved to the edge of the blanket and sat back to watch my sisters and brothers giggle and climb. Dad leaned forward, then down on hands and knees, all those laughing children on his back. That was when I noticed grey hairs hiding in his side-burns. I went to my room, dug out his boxing pictures, and cried.

I was about ten at the time, my dad about twenty-nine, and my mother twenty-eight. After that summer I never again played like that with the others. I felt too old, and instead I stood back and watched. I watched my sisters and brothers grow up. I watched him grow older, fighting all the way.

When he went to school, he tells us, he spoke only Ojibway[4] and a bit of French. His grandmother was French. The only English he knew was yes and no. Indian kids, in those days, were not allowed to speak anything but English in school. So besides being punished for speaking Ojibway, he was also punished for giving the wrong answer which was either yes or no.

He says he eventually learned to read, write, and do arithmetic, and he laughs when he tells us how he would get on the teacher's good side and then steal test answers for the rest of the class. She never had to keep any of them in after class, but then she never realized how they had cheated and helped each other. She never realized what a bunch of stupid kids she graduated.

My Dad never graduated. He learned enough to be able to go out and get a job.

Once, Dad was working in Toronto as an industrial painter (Indian men are noted for their surefootedness in high places). Mom, the kids, and I sat around the supper table. We didn't expect him home until the weekend, but there he was, standing in the doorway with his suitcase. Later that evening, I heard him confiding to Mom his reason for coming home.

He had beat up a fellow worker, a wisecracking whiteman, who had been bugging him for weeks. The ambulance was being called for when he left. My dad was afraid, afraid because he was Indian and because he had once been a boxer.

In between the various jobs on the reserve or high-painting and ironwork off in some big city, there were bouts of drinking and bouts of fanatical Christianity with thunderous preaching. We cowered every weekend waiting for him to erupt.

"Damn you, goddamn you," I would curse under my breath. "Why do you make our lives so miserable?"

We grew up as Christians, something I shall never forgive those Catholic missionaries for, although for a time it was the most settling thing in our lives. Dad made sure, in spite of everything else, his kids went to church. If he couldn't be a good father to us, then God would. But God wasn't an Indian, or a boxer, and my dad was. His visits to the Parish priest taught him fear of the Lord. But we went faithfully to church because of fear of our Dad, and fear for our furniture.

We should all be good at sports because Indians are known for that. Look at Jim Thorpe, Tom Longboat, George Armstrong.[5] We should all get a good education and not be stupid like him. We should all go to church every Sunday and not drink like him...he'd preach.

I got fed up with things, eventually. I was no good at sports. School was boring. I stopped going to church and even dared to argue with my dad. Finally, Mom and Dad had the priest come talk to me, to get me to go back to church and school.

The old man would listen when I told him that I would like to pray under the trees. He laughed. We argued. He laughed again, shook his head, and said something about excommunication. I told him off, that I would rather go to hell and burn with the rest of my heathen savage ancestors because there would be too few Indians in heaven and I'd probably get lonely. The old missionary wobbled into the house, quite shaken, and told my dad that I was "lost." Dad came out, white-faced, and beat me. He told me to leave, that he had other kids to worry about.

I settled into my own life, fighting bouts of my own, but continued hearing of his through letters and phone calls.

Was there no end? Mom and the kids kept looking to me for answers, as if I were the referee. I'd listen, but offer no solution. I was beginning to see what was driving him. I was beginning to understand that he was fighting the world, and there was no way I'd turn on him behind his back.

Afraid at first, I began to meet him blow for blow. People would say that I was like my dad. I thought I was like myself. I never did learn to box. He always laughed at the way I clenched my fists. I never was really interested in boxing. Being the eldest daughter of a boxer was enough, quite enough. But I can, however, thunder as loud as he can.

He's mellowed somewhat. And there have been times in quiet talk when he has acknowledged his weaknesses, his aspirations and exasperations for all of us in our effort to grow up and become educated. I guess these talks are what comes with being the oldest of ten.

Thundering rages, subtle tears...I have seen him cry with frustration, cry out in anger, and in pride, pride in his beautiful young looking wife and her accomplishments, his kids and grandchildren. Yet, the tears that touch me the most are those that roll down his cheeks when he talks of Nanabush.

Good ole Nanabush, the paradox, the son of a mortal woman and the thundering West Wind, a boy raised by his grandmother, the best loved of all Ojibway spirits. It was through his transgressions as well as his virtue that Nanabush taught his people. And they never negated or attempted to cover up his imperfections. Dad cries when he talks of Nanabush.

I dreamed of Dad. This was after he had argued and I told him why I would never go to church and how I could not understand why he still went. After all, the church like the government, had set out to break the Indian, to make him feel less than what he was. I did not hold back that time and told him everything I had ever felt or thought about concerning our people. He couldn't answer and politely admitted, "You've got me. But I can't argue with you now, I'll answer you when I'm not drinking."

This was the first time I had won an argument against him, and it didn't dawn on me until days later. We had talked, sipping our beer and not shouting. Arguments in our house were usually won by whomever could shout the loudest.

In my dreams I was fighting. Someone or something evil, disguised, was pushing me the wrong way, trying to make me do something I did not want to do. Thinking to expose this by disrobing it, I reached out and tugged. It turned to fend me off and guard its robe fiercely. We struggled until I stood alone with a bundle of clothes and flesh in my arms, and dread realization that I had killed another human being. Overwhelmed with guilt, I started to cry. Who would believe this act was unintentional? Then I saw him off in the distance, standing alone, his boxer's dressing-gown over his shoulders.

I could tell him. I could tell him everything. But would he listen? Understand? Lowering my burden, covering and folding it carefully I cowered toward him. His head was down, his shoulders slouched. He didn't see me until I spoke.

"Dad," I sobbed, "I killed someone who was pushing me the wrong way. I didn't mean to do it, Dad, help me."

He put his arms around me, tightly.

"I'll beat the world," he said and punched at the air.

NOTES

[1] prowess: skill.

[2] fresh with child: newly pregnant.

[3] Nanabush is a figure from Ojibway mythology; it is explained later in the story that he is "the son of a mortal woman and the thundering West Wind."

[4] Ojibway is the language of the Ojibway tribe, originally from around Lake Superior.

[5] Jim Thorpe (1887–1953), athlete of the Sauk and Fox tribes, was the winner of the gold medal for pentathlon and decathlon in the 1912 Stockholm Olympics, and also a professional baseballer from 1913 to 1919. Tom Longboat (1887–1949) was a distance runner from the Onandaga tribe. George Armstrong (1930–), originally from the Six Nations Reserve, was captain of the Toronto Maple Leafs when they won the Stanley Cup in 1967.

QUESTIONS

1. In the opening paragraph, Keeshig-Tobias says that she "learned to love, hate [her father] all in same breath." How does she use specific details to help us understand her ambivalent response to her father?

2. How and why do her feelings about her father change as she grows older?

3. What does boxing mean to Keeshig-Tobias' father? To Keeshig-Tobias herself? Why does she begin and end the essay with boxing?

4. In what ways is her father like Nanabush? How important are these similarities?

5. What prompts Keeshig-Tobias' dream about her father? How does this dream help us to understand her feelings about him when she is an adult?

6. How closely connected are boxing and tears in Keeshig-Tobias' memories of her father?

7. What is the thesis of this essay? Do you think Keeshig-Tobias' decision to imply her thesis rather than state it directly strengthens or weakens her essay?

SUGGESTION FOR WRITING

Sometimes you can get a perspective on a person you want to write about by developing the implications of a particular activity (cooking, gardening, fixing the plumbing, taking photographs) that you associate with him or her. Choose a family member and write an essay that imitates some of the techniques you have observed in "He Was a Boxer When I Was Small." Remember that you will need to work out your thesis even though you may not state it explicitly.

PROFITS BY THE TRUCKLOAD

Ross Laver

The history of economics is full of irrational buying frenzies and other such examples of the madness of crowds. There was the notorious tulip bulb craze in 17th-century Holland, the South Sea Bubble of 1720,[1] the 1920s stock market frenzy and the speculative real estate binge of the late 1980s.

To that list, add one more: the great four-wheel-drive truck craze of the 1990s.

The evidence is on every downtown street and suburban parking lot. Where once there were cars, now there are hulking GMC Suburbans, Ford Explorers, Jeep Grand Cherokees and Land Rovers—gas-guzzling, wilderness-conquering sport utility vehicles that in the hands of most owners never venture farther off-road than the local car wash.

For the auto industry, the sport utility fad is a gold mine. In 1990, North Americans bought 700,000 SUVs. Last year, the total hit two million, and some manufacturers believe it will swell to 2.5 million in three years, representing one out of every six vehicles sold.

Not only that, but there seems to be no limit to the cost increases that image-conscious truck buyers are willing to absorb. In 1993, the sticker price on a Jeep Grand Cherokee Limited, with leather seats and other luxury appointments, was $33,555. Today it's $42,305, and buyers still can't get enough of them. In the same period, the list price of a Chevy Blazer SLE jumped from $20,898 to $30,335, while the Nissan Pathfinder SE went from $25,790 to $35,998.

To be fair, almost every sport utility on the market has been substantially upgraded in recent years, with new equipment and safety features like airbags and protective side-door beams. But even allowing for that, the price increases for SUVs have far outstripped those for cars. The Ford Explorer XLT, for example, now lists for 35 per cent more than the 1993 model, compared with the 27 per cent increase on a redesigned Ford Taurus GL sedan. "It's like everything else in this world—it's what the

Ross Laver worked for five years as a reporter for *The Globe and Mail* before moving to *Maclean's*, where he is currently the assistant managing editor. He is coauthor of *Savage Messiah* (1993), a biography of Quebec-born cult leader Roch Theriault. "Profits by the Truckload" is reprinted with permission of Maclean's Magazine.

market will bear," says a spokesman for a rival automaker, acknowledging that his company, too, has been quick to exploit the SUV craze.

But how long can it last? The manufacturers' profit on a sport utility currently runs anywhere from $5000 to $13,000—an astonishing margin by industry standards. Traditional four-door sedans, by comparison, have become commodity products, yielding a few hundred dollars at best after rebates and low-interest lease deals. Many smaller car models actually lose money and are kept in production only to satisfy U.S. government standards for average fleet fuel economy.

The optimists in the car industry predict that four-wheel-drives will remain lucrative for years to come. As proof, they point to surveys of younger car buyers. Among those born since the end of the baby boom, well over 60 per cent select an SUV as their preferred vehicle. (Minivans are out because their parents drove them.)

But that only takes account of the demand side of the equation. Those fat profit margins ultimately depend on a shortage of supply, which won't last forever. Last month, Chrysler announced a $1.3-billion investment in six Detroit factories, primarily to increase truck production capacity. Chrysler is also converting a car plant in Delaware to begin production this summer of the Dodge Durango, a new mid-sized SUV. Meanwhile, Ford will soon launch the high-end Lincoln Navigator—with polished walnut dashboard and acres of chrome—to compete against Mercedes-Benz's new M-class. Chrysler, Ford and GM are also mulling plans for compact sport-utes that could go up against the recently launched Toyota RAV4 and Honda CR-V, as well as the forthcoming Subaru Forester. All told, says Jim Hall, vice-president of the market research firm AutoPacific Inc., the number of sport-utility models is forecast to grow from 34 in 1996 to 55 in the year 2005.

With profits so high, it's not surprising that everyone wants in on the action. But if history teaches anything, it is that markets this hot inevitably flame out.

NOTE

[1] These are examples, as are the two that follow, of schemes in which eager but misguided investment frenzy was followed by market collapse.

QUESTIONS

1. In this article, Laver makes three main points about sport utility vehicles (SUVs): they are very popular, they are increasingly expensive, and they make lots of money for manufacturers. Are these points arranged in an order of increasing importance? Explain your answer.

2. What main kind of evidence does Laver use to support these assertions? Is this evidence convincing?

3. Does he include any evidence to support his final comment that "markets this hot inevitably flame out"?

4. Do you think Laver's overall purpose is to explain or to persuade?

5. Laver explains why SUVs are so popular with manufacturers, but he doesn't say much about why they are so popular with consumers. What do you think?

SUGGESTION FOR WRITING

If you had plenty of money, what kind of vehicle would enable you to express your personality and fulfill your fantasies? Write a short essay describing the vehicle (it does not have to have four wheels) of your dreams.

UNCHOPPING A TREE

W. S. Merwin

Start with the leaves, the small twigs, and the nests that have been shaken, ripped, or broken off by the fall; these must be gathered and attached once again to their respective places. It is not arduous work, unless major limbs have been smashed or mutilated. If the fall was carefully and correctly planned, the chances of anything of the kind happening will have been reduced. Again, much depends upon the size, age, shape, and species of the tree. Still, you will be lucky if you can get through this stage without having to use machinery. Even in the best of circumstances it is a labor that will make you wish often that you had won the favor of the universe of ants, the empire of mice, or at least a local tribe of squirrels, and could enlist their labors and their talents. But no, they leave you to it. They have learned, with time. This is men's work. It goes without saying that if the tree was hollow in whole or in part, and contained old nests of bird or mammal or insect, or hoards of nuts or such structures as wasps or bees build for their survival, the contents will have to be repaired where necessary, and reassembled, insofar as possible, in their original order, including the shells of nuts already opened. With spiders' webs you must simply do the best you can. We do not have the spider's weaving equipment, nor any substitute for the leaf's living bond with its point of attachment and nourishment. It is even harder to simulate the latter when the leaves have once become dry—as they are bound to do, for this is not the labor of a moment. Also it hardly needs saying that this is the time for repairing any neighboring trees or bushes or other growth that may have been damaged by the fall. The same rules apply. Where neighboring trees were of the same species it is difficult not to waste time conveying a detached leaf back to the wrong tree. Practice, practice. Put your hope in that.

Now the tackle must be put into place or the scaffolding, depending on the surroundings and the dimensions of the tree. It is ticklish work. Almost always it involves, in itself, further damage to the area, which will have to be corrected later. But as you've heard, it can't be helped. And care now is likely to

W. S. Merwin was born in New York in 1927 and is principally known for his poetry, though he won the P.E.N. Translation Prize in 1968 for his book *Selected Translations 1948–1968*. He won the Pulitzer Prize in 1970 for his book of poetry *The Carrier of Ladders* and gave the Pulitzer Prize money to the draft resistance. "Unchopping a Tree" is from his 1970 collection of prose, *The Miner's Pale Children*. Reprinted by permission of Georges Borchardt Inc. for the author. Copyright 1969, 1970, 1994 by W. S. Merwin.

save you considerable trouble later. Be careful to grind nothing into the ground.

At last the time comes for the erecting of the trunk. By now it will scarcely be necessary to remind you of the delicacy of this huge skeleton. Every motion of the tackle, every slight upward heave of the trunk, the branches, their elaborately reassembled panoply of leaves (now dead) will draw from you an involuntary gasp. You will watch for a leaf or a twig to be snapped off yet again. You will listen for the nuts to shift in the hollow limb and you will hear whether they are indeed falling into place or are spilling in disorder—in which case, or in the event of anything else of the kind—operations will have to cease, of course, while you correct the matter. The raising itself is no small enterprise, from the moment when the chains tighten around the old bandages until the bole hangs vertical above the stump, splinter above splinter. Now the final straightening of the splinters themselves can take place (the preliminary work is best done while the wood is still green and soft, but at times when the splinters are not badly twisted most of the straightening is left until now, when the torn ends are face to face with each other). When the splinters are perfectly complementary the appropriate fixture is applied. Again we have no duplicate of the original substance. Ours is extremely strong, but it is rigid. It is limited to surfaces, and there is no play in it. However the core is not the part of the trunk that conducted life from the roots up into the branches and back again. It was relatively inert. The fixative for this part is not the same as the one for the outer layers and the bark, and if either of these is involved in the splintered section they must receive applications of the appropriate adhesives. Apart from being incorrect and probably ineffective, the core fixative would leave a scar on the bark.

When all is ready the splintered trunk is lowered onto the splinters of the stump. This, one might say, is only the skeleton of the resurrection. Now the chips must be gathered, and the sawdust, and returned to their former positions. The fixative for the wood layers will be applied to chips and sawdust consisting only of wood. Chips and sawdust consisting of several substances will receive applications of the correct adhesives. It is as well, where possible, to shelter the materials from the elements while working. Weathering makes it harder to identify the smaller fragments. Bark sawdust in particular the earth lays claim to very quickly. You must find your own ways of coping with this problem. There is a certain beauty, you will notice at moments, in the pattern of the chips as they are fitted back into place. You will wonder to what extent it should be described as natural, to what extent manmade. It will lead you on to speculations about the parentage of beauty itself, to which you will return.

The adhesive for the chips is translucent, and not so rigid as that for the splinters. That for bark and its subcutaneous layers is transparent and runs into the fibres on either side, partially dissolving them into each other. It does not set the sap flowing again but it does pay a kind of tribute to the preoccupations of the ancient thoroughfares. You could not roll an egg over the joints but some of the mineshafts would still be passable, no doubt. For the first exploring insect who raises its head in the tight echoless passages. The day comes when it is all restored, even to the moss (now dead) over the wound. You will sleep badly, thinking of the removal of the scaffolding that must begin the next morning. How you will hope for sun and a still day!

The removal of the scaffolding or tackle is not so dangerous, perhaps, to the surroundings, as its installation, but it presents problems. It should be taken from the spot piece by piece as it is detached, and stored at a distance. You have come to accept it there, around the tree. The sky begins to look naked as the chains and struts one by one vacate their positions. Finally the moment arrives when the last sustaining piece is removed and the tree stands again on its own. It is as though its weight for a moment stood on your heart. You listen for a thud of settlement, a warning creak deep in the intricate joinery. You cannot believe it will hold. How like something dreamed it is, standing there all by itself. How long will it stand there now? The first breeze that touches its dead leaves all seems to flow into your mouth. You are afraid the motion of the clouds will be enough to push it over. What more can you do? What more can you do?

But there is nothing more you can do.

Others are waiting.

Everything is going to have to be put back.

QUESTIONS

1. How well does "Unchopping a Tree" satisfy the requirements for step-by-step instructions and precise, easy-to-visualize detail in the "how-to" process analysis essay?

2. At what point did you first realize that these instructions are, in fact, impossible to carry out? Is process analysis an effective way to make this point? Why?

3. Reread the first paragraph and analyze the rhythm Merwin creates through his use of sentence lengths and sentence patterns. How does this rhythm help to establish the tone of the essay?

4. Note Merwin's use of figurative language throughout this essay (for more on this, see the sample essay on Merwin and Suzuki). How does this language develop and strengthen Merwin's thesis?

5. Throughout the essay, Merwin adopts the persona of a teacher instructing the reader-student. Where is this persona most evident? What purposes does it serve?

6. Merwin creates irony by leaving the obvious unsaid: that it is impossible to unchop a tree. How similar is Merwin's irony to Swift's in "A Modest Proposal"? Do you think irony is an effective strategy for persuasion? Is irony ever risky?

SUGGESTION FOR WRITING

Using "Unchopping a Tree" as a model, write an essay in which the impossibility of carrying out your instructions makes a persuasive point. Remember that in an ironic essay, your real thesis is the opposite of what you seem to be saying. You will find this irony easier to create and sustain if, like Merwin, you adopt the persona of the teacher who encourages the students but who provides impossibly complex instructions. Like Merwin, you should develop your essay as a process analysis, so be sure to include transitions that help your readers to follow the steps in your procedure.

SHOOTING AN ELEPHANT

George Orwell

In Moulmein, in lower Burma,[1] I was hated by large numbers of people—the only time in my life that I have been important enough for this to happen to me. I was sub-divisional police officer of the town, and in an aimless, petty kind of way anti-European feeling was very bitter. No one had the guts to raise a riot, but if a European woman went through the bazaars alone somebody would probably spit betel juice[2] over her dress. As a police officer[3] I was an obvious target and was baited whenever it seemed safe to do so. When a nimble Burman tripped me up on the football field and the referee (another Burman) looked the other way, the crowd yelled with hideous laughter. This happened more than once. In the end the sneering yellow faces of young men that met me everywhere, the insults hooted after me when I was at a safe distance, got badly on my nerves. The young Buddhist priests were the worst of all. There were several thousands of them in the town and none of them seemed to have anything to do except stand on street corners and jeer at Europeans.

All this was perplexing and upsetting. For at that time I had already made up my mind that imperialism[4] was an evil thing and the sooner I chucked up my job and got out of it the better. Theoretically—and secretly, of course—I was all for the Burmese and all against their oppressors, the British. As for the job I was doing, I hated it more bitterly than I can perhaps make clear. In a job like that you see the dirty work of Empire at close quarters. The wretched prisoners huddling in the stinking cages of the lock-ups, the gray, cowed faces of the long-term convicts, the scarred buttocks of the men who had been flogged with bamboos—all these oppressed me with an intolerable sense of guilt. But I could get nothing into perspective. I was young and ill educated and I had had to think out my problems in the utter silence that is imposed on every Englishman in the East. I did not even know that the British Empire is dying, still less did I

George Orwell (1903–1950) was born in India as Eric Arthur Blair. Primarily a writer and a journalist, he worked as a police officer for the Indian Imperial Police in Burma from 1922 to 1927. His fiction includes *Animal Farm* (1945) and *Nineteen Eighty-Four* (1949). He also wrote many essays, often exploring his ideas about democracy and socialism; collections include *Inside the Whale and Other Essays* (1940) and *Shooting an Elephant and Other Essays* (1950). "Shooting an Elephant" was first published in the journal *New Writing* in 1936. Copyright © Mark Hamilton as the literary executor of the estate of the late Sonia Brownell Orwell and Martin Secker and Warburg Ltd.

know that it is a great deal better than the younger empires that are going to supplant it. All I knew was that I was stuck between my hatred of the empire I served and my rage against the evil-spirited little beasts who tried to make my job impossible. With one part of my mind I thought of the British Raj[5] as an unbreakable tyranny, as something clamped down, in *saecula saeculorum*,[6] upon the will of prostrate peoples; with another part I thought that the greatest joy in the world would be to drive a bayonet into a Buddhist priest's guts. Feelings like these are the normal by-products of imperialism; ask any Anglo-Indian official, if you can catch him off duty.

One day something happened which in a roundabout way was enlightening. It was a tiny incident in itself; but it gave me a better glimpse than I had had before of the real nature of imperialism—the real motives for which despotic[7] governments act. Early one morning the sub-inspector at a police station the other end of the town rang me up on the 'phone and said that an elephant was ravaging the bazaar. Would I please come and do something about it? I did not know what I could do, but I wanted to see what was happening and I got on to a pony and started out. I took my rifle, an old .44 Winchester and much too small to kill an elephant, but I thought the noise might be useful *in terrorem*.[8] Various Burmans stopped me on the way and told me about the elephant's doings. It was not, of course, a wild elephant, but a tame one which had gone "must."[9] It had been chained up, as tame elephants always are when their attack of "must" is due, but on the previous night it had broken its chain and escaped. Its mahout,[10] the only person who could manage it when it was in that state, had set out in pursuit, but had taken the wrong direction and was now twelve hours' journey away, and in the morning the elephant had suddenly reappeared in the town. The Burmese population had no weapons and were quite helpless against it. It had already destroyed somebody's bamboo hut, killed a cow and raided some fruitstalls and devoured the stock; also it had met the municipal rubbish van and, when the driver jumped out and took to his heels, had turned the van over and inflicted violences upon it.

The Burmese sub-inspector and some Indian constables were waiting for me in the quarter where the elephant had been seen. It was a very poor quarter, a labyrinth of squalid bamboo huts, thatched with palm-leaf, winding all over a steep hillside. I remember that it was a cloudy, stuffy morning at the beginning of the rains.[11] We began questioning the people as to where the elephant had gone and, as usual, failed to get any definite information. That is invariably the case in the East; a story always sounds clear enough at a distance, but the nearer you get to the scene of events the vaguer it becomes. Some of the people said that the elephant had gone in one direction, some said that he had gone in another, some professed not even to have heard of any elephant. I had almost made up my mind that the whole story was a pack of lies, when we heard yells a little distance away. There was a loud, scandalized cry of "Go away, child! Go away this instant!" and an old woman with a switch in her hand came round the corner of a hut, violently shooing away a crowd of naked children. Some more women followed, clicking their tongues and exclaiming; evidently there was something that the children ought not to have seen. I rounded the hut and saw a man's dead body sprawling in the mud. He was an Indian, a black Dravidian coolie,[12] almost naked, and he could not have been dead many minutes. The people said that the elephant had come suddenly upon him round the corner of the hut, caught him with its trunk, put its foot on his back and ground him into the earth. This was the rainy season and the ground was soft, and his face had scored a trench a foot deep and a couple of yards long. He was lying on his belly with arms crucified and head sharply twisted to one side. His face was coated with mud, the eyes wide open, the teeth bared and grinning with an expression of unendurable agony. (Never tell me, by the way, that the dead look peaceful. Most of the corpses I have seen looked devilish.) The friction of the great beast's foot had stripped the skin from his back as neatly as one skins a rabbit. As soon as I saw the dead man I sent an orderly to a friend's house nearby to borrow an elephant rifle. I had already sent back the pony, not wanting it to go mad with fright and throw me if it smelt the elephant.

The orderly came back in a few minutes with a rifle and five cartridges, and meanwhile some Burmans had arrived and told us that the elephant was in the paddy fields[13] below, only a few hundred yards away. As I started forward practically the whole population of the quarter flocked out of the houses and followed me. They had seen the rifle and were all shouting excitedly that I was going to shoot the elephant. They had not shown much interest in the elephant when he was merely ravaging their homes, but it was different now that he was going to be shot. It was a bit of fun to them, as it would be to an English crowd; besides they wanted the meat. It made me vaguely uneasy. I had no intention of shooting the elephant—I had merely sent for the rifle to defend myself if necessary—and it is always unnerving to have a crowd following you. I marched down the hill, looking and feeling a fool, with the rifle over my shoulder and an ever-growing army of people jostling at my heels. At the bottom, when you got away from the huts, there was a metalled road and beyond that a miry waste of paddy fields a thousand yards across, not yet ploughed but soggy from the first rains and dotted with coarse grass. The elephant was standing eight yards from the road, his left side toward us. He took not the slightest notice of the crowd's approach. He was tearing up bunches of grass, beating them against his knees to clean them, and stuffing them into his mouth.

I had halted on the road. As soon as I saw the elephant I knew with perfect certainty that I ought not to shoot him. It is a serious matter to shoot a working elephant—it is comparable to destroying a huge and costly piece of machinery—and obviously one ought not to do it if it can possibly be avoided. And at that distance, peacefully eating, the elephant looked no more dangerous than a cow. I thought then and I think now that his attack of "must" was already passing off; in which case he would merely wander harmlessly about until the mahout came back and caught him. Moreover, I did not in the least want to shoot him. I decided that I would watch him for a little while to make sure that he did not turn savage again, and then go home.

But at that moment I glanced round at the crowd that had followed me. It was an immense crowd, two thousand at the least and growing every minute. It blocked the road for a long distance on either side. I looked at the sea of yellow faces above the garish clothes—faces all happy and excited over this bit of fun, all certain that the elephant was going to be shot. They were watching me as they would watch a con-jurer about to perform a trick. They did not like me, but with the magi-cal rifle in my hands I was momentarily worth watching. And suddenly I realized that I should have to shoot the elephant after all. The people expected it of me and I had got to do it; I could feel their two thousand wills pressing me forward, irresistibly. And it was at this moment, as I stood there with the rifle in my hands, that I first grasped the hollow-ness, the futility of the white man's dominion in the East. Here was I, the white man with his gun, standing in front of the unarmed native crowd—seemingly the leading actor of the piece; but in reality I was only an absurd puppet pushed to and fro by the will of those yellow faces behind. I perceived in this moment that when the white man turns tyrant it is his own freedom that he destroys. He becomes a sort of hollow, posing dummy, the conventionalized figure of a sahib.[14] For it is the condition of his rule that he shall spend his life in trying to im-press the "natives," and so in every crisis he has got to do what the "natives" expect of him. He wears a mask, and his face grows to fit it. I had got to shoot the elephant. I had committed myself to doing it when I sent for the rifle. A sahib has got to act like a sahib; he has got to ap-pear resolute, to know his own mind and do definite things. To come all that way, rifle in hand, with two thousand people marching at my heels, and then to trail feebly away, having done nothing—no, that was impossible. The crowd would laugh at me. And my whole life, every white man's life in the East, was one long struggle not to be laughed at.

But I did not want to shoot the elephant. I watched him beating his bunch of grass against his knees with that preoccupied grandmotherly air that elephants have. It seemed to me that it would be murder to shoot him. At that age I was not squeamish about killing animals, but I had never shot an elephant and never wanted to. (Somehow it always seems worse to kill a *large* animal.) Besides, there was the beast's owner to be considered. Alive, the elephant was worth at least a hundred pounds; dead, he would only be worth the value of his tusks, five pounds, possibly. But I had got to act quickly. I turned to some experienced-looking Burmans who had been there when we arrived, and asked them how the elephant had been behaving. They all said the same thing: he took no notice of you if you left him alone, but he might charge if you went too close to him.

It was perfectly clear to me what I ought to do. I ought to walk up to within, say, twenty-five yards of the elephant and test his behavior. If he charged, I could shoot; if he took no notice of me, it would be safe to leave him until the mahout came back. But also I knew that I was going to do no such thing. I was a poor shot with a rifle and the ground was soft mud into which one would sink at every step. If the elephant charged and I missed him, I should have about as much chance as a toad under a steam-roller. But even then I was not thinking particularly of my own skin, only of the watchful yellow faces behind. For at that moment, with the crowd watching me, I was not afraid in the ordinary sense, as I would have been if I had been alone. A white man mustn't be frightened in front of "natives'"; and so, in general, he isn't frightened. The sole thought in my mind was that if anything went wrong those two thousand Burmans would see me pursued, caught, trampled on, and reduced to a grinning corpse like that Indian up the hill. And if that happened it was quite probable that some of them would laugh. That would never do. There was only one alternative. I shoved the cartridges into the magazine and lay down on the road to get a better aim.

The crowd grew very still, and a deep, low, happy sigh, as of people who see the theater curtain go up at last, breathed from innumerable throats. They were going to have their bit of fun after all. The rifle was a beautiful German thing with cross-hair sights. I did not then know that in shooting an elephant one would shoot to cut an imaginary bar running from ear-hole to ear-hole. I ought, therefore, as the elephant was sideways on, to have aimed straight at his ear-hole; actually I aimed several inches in front of this, thinking the brain would be further forward.

When I pulled the trigger I did not hear the bang or feel the kick—one never does when a shot goes home—but I heard the devilish roar of glee that went up from the crowd. In that instant, in too short a time, one would have thought, even for the bullet to get there, a mysterious, terrible change had come over the elephant. He neither stirred, nor fell, but every line of his body had altered. He looked suddenly stricken, shrunken, immensely old, as though the frightful impact of the bullet had paralyzed him without knocking him down. At last, after what seemed a long time—it might have been five seconds, I dare say—he sagged flabbily to his knees. His mouth slobbered. An enormous senility seemed to have settled upon him. One could have imagined him thousands of years old. I fired again into the same spot. At the second shot he did not collapse but climbed with desperate slowness to his feet and stood weakly upright, with legs sagging and head drooping. I fired a third time. That was the shot that did for him. You could see the agony of it jolt his whole body and knock the last remnant of strength from his legs. But in falling he seemed for a moment to rise, for as his hind legs collapsed beneath him he seemed to tower upward like a huge rock toppling, his trunk reaching skyward like a tree. He trumpeted, for the first and only time. And then down he came, his belly toward me, with a crash that seemed to shake the ground even where I lay.

I got up. The Burmans were already racing past me across the mud. It was obvious that the elephant would never rise again, but he was not dead. He was breathing very rhythmically with long rattling gasps, his great mound of a side painfully rising and falling. His mouth was wide open—I could see far down into caverns of pale pink throat. I waited for a long time for him to die, but his breathing did not weaken. Finally I fired my two remaining shots into the spot where I thought his heart must be. The thick blood welled out of him like red velvet, but still he did not die. His body did not even jerk when the shots hit him, the tortured breathing continued without a pause. He was dying, very slowly and in great agony, but in some world remote from me where not even a bullet could damage him further. I felt that I had got to put an end to that dreadful noise. It seemed dreadful to see the great beast lying there, powerless to move and yet powerless to die, and not even to be able to finish him. I sent back for my small rifle and poured shot after shot into his heart and down his throat. They seemed to make no impression. The tortured gasps continued as steadily as the ticking of a clock.

In the end I could not stand it any longer and went away. I heard later that it took him half an hour to die. Burmans were bringing dahs[15] and baskets even before I left, and I was told they had stripped his body almost to the bones by the afternoon.

Afterward, of course, there were endless discussions about the shooting of the elephant. The owner was furious, but he was only an Indian and could do nothing. Besides, legally I had done the right thing, for a mad elephant has to be killed, like a mad dog, if its owner fails to control it. Among the Europeans opinion was divided. The older men said I was right, the younger men said it was a damn shame to shoot an elephant for killing a coolie, because an elephant was worth more than any damn Coringhee coolie. And afterward I was very glad that the coolie had been killed; it put me legally in the right and it gave me a sufficient pretext for shooting the elephant. I often wondered whether any of the others grasped that I had done it solely to avoid looking a fool.

NOTES

1 Burma (Union of Myanmar) is a country in Southeast Asia, and was part of the British Empire at the time to which Orwell is referring.

2 Betel juice is produced by chewing the leaf of the betel plant wrapped around parings of the areca nut.

3 As an officer in the Indian Imperial Police, Orwell was an agent of the Empire, and thus often resented by the local population.

4 Imperialism: the principle, spirit or ideology by which the existence of an empire, or the extension of territory in the name of protection of existing trading or economic interests, is justified.

5 British Raj: British rule in the Indian subcontinent prior to 1947.

6 For ever and ever.

7 Oppressive or tyrannical.

8 As a warning.

9 "Must" is a state of dangerous frenzy to which certain male animals, especially elephants and camels, are subject at infrequent intervals.

10 A *mahout* is an elephant driver.

11 The rainy season.

12 Coolie is a European word used to describe natives in India and elsewhere who are hired as labourers or burden carriers. Dravidia and Coringhee are both areas of India.

13 Paddy fields are fields of rice.

14 *Sahib* is a respectful term of address used by Indians and Asians to Europeans, equivalent to "Sir."

15 A *dah* is a short heavy sword, also used as a knife.

QUESTIONS

1. Reread the first two paragraphs of "Shooting an Elephant." What are Orwell's attitudes towards the Burmese, the British, and his own position in Burma? How does Orwell use descriptive details and diction to establish his perspective and create the tone of this essay?

2. Note the description of the man killed by the elephant (fourth paragraph). What purposes does this description serve in the essay as a whole?

3. Make a list of Orwell's reasons for not shooting the elephant. Then make a list of the reasons he gives for shooting the elephant. Are you convinced that Orwell was justified in shooting the elephant? What would you have done if you had been in his situation?

4. Note the detailed and graphic description of the elephant's death. What purposes does this description serve? What does the elephant symbolize?

5. Where does Orwell indicate his subject? What insights into the real motives for which imperialist governments act does Orwell actually gain from his experience? What is his thesis?

6. How similar are Orwell's ideas about colonialism to Frederic Raphael's in "Special English"?

7. Do you think Orwell uses narration effectively as a persuasive strategy in this essay?

8. How does Orwell use descriptive details and diction to establish his perspective and create the tone of this essay?

SUGGESTION FOR WRITING

Like Orwell, most of us have done something we are rather ashamed of but have never forgotten because it taught us something important. Using Orwell's essay as a model, write a narrative essay in which you tell a story about a single incident. Be sure this incident has a definite beginning, middle, and end. Try to begin by establishing the context of the incident (how old you were, where it happened, why it was especially important). Include plenty of vivid, precise descriptive detail. You can imitate the structure of "Shooting an Elephant" by leading up to your thesis, which you may choose to imply rather than state explicitly.

THE PHILOSOPHY OF COMPOSITION

tongue-in-cheek to critics.

Edgar Allan Poe

. . . I have often thought how interesting a magazine paper might be written by any author who would—that is to say, who could—detail, step by step, the processes by which any one of his compositions attained its ultimate point of completion. Why such a paper has never been given to the world, I am much at a loss to say—but, perhaps, the autorial[1] vanity has had more to do with the omission than any one other cause. Most writers—poets in especial—prefer having it understood that they compose by a species of fine frenzy—an ecstatic intuition—and would positively shudder at letting the public take a peep behind the scenes, at the elaborate and vacillating crudities of thought—at the true purposes seized only at the last moment—at the innumerable glimpses of idea that arrived not at the maturity of full view—at the fully matured fancies discarded in despair as unmanageable—at the cautious selections and rejections—at the painful erasures and interpolations—in a word, at the wheels and pinions—the tackle for scene-shifting—the step-ladders and demon-traps—the cock's feathers, the red paint and the black patches, which, in ninety-nine cases out of the hundred, constitute the properties of the literary *histrio*.[2]

I am aware, on the other hand, that the case is by no means common, in which an author is at all in condition to retrace the steps by which his conclusions have been attained. In general, suggestions, having arisen pell-mell, are pursued and forgotten in a similar manner.

For my own part, I have neither sympathy with the repugnance alluded to, nor, at any time, the least difficulty in recalling to mind the progressive steps of any of my compositions; and, since the interest of an analysis, or reconstruction, such as I have considered a *desideratum*,[3] is quite independent of any real or fancied interest in the thing analyzed, it will not be regarded as a breach of decorum on my part to show the *modus operandi*[4] by which some one of my own works was put together. I select "The Raven," as the most generally known. It is my design to render it manifest that no one point in its composition

Edgar Allan Poe (1809–1849) was born in Boston, Massachusetts. He was a poet, short-story writer, essayist, and critic who initially published much of his work in periodicals. Among his best-known works are the poems "The Raven" and "Annabel Lee" and the stories "The Fall of the House of Usher" and "The Pit and the Pendulum." "The Philosophy of Composition" was first published in *Graham's Magazine* in 1846.

is referable either to accident or intuition—that the work proceeded, step by step, to its completion with the precision and rigid consequence of a mathematical problem.

Let us dismiss, as irrelevant to the poem, *per se*,[5] the circumstance—or say the necessity—which, in the first place, gave rise to the intention of composing *a* poem that should suit at once the popular and the critical taste.

We commence, then, with this intention.

The initial consideration was that of extent. If any literary work is too long to be read at one sitting, we must be content to dispense with the immensely important effect derivable from unity of impression—for, if two sittings be required, the affairs of the world interfere, and everything like totality is at once destroyed. But since, *ceteris paribus*,[6] no poet can afford to dispense with *anything* that may advance his design, it but remains to be seen whether there is, in extent, any advantage to counterbalance the loss of unity which attends it. Here I say no, at once. What we term a long poem is, in fact, merely a succession of brief ones—that is to say, of brief poetical effects. It is needless to demonstrate that a poem is such, only inasmuch as it intensely excites, by elevating, the soul; and all intense excitements are, through a psychal necessity, brief. For this reason, at least one half of the "Paradise Lost"[7] is essentially prose—a succession of poetical excitements interspersed, *inevitably*, with corresponding depressions—the whole being deprived, through the extremeness of its length, of the vastly important artistic element, totality, or unity, of effect.

It appears evident, then, that there is a distinct limit, as regards length, to all works of literary art—the limit of a single sitting—and that, although in certain classes of prose composition, such as "Robinson Crusoe"[8] (demanding no unity), this limit may be advantageously overpassed, it can never properly be overpassed in a poem. Within this limit, the extent of a poem may be made to bear mathematical relation to its merit—in other words, to the excitement or elevation—again in other words, to the degree of true poetical effect which it is capable of inducing; for it is clear that the brevity must be in direct ratio of the intensity of the intended effect:—this, with one proviso—that a certain degree of duration is absolutely requisite for the production of any effect at all.

Holding in view these considerations, as well as that degree of excitement which I deemed not above the popular, while not below the critical, taste, I reached at once what I conceived the proper *length* for my intended poem—a length of about one hundred lines. It is, in fact, a hundred and eight.

My next thought concerned the choice of an impression, or effect, to be conveyed: and here I may as well observe that, throughout the construction, I kept steadily in view the design of rendering the work *universally* appreciable. I should be carried too far out of my immediate topic were I to demonstrate a point upon which I have repeatedly insisted, and which, with the poetical, stands not in the slightest need of demonstration—the point, I mean, that Beauty is the sole legitimate province of the poem. A few words, however, in elucidation of my real meaning, which some of my friends have evinced a disposition to misrepresent. That pleasure which is at once the most intense, the most elevating, and the most pure, is, I believe, found in the contemplation of the beautiful. When, indeed, men speak of Beauty, they mean, precisely, not a quality, as is supposed, but an effect—they refer, in short, just to that intense and pure elevation of *soul—not* of intellect, or of heart—upon which I have commented, and which is experienced in consequence of contemplating "the beautiful." Now I designate Beauty as the province of the poem, merely because it is an obvious rule of Art that effects should be made to spring from direct causes—that objects should be attained through means best adapted for their attainment— no one as yet having been weak enough to deny that the peculiar elevation alluded to is *most readily* attained in the poem. Now the object Truth, or the satisfaction of the intellect, and the object Passion, or the excitement of the heart, are, although attainable, to a certain extent, in poetry, far more readily attainable in prose. Truth, in fact, demands a precision, and Passion, a *homeliness* (the truly passionate will comprehend me) which are absolutely antagonistic to that Beauty which, I maintain, is the excitement, or pleasurable elevation, of the soul. It by no means follows from anything here said, that passion, or even truth, may not be introduced, and even profitably introduced, into a poem— for they may serve in elucidation, or aid the general effect, as do discords in music, by contrast—but the true artist will always contrive, first, to tone them into proper subservience to the predominant aim, and, secondly, to enveil them, as far as possible, in that Beauty which is the atmosphere and the essence of the poem.

Regarding, then, Beauty as my province, my next question referred to the *tone* of its highest manifestation—and all experience has shown that this tone is one of *sadness*. Beauty of whatever kind, in its supreme development, invariably excites the sensitive soul to tears. Melancholy is thus the most legitimate of all the poetical tones.

The length, the province, and the tone, being thus determined, I betook myself to ordinary induction, with the view of obtaining some artistic piquancy which might serve me as a key-note in the construction of the poem—some pivot upon which the whole structure might turn. In carefully thinking over all the usual artistic effects—or more properly *points*, in the theatrical sense—I did not fail to perceive immediately that no one had been so universally employed as that of the *refrain*. The universality of its employment sufficed to assure me of its intrinsic value, and spared me the necessity of submitting it to analysis. I considered it, however, with regard to its susceptibility of improvement, and soon saw it to be in a primitive condition. As commonly used, the *refrain*, or burden, not only is limited to lyric verse, but depends for its impression upon the force of monotone—both in sound and thought. The pleasure is deduced solely from the sense of identity—of repetition. I resolved to diversify, and so vastly heighten, the effect, by adhering, in general, to the monotone of sound, while I continually varied that of thought: that is to say, I determined to produce continuously novel effects, by the variation of *the application* of the *refrain*—the *refrain* itself remaining, for the most part, unvaried.

These points being settled, I next bethought me of the *nature* of my *refrain*. Since its application was to be repeatedly varied, it was clear that the *refrain* itself must be brief, for there would have been an insurmountable difficulty in frequent variations of application in any sentence of length. In proportion to the brevity of the sentence, would, of course, be the facility of the variation. This led me at once to a single word as the best *refrain*.

The question now arose as to the *character* of the word. Having made up my mind to a *refrain*, the division of the poem into stanzas was, of course, a corollary: the *refrain* forming the close to each stanza. That such a close, to have force, must be sonorous and susceptible of protracted emphasis, admitted no doubt: and these considerations inevitably led me to the long *o* as the most sonorous vowel, in connection with *r* as the producible consonant.

The sound of the *refrain* being thus determined, it became necessary to select a word embodying this sound, and at the same time in the fullest possible keeping with that melancholy which I had predetermined as the tone of the poem. In such a search it would have been absolutely impossible to overlook the word "Nevermore." In fact, it was the very first which presented itself.

The next *desideratum* was a pretext for the continuous use of the one word "nevermore." In observing the difficulty which I at once found in inventing a sufficiently plausible reason for its continuous repetition, I did not fail to perceive that this difficulty arose solely from the pre-assumption that the word was to be so continuously or monotonously spoken by a *human* being—I did not fail to perceive, in short, that the difficulty lay in the reconciliation of this monotony with the exercise of reason on the part of the creature repeating the word. Here, then, immediately arose the idea of a *non*-reasoning creature capable of speech; and, very naturally, a parrot, in the first instance, suggested itself, but was superseded forthwith by a Raven, as equally capable of speech, and infinitely more in keeping with the intended *tone*.

I had now gone so far as the conception of a Raven—the bird of ill omen—monotonously repeating the one word, "Nevermore," at the conclusion of each stanza, in a poem of melancholy tone, and in length about one hundred lines. Now, never losing sight of the object *supremeness*, or perfection, at all points, I asked myself—"Of all melancholy topics, what, according to the *universal* understanding of mankind, is the *most* melancholy?" Death—was the obvious reply. "And when," I said, "is this most melancholy of topics most poetical?" From what I have already explained at some length, the answer, here also, is obvious—"When it most closely allies itself to *Beauty*: the death, then, of a beautiful woman is, unquestionably, the most poetical topic in the world—and equally is it beyond doubt that the lips best suited for such topic are those of a bereaved lover."

I had now to combine the two ideas, of a lover lamenting his deceased mistress and a Raven continuously repeating the word "Nevermore"—I had to combine these, bearing in mind my design of varying, at every turn, the *application* of the word repeated; but the only intelligible mode of such combination is that of imagining the Raven employing the word in answer to the queries of the lover. And here it was that I saw at once the opportunity afforded for the effect on which I had been depending—that is to say, the effect of the *variation of application*. I saw that I could make the first query propounded by the lover—the first query to which the Raven should reply "Nevermore"—that I could make this first query a commonplace one— the second less so—the third still less, and so on—until at length the lover, startled from his original *nonchalance* by the melancholy character of the word itself—by its frequent repetition—and by a consideration of the ominous reputation of the fowl that uttered it—is at length excited to superstition, and wildly propounds queries of a far different character—queries whose solution he has passionately at heart—propounds them half in superstition and half in that species of despair which delights in self-torture—propounds them not altogether because he believes in the prophetic or demoniac character of the bird (which, reason assures him, is merely repeating a lesson learned by rote) but because he experiences a phrenzied[9] pleasure in so modeling his questions as to receive from the *expected* "Nevermore" the most delicious because the most intolerable of sorrow. Perceiving the opportunity thus afforded me—or, more strictly, thus forced upon me in the progress of the construction—I first established in mind the climax, or concluding query—that query to which "Nevermore" should be in the last place an answer—that in reply to which this word "Nevermore" should involve the utmost conceivable amount of sorrow and despair.

Here then the poem may be said to have its beginning—at the end, where all works of art should begin—for it was here, at this point of my preconsiderations, that I first put pen to paper in the composition of the stanza:

> "Prophet," said I, "thing of evil! prophet still if bird or devil!
> By that heaven that bends above us—by that God we both
>   adore,
> Tell this soul and sorrow laden, if within the distant Aidenn,
> It shall clasp a sainted maiden whom the angels name
>   Lenore—
> Clasp a rare and radiant maiden whom the angels name
>   Lenore."
> Quoth the raven "Nevermore."

I composed the stanza, at this point, first that, by establishing the climax, I might the better vary and graduate, as regards seriousness and importance, the preceding queries of the lover—and, secondly, that I might definitely settle the rhythm, the metre, and the length and general arrangement of the stanza—as well as graduate the stanzas which were to precede, so that none of them might surpass this in rhythmical effect. Had I been able, in the subsequent composition, to construct more vigorous stanzas, I should, without scruple, have purposely enfeebled them, so as not to interfere with the climacteric effect.

And here I may as well say a few words of the versification. My first object (as usual) was originality. The extent to which this has been neglected, in versification, is one of the most unaccountable things in the world. Admitting that there is little possibility of variety in mere *rhythm*, it is still clear that the possible varieties of metre and stanza are absolutely infinite—and yet, *for centuries, no man, in verse, has ever done, or ever seemed to think of doing, an original thing.* The fact is, originality (unless in minds of very unusual force) is by no means a matter, as some suppose, of impulse or intuition. In general, to be found, it must be elaborately sought, and although a positive merit of the highest class, demands in its attainment less of invention than negation.

Of course, I pretend to no originality in either the rhythm or metre of the "Raven." The former is trochaic—the latter is octameter acatalectic, alternating with heptameter catalectic repeated in the *refrain* of the fifth verse, and terminating with tetrameter catalectic. Less pedantically—the feet employed throughout (trochees) consist of a long syllable followed by a short: the first line of the stanza consists of eight of these feet—the second of seven and a half (in effect two-thirds)—the third of eight—the fourth of seven and a half—the fifth the same—the sixth three and a half. Now, each of these lines, taken individually, has been employed before, and what originality the "Raven" has, is in their *combination into stanza*; nothing even remotely approaching this combination has ever been attempted. The effect of this originality of combination is aided by other unusual, and some altogether novel effects, arising from an extension of the application of the principles of rhyme and alliteration.

The next point to be considered was the mode of bringing together the lover and the Raven—and the first branch of this consideration was the *locale*. For this the most natural suggestion might seem to be a forest, or the fields—but it has always appeared to me that a close *circumscription of space* is absolutely necessary to the effect of insulated incident:—it has the force of a frame to a picture. It has an indisputable moral power in keeping concentrated the attention, and, of course, must not be confounded with mere unity of place.[10]

I determined, then, to place the lover in his chamber—in a chamber rendered sacred to him by memories of her who had frequented it. The room is represented as richly furnished—this is mere pursuance of the ideas I have already explained on the subject of Beauty, as the sole true poetical thesis.

The *locale* being thus determined, I had now to introduce the bird—and the thought of introducing him through the window, was inevitable. The idea of making the lover suppose, in the first instance, that the flapping of the wings of the bird against the shutter, is a "tapping" at the door, originated in a wish to increase, by prolonging, the reader's curiosity, and in a desire to admit the incidental effect arising from the lover's throwing open the door, finding all dark, and thence adopting the half-fancy that it was the spirit of his mistress that knocked.

I made the night tempestuous, first, to account for the Raven's seeking admission, and secondly, for the effect of contrast with the (physical) serenity within the chamber.

I made the bird alight on the bust of Pallas,[11] also for the effect of contrast between the marble and the plumage—it being understood that the bust was absolutely *suggested* by the bird—the bust of *Pallas* being chosen, first, as most in keeping with the scholarship of the lover, and, secondly, for the sonorousness of the word, Pallas, itself.

About the middle of the poem, also, I have availed myself of the force of contrast, with a view of deepening the ultimate impression. For example, an air of the fantastic—approaching as nearly to the ludicrous as was admissible—is given to the Raven's entrance. He comes in "with many a flirt and flutter."

> Not the *least obeisance made he*—not a moment stopped or
> stayed he,
> But with *mien of lord or lady*, perched above my chamber
> door.

In the two stanzas which follow, the design is more obviously carried out:—

> Then this ebony bird beguiling my sad fancy into smiling
> By the *grave and stern decorum of the countenance it wore,*
> "Though thy *crest be shorn and shaven* thou," I said, "art
> sure no craven,
> Ghastly grim and ancient Raven wandering from the nightly
> shore—
> Tell me what thy lordly name is on the Night's Plutonian
> shore!"
> Quoth the Raven "Nevermore."
>
> Much I marvelled *this ungainly fowl* to hear discourse so
> plainly,
> Though its answer little meaning—little relevancy bore;
> For we cannot help agreeing that no living human being
> *Ever yet was blessed with seeing bird above his chamber
> door—*
> *Bird or beast upon the sculptured bust above his chamber
> door,*
> With such name as "Nevermore."

The effect of the *dénouement* being thus provided for, I immediately drop the fantastic for a tone of the most profound seriousness:—this tone commencing in the stanza directly following the one last quoted, with the line,

> But the Raven, sitting lonely on that placid bust, spoke only,
> etc.

From this epoch the lover no longer jests—no longer sees anything even of the fantastic in the Raven's demeanor. He speaks of him as a "grim, ungainly, ghastly, gaunt, and ominous bird of yore," and feels the "fiery eyes" burning into his "bosom's core." This revolution of thought, or fancy, on the lover's part, is intended to induce a similar one on the part of the reader—to bring the mind into a proper frame for the *dénouement*—which is now brought about as rapidly and as *directly* as possible.

With the *dénouement* proper—with the Raven's reply, "Nevermore," to the lover's final demand if he shall meet his mistress in another world—the poem, in its obvious phase, that of a simple narrative, may be said to have its completion. So far, everything is within the limits of the accountable—of the real. A raven, having learned by rote the single word "Nevermore," and having escaped from the custody of its owner, is driven at midnight, through the violence of a storm, to seek admission at a window from which a light still gleams—the chamber-window of a student, occupied half in poring over a volume, half in dreaming of a beloved mistress deceased. The casement being thrown open at the fluttering of the bird's wings, the bird itself perches on the most convenient seat out of the immediate reach of the student, who, amused by the incident and the oddity of the visitor's demeanor, demands of it, in jest and without looking for a reply, its name. The raven addressed, answers with its customary word, "Nevermore"—a word which finds immediate echo in the melancholy heart of the student, who, giving utterance aloud to certain thoughts suggested by the occasion, is again startled by the fowl's repetition of "Nevermore." The student now guesses the state of the case, but is impelled, as I have before explained, by the human thirst for self-torture, and in part by superstition, to propound such queries to the bird as will bring him, the lover, the most of the luxury of sorrow, through the anticipated answer "Nevermore." With the indulgence, to the extreme, of this self-torture, the narration, in what I have termed its first or obvious phase, has a natural termination, and so far there has been no overstepping of the limits of the real.

But in subjects so handled, however skilfully, or with however vivid an array of incident, there is always a certain hardness or nakedness, which repels the artistical eye. Two things are invariably required—first, some amount of complexity, or more properly, adaptation; and, secondly, some amount of suggestiveness—some undercurrent, however indefinite, of meaning. It is this latter, in especial, which imparts to a work of art so much of that *richness* (to borrow from colloquy[12] a forcible term) which we are too fond of confounding with *the ideal*. It is the *excess* of the suggested meaning—*it is* the rendering this the upper instead of the undercurrent of the theme—which turns into prose (and that of the very flattest kind) the so called poetry of the so called transcendentalists.[13]

Holding these opinions, I added the two concluding stanzas of the poem—their suggestiveness being thus made to pervade all the narrative which has preceded them. The undercurrent of meaning is rendered first apparent in the lines—

> "Take thy beak from out my heart, and take thy form from
> off my door!"
> Quoth the Raven "Nevermore!"

It will be observed that the words, "from out my heart," involve the first metaphorical expression in the poem. They, with the answer, "Nevermore," dispose the mind to seek a moral in all that has been previously narrated. The reader begins now to regard the Raven as emblematical—but it is not until the very last line of the very last stanza, that the intention of making him emblematical[14] of *Mournful and Never-ending Remembrance* is permitted distinctly to be seen:

> And the Raven, never flitting, still is sitting, still is sitting,
> On the pallid bust of Pallas, just above my chamber door;
> And his eyes have all the seeming of a demon's that is
>   dreaming,
> And the lamplight o'er him streaming throws his shadow on
>   the floor;
> And my soul *from out that shadow* that lies floating on the
>   floor
> Shall be lifted—nevermore.

NOTES

[1] Autorial: authorial, belonging to writers.

[2] *Histrio* is a Latin-derived term for actor. Poe's extensive use of Latin terms in this essay can partly be ascribed to nineteenth-century practice, but also to his desire to make his discussion appear weighty and important.

[3] Latin for "that which is desired."

[4] Latin for "a mode of operating," a method of doing things.

[5] Latin for "as such."

[6] Latin for "other things being equal."

[7] A long poem by the English religious poet John Milton (1608–1674).

[8] The novel by Daniel Defoe (1660–1731).

[9] Old-fashioned spelling of "frenzied."

[10] The literary doctrine that claims all the work's action should happen in the same place.

[11] Probably a reference to Pallas Athena, the warrior goddess in Greek mythology.

[12] An old-fashioned word for conversation.

[13] In nineteenth-century America, transcendentalism was an idealistic philosophy associated in particular with Ralph Waldo Emerson.

[14] Serving as a symbol.

VOCABULARY

vacillating—fluctuating, wavering between different ideas

interpolations—insertions of new material into a text

pinions—wings

corollary—something that follows naturally, the next step

sonorous—having a full, rich and strong sound

locale—locality, place

obeisance—bodily act or gesture indicative of submission, such as a bow

dénouement—the unravelling of complications of a plot

QUESTIONS

1. According to some critics, artists must make conscious, rational choices; according to other critics, artists rely mostly on intuition and inspiration. What is Poe's stand in this debate?

2. Poe develops and organizes his essay as a process analysis. Locate the transitional words and phrases that make the steps in this procedure obvious to a reader.

3. How does the structure of this essay reflect Poe's views on composition?

4. Do you think Poe gives aspiring poets good advice on how to write poetry? Is Poe's advice valuable for writers of essays?

5. Does the literary quality of "The Raven" justify Poe's approach to composition? Did Poe's essay change your opinion of this poem?

SUGGESTIONS FOR WRITING

1. Use your responses to Poe's theory of composition as a starting point for a short essay on your own philosophy of composition. If you have written poetry, songs, stories, you can compare your experience in composition with Poe's. Are your ideas about the process of composition always consistent with your practice?

2. Write a short essay in which you compare Poe's use of process analysis to develop and organize his ideas in "The Philosophy of Composition" with Merwin's in "Unchopping a Tree."

SPECIAL ENGLISH

Frederic Raphael

When they first met, leaning on the saline rail of a winter steamer, she had no English. He took her, his prize, to a remote island, where they rented a cottage from a peasant who had never before seen a typewriter. Each evening they listened, on a transistor radio, to broadcasts in special English from the American airbase on the larger island across the wine-dark sea. These broadcasts were slanted towards those who did not understand English very well. They were delivered in slow tempo and the vocabulary was instructively simple. They were, however, news broadcasts and the main news of the moment was a series of atrocities and counter atrocities committed in the course of a colonial war. Every night brought distinct variations on the gruesome theme. The lovers listened in the warming lamplight to unhurried stories of murder and mutilation. As day succeeded day, evening evening, the remote girl understood more and more. He watched her, smiling in the golden light of the paraffin, as her eyes kindled with closer comprehension. There was pride in her glance, for soon she would be able to follow his work and her chances of holding his love would, no doubt, be enhanced. Thus she would sometimes laugh, with newly educated vanity, as the tales of ambush and fratricide, or massacre and reprisal, grew more and more clear to her. Slowly then, and in pace with that unhurried, educating voice on the radio, the vocabulary of their understanding was stained with the world's blood, and slowly, as she smiled across at him each night with dawning confidence, he read eyes eloquent with bright knowledge of special English: he learned, at funeral speed, to hate her.

Frederic Raphael was born in 1931 and educated at Charterhouse and St. John's College, Cambridge. He is the author of, among other works, the novels *The Earlsdon Way* (1958) and *The Limits of Love* (1960), screenplays of *Far From the Madding Crowd* (1964) and *Daisy Miller* (1974), a biography of Somerset Maugham and a translation of *The Poems of Catullus* (1976). The following short story was first published in 1979. "Special English" from *Sleeps Six and Other Stories* by Frederic Raphael. Copyright © 1979 by Volatic Ltd. Reproduced by permission of the author c/o Rogers, Coleridge & White Ltd., 20 Powis Mews, London WII IJN

STARVING FOR THE GOLD

Laura Robinson

IMAGINE for a moment you are an Olympic athlete. If you pictured a male athlete, try again. Actually, you are a woman, engaged in rigorous year-round training. Now, imagine that your body-fat percentage is less than half the average for a reasonably active woman your age. As a result, your menstrual cycle has stopped; you no longer have a period. You are a textbook case of anorexia nervosa, obsessed with weight and body shape. Perhaps you are bulimic, and resort to compulsive binge eating, followed by violent purging—vomiting, fasting or the taking of laxatives and diuretics. If you are a junior athlete, in your early teens, you are effectively delaying the onset of puberty and stunting normal growth.

A rational observer would conclude that you are seriously ill. A rational observer would not suspect that you had been driven to these life-threatening disorders by your coach.

thesis statement

According to five women, former members of Canada's national sports teams, their coaches' insistence on excessive thinness threatened their physical health. The athletes' identities have been disguised, for reasons that will presently be made clear.

The first woman, while still a junior, was told by her coach that she should "think about" losing weight. "I was 5-foot-5 and weighed 135, but he said, 'Look, all the top women, all the senior women are thin.' So I thought, 'Maybe I am a little chubby.' I started to train for the Calgary Olympics. By late 1987, I weighed less than 110. I was constantly hungry, but I told myself, 'This is a good feeling.' I lost another five pounds the week before our qualifying competition, but I felt extremely weak and didn't make the team." Her standing began to suffer and, two years later, she retired from active competition.

Says another woman: "Looking back, I can see how stupid it was. The coaches were saying, 'Hey, we've got the thinnest team around; the girls are looking great.' We didn't have good results, but that didn't seem to matter. I was just a teenager, and a coach's

Laura Robinson, born in 1958 and presently a recreational ski racer, belonged to Canada's national cycling team in the mid 1970s. She threatened to resign from the team to protest chauvinistic behaviour on the part of coaches and team members. This essay appeared in *The Globe and Mail*, Saturday, April 11, 1992, D1, D5. "Starving for the Gold" courtesy of Laura Robinson.

attitude means everything when you're young. Now, I'm angry. They screwed up my mind, and I'll never be able to look at food again the way I did before."

A third athlete, now attending university, wrote in a study of athletic amenorrhea (cessation of the menstrual period): "Pressure was always felt to be lean, and considerable emphasis was placed on being beneath 12-per-cent body fat.[1] It seemed that the primary goal was to maintain a low body-fat composition. Often, it was felt this was more important than actual performance."

This pressure was applied in unmistakable ways. One coach held contests to see who could leave the most food uneaten on her plate at training camp. Yet another athlete experienced anxiety attacks over the caliper tests and pool dunking (total submersion in order to accurately gauge a subject's body fat). "After the tests, we'd compare results," she says. "Our coach would announce at dinner who had the lowest fat percentage, and the roller-coaster eating would start all over again."

ONE'S first reaction to these charges is a measure of disbelief. We hesitate to think that coaches would do such things—but not so long ago, our athletes were supplied with anabolic steroids because it was "necessary" in order to win, because "everyone else did it." A conspiracy of silence surrounded these activities. Ben Johnson's and Angella Issajenko's physiques were obviously artificial; the changes in their bodies couldn't be attributed to natural causes. Every athlete, every sports journalist and sports official had ample cause for suspicion. No one spoke up.

Next, one might ask: Where are the women coaches, who presumably wouldn't participate in this nonsense? An answer is suggested by the dismissal in February of Ken Porter, Athletics Canada's former director of track and field technical programs. Mr. Porter claimed that he was fired in part because he wished to promote black and women coaches, and deplored the relegation of women to "a ghetto-type position as team chaperone."

Third, why hasn't coaching malfeasance come to light? Well, it has. The Dubin Report, commissioned after Ben Johnson tested positive for anabolic steroids at the 1988 Seoul Olympics, concluded that coaches must assume responsibility for the "health, welfare, moral education and preparation for life of the athlete." Since then, another report, prepared for the federal Minister of Fitness and Amateur Sport, found that athletes feel they are coerced into "harmful practices ... and believe their concerns on the subject of personal harm are ignored." A third report, undertaken on behalf of the same ministry, is due within the next month. It is said to address the issue of physical and sexual abuse.

The reports stack up, the problems are studied to death, and the bad-apple coaches are seldom weeded out.

According to Marion Lay, manager of the Women's Program at Sport Canada (the funding agent for our national teams), "Coaches who manipulate through food and body image are robbing women of their self-esteem and self-respect. But what safe place is there for an athlete who feels abused?"

The women who confided in me asked for anonymity because some of them intend to work within the system; but even those who maintain only a casual interest fear that if they speak out they will be perceived as "traitors" to sport. Ms. Lay's reaction says it all: "Of course, they can't reveal their identities. There's no mechanism to protect them."

Why this particular form of abuse? Helen Lenskyj, a sports sociologist at the Ontario Institute for Studies in Education, cites the emergence during the 1970s of a prepubescent body type—the very young, very thin gymnast, minus hips and breasts, whose appearance continues to influence judges when it comes to awarding points for artistic merit in the so-called esthetic sports. As a result, coaches everywhere decided that their athletes should look like Soviet gymnast Olga Korbut. In fact, leanness is a factor in both esthetic and endurance sports—to a point. Athletes shouldn't carry extra pounds. The trouble is that not everyone is prepubescent, and can't possibly look that way, no matter what she does.

Another factor, according to Marion Lay, is simply resistance to change. The last two decades have seen a dramatic increase in the number of female competitors. Ms. Lay feels that often coaches haven't come to terms with this fact: "There's an attitude of, 'yes, we'll let you in, but you have to play the game our way, look the way we want you to look.' Women have to give things up in order to enter sports." In other words, the predominant view (because men control sports) is that sports are male. If a woman is going to take part, she'd better resemble a man. If she's got womanly hips, she can't really be an athlete, because real athletes aren't women—and so on, all round the vicious circle.

Little wonder that even so cautious an organization as the Coaching Association of Canada (CAC) raises the shocking notion that nearly one-third of all women athletes have some sort of eating disorder. This figure, culled from unspecified studies, appears in the National Coaching Certification Program's Level III Course—mandatory at the national-team level. The course describes the symptoms of anorexia and bulimia, and provides checklists for their detection, but assumes that the person studying the materials isn't the source of the difficulty. According to Tom Kinsman, the CAC's executive director, "These are problems that weren't talked about before, so we didn't write about them. I hope a new awareness will go a long way in helping people raise the issues with dignity and security. But I can tell you the process won't be nice, clean and clear-cut."

Apparently not. In fact, these issues were under discussion when I began competing over 20 years ago. One of the problems has always been, as Mr. Kinsman admits, if a coach acts improperly, it's up to the sport's governing body, not the CAC, to discipline him—an unlikely scenario if athletes are too intimidated to lodge complaints, and "believe their concerns are ignored" when and if they do so.

It is important not to trivialize the issue here. Demeaning comments and sexist behaviour aren't confined to the world of sports. Yes, it's crude and counterproductive to criticize an athlete in front of her peers. If a coach's first reaction to every woman who passes by is "What a lardass," the message sinks in. These things are wounding, but women everywhere face similar indignities daily. Nor do I suggest that every coach is like Charlie Francis, Ben Johnson's steroid supplier.

A skeptic would argue that plenty of non-athletic teen-agers are anorectic, that countless women punish their bodies for doubtful ends (silicone implants and face-lifts spring to mind), that a certain number of women athletes would succumb to eating disorders even with the most supportive and caring coach. As well, an athlete places such extraordinary demands on her body that it's hard to pinpoint cause and effect.

All this may be so. But it can't be denied that Canada's most senior coaches are exacerbating—if not creating—a problem of terrible magnitude.

With devastating results. First, long-term amenorrheics are susceptible to a loss in bone density or osteoporosis (abnormally porous or weakened bones). If these conditions persist, one in three such athletes, depending on her sport, will suffer a fracture. A 1985 study found that even athletes with irregular (as opposed to nonexistent) periods were nearly four times more prone to stress fractures than those whose periods were uninterrupted.

Next, and more serious, is the fact that athletes engage in regular aerobic activity, which reduces low-density lipoprotein-cholesterol. So far, so good—LDL-C is a contributing factor in coronary ailments. But, because an amenorrheic woman's estrogen secretions are low, this positive effect is reversed. Up go the LDL-C levels; up goes the risk of heart disease.

Lastly, it's been predicted that almost 15 per cent of anorectics and bulimics will die over the course of 30 years as a direct result of their disorders. There hasn't been a verifiable instance yet among Canadian athletes—but these are early days.

SO the question remains: Why would a coach encourage such dangerous behaviour? Anorectic athletes are too unhealthy to do well over
the long haul; you can't compete at the international level if you're
starving yourself. Many athletes eventually break down and disappear
from view. Unless they're household names, no one notices. They're
interchangeable; there are plenty more where they came from.

One answer has been suggested by Ms. Lenskyj, the OISE sports
psychologist: it's imitative crime. In addition to underage gymnasts like
Olga Korbut, a fair number of older European athletes are much too
thin. I could name an entire cycling team whose members are plainly
anorectic. They're fast on the road, but they're burning out even faster.
Watch for them at the Barcelona Olympics, because they won't be
competing in a couple of years.

But Marion Lay's comments earlier about forced make-overs may
be closer to the mark. Notes Karin Jasper, a Toronto psychotherapist:
"The athletic look is lean with narrow hips, and we have learned that
women dislike the size of their hips, stomachs and thighs, those areas
most connected with pregnancy." Constant harping on these areas—
the first ones to catch a male coach's eye—is enough to stir up instant
insecurity. "The ideal male athlete has narrow hips, but that's not normal for women," says Ms. Lenskyj. "Dieting can't change skeletal structure. Only a few girls have bodies that correspond to a male's in terms
of leanness. If coaches use weight and fat percentages as a tool to manipulate athletes, it is a form of sexual abuse." weaknesses

The inescapable conclusion is that the coach, unused to women in
sport, wants them to look like boys. Or, failing that, like little girls.
This syndrome assumes even more ominous overtones when you consider the inordinate number of women athletes and coaches who wind
up as romantic items. I remember a Canadian national team where
every member was living with or married to her coach or technical ad-
viser. One hesitates to speculate on these unions. According to Karin
Jasper, an unfortunate side-effect of self-starvation is often a loss of
sexual drive. The coach gets less than he bargained for in that department. The other possibility is that his fondest wish has come true—he
has found someone who's lost all outward signs of womanhood—no
breasts, no hips, no period. It makes you wonder whether he might not
be happier coaching little boys.

The real imperative here is obviously control over someone less
powerful, someone malleable and eager to please. Given that girls
begin their athletic careers very young, they don't get a chance to develop into well-rounded human beings in any sense. I personally believe that many male coaches don't like, and are ill-equipped to deal
with, grown women. There's no other explanation for the ceaseless humiliation and ridicule—the construction of a closed system where

trauma becomes a tool to produce great-looking girls, the thinnest team around.

Is change possible in the world of organized sports? Let's give coaches the benefit of the doubt. Maybe they think that all these things will actually help us bring home lots of medals. Remember the outcry when Canada's skaters "failed to win Gold," and had to "settle for" Bronze. Third-best in the world translated as "not good enough." (The logical extension of this sort of thinking is that, whatever an athlete's body is like, it's never right. It's too fat, too thin, too this or too that.)

When our athletes, being human, made mistakes, they were savagely criticized by the media. As a result, every athlete, man or woman, becomes a performance machine. Karin Jasper is not surprised: "We talk to girls and women about overcoming perfectionism, about not basing their evaluation of themselves on all-or-nothing standards. But athletes are taught to see themselves this way. Either they win, or they don't. When their entire value is based on performance, they won't be viewed as a whole person, they're one-dimensional."

Under these conditions, even an influx of women coaches would do little good. Until the system asks what's best for a given person, not an athlete, it's stuck in the all-or-nothing groove. For male coaches to change, they'd have to re-examine their priorities, their own sexuality, their entire basis for coaching. That's not going to happen.

The real tragedy is that sports can feel so good, so refreshing and exciting and freeing. I entered organized sports when I was 14. I was lucky. I had people who made sure I got to the races on time, but also gave me plenty of books to read. Still, I couldn't help but be affected to some degree. I was obsessed with exercise; I overtrained. That was my response to the pressure, and it wasn't healthy. Even now, I tend to avoid scales. I have to think twice if someone asks me if I consider myself thin. I escaped the worst of it, but my attitudes remain.

One of the women whose own sad story I recounted earlier has started to coach girls between the ages of 12 and 16.[2] "They ask me if they're overweight," she says, "and I tell them, 'If you think you can work with your weight, then you're fine. This is the body God has given you, so enjoy it.'" That's encouraging, as far as it goes—although the fact that 12-year-old athletes anguish about their weight is food for thought. But, because of her experiences, this woman is incapable of saying, "This is the body God has given me, so I'll enjoy it." That has been taken from her, and nothing can compensate her for such a loss.

NOTES

[1] Normal percentage of body fat for college-level female athletes is between 10% and 15%.

[2] The majority of anorectics (85%) are women and the majority of those are between the ages of 12 and 18. It is estimated that between 0.4% and 1% of all women in the United States

between the ages of 16 and 18 will suffer from anorexia and that the condition is responsible for as many as 3,750 deaths each year. (Michael Maloney and Rachel Kranz, *Straight Talk About Eating Disorders*. N.Y.: Facts On File, 1991.)

QUESTIONS

1. For the most part, Robinson develops her explanation of eating disorders among female athletes as causal analysis. According to Robinson, what are the main causes of eating disorders among female athletes?

2. Does this causal analysis provide convincing evidence to support her evaluation of sports in Canada? What standards of evaluation does she employ?

3. How would you describe the tone of this essay? Be specific about Robinson's attitudes to her subject, herself, and her reader.

SUGGESTION FOR WRITING

How do you think Robinson would respond to Maggie Helwig's essay "A Certain Hunger: The Body Language of Anorexia"? Imagine that you are Robinson and write a reply to Helwig. Or imagine that these two writers are having coffee and write a dialogue that captures the conversation about voluntary starvation they might be having.

SENSUAL EDUCATION

Robert S. Root-Bernstein

Music has long exerted unusual power over the scientific temperament. The French mathematician Joseph Louis Lagrange proclaimed that he worked best to the sound of music. Einstein's avocational devotion to the violin is legendary. The American chemist Charles Martin Hall was an accomplished pianist who, according to his sister, would rush to his piano whenever he encountered an intractable problem. Even "while playing with such charm and feeling," she wrote, "he was thinking steadily of his work, and thinking the more clearly because of [the music]." Some scientists, indeed, have found music overly stimulating: in his later years Charles Darwin found concerts painful to attend because they set his mind off into "too rapid perambulations."

Countless investigators from every field of science recall the inspiration they gained from growing up in musical families. The MIT[1] physicist Victor F. Weisskopf recalled in an interview how, as a child, he would listen to the practicing of his great-aunt Tony, a concert pianist: "I remember as a little boy sitting under the piano when she played Beethoven, and it came down like water, and I was sitting in that sea of sound." The Swedish physiologist P.F. Scholander recounted virtually the same experience: "Emotion has certainly been a strong ingredient in my life, whether in music or science. As a small boy I crawled underneath my mother's Steinway when she practiced, smothered by waves of emotion in the music of Bach, Grieg, Sinding."[2]

To be sure, a childhood seat beneath the Steinway does not ensure later achievement in science. Yet what is it about music that so inspires? Why this conjoining of the musical and the scientific muses? These thoughts flooded my mind recently as I listened to the music of the pianist Lorin Hollander. I was among a dozen other scientists and artists, musicians and educators brought together by the Society for the Advancement of Gifted Education in conjunction with the Teachers College of Columbia University. Our mission was to discuss a curriculum for highly talented Israeli high school students that would integrate the arts and the sciences. The Israel Arts and Sciences Academy, being built in Jerusalem, hopes to produce not just scientists, as does the Bronx High

Robert S. Root-Bernstein, the author of *Discovering* (1989), is a physiologist at Michigan State University in East Lansing, and a former MacArthur Fellow. He is engaged primarily in AIDS research. This article is reprinted by permission of THE SCIENCES and is from the September/October 1990 issue. The Sciences, 2 East 63rd Street, New York, NY 10021.

School of Science in New York, or just artists and musicians, as does the Fiorello H. LaGuardia High School of the Performing Arts, also in New York; rather it hopes to instill in students an understanding of and ability in both sets of disciplines.

As Hollander's music enveloped me, I mused about the simple rationale for this admittedly quixotic undertaking. The organizers of the Israeli academy believe that to deal with modern global issues people must be educated to combine technical knowledge and problem-solving techniques from many fields. But my colleagues at the symposium had been skeptical. Was it really wise to create such a truly integrated arts and sciences curriculum? How could one know it would work? If it was possible, why had no one done it before? Could the rare understanding of the few people who have excelled in both science and art be captured for even the handpicked elite, let alone for the many? Under the spell of Hollander's playing, I caught a glimpse of an approach to our aim.

The act of understanding, whether it concerns art, history, music or science, is not purely an intellectual experience but a sensual one as well. Insight in any discipline is usually accompanied by intense physical and emotional feelings, often expressed in aural, kinesthetic[3] or visual terms. Such feelings cannot be separated from the act of discovery itself. The intellect does not operate without the commitment of the individual as a whole, and so science will flourish only in the minds of sensitive and emotional people. "It may be odd to claim the same personal engagement for the scientist [as for the artist]," wrote the mathematician and poet Jacob Bronowski, "yet in this the scientist stands to the technician much as the artist stands to the craftsman." The best science, it seems, arises from the combination of an analytic mind with aesthetic sensitivity, a combination that might be called sensual science. It is this personal engagement in science, I reflected, that curriculum planners must consider and educators need to convey.

The notion of sensual science may strike many people as odd, even sacrilegious. In popular conceptions the scientist is an engine of logical inquiry: empirical observations are made, hypotheses developed and tested, solutions cleanly deduced. One might argue that the whole object of science is to eliminate personal, intuitive or otherwise subjective preconceptions from interfering with the objective analysis of the world. Yet this portrait of science focuses only on how insights are communicated and ignores the process by which they are gained.

According to the physicist and philosopher Michael Polanyi, understanding begins with "personal knowledge," the ability to mentally extend or project oneself into the object of study. The subject of inquiry ceases to be external; through an act of imagination the observer identifies with that subject and dwells within it. Possibly the best-known example is Einstein's use of the *Gedankenexperiment*, or thought experiment, which he described in a letter to his colleague Jacques Hadamard: "The psychical entities which seem to serve as elements in thought are certain signs and more or less clear images which can be 'voluntarily' reproduced and combined." Thus in formulating his ideas about the influence of gravity on time, Einstein pictured himself inside a falling elevator with a ray of light bouncing back and forth between opposite walls; in examining the special theory of relativity, he imagined what a moving light ray would look like if he pursued one at the speed of light. In short, his "muscular" visual images included him as an active participant. By exploiting such personal knowledge, Einstein was able to study the deepest implications of his theory of relativity.

Einstein's well-documented example notwithstanding, the technique appears to be rare among scientists. In *The Psychology of Invention in the Mathematical Field* [1954], Hadamard mentions that although various visual images were common among the mathematicians he investigated, kinesthetic feelings and auditory impressions were not. Similarly the psychologist Anne Roe, who conducted some of the first psychological studies of biologists and physicists of the postwar era, notes in *The Making of a Scientist* [1953], that almost half of her interviewees employed concrete visual images in their work, yet none reported the regular use of kinesthetic thinking to solve problems. In a study I helped direct at UCLA[4] a few years ago, only four out of forty scientists thought kinesthetically and then only rarely. Ironically Einstein's muscular mechanisms of thought do not seem to be accessible to the majority of the people—physicists and their students—who want to understand his results.

Nevertheless, many prominent scientists have shown a remarkable ability to empathize with their subject matter. Through an exercise of the imagination, scientific investigation becomes a kind of drama in which the scientist plays the leading role. Cyril Stanley Smith, who directed the metallurgical aspects of the atomic bomb project at Los Alamos[5] during the Second World War, gave one of the most detailed descriptions of the discovery process in a letter to a friend. In the course of developing alloys, Smith wrote, he gained

> a feeling of how I would behave if I were a certain alloy, a sense of hardness and softness and conductibility and fusibility and deformability and brittleness—all in a curiously internal and quite literally sensual way, even before I had sensual contact with the alloy itself ... All the work I did on interfaces really began with a combination of an aesthetic feeling for a balanced structure and a muscular feeling of the interfaces pulling against each other!

The use of scientific terminology, he wrote, was secondary to his tactual explorations: "The stage of *discovery* was entirely sensual and mathematics was only necessary to be able to communicate with other people. Perhaps discovery is always this way."

Perhaps it is. The American mathematician Stanislaw M. Ulam wrote of his "attempts to calculate, not by numbers and symbols, but by almost tactile feelings combined with reasoning." Likewise the Swedish physicist and Nobel laureate Hannes Alvén has recounted that, instead of meditating on equations, he prefers "to sit and ride on each electron and ion and try to imagine what the world is like from its point of view and what forces push [it] to the left or to the right."

Many biologists conduct their research in equally anthropomorphic ways. The Nobel prize-winning geneticist Barbara McClintock, in her biography by the historian Evelyn Fox Keller,[6] attributed her own revolutionary insights to an unusually well developed "feeling for the organism." Similarly, the English neurologist Charles Scott Sherrington raised the specter of personal knowledge in regard to the neuroanatomist and Nobel laureate Santiago Ramón y Cajal:

> He treated the microscopic scene as though it were alive and were inhabited by beings which felt and did and hoped and tried even as we do ... He would envisage the sperm cells as activated by a sort of passionate urge in their rivalry for penetration into the ovum-cell.

"Listening to him," Sherrington noted, "I asked myself how far this capacity for anthropomorphizing might not contribute to his success as an investigator."

So crucial is this approach that Joshua Lederberg, a former president of Rockefeller University and a Nobel laureate in medicine or physiology, has concluded that every scientist needs

> the ability to strip to the essential attributes some actor in a process, the ability to imagine oneself *inside* a biological situation; I literally had to be able to think for example, "What would it be like if I were one of the chemical pieces of a bacterial chromosome?" And [I had to] try to understand what my environment was, try to know *where* I was, try to know when I was supposed to function in a certain way, and so forth.

In other words, Lederberg maintains, a scientist requires much the same skills as a first-rate playwright, novelist or thespian. It is not enough that the plots of nature be sketched out, the characters clothed and their lines written down; they must be brought to life. Only a sensual imagination can vivify the sterile, motionless symbols and words through which scientists are forced to convey the shadows of their understanding.

Is it by chance, then, that not a few of the most insightful scientists of the past two centuries have developed their keen powers of observation, their sense of the harmony of data, their appreciation of form, symmetry and the beauty of a theory, their visceral understanding of the relation between theory and observation outside the course of their regular scientific training? In the nineteenth century the Frenchman Claude Bernard became one of the founders of modern physiology only after failing to find a niche as a playwright. Before his groundbreaking work on the mathematical study of genetics and enzymology, J.B.S. Haldane had acted in the plays of his sister, Naomi Mitchison, and had become a successful essayist and novelist. And stories abound of the unusual physical achievements of scientists: the gymnastic skills of Ramón y Cajal and the physicist Luis Alvarez, the tennis championships of the physicists Albert W. Michelson and Frederick A. Lindemann. Even Einstein has been described by C.P. Snow as having a surprisingly well developed physique, which could have resulted only from daily exercise: "It was a massive body, very heavily muscled. [He was] an unusually strong man."

Jacob Shaham, a physicist at Columbia University, has commented on the influence an early course in acting had on his scientific career. Shaham was to play a beggar, and, while he was learning his lines, it dawned on him that he had to bring the experiences of a beggar to the part. He then spent several weeks following beggars through the streets of Jerusalem, studying their gestures and their facial expressions and making their thoughts his own. This experience, Shaham recalls, never left him:

> For every equation, statement or idea I would study or come
> by, I would always try to look around it, see what follows,
> what may be related to it, what is missing … It is something
> that some of my science teachers did their best to give us a
> feel for, but only now, after having been doing science for
> over 20 years, do I realize how close to it I actually was from
> the start because of that dramatic role.

The implication of such examples seems to be that the usual modes of scientific training are inadequate by themselves for producing creative scientists; skills beyond verbal and mathematical fluency are required. Maybe it is too much to expect that educators or scientists will readily accept the idea that science might be taught through experiences in the arts, drama, literature, music or perhaps even athletics or other superficially unrelated disciplines. Nevertheless, students of the sciences must somehow learn the successful methods of their predecessors. If those methods include personal knowledge and sensual science, an effort of some kind must be made to codify and convey these ways of knowing.

Intriguingly, a handful of scientists have already attempted to translate some of those principles into functioning technologies. The chemist Robert C. Morrison of East Carolina University in North Carolina, among others, has developed computer programs that will translate patterns of numerical data into audible tones. As Morrison has pointed out, the ear is a much more sensitive instrument than the eye for recognizing patterns. Through the medium of music, then, an investigator would be able to distinguish recurrent themes in chemical analyses, economic indicators and other data bases too complex, both mathematically and visually, to allow ready analysis. Susumu Ohmo, a geneticist with the Beckman Research Institute of the City of Hope in Duarte, California, has even transcribed DNA sequences into evocative melodies.

Scientists and engineers elsewhere hope to bring the sense of touch into play. At the IBM Thomas J. Watson Research Center in Yorktown Heights, New York, David W. Abraham, Ralph L. Hollis and Septimiu E. Salcudean have developed a "magic wrist" that converts images from a scanning-tunneling microscope—a device that can resolve the atoms at the surface of a material—into three-dimensional movements. Thus a person wearing the device can actually feel the atomic surface structures of, say, metals and alloys. The IBM group has plans to attach their magic wrist to an atomic-force microscope—a device capable of measuring the attractive forces that bind molecules together—thereby enabling an investigator to experience chemical affinities firsthand.

Such devices may eventually enable workers to manipulate materials on a very small scale, and for this reason they are of particular interest to medicine. One eye surgeon is evaluating the magic wrist for the removal of retinal scar tissue from diabetic patients. A similar tele-microrobotic system, developed by Ian W. Hunter of McGill University in collaboration with engineering colleagues at MIT and the University of Auckland, can manipulate individual muscle cells. Biology students can thereby gain a direct kinesthetic knowledge of the human muscular system.

Similarly, one can imagine fostering an educational environment in which aural, kinesthetic and visual experience is intimately tied to the teaching of theory. The student laboratory, of course, is the traditional answer to the educational need for sensual contact with fundamental principles, and it is a tradition whose benefits should not be underestimated. But the behavior of mathematical functions—for instance, the path of a set of light rays through a complex optical system, or the configuration of a large organic molecule as it passes through a channel in the membrane of a cell—all can be inspected graphically on a computer monitor. More mundane techniques from the traditional humanities also could be enlisted. With the help of a choreographer,

Marvin L. Cohen, who is a professor of physics at the University of California at Berkeley, recently created *The Dance of the Electrons*, a stage adaptation of quantum mechanics that provides viewers and participants with a direct feel for how electrons behave in a superconductor. Similarly, why not encourage students to follow Jacob Shaham's lead and view equations as scripts? Why not at least insist that they write descriptions of physical processes, to paraphrase Richard Feynman, so that a high school student could understand them? To translate the undigested equations of the theory into metaphor, homespun analogy and the essentials of insight would be an exercise worthy of a station in Einstein's gym.

These devices and others yet to be invented are an exciting recognition of the need for sensual science, and they hold great promise as learning tools for the uninitiated. Yet the satisfaction of the quest for personal knowledge and the thrill of scientific discovery that so many investigators thrive on cannot be taught merely through mechanical devices. If today's scientists are to captivate the minds and souls of future generations, they must convey firsthand the joy of their research and the splendor of its sensuality.

What could be sadder than to learn of the following confession by the mathematician I.M. Singer: "I've never before lectured on personal matters like my own emotions toward research." How many other scientists could make the same admission? How many would have the courage? And how many confuse the admirable tradition of dryly and carefully eschewing hype and overstatement with the rather macho tendency to keep a straight face about how it feels to do science? No wonder so many students find science a dull, inhuman subject. Why not let them know about the many satisfactions Singer himself found in creativity? "I ... feel a kinship," he said, "with artists and scientists the world over. A Matisse[7] exhibit thrills and inspires me. I rush home and attack my own research problems with zest, feeling I am part of the world of Matisse. A good ballet affects me the same way."

Whatever else a scientific education does, it should inspire students to explore the varieties and virtues of personal, creative insight. For ultimately, as the English biologist C.H. Waddington said in 1969, "The acute problems of the world can be solved only by *whole* men, not by people who refuse to be, publicly, anything more than a technologist, or a pure scientist, or an artist. In the world of today you have got to be everything or you are going to be nothing." Young scientists, as much as budding artists or musicians, must learn to integrate the languages of self and nature; a scientist must learn to feel in order to think. Precisely how sensual science will be conveyed to the students of the Israeli academy remains to be seen. Judging from the number of past scientists who somehow learned to adopt it, however, it is clear that the set of educational solutions is not empty.

NOTES

[1] Massachusetts Institute of Technology.

[2] Johann Sebastian Bach, 1685–1750; Edvard Grieg, 1843–1907, Norwegian composer; Christian Sinding, 1856–1941, Danish composer.

[3] Relating to bodily reactions or motor memory.

[4] University of California, Los Angeles.

[5] Located on a mesa 30 miles from Santa Fe, New Mexico, Los Alamos is the site of the United States's most secret atomic bomb laboratory. The nearby Trinity Site was the location of the first nuclear explosion. Today it is one of the best-equipped physics labs anywhere.

[6] *A Feeling for the Organism: The Life and Work of Barbara McClintock* (San Francisco: Freeman, 1983).

[7] Henri Matisse, French painter, 1869–1954.

QUESTIONS

1. Essays are often written in response to a particular occasion or situation. The occasion for this essay was a gathering of "scientists and artists, musicians and educators" whose mission was to discuss a high school curriculum that "would integrate the arts and the sciences." Does this context illuminate the attitudes and concerns Root-Bernstein presents in this essay?

2. What is Root-Bernstein's thesis? Is it a thesis about science, about education, about intellectual understanding in general, or about all of these subjects? Is the thesis evaluative, and, if so, what standard(s) of evaluation does he use?

3. Root-Bernstein seems to pay particular attention to paragraph transitions. Examine the first sentence of each paragraph and underline words or phrases that create continuity with the previous paragraph.

4. Presumably few of Root-Bernstein's readers would be familiar with all of the disciplines from which he draws examples. Is this range of examples a weakness in the essay?

5. Throughout this essay, Root-Bernstein argues that experiences in the arts enhance work in the sciences. Do you agree? Do you think the reverse is also true? Do you know of any artists who are also scientists? Does scientific knowledge enhance your own endeavours in the arts?

6. Compare Root-Bernstein's account of scientific discovery with that found in Vivian Gornick's "Two Women…." Do you see any similarities?

SUGGESTION FOR WRITING

What are the arguments against integrating the arts and sciences in either secondary or post-secondary school curriculums? If you prefer to specialize in either the arts or the sciences, write a letter to Root-Bernstein expressing your views.

THE MEN WE CARRY IN OUR MINDS

Scott Russell Sanders

"This must be a hard time for women," I say to my friend Anneke. "They have so many paths to choose from, and so many voices calling them."

"I think it's a lot harder for men," she replies.

"How do you figure that?"

"The women I know feel excited, innocent, like crusaders in a just cause. The men I know are eaten up with guilt."

We are sitting at the kitchen table drinking sassafras tea,[1] our hands wrapped around the mugs because this April morning is cool and drizzly. "Like a Dutch morning," Anneke told me earlier. She is Dutch herself, a writer and midwife and peacemaker, with the round face and sad eyes of a woman in a Vermeer painting[2] who might be waiting for the rain to stop, for a door to open. She leans over to sniff a sprig of lilac, pale lavender, that rises from a vase of cobalt blue.

"Women feel such pressure to be everything, do everything," I say. "Career, kids, art, politics. Have their babies and get back to the office a week later. It's as if they're trying to overcome a million years' worth of evolution in one lifetime."

"But we help one another. We don't try to lumber on alone, like so many wounded grizzly bears, the way men do." Anneke sips her tea. I gave her the mug with the owls on it, for wisdom. "And we have this deep-down sense that we're in the *right*—we've been held back, passed over, used—while men feel they're in the wrong. Men are the ones who've been discredited, who have to search their souls."

I search my soul. I discover guilty feelings aplenty—towards the poor, the Vietnamese, Native Americans, the whales, an endless list of debts—a guilt in each case that is as bright and unambiguous as a neon sign. But toward women I feel something more confused, a snarl of shame, envy, wary tenderness, and amazement. This muddle troubles me. To hide my unease I say, "You're right, it's tough being a man these days."

"Don't laugh." Anneke frowns at me, mournful-eyed, through the sassafras steam.

Scott Russell Sanders (1945–) was born in Memphis, Tennessee. In addition to working as a professor of English at Indiana University, Sanders is a fiction writer, essayist, and critic. Among his publications are *Fetching the Dead: Stories* (1984), *Stone Country* (1985), and *The Paradise of Bombs* (1987), from which "The Men We Carry in Our Minds" is reprinted. Copyright © 1984 by Scott Russell Sanders; first appeared in *Milkweed Chronicle*; reprinted by permission of the author and Virginia Kidd Agency, Inc.

"I wouldn't be a man for anything. It's much easier being the victim. All the victim has to do is break free. The persecutor has to live with his past."

How deep is that past? I find myself wondering after Anneke has left. How much of an inheritance do I have to throw off? Is it just the beliefs I breathed in as a child? Do I have to scour memory back through father and grandfather? Through St. Paul?[3] Beyond Stonehenge[4] and into the twilit caves? I'm convinced the past we must contend with is deeper even than speech. When I think back on my childhood, on how I learned to see men and women, I have a sense of ancient, dizzying depths. The back roads of Tennessee and Ohio where I grew up were probably closer, in their sexual patterns, to the camp-sites of Stone Age hunters than to the genderless cities of the future into which we are rushing.

The first men, besides my father, I remember seeing were black convicts and white guards, in the cottonfield across the road from our farm on the outskirts of Memphis. I must have been three or four. The prisoners wore dingy gray-and-black zebra suits, heavy as canvas, sodden with sweat. Hatless, stooped, they chopped weeds in the fierce heat, row after row, breathing the acrid dust of boll-weevil poison.[5] The overseers wore dazzling white shirts and broad shadowy hats. The oiled barrels of their shotguns flashed in the sunlight. Their faces in memory are utterly blank. Of course those men, white and black, have become for me an emblem of racial hatred. But they have also come to stand for the twin poles of my early vision of manhood—the brute toiling animal and the boss.

When I was a boy, the men I knew labored with their bodies. They were marginal farmers, just scraping by, or welders, steel-workers, carpenters; they swept floors, dug ditches, mined coal, or drove trucks, their forearms ropy with muscle; they trained horses, stoked furnaces, built tires, stood on assembly lines wrestling parts onto cars and refrigerators. They got up before light, worked all day long whatever the weather, and when they came home at night they looked as though somebody had been whipping them. In the evenings and on weekends they worked on their own places, tilling gardens that were lumpy with clay, fixing broken-down cars, hammering on houses that were always too drafty, too leaky, too small.

The bodies of the men I knew were twisted and maimed in ways visible and invisible. The nails of their hands were black and split, the hands tattooed with scars. Some had lost fingers. Heavy lifting had given many of them finicky backs and guts weak from hernias. Racing against conveyor belts had given them ulcers. Their ankles and knees ached from years of standing on concrete. Anyone who had worked for long around machines was hard of hearing. They squinted, and the skin of their faces was creased like the leather of old work gloves. There were times, studying them, when I dreaded growing up. Most of them coughed, from dust or cigarettes, and most of them drank cheap wine or whiskey, so their eyes looked bloodshot and bruised. The fathers of my friends always seemed older than the mothers. Men wore out sooner. Only women lived into old age.

As a boy I also knew another sort of men, who did not sweat and break down like mules. They were soldiers, and so far as I could tell they scarcely worked at all. During my early school years we lived on a military base, an arsenal[6] in Ohio, and every day I saw GIs in the guardshacks, on the stoops of barracks, at the wheels of olive drab Chevrolets. The chief fact of their lives was boredom. Long after I left the Arsenal I came to recognize the sour smell the soldiers gave off as that of souls in limbo.[7] They were all waiting—for wars, for transfers, for leaves, for promotions, for the end of their hitch—like so many braves waiting for the hunt to begin. Unlike the warriors of older tribes, however, they would have no say about when the battle would start or how it would be waged. Their waiting was broken only when they practiced for war. They fired guns at targets, drove tanks across the churned-up fields of the military reservation, set off bombs in the wrecks of old fighter planes. I knew this was all play. But I also felt certain that when the hour for killing arrived, they would kill. When the real shooting started, many of them would die. This was what soldiers were *for*, just as a hammer was for driving nails.

Warriors and toilers: those seemed, in my boyhood vision, to be the chief destinies for men. They weren't the only destinies, as I learned from having a few male teachers, from reading books, and from watching television. But the men on television—the politicians, the astronauts, the generals, the savvy lawyers, the philosophical doctors, the bosses who gave orders to both soldiers and laborers—seemed as remote and unreal to me as the figures in tapestries. I could no more imagine growing up to become one of these cool, potent creatures than I could imagine becoming a prince.

A nearer and more hopeful example was that of my father, who had escaped from a red-dirt farm to a tire factory, and from the assembly line to the front office. Eventually he dressed in a white shirt and tie. He carried himself as if he had been born to work with his mind. But his body, remembering the earlier years of slogging work, began to give out on him in his fifties, and it quit on him entirely before he turned sixty-five. Even such a partial escape from man's fate as he had accomplished did not seem possible for most of the boys I knew. They joined the army, stood in line for jobs in the smoky plants, helped build highways. They were bound to work as their fathers had worked, killing themselves or preparing to kill others.

A scholarship enabled me not only to attend college, a rare enough feat in my circle, but even to study in a university meant for the children of the rich. Here I met for the first time young men who had assumed from birth that they would lead lives of comfort and power. And for the first time I met women who told me that men were guilty of having kept all the joys and privileges of the earth for themselves. I was baffled. What privileges? What joys? I thought about the maimed, dismal lives of most of the men back home. What had they stolen from their wives and daughters? The right to go five days a week, twelve months a year, for thirty or forty years to a steel mill or a coal mine? The right to drop bombs and die in war? The right to feel every leak in the roof, every gap in the fence, every cough in the engine, as a wound they must mend? The right to feel, when the lay-off comes or the plant shuts down, not only afraid but ashamed?

I was slow to understand the deep grievances of women. This was because, as a boy, I had envied them. Before college, the only people I had ever known who were interested in art or music or literature, the only ones who read books, the only ones who ever seemed to enjoy a sense of ease and grace were the mothers and daughters. Like the menfolk, they fretted about money, they scrimped and made-do. But, when the pay stopped coming in, they were not the ones who had failed. Nor did they have to go to war, and that seemed to me a blessed fact. By comparison with the narrow, ironclad days of fathers, there was an expansiveness, I thought, in the days of mothers. They went to see neighbors, to shop in town, to run errands at school, at the library, at church. No doubt, had I looked harder at their lives, I would have envied them less. It was not my fate to become a woman, so it was easier for me to see the graces. Few of them held jobs outside the home, and those who did filled thankless roles as clerks and waitresses. I didn't see, then, what a prison a house could be, since houses seemed to me brighter, handsomer places than any factory. I did realize—because such things were never spoken of—how often women suffered from men's bullying. I did learn about the wretchedness of abandoned wives, single mothers, widows; but I also learned about the wretchedness of lone men. Even then I could see how exhausting it was for a mother to cater all day to the needs of young children. But if I had been asked, as a boy, to choose between tending a baby and tending a machine, I think I would have chosen the baby. (Having now tended both, I know I would choose the baby.)

So I was baffled when the women at college accused me and my sex of having cornered the world's pleasures. I think something like my bafflement has been felt by other boys (and by girls as well) who grew up in dirt-poor farm country, in mining country, in black ghettos, in Hispanic barrios,[8] in the shadows of factories, in Third World nations—

any place where the fate of men is as grim and bleak as the fate of women. Toilers and warriors. I realize now how ancient these identities are, how deep the tug they exert on men, the undertone of a thousand generations. The miseries I saw, as a boy, in the lives of nearly all men I continue to see in the lives of many—the body-breaking toil, the tedium, the call to be tough, the humiliating powerlessness, the battle for a living and for territory.

When the women I met at college thought about the joys and privileges of men, they did not carry in their minds the sort of men I had known in my childhood. They thought of their fathers, who were bankers, physicians, architects, stockbrokers, the big wheels of the big cities. These fathers rode the train to work or drove cars that cost more than any of my childhood houses. They were attended from morning to night by female helpers, wives, and nurses and secretaries. They were never laid off, never short of cash at month's end, never lined up for welfare. These fathers made decisions that mattered. They ran the world.

The daughters of such men wanted to share in this power, this glory. So did I. They yearned for a say over their future, for jobs worthy of their abilities, for the right to live at peace, unmolested, whole. Yes, I thought, yes yes. The difference between me and these daughters was that they saw me, because of my sex, as destined from birth to become like their fathers, and therefore as an enemy to their desires. But I knew better. I wasn't an enemy, in fact or in feeling. I was an ally. If I had known, then, how to tell them so, would they have believed me? Would they now?

NOTES

1 Sassafras tea is made from the root of the sassafras tree, a small tree native to North America.

2 Jan Vermeer (1932–1975) was a Dutch painter known in particular for his depiction of peaceful domestic scenes.

3 St. Paul, author of one of the biblical Epistles, is known for his stern views on Christian belief and behaviour.

4 Stonehenge is a prehistoric circle of stones on Salisbury Plain in England.

5 The boll-weevil beetle is a beetle that attacks the seed vessels of cotton, a major crop in the American South.

6 An arms repository or store.

7 A place between heaven and hell, where the souls of the unbaptized are supposed to reside.

8 Spanish-speaking districts of cities or towns in the United States, especially poor neighbourhoods populated by immigrants.

QUESTIONS

1. How does Sanders' account of his conversation with his friend Anneke create a framework for the rest of the essay?

2. What do the men Sanders carries in his mind—convicts and guards, marginal farmers, factory workers, labourers, soldiers—have in common? How have these men shaped Sanders' attitudes towards gender issues?

3. How does Sanders use comparison as a strategy to develop and organize his ideas in this essay?

4. Do you think Sanders makes effective use of descriptive detail?

5. If you are a female reader, did Sanders' essay make you more willing to believe that men have problems? If you are a male reader, can you identify with Sanders' account of men's lives?

SUGGESTION FOR WRITING

What men or women do you carry in your mind? How have they influenced your attitudes towards whether men or women have easier lives? Write an essay in which you describe the appearance of the men or women you grew up with and the work they did. Be sure to include a range of specific sensory detail.

IT ALWAYS COSTS

David T. Suzuki

I have long believed that we have to have greater scientific literacy at all levels of society if we are to have any hope of affecting the way science and technology are impacting on our lives. That's why I went into broadcasting.

But I have only recently realized that my underlying faith in the power of greater awareness is misplaced. First of all, we must understand that there is no such thing as a problem-free technology. However beneficent, technology always has a cost.

Think, for example, of DDT[1]—it killed malaria-carrying mosquitoes in huge numbers and without question saved millions of lives in tropical countries. But geneticists could have predicted that DDT would exert incredible selective pressure for mutations that would confer resistance to DDT in the mosquitoes and that within a few years large numbers would return. They did. But once committed to a chemical approach, we had to turn to other more toxic compounds.

The ecological damage from massive use of chemical sprays has been enormous because DDT is not specific and kills all insects. Furthermore, the compound is ingested by many organisms, so that initially minute quantities become concentrated up the food chain in a process called *biomagnification*. The final result was that DDT ended up in the shell glands of birds, affecting the thickness of egg shells and eventually causing heavy bird mortality.

There are numerous examples of how technological innovations have had detrimental side effects that eventually outweighed their benefits. It has been my assumption that what we needed was some kind of vehicle, like panels of citizens representing a broad range of interests, to do a cost/benefit analysis of all new technologies. The idea was that by carefully weighing the benefits and bad side effects, we could make a more informed decision on whether to allow a new technology to be used. My belief that this would help us avoid future problems was based on faith in our predictive capabilities. Indeed, much of the testing of environmental and health impacts is made on that faith. But we can't rely on such a system.

David Takayoshi Suzuki, born in Vancouver in 1936, is a university teacher and researcher in genetics, but is better known as a TV and radio broadcaster of programs on science and ecology, and as a columnist for the *Toronto Star* and, formerly, *The Globe and Mail*. He is the author of numerous books, including *An Introduction to Genetic Analysis* (4th ed., 1989), *Wisdom of the Elders* (1992), and *Inventing the Future* (1989). "It Always Costs," taken from *Inventing the Future*, by David Suzuki. Reprinted with the permission of Stoddart Publishing Co. Limited, North York, Ontario.

For one thing, our assessments are always limited. For example, suppose we do an environmental impact assessment of drilling for oil in the high Arctic. The studies, of necessity, are carried out in a limited time within a restricted area. It is simply assumed that scaling up the observed effects of the two drill holes by a factor of one hundred or more gives a reasonable estimate of the impact of major exploration.

Well, there are effects called *synergistic*; several components interact to give new or greater effects than the sum of their individual impact. Also, during an assessment, you can bet industry will be on its best behaviour, so the results will always be on the conservative side.

It is also true that even if a study is made over ten years (which it won't be) we could never anticipate all the fluctuation of conditions in this sensitive area. I've known colleagues who have studied populations of animals or plants over decades and find nice cycles and patterns that are predictable until suddenly completely unexpected fluctuations occur. They get out more publications that way, but we ought, then, to be a lot more humble about how *little* we know.

Finally, we know that major blowouts, spills or accidents are relatively rare. Suppose one happens an average of once every twenty holes. By studying *two* holes and finding no effect, we are not justified in concluding that drilling one hundred holes will also be accident free. It would be just as invalid were an accident to happen in one of the test holes to conclude that half of all drilling sites will have a bad episode. The numbers are statistically meaningless.

Food additives, pesticides and drugs are extensively tested before they are approved for use. But numerous cases inform us that we can't anticipate all the effects. The DDT example is classic—at the time it was used, we didn't even know about biomagnification, let alone its concentration in bird shell glands.

Remember thalidomide[2] or DES?[3] Or consider the oral contraceptive. It had been extensively tested (in Puerto Rico, of course) and shown to be efficacious without detrimental side effects. It was only after millions of healthy, normal women had taken the pill for years that epidemiologists[4] could see negative effects. No amount of pretesting could have anticipated them.

So we come to a terrible conclusion. Technology has enormous benefits. They are undeniable—that's why we're hooked on it. Once technology is in place, it becomes impossible to do without it and we can't go back to doing things the old way. But the pretesting of any new technology is flawed because it provides only a limited assessment of its impact. The tests are restricted in size, scope and time and are based on what we decide a priori[5] might be a possible effect.

But how can we test for something that we don't know will happen? If every technology has a cost, the more powerful the technology, the greater its potential cost. We have to build into our judgements a large leeway for our ignorance and err on the side of extreme caution. And perhaps it's time to realize we don't have to do everything just because we can.

NOTES

[1] DDT—dichlorodiphenyltrichloroethane has been used extensively as an insecticide, particularly in combatting malarial mosquitoes. It is a persistent pesticide (it does not break down readily) and is stored in human fat almost indefinitely. Tolerance to DDT is widely variant in humans and its use has led to much controversy. It has been shown, in laboratory experiments, to be an "enzyme inducer" that breaks down estrogen, which in birds mediates calcium metabolism. It is also readily passed through the placenta into the foetus. The use of DDT is now banned in Canada and the United States, though it is still manufactured for export.

[2] Thalidomide, or alpha phthaloyl glutarimide, is a close relative of aminopteria, a drug known since 1950 to have teratogenic (causing monstrous genetic defect) properties. Thalidomide was introduced for sale in Britain in April, 1958. It was released for sale despite an almost complete lack of chemical and pharmacological testing, and of research into the scientific literature. It was touted as being perfectly safe as a sedative for pregnant women despite testing that indicated that it could completely shut down thyroid function. It caused birth defects such as shortened or absent limbs and flipper-like appendages in more than 450 births as well as nerve damage in more than 400 adults and children. Despite medical evidence of its effects, it continued to be sold until its withdrawal in November, 1961.

[3] DES or diethylstilbestrol is a chemical with many of the properties of estrogen. It was widely used as a "morning after" contraceptive as well as a treatment for menopausal symptoms, cancer of the prostate, and certain uterine disorders. DES has also been used since 1954 for fattening cattle and promoting growth in chickens. It has since been found to be related to, if not the cause of, an increase in uterine cancer in women who previously did not get such cancers, and of an increase in cancer of the testes.

[4] Epidemiology deals with the incidence, distribution, and control of diseases in large populations.

[5] *A priori* here means being knowable by reasoning from something that is considered self-evident or presupposed from general experience.

QUESTIONS

1. Suzuki's title "It [technology] Always Costs" is also his thesis. How is his essay organized to support this thesis?

2. Why does Suzuki include his reassessments of the value of scientific research in his essay? How do these inclusions affect his tone? Be specific about his attitudes to himself, his readers, and his subject.

3. What does Suzuki's comment that the oral contraceptive was tested "in Puerto Rico, of course" reveal about his attitude to the scientific establishment? Do you think this comment affects Suzuki's credibility?

4. Is this essay written for the scientific industry, for specialists in environmental issues, or for the general public? Does Suzuki's style define the audience he is aiming for? (For more on Suzuki's style, see the sample essay comparing Suzuki with Merwin.)

SUGGESTION FOR WRITING

Do you agree that scientific advances *always* have costs? Write a letter to Suzuki expressing your views on the costs and/or benefits of recent developments in science and technology, such as cloning, digital television screens, voice mail, Web pages, one or more features of the Internet.

A MODEST PROPOSAL

For preventing the Children of Poor People
from being a Burthen to
their Parents, or the Country,
and for making them
Beneficial to the Publick.

Jonathan Swift

It is a melancholly Object to those, who walk through this great Town,[1] or travel in the Country, when they see the *Streets*, the *Roads*, and *Cabbin-Doors*, crowded with *Beggars* of the female Sex, followed by three, four, or six Children, *all in Rags*, and importuning every Passenger for an Alms. These *Mothers* instead of being able to work for their honest Livelyhood, are forced to employ all their time in Stroling, to beg Sustenance for their *helpless Infants*, who, as they grow up, either turn *Thieves* for want of work, or leave their *dear native Country to fight for the Pretender in Spain*,[2] or sell themselves to the *Barbadoes*.[3]

I think it is agreed by all Parties, that this prodigious number of Children, in the Arms, or on the Backs, or at the *Heels* of their *Mothers*, and frequently of their *Fathers*, is *in the present deplorable state of the Kingdom*,[4] a very great additional grievance; and therefore whoever could find out a fair, cheap and easy method of making these Children sound and useful Members of the Commonwealth would deserve so well of the publick, as to have his Statue set up for a Preserver of the Nation.

But my Intention is very far from being confined to provide only for the Children of *professed Beggars*: It is of a much greater extent, and shall take in the whole number of Infants at a certain Age, who are born of Parents in effect as little able to support them, as those who demand our Charity in the Streets.

As to my own part, having turned my thoughts, for many Years, upon this important Subject, and maturely weighed the several *Schemes of other Projectors*, I have always found them grossly mistaken in their computation. It is true a Child, *just dropt*

Jonathan Swift (1667–1745) is often regarded as the foremost prose satirist to write in English. Born in Ireland of English parents, he was educated at Trinity College, Dublin, and then attempted a career in writing, politics, and the church in England. Most of his best-known works, including "A Modest Proposal" (1729) and the Utopian fiction, *Gulliver's Travels* (1726), were written during the thirty years from his appointment as Dean of St. Patrick's (Anglican) Cathedral in Dublin in 1714 to his death in 1745, a period in which he more and more took on the role of defender of Ireland against English absentee landlords and their Irish collaborators.

from its Dam, may be supported by her Milk, for a Solar year with little other Nourishment, at most not above the Value of two Shillings, which the Mother may certainly get, or the Value in *Scraps*, by her lawful Occupation of begging, and it is exactly at one Year old that I propose to provide for them, in such a manner, as, instead of being a Charge upon their *Parents*, or the *Parish*, or *wanting Food and Raiment* for the rest of their Lives, they shall, on the Contrary, contribute to the Feeding and partly to the Cloathing of many Thousands.

There is likewise another great Advantage in my Scheme, that it will prevent those *voluntary Abortions*, and that horrid practice of *Women murdering their Bastard Children*; alas! too frequent among us; sacrificing the *poor innocent Babes*, I doubt, more to avoid the Expence, than the Shame; which would move Tears and Pity in the most Savage and inhuman breast.

The Number of Souls in this Kingdom being usually reckoned one Million and a half; of these I calculate there may be about two hundred thousand Couple whose Wives are Breeders; from which number I Subtract thirty Thousand Couples, who are able to maintain their own Children, although I apprehend there cannot be so many under *the present distresses of the Kingdom*; but this being granted, there will remain an Hundred and Seventy Thousand Breeders. I again Subtract fifty Thousand for those Women who miscarry, or whose Children dye by accident, or disease within the Year. There only remain an hundred and twenty thousand Children of poor Parents annually born: The question therefore is, how this number shall be reared, and provided for, which, as I have already said, under the present Situation of Affairs, is utterly impossible by all the methods hitherto proposed, for we can *neither employ them in Handicraft*, or *Agriculture*; we neither build Houses, (I mean in the Country) nor cultivate Land: They can very seldom pick up a Livelyhood *by Stealing* till they arrive at six years Old, except where they are of towardly parts, although, I confess they learn the Rudiments much earlier, during which time, they can however be properly looked upon only as *Probationers*, as I have been informed by a principal Gentleman in the County of *Cavan*,[5] who protested to me, that he never knew above one or two Instances under the Age of six, even in a part of the Kingdom *so renowned for the quickest proficiency in that Art*.

I am assured by our Merchants, that a Boy or Girl, before twelve Years old, is no saleable Commodity, and even when they come to this Age, they will not yield above three Pounds, or three Pounds and half a Crown at most on the Exchange, which cannot turn to Account either to the Parents or the Kingdom, the Charge of Nutriment and Rags having been at least four times that Value.

I shall now therefore humbly propose my own thoughts, which I hope will not be liable to the least Objection.

I have been assured by a very knowing *American* of my acquaintance in *London*, that a young healthy Child well Nursed is at a Year old a most delicious, nourishing, and wholesome Food, whether *Stewed, Roasted, Baked, or Boiled*, and I make no doubt that it will equally serve in a *Fricasie*, or a *Ragoust*.

I do therefore humbly offer it to *publick consideration*, that of the hundred and twenty thousand Children, already computed, twenty thousand may be reserved for Breed, whereof only one fourth part to be Males, which is more than we allow to *Sheep, black Cattle*, or *Swine*, and my reason is that these Children are seldom the Fruits of Marriage, *a Circumstance not much regarded by our Savages*, therefore *one Male* will be sufficient to serve *four females*. That the remaining hundred thousand may at a Year old be offered in Sale to the *persons of Quality*, and *Fortune*, through the Kingdom, always advising the Mother to let them Suck plentifully in the last Month, so as to render them Plump, and Fat for a good Table. A Child will make two Dishes at an Entertainment for Friends, and when the Family dines alone, the fore or hind Quarter will make a reasonable Dish, and seasoned with a little Pepper or Salt will be very good Boiled on the fourth Day,[6] especially in Winter.

I have reckoned upon a Medium, that a Child just born will weigh 12 pounds, and in a solar Year if tolerably nursed encreaseth to twenty eight Pounds.

I grant this food will be somewhat dear, and therefore very *proper for Landlords*, who, as they have already devoured most of the Parents, seem to have the best Title to the Children.

Infant's flesh will be in Season throughout the Year, but more plentiful in *March*, and a little before and after, for we are told by a grave Author[7] an eminent *French* Physitian, that *Fish being a prolifick Dyet*, there are more Children born in *Roman Catholick Countries* about nine Months after *Lent*, than at any other Season: Therefore reckoning a Year after *Lent*, the Markets will be more glutted than usual, because the number of *Popish Infants*, is at least three to one in this Kingdom, and therefore it will have one other Collateral advantage by lessening the Number of *Papists*[8] among us.

I have already computed the Charge of nursing a Beggars Child (in which list I reckon all *Cottagers, Labourers*, and four fifths of the *Farmers*) to be about two Shillings *per Annum*, Rags included, and I believe no Gentleman would repine to give Ten Shillings for the *Carcass of a good fat Child*, which, as I have said will make four Dishes of excellent Nutritive Meat, when he hath only some particular friend, or his own Family to Dine with him. Thus the Squire will learn to be a good Landlord, and grow popular among his Tenants, the Mother will have Eight Shillings net profit, and be fit for Work till she produceth another Child.

Those who are more thrifty (*as I must confess the Times require*) may flay the Carcass; the Skin of which, artificially dressed, will make admirable *Gloves for Ladies*, and *Summer Boots for fine Gentlemen*.

As to our City of *Dublin*, Shambles may be appointed for this purpose, in the most convenient parts of it, and Butchers we may be assured will not be wanting, although I rather recommend buying the Children alive, and dressing them hot from the Knife, as we do *roasting Pigs*.

A very worthy Person, *a true Lover of his Country*,[9] and whose Virtues I highly esteem, was lately pleased, in discoursing on this matter, to offer a Refinement upon my Scheme. He said, that many Gentlemen of this Kingdom, having of late destroyed their Deer, he conceived that the want of Venison might be well supplied by the Bodies of young Lads and Maidens, not exceeding fourteen Years of Age, nor under twelve, so great a Number of both Sexes in every Country being now ready to Starve, for want of Work and Service: And these to be disposed of by their Parents if alive, or otherwise by their nearest Relations. But with due deference to so excellent a friend, and so deserving a Patriot, I cannot be altogether in his Sentiments, for as to the Males, my *American* acquaintance assured me from frequent Experience, that their flesh was generally Tough and Lean, like that of our Schoolboys, by continual exercise, and their Taste disagreeable, and to Fatten them would not answer the Charge. Then as to the Females, it would, I think with humble Submission, *be a loss to the Publick*, because they soon would become Breeders themselves: And besides it is not improbable that some scrupulous People might be apt to Censure such a Practice, (although indeed very unjustly) as a little bordering upon Cruelty, which, I confess, hath always been with me the strongest objection against any Project, however so well intended.

But in order to justify my friend, he confessed, that this expedient was put into his head by the famous *Sallmanaazor*, a Native of the Island *Formosa*,[10] who came from thence to *London*, above twenty Years ago, and in Conversation told my friend, that in his Country when any young Person happened to be put to Death, the Executioner sold the Carcass to *Persons of Quality*, as a prime Dainty, and that, in his Time, the Body of a plump Girl of fifteen, who was crucified for an attempt to Poison the Emperor, was sold to his Imperial *Majesty's prime Minister of State*, and other great *Mandarins* of the Court, *in Joints from the Gibbet*, at four hundred Crowns. Neither indeed can I deny, that if the same use were made of several plump young Girls in this Town, who, without one single Groat[11] to their Fortunes, cannot stir abroad without a Chair, and appear at the *Play-House*, and *Assemblies* in Foreign fineries, which they never will Pay for; the Kingdom would not be the worse.

Some Persons of a desponding Spirit are in great Concern about that vast Number of poor People, who are aged, diseased, or maimed, and I have been desired to imploy my thoughts what Course may be taken, to ease the Nation of so grievous an Incumbrance. But I am not in the least pain about the matter, because it is very well known, that they are every Day *dying*, and *rotting*, by *cold*, and *famine*, and *filth*, and *vermin*, as fast as can be reasonably expected. And as to the younger Labourers they are now in almost as hopeful a Condition. They cannot get Work, and consequently pine away for want of Nourishment, to a degree, that if at any time they are accidentally hired to common Labour, they have not strength to perform it, and thus the Country and themselves are happily delivered from the Evils to come.

I have too long digressed, and therefore shall return to my subject. I think the advantages by the Proposal which I have made, are obvious, and many, as well as of the highest importance.

For, *First*, as I have already observed, it would greatly lessen *the Number of Papists*, with whom we are yearly over-run, being the principal Breeders of the Nation, as well as our most dangerous Enemies, and who stay at home on purpose with a design *to deliver the Kingdom to the Pretender*, hoping to take their Advantage by the absence *of so many good Protestants*, who have chosen rather to leave their Country, than stay at home, and pay Tithes against their Conscience, to an *Episcopal Curate*.

Secondly, the poorer Tenants will have something valuable of their own, which by Law may be made liable to Distress,[12] and help to pay their Landlord's Rent, their Corn and Cattle being already seazed, and *Money a thing unknown*.

Thirdly, Whereas the Maintenance of an Hundred Thousand Children, from two Years old, and upwards, cannot be computed at less than Ten Shillings a piece *per Annum*, the Nation's Stock will be thereby encreased fifty thousand pounds *per Annum*, besides the profit of a new Dish, introduced to the Tables of all *Gentlemen of Fortune* in the Kingdom, who have any refinement in Taste, and the Money will circulate among ourselves, the Goods being entirely of our own Growth and Manufacture.

Fourthly, The constant Breeders, besides the gain of Eight Shillings *per Annum*, by the Sale of their Children, will be rid of the Charge of maintaining them after the first Year.

Fifthly, This food would likewise bring great *Custom to Taverns*, where the Vintners will certainly be so prudent as to procure the best receipts for dressing it to perfection, and consequently have their Houses frequented by all the *fine Gentlemen*, who justly value themselves upon their Knowledge in good *Eating*, and a skillful Cook, who understands how to oblige his Guests, will contrive to make it as expensive as they please.

Sixthly, This would be a great Inducement to Marriage, which all wise Nations have either encouraged by Rewards, or enforced by Laws and Penalties. It would encrease the care and tenderness of Mothers towards their Children, when they were sure of a Settlement for Life, to the poor Babes, provided in some sort by the Publick to their annual Profit instead of Expence. We should soon see an honest Emulation among the married Women, *which of them could bring the fattest Child to the Market.* Men would become as fond of their *Wives*, during the Time of their Pregnancy, as they are now of their *Mares* in Foal, their *Cows* in Calf, or *Sows* when they are ready to Farrow, nor offer to Beat or Kick them (as it is too frequent a practice) for fear of a Miscarriage.

Many other advantages might be enumerated. For Instance, the addition of some thousand Carcases in our exportation of barreled Beef: The Propagation of *Swines Flesh*, and Improvement in the Art of making good *Bacon*, so much wanted among us by the great destruction of *Pigs*, too frequent at our Tables, which are no way comparable in Taste, or Magnificence to a well grown, fat Yearling Child, which Roasted whole will make a considerable Figure at a *Lord Mayor's Feast*, or any other Publick Entertainment. But this, and many others I omit, being studious of Brevity.

Supposing that one thousand Families in this City, would be constant Customers for Infants Flesh, besides others who might have it at *Merry-meetings*, particularly *Weddings* and *Christenings*, I compute that *Dublin* would take off annually about Twenty Thousand Carcases, and the rest of the Kingdom (where probably they will be sold somewhat cheaper) the remaining Eighty Thousand.

I can think of no one Objection, that will possibly be raised against this Proposal, unless it should be urged that the Number of People will be thereby much lessened in the Kingdom. This I freely own, and it was indeed one principal Design in offering it to the World. I desire the Reader will observe, that I Calculate my Remedy *for this one individual Kingdom of IRELAND, and for no other that ever was, is, or, I think, ever can be upon Earth.* Therefore let no Man talk to me of other Expedients: *Of taxing our Absentees at five Shillings a pound: Of using neither Cloaths, nor household Furniture, except what is of our own Growth and Manufacture: Of utterly rejecting the Materials and Instruments that promote Foreign Luxury: Of curing the Expensiveness of Pride, Vanity, Idleness, and Gaming in our Women:*

Of introducing a Vein of Parsimony, Prudence and Temperance: Of learning to Love our Country, wherein we differ even from LAPLAN- DERS, and the Inhabitants of TOPINAMBOO:[13] *Of quitting our Animosities, and Factions, nor Act any longer like the Jews, who were Murdering one another at the very moment their City was taken:*[14] *Of being a little Cautious not to Sell our Country and Consciences for nothing: Of teaching Landlords to have at least one degree of Mercy towards their Tenants. Lastly of putting a Spirit of Honesty, Industry and Skill into our Shopkeepers, who, if a Resolution could now be taken to Buy only our Native Goods, would immediately unite to Cheat and Exact upon us in the Price, the Measure, and the Goodness, nor could ever yet be brought to make one fair Proposal of just dealing, though often and earnestly invited to it.*

Therefore I repeat, let no Man talk to me of these and the like Expedients, till he hath at least some Glimpse of Hope, that there will ever be some hearty and sincere Attempt to put them in Practice.

But as to my self, having been wearied out for many Years with of- fering vain, idle, visionary thoughts, and at length utterly despairing of Success, I fortunately fell upon this Proposal, which as it is wholly new, so it hath something Solid and Real, of no Expence and little Trouble, full in our own Power, and whereby we can incur no Danger in *dis- obliging* England. For this kind of Commodity will not bear Exportation, the Flesh being of too tender a Consistance, to admit a long continuance in Salt, *although perhaps I could name a Country, which would be glad to Eat up our whole Nation without it.*

After all, I am not so violently bent upon my own Opinion, as to re- ject any Offer, proposed by wise Men, which shall be found equally in- nocent, cheap, easy and effectual. But before something of that kind shall be advanced in Contradiction to my Scheme, and offering a bet- ter, I desire the Author, or Authors will be pleased maturely to con- sider two points. *First*, as things now stand, how they will be able to find Food and Raiment for an hundred thousand useless Mouths and Backs. And *Secondly*, there being a round Million of Creatures in human Figure, throughout this Kingdom, whose whole Subsistance put into a common Stock, would leave them in Debt of two Million of Pounds *Sterling*, adding those, who are Beggars by Profession, to the Bulk of Farmers, Cottagers and Labourers with their Wives and Children, who are Beggars in Effect; I desire those *Politicians*, who dis- like my Overture, and may perhaps be so bold to attempt an Answer, that they will first ask the Parents of these Mortals, whether they would not at this Day think it a great Happiness to have been sold for Food at a year Old, in the manner I prescribe, and thereby have avoided such a perpetual Scene of Misfortunes, as they have since gone through, by the *Oppression of Landlords*, the Impossibility of paying Rent without Money or Trade, the want of common Sustenance, with neither House nor Cloaths to cover them from Inclemencies of Weather, and the most inevitable Prospect of intailing the like, or greater Miseries upon their Breed for ever.

I Profess in the sincerity of my Heart that I have not the least personal Interest, in endeavouring to promote this necessary Work; having no other Motive than the *publick Good of my Country,* by *advancing our Trade, providing for Infants, relieving the Poor, and giving some Pleasure to the Rich.* I have no Children, by which I can propose to get a single Penny; the youngest being nine Years old, and my Wife past Childbearing.

NOTES

[1] Dublin

[2] The Pretender is James Edward Stuart, who claimed (or "pretended" to) the throne lost by his father, James II, in 1688. The French upheld James Stuart's claim because of his Roman Catholicism, and, by the Limerick Treaty of 1691, Irish Roman Catholics were granted the right to bear arms in the service of France, and thus, by affiliation, in the service of the Pretender.

[3] Because of the poverty in Ireland many Irish immigrated to British colonies in America and the Indies, indenturing themselves to plantation owners for their passage.

[4] Ireland had just suffered three successive bad harvests.

[5] Soil conditions in county Cavan are particularly unsuited to tillage and require a great deal of capital to manage. It also had a long history of high rents and exploitation.

[6] Boiling was a way to render meat edible if it was beginning to turn bad.

[7] Francois Rabelais (1494–1553) was a French humorist and satirist and anything but "grave."

[8] Swift was an Anglican clergyman.

[9] It is not clear whether the "true lover of his country" refers to an actual person or not.

[10] George Psalmanazar was a Frenchman who posed as a Formosan. His fictitious accounts, *Historical and Geographical History of Formosa* (1704) and *A Dialogue between a Japanese and a Formosan about some points of the religion of the time* (1707), contained passages describing human sacrifice and cannibalism. The remainder of this paragraph is a paraphrase of one of the stories told by Psalmanazar.

[11] A groat is a small British coin worth four pence.

[12] Distress or distraint is the act of distraining or legally forcing a person to give up personal goods to be used as payment against debts.

[13] The Tupinamba were a group of tribes, now extinct, that lived on the coast of Brazil from the mouth of the Amazon to the southern part of the State of Sao Paulo. Swift says that even those who live in places of extreme cold and heat love their countries better than the Anglo-Irish.

[14] In A.D. 70, the Roman Emperor Titus laid siege to, captured, and destroyed Jerusalem. Throughout the period of siege and capture, the city was being torn apart internally by warring religious factions.

VOCABULARY

alms—anything given freely to relieve want

artificially—with skill or artifice

crown—a coin worth five shillings, a shilling being worth 1/20 of a pound or five pence. Half a crown is, therefore, a coin worth 12 1/2 pence.

dressing—preparing meat for the market, usually by bleeding and cleaning it

emulation—an attempt to equal or excel, here perhaps each other

gibbet—a gallows

importuning—pressing or urging with unreasonable requests

intailing (or usually, entailing)—settling something (e.g., land, title, obligation) on a number of persons in succession so that it cannot be bequeathed to another person

joints—a large section of meat usually including a large bone or joint

probationers—those whose fitness is being tested

repine—to complain or fret

shambles—a slaughterhouse

squire—a country gentleman, particularly the principal landowner of a district

towardly—dutiful, tractable

vintner—not only the maker but also the seller of wines

QUESTIONS

1. In this essay, is Swift speaking in his own voice or through a persona (a mask, or second self, created by the author)? How do you know?

2. List the main interests and characteristics of Swift's persona.

3. How does Swift use the gap between his own feelings and opinions and those of his persona to create and sustain the irony throughout the essay? What standard(s) of evaluation does the persona employ as he presents his solution to the terrible poverty in Ireland? What standards does Swift imply?

4. Can you identify any places where Swift steps out from behind his mask?

5. For what reasons, literary or otherwise, do you think Swift chose irony, rather than direct statement, as a strategy to persuade his audience to alleviate poverty in Ireland?

6. In a satiric essay, writers achieve their purpose by undermining the apparent thesis rather than by supporting it. What is the apparent thesis of "A Modest Proposal"? How does Swift undermine it?

7. Matters like spelling, punctuation, capitalization, and the use of italics were far less standardized in Swift's day than in ours. Do these or other features of Swift's style affect your reading of this essay? If so, how?

SUGGESTION FOR WRITING

Using Swift's essay as a model, write a "modest proposal" in which you present an outrageous solution to a current social problem. Follow the structure of "A Modest Proposal" and feel free to include verbal echoes from it. Remember that you will need to adopt a persona whose attitudes and values present to your readers an exaggerated version of their own. Like Swift, you want to shock your readers into a recognition of their moral inadequacies in not responding to a social need.

NOTES ON PUNCTUATION

Lewis Thomas

There are no precise rules about punctuation (Fowler lays out some general advice (as best he can under the complex circumstances of English prose (he points out, for example, that we possess only four stops (the comma, the semicolon, the colon and the period (the question mark and exclamation point are not, strictly speaking, stops; they are indicators of tone (oddly enough, the Greeks employed the semicolon for their question mark (it produces a strange sensation to read a Greek sentence which is a straightforward question: Why weepest thou; (instead of Why weepest thou? (and, of course, there are parentheses (which are surely a kind of punctuation making this whole matter much more complicated by having to count up the left-handed parentheses in order to be sure of closing with the right number (but if the parentheses were left out, with nothing to work with but the stops, we would have considerably more flexibility in the deploying of layers of meaning than if we tried to separate all the clauses by physical barriers (and in the latter case, while we might have more precision and exactitude for our meaning, we would lose the essential flavor of language, which is its wonderful ambiguity)))))))))))).

The commas are the most useful and usable of all the stops. It is highly important to put them in place as you go along. If you try to come back after doing a paragraph and stick them in the various spots that tempt you you will discover that they tend to swarm like minnows into all sorts of crevices whose existence you hadn't realized and before you know it the whole long sentence becomes immobilized and lashed up squirming in commas. Better to use them sparingly, and with affection, precisely when the need for each one arises, nicely, by itself.

I have grown fond of semicolons in recent years. The semicolon tells you that there is still some question about the preceding full sentence; something needs to be added; it reminds you sometimes of the Greek usage. It is

Lewis Thomas (1913–) has had a distinguished career as a doctor, and as president and chancellor of the Memorial Sloan-Kettering Cancer Center in New York. He started writing essays for *The New England Journal of Medicine*, and his essays have been collected in *The Lives of a Cell* (1974), *The Medusa and the Snail* (1979), from which "Notes on Punctuation" comes, and *Late Night Thoughts on Listening to Mahler's Ninth Symphony* (1983). His latest book is *The Fragile Species* (1992). "Notes on Punctuation," copyright 1979 by Lewis Thomas, from *The Medusa and the Snail* by Lewis Thomas. Used by permission of Viking Penguin, a division of Penguin Books USA Inc.

almost always a greater pleasure to come across a semicolon than a period. The period tells you that that is that; if you didn't get all the meaning you wanted or expected, anyway you got all the writer intended to parcel out and now you have to move along. But with a semicolon there you get a pleasant little feeling of expectancy; there is more to come; read on; it will get clearer.

Colons are a lot less attractive, for several reasons: firstly, they give you the feeling of being rather ordered around, or at least having your nose pointed in a direction you might not be inclined to take if left to yourself, and, secondly, you suspect you're in for one of those sentences that will be labeling the points to be made: firstly, secondly and so forth, with the implication that you haven't sense enough to keep track of a sequence of notions without having them numbered. Also, many writers use this system loosely and incompletely, starting out with number one and number two as though counting off on their fingers but then going on and on without the succession of labels you've been led to expect, leaving you floundering about searching for the ninethly or seventeenthly that ought to be there but isn't.

Exclamation points are the most irritating of all. Look! they say, look at what I just said! How amazing is my thought! It is like being forced to watch someone else's small child jumping up and down crazily in the center of the living room shouting to attract attention. If a sentence really has something of importance to say, something quite remarkable, it doesn't need a mark to point it out. And if it is really, after all, a banal sentence needing more zing, the exclamation point simply emphasizes its banality!

Quotation marks should be used honestly and sparingly, when there is a genuine quotation at hand, and it is necessary to be very rigorous about the words enclosed by the marks. If something is to be quoted, the *exact* words must be used. If part of it must be left out because of space limitations, it is good manners to insert three dots to indicate the omission, but it is unethical to do this if it means connecting two thoughts which the original author did not intend to have tied together. Above all, quotation marks should not be used for ideas that you'd like to disown, things in the air so to speak. Nor should they be put in place around cliché; if you want to use a cliché you must take full responsibility for it yourself and not try to job it off on anon., or on society. The most objectionable misuse of quotation marks, but one which illustrates the dangers of misuse in ordinary prose, is seen in advertising, especially in advertisements for small restaurants, for example "just around the corner," or "a good place to eat." No single, identifiable, citable person ever really said, for the record, "just around the corner," much less "a good place to eat," least likely of all for restaurants of the type that use this type of prose.

The dash is a handy device, informal and essentially playful, telling you that you're about to take off on a different tack but still in some way connected with the present course—only you have to remember that the dash is there, and either put a second dash at the end of the notion to let the reader know that he's back on course, or else end the sentence, as here, with a period.

The greatest danger in punctuation is for poetry. Here it is necessary to be as economical and parsimonious with commas and periods as with the words themselves, and any marks that seem to carry their own subtle meanings, like dashes and little rows of periods, even semicolons and question marks, should be left out altogether rather than inserted to clog up the thing with ambiguity. A single exclamation point in a poem, no matter what else the poem has to say, is enough to destroy the whole work.

The things I like best in T.S. Eliot's poetry, especially in the *Four Quartets*, are the semicolons. You cannot hear them, but they are there, laying out the connections between the images and ideas. Sometimes you get a glimpse of a semicolon coming, a few lines farther on, and it is like climbing a steep path through woods and seeing a wooden bench just at a bend in the road ahead, a place where you can expect to sit for a moment, catching your breath.

Commas can't do this sort of thing; they can only tell you how the different parts of a complicated thought are to be fitted together, but you can't sit, not even take a breath, just because of a comma,

QUESTIONS

1. What principles govern the paragraph divisions and the paragraph sequence in this essay?

2. Where does Thomas use his own punctuation to demonstrate the points he is making about various punctuation marks? Why does his own punctuation seem quite unorthodox in some parts of the essay?

3. A number of Thomas' comments on punctuation marks are evaluative. What standard(s) of evaluation is he using? According to Thomas, what makes punctuation effective?

4. The essays by Pico Iyer and Lewis Thomas provide a different sort of information on punctuation than you would find in a handbook (see, for example, Part 2, Handbook for Final Editing sections on punctuation in this text). Which approach to punctuation do you find more useful? Why?

SUGGESTION FOR WRITING

Write an evaluative essay comparing "Notes on Punctuation" with Pico Iyer's "In Praise of the Humble Comma." How do these essays differ in structure and tone? What other similarities or differences can you find? Which essay is more effective? Which provides better advice on punctuation? Be sure to make your own standard(s) of evaluation clear.

ECONOMY

Henry David Thoreau

When I wrote the following pages, or rather the bulk of them, I lived alone, in the woods, a mile from any neighbor, in a house which I had built myself, on the shore of Walden Pond, in Concord, Massachusetts, and earned my living by the labor of my hands only. I lived there two years and two months. At present I am a sojourner in civilized life again.

I should not obtrude my affairs so much on the notice of my readers if very particular inquiries had not been made by my townsmen concerning my mode of life, which some would call impertinent, though they do not appear to me at all impertinent, but, considering the circumstances, very natural and pertinent. Some have asked what I got to eat; if I did not feel lonesome; if I was not afraid; and the like. Others have been curious to learn what portion of my income I devoted to charitable purposes; and some, who have large families, how many poor children I maintained. I will therefore ask those of my readers who feel no particular interest in me to pardon me if I undertake to answer some of these questions in this book.[1] In most books, the *I*, or first person, is omitted; in this it will be retained; that, in respect to egotism, is the main difference. We commonly do not remember that it is, after all, always the first person that is speaking. I should not talk so much about myself if there were any body else whom I knew as well. Unfortunately, I am confined to this theme by the narrowness of my experience. Moreover, I, on my side, require of every writer, first or last, a simple and sincere account of his own life, and not merely what he has heard of other men's lives; some such account as he would send to his kindred from a distant land; for if he has lived sincerely, it must have been in a distant land to me. Perhaps these pages are more particularly addressed to poor students. As for the rest of my readers, they will accept such portions as apply to them. I trust that none will stretch the seams in putting on the coat, for it may do good service to him whom it fits....

Henry David Thoreau (1817–1862) was an American naturalist and essayist. His books include *A Week on the Concord and Merrimac Rivers* (1849) and *Walden: Or, Life in the Woods* (1854). The essay we reprint is excerpted from "Economy," a section of *Walden.*

I see young men, my townsmen, whose misfortune it is to have inherited farms, houses, barns, cattle, and farming tools; for these are more easily acquired than got rid of. Better if they had been born in the open pasture and suckled by a wolf, that they might have seen with clearer eyes what field they were called to labor in. Who made them serfs of the soil? Why should they eat their sixty acres, when man is condemned to eat only his peck of dirt? Why should they begin digging their graves as soon as they are born? They have got to live a man's life, pushing all these things before them, and get on as well as they can. How many a poor immortal soul have I met well nigh crushed and smothered under its load, creeping down the road of life, pushing before it a barn seventy-five feet by forty, its Augean stables[2] never cleansed, and one hundred acres of land, tillage, mowing, pasture, and wood-lot! The portionless, who struggle with no such unnecessary inherited encumbrances, find it labor enough to subdue and cultivate a few cubic feet of flesh.

But men labor under a mistake. The better part of the man is soon ploughed into the soil for compost. By a seeming fate, commonly called necessity, they are employed, as it says in an old book, laying up treasures which moth and rust will corrupt and thieves break through and steal. It is a fool's life, as they will find when they get to the end of it, if not before....

Most men, even in this comparatively free country, through mere ignorance and mistake, are so occupied with the factitious cares and superfluously coarse labors of life that its finer fruits cannot be plucked by them. Their fingers, from excessive toil, are too clumsy and tremble too much for that. Actually, the laboring man has not leisure for a true integrity day by day; he cannot afford to sustain the manliest relations to men; his labor would be depreciated in the market. He has no time to be any thing but a machine. How can he remember well his ignorance— which his growth requires—who has so often to use his knowledge? We should feed and clothe him gratuitously sometimes, and recruit him with our cordials, before we judge of him. The finest qualities of our nature, like the bloom on fruits, can be preserved only by the most delicate handling. Yet we do not treat ourselves nor one another thus tenderly....

The mass of men lead lives of quiet desperation. What is called resignation is confirmed desperation. From the desperate city you go into the desperate country, and have to console yourself with the bravery of minks and muskrats. A stereotyped but unconscious despair is concealed even under what are called the games and amusements of mankind. There is no play in them, for this comes after work. But it is a characteristic of wisdom not to do desperate things.

When we consider what, to use the words of the catechism, is the chief end of man, and what are the true necessaries and means of life, it appears as if men had deliberately chosen the common mode of living because they preferred it to any other. Yet they honestly think there is no choice left. But alert and healthy natures remember that the sun rose clear. It is never too late to give up our prejudices. No way of thinking or doing, however ancient, can be trusted without proof.

What every body echoes or in silence passes by as true to-day may turn out to be falsehood to-morrow, mere smoke of opinion, which some had trusted for a cloud that would sprinkle fertilizing rain on their fields. What old people say you cannot do you try and find that you can. Old deeds for old people, and new deeds for new. Old people did not know enough once, perchance, to fetch fresh fuel to keep the fire a-going; new people put a little dry wood under a pot, and are whirled round the globe with the speed of birds, in a way to kill old people, as the phrase is. Age is no better, hardly so well, qualified for an instructor as youth for it has not profited so much as it has lost. One may almost doubt if the wisest man has learned any thing of absolute value by living. Practically, the old have no very important advice to give the young, their own experience has been so partial, and their lives have been such miserable failures, for private reasons, as they must believe; and it may be that they have some faith left which belies that experience, and they are only less young than they were. I have lived some thirty years on this planet, and I have yet to hear the first syllable of valuable or even earnest advice from my seniors. They have told me nothing, and probably cannot tell me any thing, to the purpose. Here is life, an experiment to a great extent untried by me; but it does not avail me that they have tried it. If I have any experience which I think valuable, I am sure to reflect that this my Mentors said nothing about.

One farmer says to me, "You cannot live on vegetable food solely, for it furnishes nothing to make bones with;" and so he religiously devotes a part of his day to supplying his system with the raw materials of bones; walking all the while he talks behind his oxen, which, with vegetable-made bones, jerk him and his lumbering plough along in spite of every obstacle. Some things are really necessaries of life in some circles, the most helpless and diseased, which in others are luxuries merely, and in others still are entirely unknown....

Let us consider for a moment what most of the trouble and anxiety which I have referred to is about, and how much it is necessary that we be troubled, or, at least, careful. It would be some advantage to live a primitive and frontier life, though in the midst of an outward civilization, if only to learn what are the gross necessaries of life and what methods have been taken to obtain them; or even to look over the old day-books of the merchants, to see what it was that men most commonly bought at the stores, what they stored, that is, what are the grossest groceries. For the improvements of ages have had but little influence on the essential laws of man's existence; as our skeletons, probably, are not to be distinguished from those of our ancestors.

By the words, *necessary of life*, I mean whatever, of all that man obtains by his own exertions, has been from the first, or from long use has become, so important to human life that few, if any, whether from savageness, or poverty, or philosophy, ever attempt to do without it. To many creatures there is in this sense but one necessary of life, Food.[3] To the bison of the prairie it is a few inches of palatable grass, with water to drink; unless he seeks the Shelter of the forest or the mountain's shadow. None of the brute creation requires more than Food and Shelter. The necessaries of life for man in this climate may, accurately enough, be distributed under the several heads of Food, Shelter, Clothing, and Fuel; for not till we have secured these are we prepared to entertain the true problems of life with freedom and a prospect of success. Man has invented, not only houses, but clothes and cooked food; and possibly from the accidental discovery of the warmth of fire, and the consequent use of it, at first a luxury, arose the present necessity to sit by it. We observe cats and dogs acquiring the same second nature. By proper Shelter and Clothing we legitimately retain our own internal heat; but with an excess of these, or of Fuel, that is, with an external heat greater than our own internal, may not cookery properly be said to begin? Darwin,[4] the naturalist, says of the inhabitants of Tierra del Fuego,[5] that while his own party, who were well clothed and sitting close to a fire, were far from too warm, these naked savages, who were farther off, were observed, to his great surprise, "to be streaming with perspiration at undergoing such a roasting." So, we are told, the New Hollander[6] goes naked with impunity, while the European shivers in his clothes. Is it impossible to combine the hardiness of these savages with the intellectualness of the civilized man? According to Liebig,[7] man's body is a stove, and food the fuel which keeps up the internal combustion in the lungs. In cold weather we eat more, in warm less. The animal heat is the result of a slow combustion, and disease and death take place when this is too rapid; or for want of fuel, or from some defect in the draught, the fire goes out. Of course the vital heat is not to be confounded with fire; but so much for analogy. It appears, therefore, from the above list, that the expression, *animal life*, is nearly synonymous with the expression, *animal heat*; for while Food may be regarded as the Fuel which keeps up the fire within us,—and Fuel serves only to prepare that Food or to increase the warmth of our bodies by addition from without,—Shelter and Clothing also serve only to retain the *heat* thus generated and absorbed.

The grand necessity, then, for our bodies, is to keep warm, to keep the vital heat in us. What pains we accordingly take, not only with our Food, and Clothing, and Shelter, but with our beds, which are our night-clothes, robbing the nests and breasts of birds to prepare this shelter within a shelter, as the mole has its bed of grass and leaves at the end of its burrow! The poor man is wont to complain that this is a cold world; and to cold, no less physical than social, we refer directly a great part of our ails. The summer, in some climates, makes possible to man a sort of Elysian[8] life. Fuel, except to cook his Food, is then unnecessary; the sun is his fire, and many of the fruits are sufficiently cooked by its rays; while Food generally is more various, and more easily obtained; and Clothing and Shelter are wholly or half unnecessary. At the present day, and in this country, as I find by my own experience, a few implements, a knife, an axe, a spade, wheelbarrow, etc., and for the studious, lamplight, stationery, and access to a few books, rank next to necessaries, and can all be obtained at a trifling cost. Yet some, not wise, go to the other side of the globe, to barbarous and unhealthy regions, and devote themselves to trade for ten or twenty years, in order that they may live,—that is, keep comfortably warm,—and die in New England at last. The luxuriously rich are not simply kept comfortably warm, but unnaturally hot; as I implied before, they are cooked, of course *à la mode*.

Most of the luxuries, and many of the so called comforts of life, are not only not indispensable, but positive hinderances to the elevation of mankind. With respect to luxuries and comforts, the wisest have ever lived a more simple and meagre life than the poor. The ancient philosophers, Chinese, Hindoo, Persian, and Greek, were a class than which none has been poorer in outward riches, none so rich in inward. We know not much about them. It is remarkable that *we* know so much of them as we do. The same is true of the more modern reformers and benefactors of their race. None can be an impartial or wise observer of human life but from the vantage ground of what *we* should call voluntary poverty. Of a life of luxury the fruit is luxury, whether in agriculture, or commerce, or literature, or art. There are nowadays professors of philosophy, but not philosophers. Yet it is admirable to profess because it was once admirable to live. To be a philosopher is not merely to have subtle thoughts, nor even to found a school, but so to love wisdom as to live according to its dictates, a life of simplicity, independence, magnanimity, and trust. It is to solve some of the problems of life, not only theoretically, but practically. The success of great scholars and thinkers is commonly a courtier-like success, not kingly, not manly. They make shift to live merely by conformity, practically as their fathers did, and are in no sense the progenitors of a nobler race of men. But why do men degenerate ever? What makes families run out? What is the nature of the luxury which enervates and destroys nations? Are we sure that there is none of it in our own lives? The philosopher is in advance of his age even in the outward form of his life. He is not fed, sheltered, clothed, warmed, like his contemporaries. How can a man be a philosopher and not maintain his vital heat by better methods than other men?

When a man is warmed by the several modes which I have described, what does he want next? Surely not more warmth of the same kind, as more and richer food, larger and more splendid houses, finer and more abundant clothing, more numerous incessant and hotter fires, and the like. When he has obtained those things which are necessary to life, there is another alternative than to obtain the superfluities; and that is, to adventure on life now, his vacation from humbler toil having commenced. The soil, it appears, is suited to the seed, for it has sent its radicle downward, and it may now send its shoot upward also with confidence. Why has man rooted himself thus firmly in the earth, but that he may rise in the same proportion into the heavens above?—for the nobler plants are valued for the fruit they bear at last in the air and light, far from the ground, and are not treated like the humbler esculents, which, though they may be biennials, are cultivated only till they have perfected their root, and often cut down at top for this purpose, so that most would not know them in their flowering season.

I do not mean to prescribe rules to strong and valiant natures, who will mind their own affairs whether in heaven or hell, and perchance build more magnificently and spend more lavishly than the richest, without ever impoverishing themselves, not knowing how they live,—if, indeed, there are any such, as has been dreamed; nor to those who find their encouragement and inspiration in precisely the present condition of things, and cherish it with the fondness and enthusiasm of lovers,—and, to some extent, I reckon myself in this number; I do not speak to those who are well employed, in whatever circumstances, and they know whether they are well employed or not;—but mainly to the mass of men who are discontented, and idly complaining of the harness of their lot or of the times, when they might improve them. There are some who complain most energetically and inconsolably of any, because they are, as they say, doing their duty. I also have in my mind that seemingly wealthy, but most terribly impoverished class of all, who have accumulated dross, but know not how to use it, or get rid of it, and thus have forged their own golden or silver fetters.

NOTES

[1] Referring to *Walden* (see biographical note).

[2] From the story of Hercules, who had to clean abominably dirty stables as one of his tasks.

[3] In writing of the nineteenth century and before, capitalization is often used to emphasize prominent nouns.

[4] Charles Darwin (1809–1882) developed the theory of evolution in *Origin of Species* (1859) and *Descent of Man* (1871).

[5] Islands at the southernmost tip of South America.

[6] Native inhabitants of the Pennsylvania area.

[7] Baron Justus von Liebig (1803–1873) was a German chemist.

[8] Heavenly. The Elysian Fields, according to classical mythology, were the abode of the Blessed after death.

VOCABULARY

sojourner—a temporary resident, a visitor passing through

obtrude—to force, thrust forward

serfs—slaves

catechism—Christian instruction book, used to raise and answer questions of faith

progenitors—producers

radicle—root

esculents—plants used for food

QUESTIONS

1. What does the title "Economy" suggest to you? Is Thoreau referring to the management of the community's resources? To the management of the individual's resources? To the careful use of resources? For more ideas on the meaning of *economy*, consult your dictionary.

2. Thoreau argues that we could all enjoy far more leisure if we limited our material needs to the necessities. How does Thoreau define *necessity*? What were the necessities of life for him?

3. Thoreau says that every writer should be prepared to provide "a simple and sincere account of his own life. . . some such account as he would send to his kindred from a distant land." Why does Thoreau think such an account is valuable? How does he make us believe that he is sincere?

4. Thoreau says, in an often-quoted comment, that "the mass of men lead lives of quiet desperation." What customs, attitudes, and beliefs create this condition? How do people enslave themselves?

5. Thoreau's friend Emerson (another important nineteenth-century American writer) once commented that Thoreau "had no temptations to fight against—no appetites, no passions, no taste for elegant trifles. A fine house, dress, the manners and talk of highly cultivated people were all thrown away on him. . . It cost him nothing to say No; indeed he found it much easier than to say Yes." Emerson also commented that Thoreau's tendency to argue against everyone else's ideas was "a little chilling to the social relations. . . I love Henry [said Emerson]. . . but I cannot like him; and as for taking his arm, I should as soon think of taking the arm of an elm-tree." Does the image Thoreau presents of himself in "Economy" fit with Emerson's comments on him?

SUGGESTION FOR WRITING

Write an essay in which you develop your own "Economy." Begin by setting out your *necessities* and explain why they are important to you. Then explain how you will manage your resources (time and physical, emotional, and spiritual energy) to secure the good life for yourself.

THE *ENGLISH* PATIENT DEBATE

The film version of The English Patient, *the prize-winning novel by Canadian author Michael Ondaatje, provoked a wide range of opinion. The following pieces, published in* The Globe and Mail *between January and March 1997, illustrate different ways of evaluating both the film and other viewers' responses.*

The Moral Superiority of *Casablanca* over *The English Patient*

Thomas Hurka[1]

Both take place during the Second World War. Both are set largely in North Africa, with the desert a powerful backdrop. But one is a morally serious movie while the other is fatuous sentimentality. I'm talking about *Casablanca* and *The English Patient*.[2]

Casablanca's moral vision is expressed in one of the many quotable lines of Rick, Humphrey Bogart's character. Rick is deeply in love with Ingrid Bergman's Ilsa and she with him. But Ilsa is married to Victor Laszlo, a leader of the anti-Nazi resistance in his home country. It's important for the fight against Nazism that Victor escape to the United States and important to Victor's work that Ilsa go with him. Though Ilsa wants to stay with Rick, he knows she can't. As he puts her and Victor on the plane, he says, "The problems of three little people don't amount to a hill of beans in this crazy world."

In *Casablanca* the political can be more important than the personal. No matter how passionate one's love—and Rick and Ilsa are certainly passionate—there are situations and dangers that must take priority. The Second World War was one such situation and Nazism one such danger.

The English Patient is based on the novel of the same name by Canadian Michael Ondaatje. Its moral vision is expressed in a line it uses twice: "Betrayals in war are childlike compared to our betrayals in peace." Or, roughly, loyalty in love is more important than loyalty in war.

The movie's central character, played by Ralph Fiennes, is Count Almasy. Just before the war Almasy gave the German army crucial desert maps that enabled them to successfully attack Tobruk[3] and almost win the war in North Africa. Now, badly burned, he is dying in a villa in Italy. One character, Caravaggio, suspects Almasy's identity and wants to kill him for his betrayal. But he changes his mind and forgives Almasy when he learns what led to the betrayal.

Almasy too was deeply in love with a married woman, Katherine. After a desert plane crash left her injured and unable to move, he carried her to a cave and promised to return with help. The only source of help was the German army. To get that help, and as the only way to keep his promise, he gave the Germans the maps.

In *The English Patient* the personal is more important than the political. Whatever the effects on the outcome of a coming war, the movie suggests, it's understandable to give priority to your personal relationships. The problems of the world, and of the millions of people threatened by Nazism, don't amount to a hill of beans beside those of two love-crazed people.

This is the immorality at the core of *The English Patient*: It exalts personal emotion at the expense of everything else. In *Casablanca* Rick's love doesn't blind him to larger issues of politics. On the contrary, only after Ilsa returns that love can he care about those issues properly. But Almasy in the desert thinks only of his own small affair. And the movie presents this as making his betrayal not only forgivable but even, as the background music swells, inspiring. When, tears streaming, he emerges from the last trip to the cave, he is treated wholly sympathetically.

Questioned about his betrayal, Almasy gives Caravaggio other excuses. After leaving Katherine in the cave he went first to the British. Staggering into their camp without identification papers and demanding a jeep, he was instead arrested as a spy. Since they betrayed him first, Almasy says, he didn't really betray them.

But what planet was the man on? He was in contested territory on the brink of war and without papers. And he expected to be given a jeep? This is again a sign of the movie's absorption in personal emotions. Almasy's blindness to the reality around him is presented not as irresponsibility but as a sign of profound and wonderful love.

In any case, the movie cheats by presenting the issue facing him as just one of loyalty, of being true to your side just because they're your own. Before the war Almasy and his cosmopolitan friends are rightly scornful of this kind of parochialism. But the other side in this case is

Nazism and that should make a difference. Rick in *Casablanca* is a neutral and faces no issue of loyalty; he's an American and the U.S. isn't yet in the war. But he sees that one side is morally odious. Almasy doesn't bother to look.

In each of two movies a man deeply in love makes a choice in the desert. Rick sacrifices his love for a larger political cause; Almasy sacrifices a cause because he cares only about his love. *Casablanca* is one of the most loved movies of all time. *The English Patient* is beautifully photographed, powerfully acted, and completely morally bankrupt.

NOTES

[1] © Thomas Hurka. Reprinted from *The Globe and Mail*.

[2] *Casablanca*, directed by Michael Curtiz, came out in 1942. (See the essay on *Casablanca* in Chapter 1.) *The English Patient* (1996), directed by Anthony Minghella, is based on a 1992 book of the same name by Canadian poet and novelist Michael Ondaatje. Both films are set in North Africa.

[3] A port town in northeastern Libya that was taken alternately by the Germans and the British between 1940 and 1942.

VOCABULARY

fatuous—silly and self-congratulatory

cosmopolitan—being of the world, sophisticated, free from national and local prejudice.

parochialism—the state of being narrow-minded, full of local prejudice

Round Two:

The English Patient Rallies (Letters)[4]

Re The Moral Superiority of *Casablanca* Over *The English Patient* (Focus, Jan 25):

Where has Thomas Hurka been for the past 15 years? Works by such people as Carol Gilligan[5] and other feminists working on the topic of morality have recognized that women, and men, too, who value relations, may speak "in a different voice" which has been undervalued, but one in which the care and response to others as a top concern has come to be seen as parallel in morality positioning to those who focus on "higher" ideals and causes.

Valuing relationships and honouring our promises to commitment to others may seem "bankrupt" to Professor Hurka but many of us have come to understand that it is allegiance to people and loving and caring about them which gives life its fullest and finest meaning. The two films of *Casablanca* and *The English Patient* may represent two different morality paths but if they do, neither should be viewed as superior or inferior to the other.

Catharine E. Warren
University of Calgary

* * *

I find I must respond to the piece of fatuous tripe appearing under the name of Thomas Hurka (The Moral Superiority of *Casablanca* Over *The English Patient* (Focus, Jan 25). According to Mr. Hurka, *Casablanca* is a "morally serious movie" or one of "moral vision" because it takes the political to be more important than the personal, whereas *The English Patient* is decried on the grounds that it "exalts personal emotion at the expense of everything else." Says Professor Hurka: "Almasy sacrifices a cause because he cares only about his love." Now let's look at the reality:

Almasy asks for a car from the British to save a dying woman, which he has promised her he will do. The British treat him abominably. Seen as a Hungarian and hence an ally of Hitler, he is shipped off to the coast. He escapes and is forced to turn to the Germans to enable him to go back to the dying woman and try to rescue her, as he had promised. To get the necessary fuel, he gives them expedition maps. Assuming him to be a spy, the British shoot him down on his return flight with the body of the woman he loved. Of course he was not a spy, but a desperate man to whom help had been refused by the "good" side. Nor had he betrayed anyone or anything.

In point of fact, Almasy had no loyalties to any nation as such (though his initial sympathies were obviously with the allies), and like most of his expedition comrades, believed that there were things more important than national loyalties, such as the human values the archeological expedition was devoted to, and yes, love—the deepest emotion of which any human being is capable. He had no national "cause," only his loves, his friendships, and his interest in the human past. (If he had had a cause, as a "loyal" Hungarian it would have to have been Hitler's! Otherwise he would have been a traitor!)

Yes there *are* things, human things, more important than national loyalties and the clash by night of ignorant armies,[6] and that is an important part of what is being said in this novel and this film.

Casablanca is a great Bogie thriller. *The English Patient* is a deep and serious moral movie.

E. J. Bond, Professor of Philosophy
Queen's University, Kingston

* * *

Thomas Hurka's accusation that the film *The English Patient* is "completely morally bankrupt" blindly equates politics, and particularly patriotism, with morality. Among the many ideas Professor Hurka chooses to ignore is the fact that the movie's so-called "absorption in personal emotions" is itself a powerful moral decision: a rejection of both war and nationalism.

"In our hearts," Graham Greene[7] once wrote, "there is a ruthless dictator, ready to contemplate the misery of a thousand strangers if it will ensure the happiness of the few we love." This truth may be terrible to contemplate, but to suggest the opposite (betray the beloved and—only perhaps—save the many unknowns) is more palatable is only the moral attitude of a bean-counter.

Mr. Hurka's crude equation: selflessness in war is morally superior to selflessness in love. If "morality" has no direct relation to love, leave me out of it.

Tim Conley, Montreal

* * *

The discussion in your pages over the past few days about *Casablanca* and *The English Patient* has been interesting, but much has been based on a fundamental misunderstanding of the choice that Rick Blaine makes at the end of *Casablanca*.

The popular notion is that Rick chooses between a woman and a cause. In fact he does not.

Rick spends most of the movie despising Ilsa, and despising the memory of Paris. He is dead inside, incapable of loving Ilsa or anyone else, and doesn't believe in fighting for any cause—not even against the Nazis ("I stick my neck out for no one"). The events of the movie conspire to change Rick, to restore his love ("We'll always have Paris. We didn't have it—we'd lost it—until you came to *Casablanca*. We got it back last night.") and his ability to fight for a cause ("But I've got a job to do . . . it doesn't take much to see that the problems of three little people don't amount to a hill of beans in this world").

In fact Rick does not choose love or glory, he chooses both, which is why the song says, "It's still the same old story, a fight for love and glory . . ."

If Rick had sent Victor Laszlo away without his wife, would it have made much of a difference to the war effort? Probably not. But in sending her away the audience understands that Rick's character has grown; he understands love, not merely romance, and he has regained his sense of justice.

Markham Cook, Toronto

NOTES

[4] Reprinted with permission from *The Globel and Mail.*

[5] Carol Gilligan is a feminist writer who compares moral development in girls and boys in her book *In a Different Voice: Psychological Theory and Women's Development* (1982).

[6] "Where ignorant armies clash by night", the final line in Matthew Arnold's poem "Dover Beach", is the Victorian poet's description of the confusions of the modern world.

[7] Graham Greene (1904–1991) wrote over thirty volumes of fiction, essays, plays, and poetry. Many of his novels deal with the conflict between differing loyalties.

When Loyalty and Friendship Collide

Editorial[8]

The practicality of philosophy has been debated at least since Socrates took on the Sophists[9] and their free-market approach to truth back in ancient Athens. Purists who believe philosophers should confine their work to classroom lectures and abstruse articles in learned periodicals have always been suspicious of those who go public with their thoughts.

The result is a regrettable polarization: Many of the disciplined thinkers in the universities expend their brainpower on topics of marginal usefulness to the wider world, while those who try to argue ethical issues in the media often favour rhetorical style over intellectual substance.

Last Saturday in the Focus section of *The Globe and Mail*, University of Calgary philosophy professor Thomas Hurka tried to bridge this gap. He took it upon himself to review the popular film *The English Patient*, based on Michael Ondaatje's prize-winning novel, from a moral standpoint. The uproar that has resulted—see the Letters page opposite, or listen to the arguments reverberating across the living rooms and common rooms of the nation—reveals just how engaging philosophy can be, when it chooses to.

And not just philosophy. Art too, when it is not retreating into self-regarding minimalism,[10] is still capable of making us re-examine our thinking on fundamental issues. And nothing could be more fundamental than the issue broached in *The English Patient*: On the eve of the Second World War, a man gives the Germans maps that are crucial to their campaign in North Africa. This betrayal of country, however, is for a greater good: In exchange for the maps, the man gets help for the woman he loves. Personal loyalties, to put it more crudely than Mr. Ondaatje would ever do, are more important than political loyalties.

"Fatuous sentimentality," pronounced Prof. Hurka, who contrasted this "morally bankrupt" message with the "morally serious" decision made by Rick, Humphrey Bogart's character in *Casablanca*. Choosing to send away the woman he loves and her resistance-leader husband while he stays behind in Casablanca, Rick says: "The problems of three little people don't amount to a hill of beans in this crazy world." In this case, with the Nazis at hand, politics must take priority over love.

The position Prof. Hurka staked out has proved decidedly unpopular, which may explain why so few professional philosophers dare to venture out from their academic lairs. What he calls sentimentality, others see as higher truths: Personal loyalties are paramount; emotional ambiguity in a time of conflict is a natural human response; it is war itself that is morally bankrupt.

A celebrated quote from E. M. Forster[11] was brought out to buttress this preference for the personal over the political: "If I had to choose between betraying my country and betraying my friend, I hope I should have the guts to betray my country." It is a point of view that by now is so firmly fixed in Western culture as to make Prof. Hurka look dangerously out of step. What living artist would dare to champion war over love, and expect to be treated seriously either as an artist or a thinker?

Yet take another look at that quote from Forster. If it seems familiar, that is because it was trotted out many times to defend the actions of the Cambridge traitors—Anthony Blunt, Kim Philby, Guy Burgess, Donald Maclean and John Cairncross—who gave secrets to the Soviet Union while working for British intelligence. Their physical and platonic relationships, formed in a university where friendship was the noblest ideal, took priority over loyalty to the abstract political entity of Britain. But all the same, they still compromised the lives of their fellow citizens by betraying secrets to the Soviet communism that their youthful and high-minded idealism preferred.

Not everyone who prefers the personal over the political is quite so hypocritical. But it is necessary to remember that the consequences of apolitical idealism are still political. War may well be morally bankrupt. Artists instinctively find it offensive because its intolerant values are so clearly antiliberal.

Yet war does not go away simply because it is intellectually and emotionally dissatisfying. If you betray secrets to help your loved one, you have put war at a distance. But that help comes at a cost. Not just your sense of betrayal, but the suffering and death of those who are affected by your betrayal.

For the ancient Greeks, such decisions were easier. They knew war and hated it, but because it was so much a part of their daily life, few citizens could ever entertain our distinction between personal and political loyalties: The two were much the same, and to shirk war was to consign your family and your values to the flames.

In the modern world, most of us are more remote from the decision-making. Politicians, not a breed seen to be sensitive to life's moral complexities, declare war. Others do the fighting. It is far too easy in this arrangement to feel detached from the warmaking, to feel the lure of the human relationships that appear so much more real and personal.

But all war is ultimately personal, as even Canadians may some day have to discover. Some wars must be opposed, it is true, for political loyalty is not the same as dumb and blind acceptance. But war itself can not be rejected, not as long as there is something in this crazy world worth defending.

NOTES

[8] Reprinted with permission from *The Globe and Mail.*

[9] The Greek philosopher Socrates (?469–399 B.C.), mentor to Plato, attacked the Sophists, a school of professional philosophers, for focusing on the technique rather than the truth of arguments.

[10] Minimalism was a movement in abstract art and music in the 1960s that emphasized extremely simplified composition. By extension, the term refers to trivializing simplification.

[11] For more information on E. M. Forster, see the biographical note attached to his essay "My Wood," reprinted earlier in this section.

VOCABULARY

abstruse—difficult, obscure.

platonic relationships—close friendships of a non-sexual nature

apolitical—detached from politics

Feminism at the Movies

Margaret Wente[12]

The English Patient is not only a big Oscar winner. It's turning into the greatest date movie of all time. The night I saw it, the theatre was packed with sobbing couples, bawling their eyes out over this tale of all-consuming passion set in a world of war and loss. It's what people used to call a three-hankie movie. Half an hour after it ended I was still leaking into my cappuccino.

There was lots of fuss over the fact that an "independent" movie swept the Academy Awards. But the triumph of *The English Patient* was completely predictable. At its core, it's hardly more than an old-fashioned love story in which the woman's job is to look ravishing, be ravished, and pay the awful price for her illicit desires. She's rather like Helen of Troy.[13] All she has to do is show up, and wreak devastation on every man in sight.

The men would have come to a much better end if Kristin/Katharine had just stayed out of that darn desert. They were quite happy doing their Egyptology[14] without her. The desert, they told her, is no place for a woman, and they were right, although what they really meant is that a men's club is no place for a woman. She is the snake in the garden, the worm in the apple.[15] The moment she slithers onto the scene, you know things are definitely heading downhill.

If you are one of the six people who haven't seen the movie yet, forgive me for revealing that it all ends badly. Kristin/Katharine bewitches Count Ralph, after which her husband kills himself out of crazed jealousy, she dies fetchingly in a cave (you should aspire to look as good as her corpse), the Count betrays the Allied cause[16] for her sake and then literally burns up for love. Before that happens, though, they get to have some really hot sex, which makes it all worth while. She looks so wonderful without her clothes that you want to run right out and get a full-body liposuction.

In terms of women's roles, *The English Patient* is deeply, hopelessly, irrevocably reactionary. It could have been made in 1930. Its lesson is: Women! They screw things up! (The other main woman is a nurse—what else?—who tends the charred Ralph.)

FOR a truly fresh take on women, I advise you to rent *Fargo*, the movie that did not win the best-picture Oscar even though it was far more daring and original.

Everything about *Fargo* is an inversion of *The English Patient*. Instead of desert and blistering heat, it has snow and numbing cold. Instead of exotic Africa, with its luxurious expat clubs and people who talk like aristocrats, you get Minnesota, with its Arby's and Hardee's and people who talk like Bob and Doug MacKenzie. Instead of gauzy gowns and scarves streaming in the wind, you get big ugly hats with earflaps.

And instead of Katharine you get Margie, who is the stupendously pregnant police chief. Margie is the moral centre of the movie, the only person who knows right from wrong. In *Fargo* it's the men who destroy order and the woman who restores it.

Instead of just standing around looking stunning, Margie (played by Frances McDormand, who won an Oscar even though the movie didn't) gets to investigate the malfeasance, pursue the bad guys, and put the world right again. Just to underline that there's no contradiction between moral authority and maternity, the scriptwriters even give her an atypical bout of morning sickness. (Note to the Coen brothers: it generally clears up after the first trimester.)

Margie is kind, reasonable and dogged. She is not afraid of any of the villains, who range from sociopathic outlaws to prosperous businessmen. (In this movie, the car dealership is America's heart of darkness.) She is not only the best person in the whole movie, she's by far the smartest.

Margie's love interest is her husband, Norm, who doesn't bear the slightest resemblance to Ralph Fiennes. Instead of making wild, sensuous love in bathtubs, they put on their PJs and sweaters and go to bed to watch nature documentaries. But it's clear their love, though domestic, is durable and deep. He gets up to fix her eggs. She stops off to find him some night crawlers.

Anyone can love a hero. But how many women can love a pudgy, bald guy whose lifetime achievement is getting his mallard on the three-cent stamp?

In *The English Patient*, Count Ralph gets the best line in the movie when he says the heart is an organ of fire. In *Fargo*, it's Margie who delivers the message when she ruminates on all the mayhem the men have wrought. "And for what?" she puzzles. "For a little bit of money. There's more to life than a little money, you know."

Margie is the woman we all try so hard to be—brave, nurturing, strong, equally employed, faithful and good. Katharine is the woman we all secretly wish we were—a love object to die for. And that's why *Fargo* is only on video, and never had a hope of winning Best Picture. Fantasy trumps feminism, every time.

NOTES

[12] Reprinted with permission of *The Globe and Mail.*

[13] Helen of Troy was the beautiful wife of the Greek king Menelaus. Her abduction by the Trojan prince, Paris, was the cause of the Trojan war.

[14] Egyptology: studies of Egypt.

[15] In the biblical strory of Adam and Eve, Satan disguises himself as a snake to seduce Eve into eating, and persuading Adam to eat, the apple of knowledge.

[16] The Allies were the countries allied against Germany, Italy, and Japan in the Second World War.

QUESTIONS

1. According to Hurka, what are the main similarities between *Casablanca* and *The English Patient?* What are the main differences?

2. In your opinion, which of the letters to the editor presents the most interesting response to Hurka's article?

3. Do you think the editorial in *The Globe and Mail* presents convincing support for Hurka's attack on *The English Patient?* Explain why.

4. What evidence does Wente present to support her argument that "in terms of women's roles, *The English Patient* is deeply, hopelessly, irrevocably reactionary"?

5. Hurka and Wente use different methods to organize their comparisons. Identify the method each uses and explain whether you think it is effective.

SUGGESTIONS FOR WRITING

1. If the responses of any of these participants prompt you to join *The English Patient* debate, write a letter to the editor expressing your own views. In your letter, make clear which standard of evaluation you are using: moral, aesthetic, logical.

2. In his essay on Joseph Conrad, Chinua Achebe also uses a moral standard to evaluate a work of art. Do you find his assessment of the weaknesses of *Heart of Darkness* more or less convincing than Hurka's attack on *The English Patient?* Formulate a thesis in which you state the most important similarity or difference in Achebe's and Hurka's criticisms. Explain why you think that similarity or difference is important.

3. Write a newspaper column in which you present your own evaluation of heroes of two films. Use Wente's column as a model.

TO PEACEKEEP OR NOT TO PEACEKEEP

James Ash

The image of a soldier in a blue beret is one that will surely characterize the nineties. Peacekeeping is a booming business, and Canada has established herself as the world leader in this endeavour. There are those, however, who criticize Canada's active support of, and enthusiastic participation in UN peacekeeping operations. They believe that our armed forces should focus on territorial defence, and that our defence dollar should be spent on the acquisition of new equipment; as for peacekeeping, they believe we should leave it to bigger powers. Such critics are mistaken. Peacekeeping is the best possible role for the Canadian Armed Forces, both from the pragmatic and the ethical point of view.

The most common objection to Canada's involvement in peacekeeping operations is that it ties up our limited military resources abroad, and leaves nothing for the defence of Canada. It is hard to deny the truth of this allegation; we have so few actual soldiers in our army that it is hard to imagine that there are any of them left in Canada, considering our many peacekeeping commitments. But whom would these soldiers be guarding against? Any foreign power that attacks Canada will have to contend with the United States, and if the U.S. were to attack us, it would be a very short war, whether our puny army was in Canada or Yugoslavia. Either we fight alongside the U.S. or against them, and in either case the American military machine dwarfs our own so badly that the issue of territorial defence is hardly an issue at all.

This is not to say that we do not want an army that can engage in large-scale violence as efficiently as the next one, both as a point of national pride (it is nice to think that we could at least put up a fight before the Stars and Stripes flies over Parliament Hill), and as a sign that we are willing to do our part for collective security with our allies.

However, as General Lewis Mackenzie pointed out in *Maclean's* magazine, peacekeeping is ideal training for war-making; it requires the same skills, and it provides the ideal environment for troops to practice them in, namely a real war. This same rationale can be used to answer the objection that our defence dollar would be better spent on new equipment. Yes, our armed forces do need new equipment. But they are far more likely to get this equipment if they are abroad on peacekeeping missions than if they are at home involved in tame training exercises. A few body bags being flown home because Yugoslavian small-arms fire can penetrate Canada's ancient armored personnel carriers, or because our helicopters are too decrepit to evacuate Canadian wounded, is probably the only incentive that will actually get Canada's military the tools it needs to do the job.

We have yet to even consider the merits of peacekeeping in and of itself. The first is that it allows Canada to play a legitimate, independent foreign policy role. Canada will never be a superpower, but it has the misfortune (at times) to live next to one. Peacekeeping is an opportunity for Canada to play a real role in the world beyond its border, without being an American puppet. We are not following the U.S. example with peacekeeping; we are setting one for them.

Setting an example is an idea that is central to this whole issue, because peacekeeping is becoming a symbol of Canada at a time when it desperately needs one. Peacekeeping allows Canada to be the best at something, to be famous, to earn awards. This argument may sound like an emotional one, but it is not entirely. Pragmatically, at a time when Canada is internally divided and economically exhausted, peacekeeping is a low-cost morale booster for a nation that seems to be wallowing in self-pity and cynicism.

Ultimately, though, all of these arguments for peacekeeping are window-dressing. The bottom line is that Canada should commit its defence resources to peacekeeping because it is the right thing to do. War is bad; we take this to be a self-evident truth. Consequently, the only ethical role for a peacetime army is to try and prevent war. It may not always work, it may even never work, but it is something that, morally, we should try our best at, anyhow. If it saves more lives than it costs, if it brings even temporary relief to parts of the world that have become living hells, if it serves merely as a small sign that the world will not stand by forever and let butchers and "ethnic cleansers" have their way, then peacekeeping should be supported by even the most hard-nosed pragmatist.

It seems, on balance, that there really is no good argument against Canada's involvement in UN sponsored peacekeeping, and several good arguments for it. Maybe it is time we gave our much-maligned government a little credit for something. It seems that we have found a government expenditure where taxpayers are getting more than their money's worth.

THE PROBLEM OF ENVIRONMENTAL COSTS:

SUZUKI VS. MERWIN

Joyce MacDonald

We live in a time of great concern for the environment. We constantly need to evaluate almost everything we buy or consume in terms of what it may be doing to our atmosphere or water supply. We have a wide range of sometimes contradictory information at our fingertips telling us how we can, or should, help the environmental cause. While both David Suzuki, in his essay "It Always Costs," and W. S. Merwin, in "Unchopping A Tree," concern themselves with the problem of environmental costs, their messages are very different. Suzuki provides a very accessible essay using well-defined technical terms and a straightforward, academic structure. His thesis, that we must just be a little more careful about the environment, is very practical. The entire tone of his essay, however, is somewhat emotionally detached. Merwin, on the other hand, provides an essay that uses complicated emotional imagery, a complex reverse-process structure and a thesis that is totally impractical: all forest harvesting must be stopped. What Merwin's article has that Suzuki's lacks is a tone of emotional connection to the question of environmental costs. This sense of emotional connection is the truly necessary feature which causes the reader to take personal responsibility for the problems of the environment.

While Suzuki's use of well-defined technical jargon makes his essay accessible to his reader, it also creates a tone of emotional distance from the subject. He uses terms like "biomagnification" and "synergistic" followed by their definitions (408; 409). These terms may be accurate but they are hardly descriptive. When Suzuki refers to "bad episodes" (409) on a drill site, he does not explain what these may be. Are they blowouts, loss of wildlife, or loss of human life? When he writes about the "negative effects" (409) of the pill, he does not elaborate on how it affects a woman's mental health or how it may increase her risks of developing cancer. By eliminating description, Suzuki produces a tone of emotional distance from his subject. One brief description of the horror a mother would experience on the birth of a severely deformed thalidomide baby would be enough to arouse some sympathy in the reader. As it stands, the technical jargon only serves to distance the reader from the subject matter. While it explains everything clearly, it provokes no emotional response. Without emotional connection to the material, no sense of personal responsibility for the environment can be established.

Merwin, in contrast, uses elaborate imagery to evoke an emotional response in the reader, creating a tone of personal involvement. He uses the language of violation, saying that the trees have been "shaken, ripped and broken off" (363), with their limbs "smashed or mutilated" (363), "the skeleton of the resurrection" (364), "tight echoless passages" (365). The death of the tree creates more of an emotional response than the fate of Suzuki's thalidomide babies. We are made to feel for the dead trees, whereas those deformed children are kept at a safe distance by nice technical language. The tone of personal emotional involvement created by Merwin is more conducive to creating a feeling of personal responsibility for those poor dead trees.

The tone created by Suzuki's academic essay structure also serves to distance the reader from the subject. The thesis, "technology always has a cost" (408), is given in the beginning. We are also handed our conclusion on a silver platter: "We must ... err on the side of extreme caution" (410). The reader never needs to search for any hidden meaning in this straightforward approach. The reader can remain emotionally detached from what he or she is reading. While use of the term "we" throughout may seem like an effort to involve the reader, closer examination shows this term to mean "the public in general" and not "you and me." Few of us will ever conduct "an environmental impact assessment" (409), so we can even further detach ourselves because the term seems to refer to the scientific community. The tone created is one of total emotional detachment in the reader. There are no conclusions to reason out. There is no personal stake in the state of the environment. No commitments need to be made by the reader.

Merwin's reverse process structure is more successful in creating a tone of personal involvement because the thesis is never stated and the conclusion is never drawn. Discovery of the point of the essay is an active process. The reader is included in the essay:

> You will watch ...
> You will listen for the nuts to shift ...
> You will hear whether they are indeed falling ... (364)

The emotions the reader is supposed to feel are carefully explained: "It is as though its weight for a moment stood on your heart ... You are afraid the motion of the clouds will be enough to push it over" (365). The sheer complexity of the process increases the reader's sense of futility:

It goes without saying that if the tree was hollow in whole or in part, and contained old nests of bird or mammal or insect, or hoards of nuts or such structures as wasps or bees build for their survival, the contents will have to be repaired where necessary, and reassembled, insofar as possible, in their original order, including the shells of nuts already opened. (363)

Recognition of the futility of the enterprise combined with the prescribed feelings dictated by Merwin leaves us emotionally involved. We are responsible for coming to our own conclusions. This sense of personal responsibility is exactly what Merwin is after. Merwin wants us to take personal responsibility for the environment. Without a sense of personal responsibility, one does not make a commitment to a cause.

In criticism of Merwin, one might say that his proposal to stop deforestation is totally impractical, whereas Suzuki seems to have a very reasonable approach. The problem with Suzuki is that he generalizes wildly in his assumption that we are "hooked" on modern technology and cannot go back to doing things the old way (409). What about the conservation movement that advocates returning to simpler methods around our own homes? Suzuki ignores the ideas of composting and recycling to reduce household wastes and using compost as an alternative to chemical fertilizers. These are certainly old ways to deal with our modern problems. In speaking about technology on a large scale, Suzuki misses these small individual efforts. Perhaps there are ways in which large scale technologies can return to simpler, less destructive techniques. Just to say that it can't be done shows a lack of faith. Merwin's proposal, on the surface seems totally impractical, until it is analysed more closely. His demand for a halt to tree chopping is an overstatement. It is almost like bartering; he asks for much more than he ever hopes to receive. If he is lucky he will get more than he has at present. Instead of asking for a halt to deforestation, he really is asking for a slowdown of the devastation. Where Merwin seems to ask for too much, Suzuki seems to show no faith, and asks for too little. Suzuki seems to buy the technological quick fix, whereas Merwin rejects it as not good enough.

While Suzuki seems to be all practicality and accessibility in his essay, he lacks the tone of personal emotional involvement achieved by Merwin. The future of the environment may depend much less on what the scientific community dictates than on the contributions made by individuals who take a personal stand on the issue and do everything in their power to make things better. Merwin asks his reader to become involved, to accept the challenge, to change the world. If we do not aim at something better than what we have, we will never have anything better and we may end up with something even worse.

COLONIALISM AND MASCULINITY IN "SPECIAL ENGLISH"

A. Smith

Frederic Raphael's "Special English" is a very short short story that appears to be about male–female relationships. We fail to grasp the significance of the story, however, unless we also recognize it as a critique of colonialism. Through setting, characterization, style, and point of view Raphael establishes parallels between masculine attitudes and colonial attitudes. In a man's growing hatred of the woman he brings to a remote island, we see the hatred of the colonizer for the colonized: hatred that erupts in a brutal colonial war.

The setting of "Special English" directly conveys Raphael's concern with colonialism. The man has taken the woman "to a remote island, where they rented a cottage from a peasant who had never before seen a typewriter" (386). The protagonist seems to be attracted to the remoteness of the island just as he is attracted to the woman, who is also described as "remote." Perhaps it is the man, not the woman and the island, who is remote, emotionally detached—a state that is easier to maintain if he thinks his surroundings and his companion have no connection with him. Raphael links the man's interest in the remote and his desire for detachment with colonial attitudes through news broadcasts that provide gory details of "a series of atrocities and counter atrocities committed in the course of a colonial war" (386). These broadcasts, designed to improve English skills, tell "unhurried stories of murder and mutilation. . . tales of ambush and fratricide, or massacre and reprisal"(386). Through the setting of "Special English," Raphael suggests that colonialism may be present not only in distant places but also in the relationship between the protagonists themselves.

The fact that characterization in this story is limited expands the connections Raphael is making between masculine attitudes and colonialism. Perhaps the man is uninterested in the woman as an individual or simply incapable of seeing her as one. Her initial inability to speak and understand English helps us to see his preference for detachment and control. She is his possession. He therefore sees his own needs and interests in her and assumes that she is learning English so that "she would be able to follow his work and her chances of holding his love would, no doubt, be enhanced" (386). She does not realize that he sees her only as a possession, a colony, and that her increasing ability to present herself as an individual is steadily turning him against her.

The parallel between masculine and colonial attitudes established by the setting and characterization in "Special English" is developed by its diction and imagery. The formal words and phrases— "saline rail," "tempo," "distinct variations," "enhanced," and "eloquent"— are reinforced by the vocabulary of teaching and learning in phrases like "instructively simple," "the vocabulary of their understanding," "her newly educated vanity," and "special English." This intellectual, detached diction pretends to be objective and inclusive: to present the woman's perceptions as well as the man's. We gradually see, however, that the man's language is that of the colonizer who assumes that his perception of reality fits both of them and that she exists to meet his needs. She is his "prize" but as remote from him as the island where he has taken her. Finally, the metaphor of the colonial war "staining the vocabulary of their understanding. . . with the world's blood" (386) merges the colonial war and male–female relationships.

The colonizer–colonized relationship between the man and woman is conveyed through the point of view in "Special English," but this becomes clear only through careful reading. At first, "Special English" seems to be told from an objective point of view as we are given external details of the couple's meeting, their journey to the cottage, and the broadcasts they listen to. The point of view then seems to shift to omniscient narration as we learn of the woman's apparent pride in her accomplishments and, finally, of the man's surprising hatred. It is only when we notice that details of the woman's state of mind are introduced through the man's watching her and "read[ing]" her smile and eyes that we realize we are getting the man's point of view, his account of the relationship. Read in this way, the objectivity of the first part of the narrative reveals his preference for emotional detachment; the latter part reveals his desire for control over others and his eventual hatred for them. These are features often associated with traditional concepts of masculinity; they also accurately describe the relationship between the colonizer and the colonized.

The parallels between masculine and colonial attitudes are developed gradually in "Special English." The setting and characterization establish the concern with colonialism quite explicitly, but Raphael makes the most interesting connections between colonialism and masculinity through the style and the point of view in this story. Both present a dominating masculine world view; both are destructive. An analysis of "Special English" suggests that both masculinity and colonialism present a view of the world that seems objective: it takes careful reading to detect the biases behind this objectivity. To question these seemingly objective attitudes towards women and those who are colonized may be the most important lesson we learn from "Special English."

TWO VIEWS OF THE BATTLE AT POWDER RIVER

B. Smith

Both Ernest Wallace's *Ranald S. Mackenzie on the Texas Frontier* and Dee Brown's *Bury My Heart at Wounded Knee* give accounts of the Powder River expedition of 1876, in which the U.S. cavalry led by Mackenzie attacked a Northern Cheyenne village. If we compare the use of structure, development, and style in the two accounts, it becomes clear that Wallace's conveys a favourable attitude towards Mackenzie and an unfavourable attitude towards the Indians, while Brown's account conveys the opposite attitude.

The structure of Wallace's account emphasizes the justice and courage of Mackenzie's expedition, while the structure of Brown's account emphasizes the injustice and cowardice of the attack. Wallace's account begins by pointing out that the attack is justified, in the military's eyes, because this band had left their reservation "in time to participate in the slaughter of Custer's troops." As the expedition gets underway, Wallace's account focuses on the courage of the cavalry. The march is undertaken in a "blinding snowstorm" and in "subzero temperatures." The large number of lodges and hides destroyed in the battle helps to suggest the strength of the Indian forces in their "stronghold." Wallace's account ends on a note of justice: the commendation that Mackenzie receives from his superior reinforces the idea that the whole expedition was just.

Brown's account, on the other hand, begins by disputing the justice of the expedition. He says that "most of these Cheyenne had not been in the Little Bighorn battle" and points out that they had left the reservation because the army had "stopped their rations." Brown emphasizes the cowardice and brutality of the attack. According to his account, many of the Cheyenne warriors were killed "as they came awake." He describes other Indians struggling to protect the women and children. His description implies that the soldiers and their Indian mercenaries are cowardly enough to attack these helpless members of the tribe. This image of a cowardly attack upon the helpless is repeated in the final image of the account: Mackenzie's destruction of the trapped ponies. This image reinforces both the cowardliness and the injustice of the attack from the Indians' point of view.

The choice of detail in the two accounts helps develop the attitudes established by the structure, since Wallace's detail emphasizes military precision while Brown's detail focuses on the Indian experience of the battle. The military precision of Wallace's account appears most obviously in the focus on exact numbers. Mackenzie, according to Wallace, starts out with "1552 men, 6 surgeons, almost 400 Indian scouts, and 168 supply wagons." For the actual expedition he takes "363 Indian scouts and 818 troops." During the battle he burns 173 lodges and loses one officer, five enlisted men, and fifteen cavalry horses. Brown, on the other hand, is much more concerned with recounting sensory impressions of the kind the Indians would likely have experienced. His description of the setting, for example, emphasizes images of coldness: the "deep snow in the shaded places and the ice-crusted snow in the open places." In his description of the battle itself, he stresses the "biting cold" the Indians face and the "furious moments of fighting." Although their emphasis is different, both authors use only observable detail; neither says what those involved are thinking or feeling.

The contrast between an emphasis on military precision and an emphasis on the Indians' sensory experience is also apparent in the two historians' styles. Wallace's style is a style for recording precise factual information. He uses long sentences to accommodate his details about the preparations for the expedition and its consequences. His vocabulary, with its "participate," "conclude" and "commend," is the vocabulary of the military. Brown's style, in contrast, focuses the reader's attention on the Indians' experience. His sentences emphasize action: Mackenzie brings his troops and strikes the Cheyenne, the Pawnee mercenaries go first, the Cheyenne warriors run out, and so on. To convey this experience from the Indian point of view, Brown uses their sense-oriented vocabulary: "Three Fingers Mackenzie" and the "Deer Rutting Moon," for example.

We can conclude then that structure, development, and style in the two accounts all contribute to conveying quite different attitudes towards the two sides in the battle at Dull Knife's village. In Wallace's account we have a well-planned, just, and courageous attack against deserving foes; in Brown's we have a careless, unjust, and brutal attack against heroic but helpless victims. This difference in attitude is conveyed not only by obvious choices in structure, development, and style, but more subtly by the way these elements combine to reflect the values of one of the sides in the battle. If historians' accounts are shaped in these ways, we must consider the possibility that so are the seemingly objective reports of journalists and other writers, upon whom later historians will depend for the records from which history is written.

WHAT DOES THE CANADIAN HEALTH-CARE SYSTEM NEED?

C. Smith

In an essay entitled "How to Preserve the Health-Care Safety Net" (*Maclean's*, December 2, 1996, 13), Barbara Amiel argues that to address problems resulting from socialized medicine, especially problems of "stratospheric health-care costs" and poor service, we need to return to a system that allows private insurance and "private medicine to co-exist with a public safety net." How convincing is this argument? The strengths of Amiel's essay, according to a logical standard of evaluation, are its unspecific but effective examples of problems, and the emotional appeal of a writer who seems to be able to put herself in the patient's place. These strengths, however, are more than offset by the essay's weaknesses in presenting solutions, namely its defective causal reasoning and its lack of convincing examples of a practical and humane alternative.

A definite strength of Amiel's essay is that her examples of problems in the Canadian health-care system, while not very specific, are wide ranging and give a good sense of the issues. Amiel's examples of problems are not just the familiar ones of people going to the doctor for the common cold and to psychiatrists for help with their love lives. They also include the cost of "million-dollar diagnostic machines," ethical dilemmas about who receives the benefits of these machines, the alleged "brain drain" of doctors, the problems of doctors opting out or migrating to urban centres, and patient problems with "endless waiting and harassed staff." No documentation or detail is provided for any of these problems, but it is hard to imagine a reader who has not experienced or read about at least one or two of them.

Amiel reinforces her examples of problems with emotional appeals, but these emotional appeals are only partly effective. At first Amiel's reader is likely to be persuaded by her reference to her experience as a student who "couldn't afford [her] insurance and happened to end up in Toronto General Hospital," and by her comments on vulnerable patients' need for "a bedpan or an understanding nurse." Comments like these, suggesting Amiel's identification with patients, create a bond between writer and reader. This sympathetic approach, however, is accompanied by claims that the "nightmarish" conceptions that the British then and Canadians now have about two-tier medicine are a "lie." This emotive language seems extreme for claims supported only by Amiel's experience as a student in hospital; it likely will make the reader suspect there are some undisclosed weaknesses in Amiel's argument.

The weaknesses in Amiel's argument are first evident in her causal reasoning, which is distinctly flawed. Amiel claims that a return to private insurance and private medicine would solve health-care problems. The flaw in her reasoning is that she has already identified "two main problems with modern medicine" and admitted that one of these—the cost of medical technology and a trained workforce—"has absolutely nothing to do with socialized medicine." Thus even if the reader accepts Amiel's argument that socialized medicine is the other half of the problem, it is obvious that eliminating the current system can only be half a solution.

An even more important weakness is the lack of adequate examples to support Amiel's claim that a two-tier health-care system would work effectively and humanely. As already noted, the one piece of support for this claim is Amiel's experience over forty years ago. The most obvious source of examples of a two-tier health system currently at work is the United States, but of health care in the United States Amiel says nothing. This seems a major flaw in her argument, since the reader must suspect that she simply cannot cite any current examples of a two-tier system working as she says it will.

We are probably all aware of problems with Canada's health-care system, and Barbara Amiel's essay does point to these problems and encourage sympathy for patients suffering from them. However, her acknowledgment that other factors besides socialized medicine are responsible for problems in the system makes her attack on socialized medicine unconvincing. Furthermore, her seeming inability to cite examples of a two-tier system working effectively damages her claims concerning solutions. For these reasons, Barbara Amiel's "How to Preserve the Health-Care Safety Net" fails to persuade us that private insurance and medicine could co-exist with a public safety net in a way that would provide a humane and effective health-care system.

THE MAKING OF THE TRAGIC HERO:

THE GRAVEYARD SCENE IN *HAMLET*

D. Smith

In William Shakespeare's tragedy *Hamlet, Prince of Denmark*, Act Five, Scene One, commonly known as the graveyard scene, marks Hamlet's reappearance after his interrupted voyage to England. The Hamlet we see in this scene is very different from the cruel, cynical prince of Acts III and IV. Most critics attribute this difference to a philosophical change in Hamlet's attitude towards death. In focusing on the thematic significance of this scene, however, they neglect its dramatic function: to engage the audience's sympathy for Hamlet before his death. Without a change in character, Hamlet would not achieve the stature of a tragic hero, because his death would not arouse the pity, fear, awe, and sense of waste common to Shakespearean tragedy. The graveyard scene engages our sympathy for Hamlet in three ways: by using the episode with the gravediggers as a means to shift the audience's perspective from the court to a humanized Hamlet; by clarifying Hamlet's relationship with Ophelia; and by symbolically foreshadowing the outcome of the duel between Hamlet and Laertes.

Most interpretations of the play fail to consider the dramatic function of the graveyard scene; instead they focus on its philosophical significance. These interpretations fall into three main groups: those that see Hamlet coming to a Christian acceptance of death; those that see his attitude as fatalistic resignation; and those that argue that the scene is a mixture of both these attitudes (Philias 226). Maynard Mack and Walter King are representative of those who favour a Christian interpretation. According to Mack, Hamlet by the last act of the play has "learned, and accepted, the boundaries in which human action, human judgment are enclosed" and therefore no longer assumes he must single-handedly set the world to rights (521). Similarly, King argues that the graveyard scene presents "affirmation of life and love as a viable center of values in a God-created and God-centered universe," but within the context of a world in which these values "are perennially in danger of being snuffed out" (146).

The view that Hamlet's attitude is totally, or at least partially, fatalistic is propounded by G. Wilson Knight, Richard Levine, and Peter

Philias. Knight sees our sympathies as being divided between the members of the court, who for all their imperfections "assert the importance of human life," and Hamlet, whose philosophy is "inevitable, blameless, and irrefutable," but whose very existence asserts "the negation of life" (60–61). Far from admitting that there is a shift in our sympathies during the graveyard scene, he asserts that "Laertes and Hamlet struggling at Ophelia's grave are like symbols of life and death contending for the prize of love" (64). Unlike Knight, Levine sees a change in Hamlet but argues that the change is negative. In his view, Hamlet's "tragic flaw, his vacillating and faulty world view," is resolved by Hamlet's rejection of traditional religious belief in favour of "an attenuated stoicism" (539, 543). Peter Philias, while less negative in his assessment of Hamlet, reaches much the same conclusion. Focusing on the episode with the gravediggers, as most of the other critics do, he concludes that "the Christian framework of the play is profoundly qualified, though not replaced, by a strong fatalistic point of view" (226).

While these interpretations give us some insight into the philosophical issues raised by the play, they do not adequately account for the presence of the gravediggers, Hamlet's farewell to Ophelia, or the struggle in the grave. Even a critic who calls it "one of the most important scenes" because it "bring[s] into dramatic focus parts of the play which are seemingly disparate" (Bennett 160) fails to adequately account for these elements. The most useful interpretation of the scene's dramatic function is that of B.D. Cheadle. Cheadle asks Coleridge's question "What reason does it contain within itself for being as it is and no other?" (89) as a guide to understanding Hamlet's confrontation with Laertes at Ophelia's grave. Asking this question for the scene as a whole will enable us to see that these elements are explained by their role in bestowing upon Hamlet the qualities of dignity, courage, and deep feeling that make his death a waste of potential greatness.

The graveyard scene opens not with Hamlet's entrance but with the conversation between the gravediggers. This opening allows for a gradual shift in sympathy from the court to Hamlet and humanizes the prince by making death a personal rather than a metaphysical concern. The shift in perspective has to be gradual because we have seen little to admire in Hamlet since the early scenes of the play. In the scenes preceding his exile, as Knight points out, Hamlet "is cruel to Ophelia and his mother"; "exults in tormenting the King by the murder of Gonzago" and "takes a demoniac pleasure in the thought of preserving his life for a more damning death"; "murders Polonius in error" and then makes disgusting, callous comments to Claudius about the body (55–56). Furthermore, the three scenes from which Hamlet is absent focus on Laertes' grief and anger over his father's death and on Ophelia's madness and suicide. If we are to mourn the death of a man who has caused such suffering, we need to see him in a more favourable light.

The gravediggers serve as a means of detaching our sympathies from the court and transferring them to Hamlet. The dramatic goings-on and highly charged language of the court scenes seem excessive when contrasted with the matter-of-fact way in which the gravediggers go about their work. Emotional indulgence, like Christian burial for a suicide, seems a privilege accorded only to those of high social position (MacDonald 312). When Hamlet enters, however, his first comment is a criticism of the first gravedigger's singing at his work. His next is an assertion of the finer feelings of those with higher status: "The hand of little employment hath the daintier sense" (V.i.66). This exchange encourages us to forget Hamlet's earlier callousness and cynicism and to see him as a person of fine sensibility. These few lines initiate what Michael Cohen sees as "two competing subtexts in the scene, one that argues that death is the ultimate leveller of all class distinctions, another that argues, with almost equal persuasiveness, that class distinctions continue even after death" (78).

But the graveyard scene does not merely shift the point of view from the court to Hamlet. It also humanizes Hamlet by making death a personal rather than a metaphysical concern. The gravediggers' debate over Ophelia's burial, as Philias points out, shifts attention away from the religious questions of salvation and damnation that were so powerful when Hamlet himself was considering suicide to the social issues of power and status (231). The reduction of death from a metaphysical to a human concern is further emphasized by the gravedigger's actions as he tosses skulls about and sings about the human cycle of love, age, and death.

Even more important in engaging our sympathy for Hamlet, however, is the dramatic tension created by his not knowing that the grave is for Ophelia. Although the discovery of Yorick's skull momentarily shows us Hamlet's deeper feelings and allows us to identify with the mixture of fond memory, revulsion, and jest in his response to this physical reminder of mortality, his ignorance of Ophelia's death allows him to remain witty and self-possessed. As a result, our image of Hamlet at the end of this episode is that of a person who is neither morbidly preoccupied with death (as he was at the beginning of the play) nor overly sentimental about it (as Laertes appears in the next part of the scene). Instead, he has accepted its reality. The episode with the gravediggers thus prepares us to see the burial of Ophelia from Hamlet's point of view.

The second half of the scene increases our sympathy for Hamlet by revealing the depth of his feeling for Ophelia and by bringing him face to face with the man we know will be the instrument of his death. The simplicity of Hamlet's "I loved Ophelia" (V.i.256) dispels the mystery surrounding their relationship. Although we hear from Ophelia of her suitor's wild dress and melancholy behaviour when his attentions are forbidden, we are not sure whether his actions are motivated by "mock-madness" or, as Knight maintains, by blighted love (53). The only two times we see Hamlet and Ophelia together—when she is acting as decoy for her father and Claudius in III.i. and when both attend the play-within-a-play in the following scene—Hamlet treats her with such contempt and cruelty that we question his regard for her. To establish the depth of Hamlet's love, Cheadle suggests, his leap into the grave should be staged so that he says "This is I" (V.i. 244) as "an avowal to the dead Ophelia that had she lived and had things been different, she would have been Queen to the Dane" (87). When a few lines later Hamlet says "I loved Ophelia," the past tense marks not only Hamlet's acceptance of the end of the relationship but also his acceptance of the death of love, a fact he could not accept in his mother's remarriage. The ending of the Ophelia subplot in this manner introduces, in a way sympathetic to Hamlet, the sense of wasted lives and lost possibilities that will become more pronounced in the final scene.

Interwoven with the burial of Ophelia is the confrontation between Hamlet and Laertes. Although their behaviour seems strange and inappropriate as an expression of grief for a woman they both loved, it makes a very powerful dramatic impact when considered as a prelude to, and symbolic foreshadowing of, their duel and deaths. Hamlet's dignity is enhanced by his initial self-control, a deliberate contrast, as Cheadle points out, to Laertes' "ranting" (89). Furthermore, Hamlet's announcing himself as "Hamlet the Dane" is both "an assertion of identity and purpose" and a direct challenge to Claudius, since only the King has the right to call himself "the Dane" (86). Claudius' plot against Hamlet makes Laertes not only Ophelia's grief-stricken brother but also the King's champion. The impact of the final duel would be much less, however, if we saw Laertes only as Claudius' instrument. It is dramatically necessary for Shakespeare to bring together Hamlet and Laertes, both of whom have vowed to avenge a father's death, so that each recognizes the justice in the other's actions and can "Exchange forgiveness," as the dying Laertes requests in the final scene. Their struggle in Ophelia's grave thus foreshadows the death blows they will deal each other and the sense of wasted nobility we will feel at their deaths.

This sense of waste, and the feelings of pity, fear, and awe that accompany it, would not be so pronounced at the end of the play without the graveyard scene to engage our sympathies. Interpretations of the scene's philosophical significance tend to overlook the dramatic impact of the gravedigger episode, of Hamlet's farewell to Ophelia, and of the struggle between Hamlet and Laertes. These critics forget, perhaps, that our response to the play, like Hamlet's to death, is personal as well as metaphysical, and equally shaped by the dramatist's art.

WORKS CITED

Bennett, William E. "The Gravedigger's Scene: A Unifying Thread in *Hamlet.*" *Upstart Crow* 5 (Fall 1984): 160–65.

Cheadle, B. D. "Hamlet at the Graveside: A Leap into Hermeneutics." *English Studies in Africa* 22.2 (1979): 83–90.

Cohen, Michael. " 'To what base uses we may return': Class and Mortality in *Hamlet* (5.1)." *Hamlet Studies* 9.1–2 (Summer–Winter 1987): 78–85.

King, Walter N. *Hamlet's Search for Meaning.* Athens, GA: U of Georgia P, 1982.

Knight, G. Wilson. "The Embassy of Death: An Essay on *Hamlet*" in *The Wheel of Fire.* 4th ed. London: Methuen, 1949. 17–46.

Levine, Richard A. "The Tragedy of Hamlet's World View." *College English* 23.7 (1962): 539–46.

MacDonald, Michael. "Ophelia's Maim'èd Rites." *Shakespeare Quarterly.* 37.3 (Autumn 1986): 309–17.

Mack, Maynard. "The World of Hamlet." *Yale Review.* 41.4 (1952): 502–23.

Philias, Peter E. "Hamlet and the Grave-Maker." *Journal of English and German Philology* 63 (1964): 226–34.

SPONTANEITY AND ENJOYMENT OF THE NATURAL WORLD

Karin Swanson

Edward Thomas' "Adlestrop" (464) and Robert Frost's "Stopping by Woods on a Snowy Evening" (463) each describe a personal account of an encounter with the natural world. Frost's speaker chooses to stop and "watch [the] woods fill up with snow" (l. 4), but is unable to enjoy the tranquillity of the forest because of his/her preoccupation with "promises" (l. 14) and other obligations. The speaker in Thomas' poem, however, relaxes and enjoys the countryside through an express train window during an "unwonted" (l. 4) stop at Adlestrop. Frost's speaker's premeditated attempt at enjoying nature is unsuccessful while Thomas' speaker is captivated by an unplanned encounter with the natural world. Through comparison of the setting, structure, and prosody of these two poems, it becomes clear that both poems suggest that spontaneity is the key to the genuine enjoyment of nature.

Setting, or more accurately the speakers' control over the setting, emphasizes the importance of spontaneity when visiting nature. Frost's speaker arrives in the woods with his "little horse" (l. 5) and deliberately chooses "to stop without a farm house near" (l. 6) where the owner "will not see [him] stopping" (l. 3). The onus is on the speaker to decide when he must leave; he has control over both the location and the length of his stay in the forest. Unfortunately, this premeditated, highly controlled approach to nature conflicts with the peaceful atmosphere of the woods, described in the phrases "easy wind and downy flake" (l. 12). This conflict ultimately impairs the speaker's ability to enjoy the natural world.

The structures of "Adlestrop" and "Stopping by Woods on a Snowy Evening" indicate shifts in the speakers' relationship regarding the natural world. At first glance, it appears that the speaker in Frost's poem is enjoying nature, only to be torn away by remembrances of obligations in the last stanza of the poem. The speaker remarks that "The woods are lovely, dark and deep / But I have promises to keep" (ll. 11–12), finally admitting to himself in the last few lines of the poem that he must leave his wooded wonderland. However, a closer examination of the organization of detail within the poem reveals that the speaker's relationship with the natural world remains static throughout the poem and that the speaker never successfully loses himself to the natural world. The speaker is constantly aware of whose property he is on (ll. 1–3) and what his horse is doing (ll. 5, 9–10). These concerns are presented before his description of the woods (ll. 11–13), which makes the actual enjoyment of the forest seem less important. These preoccupations continually interfere with his attempts to observe the loveliness of the woods, which makes the speaker's decision to leave (ll. 13–14) unsurprising.

The structure in Thomas' poem, however, indicates that the speaker undergoes a shift in awareness regarding his perception of the natural world. The speaker's observations in the first two stanzas are very limited in scope. "The steam hissed" (l. 5), "Someone cleared his throat" (l. 5), and "No-one left and no-one came / On the bare platform" (ll. 6–7) are quite unremarkable descriptions of events associated with train travel. A shift in the speaker's awareness occurs in line 9 when the speaker begins a very detailed account of the countryside outside of his window. The speaker maintains this awareness throughout the remaining two stanzas. It is the express train's "unwonted" or spontaneous (l. 4) stop which enables the speaker to lose himself in the natural world at Adlestrop.

The prosody of both poems effectively conveys the idea that an unplanned approach is most conducive to the enjoyment of nature. The meter in Frost's poem is iambic, giving the poem a very even, consistent rhythm. The meter has a forward momentum to it which contrasts with the subject of the poem, *stopping* in the woods. Frost's poem also exhibits a considerable amount of rhyme. At least three out of four lines in each stanza rhyme, contributing to the precise, disciplined tone of the poem. The meticulous rhyme and rhythm in this poem is representative of the speaker's preoccupation with order and control, which is what prevents him from enjoying his stop in the woods.

The rhythm of "Adlestrop" is less militant; its rhythm is more akin to ordinary conversation. There are no definite end stops; the ideas of each line flow into one another, giving the poem a serene, dreamlike quality. There is less rhyme in "Adlestrop" as well, making the tone of the poem less intense. The loose rhythm and reduced rhyme in "Adlestrop" convey the relaxed attitude of the speaker, and it is from this relaxed space that the speaker is able to experience the natural world.

Frost's poem conveys the message that the speaker's premeditated and controlled approach to the woods interferes with his enjoyment of the scene. Conversely, Thomas' poem implies that the speaker is able to enjoy the countryside because his arrival at Adlestrop is unplanned.

The message is subtle, but through comparison of the setting, structure, and prosody of "Adlestrop" and "Stopping by Woods on a Snowy Evening," it becomes clear that spontaneity is required to experience true enjoyment of nature.

WORKS CITED

Frost, Robert. "Stopping by Woods on a Snowy Evening." *The Norton Anthology of Poetry*. 4th ed. Ed. Margaret Ferguson et al. New York: Norton, 1996. 1131.

Thomas, Edward. "Adlestrop." *The Norton Anthology of Poetry*. 4th ed. Ed. Margaret Ferguson et al. New York: Norton, 1996. 1147.

Stopping by Woods on a Snowy Evening

Robert Frost

1   Whose woods these are I think I know,
His house is in the village though;
He will not see me stopping here
To watch his woods fill up with snow.

5   My little horse must think it queer
To stop without a farmhouse near
Between the woods and frozen lake
The darkest evening of the year.

He gives his harness bells a shake
10   To ask if there is some mistake.
The only other sound's the sweep
Of easy wind and downy flake.

The woods are lovely, dark and deep,
But I have promises to keep,
15   And miles to go before I sleep,
And miles to go before I sleep.

1923

Adlestrop

Edward Thomas

1   Yes, I remember Adlestrop—
The name, because one afternoon
Of heat the express-train drew up there
Unwontedly. It was late June.

5   The steam hissed. Someone cleared his throat.
No one left and no one came
On the bare platform. What I saw
Was Adlestrop—only the name

And willows, willow-herb, and grass,
10   And meadowsweet, and haycocks dry,

No whit less still and lonely fair
Than the high cloudlets in the sky.

And for that minute a blackbird sang
Close by, and round him, mistier,
15   Farther and farther, all the birds
Of Oxfordshire and Gloucestershire.

1917

Resources
for Writing

part four

Making Effective Use of Your Computer

Try these suggestions for getting the most out of the capabilities of your computer.

Clarifying Topics and Gathering Material

- Investigate software programs that help you come up with a topic. Some programs ask open-ended questions about your areas of interest and expertise. Others ask questions tailored to specific kinds of writing.

- Create files of discovery questions, such as the questions we suggest for content analysis and textual analysis, for each type of writing you do. Whenever you start an assignment, you can transfer the appropriate questions to the file you are working on.

- As soon as you get an assignment, open a file and type in your preliminary ideas about the topic. Add research material, new ideas, even complete paragraphs without worrying about the order. If you add to the file regularly for a week or so, you will accumulate lots of material that you can use as the starting point for an outline or a draft.

- Use databases for gathering material and recording notes, citations, and bibliographies for research papers.

- If you are writing a research paper, consider searching the Internet for secondary sources of information on your topic.

Drafting

- Freewrite drafts of your essay. (If you have trouble drafting without editing or proofreading, try covering the monitor or darkening the screen.)
- Put your comments and questions about the draft in boldface or block capitals (EVIDENCE NEEDED; IS THIS TRUE? IS THIS CLEAR?) or use the highlighting feature so that they will stand out when you revise.
- Number the drafts (Obasan1, Obasan2), save, and print them out separately so that you can compare your ideas and methods of development.

Outlining

- You can easily add, delete, and rearrange material in your planning outline.
- Set up columns for your planning outline, your draft outline, and your revision outline.

Revising

- Collaborate with others by printing out multiple copies of a draft and asking for comments, or by sending drafts to fellow students or your instructor via e-mail.
- To revise your own work, print out a hard copy so that you can begin with the larger issues in revision—content and organization.
- Some word-processing programs allow you to work back and forth between different drafts by displaying both drafts on the screen. This feature is particularly useful for writing a final draft once you have decided on the changes to make.

Editing

- Use editing programs (grammar checkers, spell checkers, thesaurus capabilities) cautiously. These programs are useful but will not eliminate all problems and errors. Grammar checkers, for instance, may produce false tags (such as highlighting every passive construction). Many spell checkers make no distinctions among homonyms (*there/their*), nor will they pick up the misuse of correctly spelled words ("One affect of pollution is …"). An editing program with a thesaurus will provide synonyms but will not tell you if a synonym is appropriate in a particular context.

- If your editing skills are weak, you might consider a software program that provides on-screen access to a handbook. On-screen versions of handbooks enable you to "pop up" answers to questions about grammar, style, punctuation, and mechanics.
- Most word-processing programs allow you either to put notes at the bottom of the page or to collect them in endnotes. The format, however, will not necessarily follow the style guide you are using. Since in-text citations are typed directly into the text, they are not affected.

Formatting

Word-processing programs make it easy to produce a neat, professional-looking essay.

- Adjust spacing and margins as required.
- Check page breaks to make sure a heading doesn't appear at the bottom of a page.
- Use a standard 12-point font. Do not set quotations in smaller type. If you wish to use a special font for a particular effect, check with your instructor.
- For more complete guidelines about various aspects of formatting, see Essay Format, Quotations, and Documentation, Part 2, Handbook for Final Editing.

Word-Processing Checklist

- Remember to save your work frequently and have two copies of your work in electronic form at all times (one of them should be on a floppy disk that is stored away from your computer). Don't delete them until you get your graded essay back from your instructor, just in case anything goes amiss with your hard copy.
- If you are working with more than one computer system or software package, make sure that the various components are compatible well in advance of your due date.
- If you share disks with others, use disks in computers other than your own, or download material from the Internet, be sure to install a memory resident virus checker on your computer to protect against computer viruses.

For extended discussion of these and other matters, see *The Computer in Composition Instruction: A Writer's Tool*, ed. William Wresch (Urbana, IL: NCTE, 1984).

Strategies for Research

What sources of reference material can I draw on for my working bibliography?

1. Annual Bibliography or Periodical Index
   a. Check library catalogue under subject and title (also for bound bibliography).
   b. Check serials list (if any) under title.
   c. Check for relevant CD-ROM and on-line bibliographies.
2. The Library On-line, Microfiche, or Card Catalogue

How do I find references in these sources?

1. Check relevant sections in each yearly volume, working backwards from the present.
2. Check under relevant subject headings, using *Library of Congress Subject Headings* volumes if necessary.
3. For Internet sources, try a variety of different search terms and search engines.

What bibliographical information do I need to record?

1. Books: Author, title, place of publication, publisher, date of publication.
2. Articles: Author, title of article, title of periodical, volume number (for scholarly journals), date, page numbers.
3. Internet: Author, title of document, date of publication or last revision, electronic address, date of access.

How do I locate books and articles?

1. Books:
   a. Check library catalogue under author or title.
   b. Record call number.
   c. Search shelves by call number, or request from closed stacks librarian.

2. Articles:
   a. Check library catalogue or serials list under title of periodical.
   b. Check holdings for volume wanted: record call number.
   c. Search shelves or request from librarian.

Websites

Be aware that Canadian conventions of English usage may differ from advice you find on American and British Websites listed here.

Writing Essays: An Overview

Writers on the Net: Classes, Tutoring and Mentoring; Writers' Groups
http://www.writers.com/

Inkspot: Writer's Resources on the Web: a good extensive range of links
http://www.inkspot.com/

Resources for Writers and Writing Instructors: another good range of links
http://www.english.upenn.edu/~jlynch/writing.html

Rensselaer Writing Centre: Handouts
http://www.rpi.edu/dept/llc/writecenter/web/handouts.html

University of Victoria's Hypertext Writer's Guide
http://webserver.maclab.comp.uvic.ca/writersguide/welcome.html

Ryerson Polytechnic University: The Writing Centre Guide #3: Writing a University Essay
http://gopher.ryerson.ca:70/0.services/.write/.essay

Essay Topics

York University Computer Assisted Writing Centre: strategies and techniques for generating ideas for your essay
http://www.yorku.ca/admin/cawc/strategies/contents.html

Handout on brainstorming by consultants at the Undergraduate
Writing Center at UT Austin
gopher://gopher.utexas.edu:3003/00/pub/uwc/Handouts/brainsto.txt

Special Types of Essays

Writing tips for specific essay forms
http://lc.byuh.edu/R_WCTR/handout.html

Grammar and Style

The classic *Elements of Style* by Strunk and White
http://www.columbia.edu/acis/bartleby/strunk

An on-line English grammar resource
http://www.edunet.com/english/grammar/toc.html

Hypergrammar: an online grammar handbook from the University of
Ottawa
http://www.uottawa.ca/academic/arts/writcent/hypergrammar
/grammar.html

Grammar Hotline Directory 1995, from Tidewater Community College:
a list of phone numbers or e-mail addresses that you can contact for
information on grammar
http://www.infi.net/tcc/tcresourc/faculty/dreiss/writcntr/hotline.html

Punctuation Guide, from NASA's *A Handbook for Technical Writers
and Editors*
http:/sti.larc.nasa.gov/html/Chapt3/Chapt3-TOC.html

Capitalization Guide, from NASA's *A Handbook for Technical Writers
and Editors*
http:sti.larc.nasa.gov/html/Chapt4/Chapt4-TOC.html

An Elementary Grammar, from The English Institute in the U.K.
http://www.hiway.co.uk/~ei/intro.html

Word Processing Style Guide
http://ourworld.compuserve.com/homepages/timg/

Gender-Free Pronoun Frequently Asked Questions (GFP FAQ)
http://www.eecis.udel.edu/~chao/gfp/

Dictionaries and Thesauruses

Webster's Dictionary
http://c.gp.cs.cmu.edu:5103/prog/webster

The Oxford English Dictionary On-line
http://www.oed/com/oetc.html

Roget's Thesaurus
http://humanities.uchicago.edu/forms_unrest/ROGET.html

Research Institute of the Humanities: extensive listing of dictionaries and thesauruses.
http://www.arts.cuhk.hk/Ref.html#dt

Carnegie-Mellon On-line Reference Works
http://www.cs.cmu.edu/Web/references.html

Documentation

Bibliography Styles Handbook: summarizes and illustrates APA and MLA styles
http://www.english.uiuc.edu/cws/wworkshop/bibliostyles.htm

The APA Crib Sheet
http://www.gasou.edu/psychweb/tipsheet/apacrib.htm

Citing Electronic Materials with the New MLA Guidelines
http://www-dept.usm.edu/~engdept/mla/rules.html

Guides for Citing Internet Sources: links
http://acm:ewu.edu/cscourse/cs315/cite.htm

Common Perspectives for Content Analysis

TYPE OF ANALYSIS	COMMON PERSPECTIVES
	Economic Perspective: Focuses on events, sets of data, phenomena, concepts, or theories as they relate to the production, circulation, or distribution of wealth, goods, or services
Systems Analysis What are the main parts of this event, set of data, phenomenon, concept, or theory? What is the nature and function of the parts? How are the parts related?	**Economic system:** **Example** *Data*: statistics on unemployment *Stages*: total labour force, number of people employed, number actively seeking work, number of "discouraged" job seekers, number of unemployed
Process Analysis What are the main stages in the evolution of this event, set of data, phenomenon, concept, or theory? What is the nature and function of these stages? How are these stages related?	**Economic process:** **Example** *Data*: statistics on unemployment *Stages*: in the rise and fall of employment; in the way unemployment figures are calculated
Causal Analysis What factors have brought about, or might have brought about, this event, set of data, phenomenon, concept, or theory? What changes have occurred, or might occur, as a result? How are these causes/effects related?	**Economic causes/effects:** **Example** *Data*: statistics showing high unemployment *Causes*: high interest rates; decrease in exports; loss of manufacturing *Effects*: rollbacks in wages and benefits; government incentives to create jobs; fewer part-time and summer jobs for students

FOR CONTENT ANALYSIS

Social Perspective: Focuses on events, sets of data, phenomena, concepts, or theories as they relate to a society, community or group	**Political Perspective:** Focuses on events, sets of data, phenomena, concepts, or theories as they relate to government, power, or authority	**Psychological Perspective:** Focuses on events, sets of data, phenomena, concepts, or theories as they relate to the needs, drives, or behaviour of individuals
Social system: **Example** *Phenomenon*: the family *Parts*: parent(s), child(ren), other relatives, other members of a household	**Political system:** **Example** *Event*: parliamentary elections *Parts*: Political parties, candidates, voters, media	**Psychological system:** **Example** *Theory*: Freud's theory of the unconscious *Parts*: concepts of the id, the ego, the superego
Social process: **Example** *Phenomenon*: the family *Stages*: in the formation of a family, such as courtship, marriage, childbirth; in the evolution of the family in Western society, such as the tribe, the extended family, the nuclear family	**Political process:** **Example** *Event*: parliamentary elections *Stages*: in the evolution of parliamentary elections; in a particular election	**Psychological process:** **Example** *Theory*: Freud's theory of the unconscious *Stages*: in Freud's process of developing the theory; in the theory of psycho-sexual development
Social causes/effects: **Example** *Phenomenon*: contemporary family *Causes*: high rates of divorce and remarriage; increased recognition of gay and lesbian families; increasing number of consensual households. *Effects*: less peer disapproval of children in non-nuclear families	**Political causes/effects:** **Example** *Event*: parliamentary election *Causes*: desire to capitalize on party's popularity; defeat of major legislation; vote of non-confidence *Effects*: shifts in regional power; minority government; increased representation of women and minorities	**Psychological causes/effects:** **Example** *Theory*: Freud's theory of the unconscious *Causes*: in Freud (self-analysis, influences of others) *Effects*: on others (therapeutic transformation)

5

General and Special Categories for Textual Analysis

GENERAL CATEGORIES	SPECIAL CATEGORIES	
	NONFICTION	**FICTION**
Subject What is the work about? **Subgenre** Does it belong to a special *kind* of text? **Context** For what audience and in what situation was it produced?	What issue, idea, event, or person is this work about? Is it a particular kind of nonfiction? For what audience and in what situation was it written?	What is the novel or short story about? Is it a particular kind of fiction? For what audience and in what situation was it written?
Methods of Development What are the particular details that give the work substance?	**Evidence and Detail** What kind of evidence does the author give to support the argument? What kind of detail to develop explanatory, narrative or descriptive writing?	A. **Setting** What is the place, time, and social environment within which events take place? B. **Characterization** What are the characters like? What techniques are used to portray them?
Structure How is the work put together?	**Structure** How is the argument, explanation, narrative and/or description selected and arranged?	**Narrative Structure** What is the principle behind the selection and arrangement of events ("plot")?

POETRY	DRAMA	FILM AND TV
What is the poem or sequence of poems about? Does it belong to a particular kind of poetry? For what audience and in what situation was it written?	What is this play about? Does it belong to a particular kind of drama? For what audience and in what situation was it written/produced?	What is the film or program about? Is it a particular kind of film or TV program? For what audience and in what situation was it written/produced?
A. Setting What is the place, time, and social environment within which the development of the poem takes place? **B. Characterization** How is (are) the speaker and/or other character(s) portrayed?	**A. Setting** What is the place, time, and social environment within which the action takes place? What do costuming, music, lighting, sets, etc., indicate about the setting? **B. Characterization** What are the characters like? How are various techniques, including dialogue and acting, used to portray them?	**A. Setting** What is the place, time, and social environment established by the locations, by music, etc.? **B. Characterization** What are the characters like? How are various techniques, including dialogue and acting, used to portray them?
Poetic Structure What is the principle behind the selection and arrangement of details in the poem?	**Dramatic Structure** What is the principle behind the selection and arrangement of events ("action")?	**Structure** What is the principle behind the selection and arrangement of events ("action")?

GENERAL CATEGORIES   SPECIAL CATEGORIES

	NONFICTION	FICTION
Style How does the author/director use the "language" of the medium?	**A. Diction** What do usage level and word choice convey? **B. Figurative Language and Allusions** Are images, symbols, and/or allusions used to comment on the subject? How? **C. Sentence Structure** What do sentence patterns indicate?	**A. Diction** What do usage level and word choice convey? **B. Figurative Language and Allusions** Do images, symbols, and/or allusions create patterns of meaning? How? **C. Sentence Structure** What do sentence patterns indicate?
Tone What is the author's/director's attitude towards self, subject, and audience, as conveyed by the work?	**Tone** What is the author's attitude to subject and reader, as conveyed by the work?	**A. Tone** What attitude does the narrator (and/or author) adopt towards the story and the reader? **B. Point of View** Who is the narrator? How does this affect the way the story is told?
Theme or Thesis What is the central idea of the work?	**Thesis** What is the central point of the work?	**Theme** What is the central idea of the novel or short story?

POETRY	DRAMA	FILM AND TV
A. **Diction** What do usage level and word choice tell me? B. **Figurative Language** Do images, symbols, and allusions create patterns of meaning? How? C. **Prosody** How are sound, rhythm, and other techniques of line and verse construction used in the poem?	A. **Diction** What do usage level and word choice in individual characters and in the play as a whole tell me? B. **Figurative Language** Do images, symbols, and allusions create patterns of meaning? How? C. **Pacing** What is the rhythm of dialogue and action?	A. **Shooting Techniques** What do camera angles, shot length, etc., convey about setting or characters? B. **Images, Symbols, Allusions** Do these create patterns of meaning? How? C. **Editing Techniques** What movement of action does the editing create?
A. **Tone** What is the tone and how does it reflect the speaker's attitude? B. **Point of View** Who is the speaker in the poem? Is the speaker a created character or an aspect of the poet? How does this affect the way the poem is written?	**Tone** (a) Playwright: What attitude to subject and audience is evident? (b) Director: What attitude to subject and audience is evident?	**Tone** What is the director's attitude to the subject and audience, as conveyed by the film or program?
Theme What is the central idea of the poem?	**Theme** What is the central idea of the play?	**Theme or Thesis** What is the central idea of the film or program?

6

Special Categories for Textual Analysis

Questions to Ask in Analyzing Nonfiction

A. Identifying Textual Features

Subject, Subgenre, Context

1. What issue, idea, event, or person is this work about?
2. Does this work belong to a particular subgenre (kind) of nonfiction writing (e.g., autobiography, argumentative essay, historical writing, scientific article)? What are the main characteristics of this subgenre?
3. Can you identify the likely audience for this work (e.g., academic, popular, special interest)? Is information about the social, historical, and/or cultural situation in which the work was produced relevant to understanding the work?

Evidence and Detail The material used to support evaluative or analytic points, or to give substance to explanation, narration, or description.

1. What material does the author use to support evaluative or analytic points? Examples? Facts? Statistics? References to, or quotations from, authorities on the subject? Imaginary situations? Predictions? (See Chapter 10 for kinds of evaluative arguments and detail.)
2. Does the author give substance to narration by extended accounts of a small number of events or by brief accounts of many events? Is description panoramic (using selected details to sum-

marize a wide range of experience), or dramatic (using lots of details to convey a particular experience)?

Structure The selection and arrangement of points, narrative incidents, and/or descriptive detail.

1. Does the work use the structure appropriate to a particular subgenre (e.g., inductive structure in personal writing)?
2. Does the work use the structure appropriate to a particular mode of discourse? For example:
   a. Is the main purpose of the work to present an evaluation (another commonly used term is argument)? If so, what principle determines the order in which points are presented (e.g., pro–con structure)?
   b. Is the main purpose of the work to present an analysis (another commonly used term is exposition)? If so, what principle determines the order in which points are presented (e.g., order of ascending interest)?
   c. Is the main purpose of the work to present a narrative or a description? If so, what principle governs its order (e.g., past to present, near to far)?
   d. If the work mixes evaluation and/or analysis with narration and/or description, what is the organizing principle?
3. Do typographic devices help to indicate structure?

Diction The author's general level of usage and particular word choices.

1. Is the general level of usage in the work that of formal, educated speech; informal, everyday speech; the colloquial speech associated with a particular dialect or subculture; or a mixture of these levels? Are there significant shifts between levels of usage?
2. Is a specialized vocabulary (e.g., the vocabulary of the biologist or the banker) important to this work?
3. Are there significant patterns of word choices (e.g., euphemisms designed to hide unpleasant facts)?

Figurative Language and Allusions Images are figures of speech and, more generally, descriptions of sensations; symbols are objects, actions, gestures, or patterns of images used to express a more abstract idea; allusions are references to literary, historical, mythological, or religious figures, events, places, or ideas.

1. Does the author use any significant figures of speech (metaphor, simile, personification) or descriptions of sensations (sight, hearing, touch, smell, taste, body movement) in discussing issues, ideas, events, or persons (e.g., the comparison of scientific investigation to a jigsaw puzzle in Vivian Gornick's "Two Women of Science")?

2. Are there any objects, actions, gestures, or images that have or take on a symbolic meaning (e.g., shooting an elephant in George Orwell's essay of that title)?

3. Are there references to literary, etc., figures (e.g., Biblical allusions in E. M. Forster's "My Wood")? Are any references repeated? Do these references form a pattern?

Sentence Structure Sentence length and type.

1. What are the characteristic features of the author's sentences? Long or short? Simple or complex? Is there a distinctive use of parallelism or of other rhetorical devices? (See Using Sentence Structure and Length to Clarify Ideas, Handbook.)

2. Are there significant exceptions to, or changes in, the author's habitual sentence structure?

Tone The author's attitude towards his or her self, subject, and readers, as conveyed in the work: the counterpart of "tone of voice" in speech.

1. Is there a narrator who is distinctly different from the author (a persona)? If so, how would you characterize the narrator's attitude towards the subject and/or the reader? Contemptuous? Confiding? Reasonable, as Swift's narrator seems in "A Modest Proposal"?

2. How would you characterize the author's attitude towards his or her subject (and narrator)? Serious? Humorous? Detached? Impassioned?

3. How would you characterize the author's attitude towards his or her readers? Friendly? Pompous? Critical? Condescending?

4. Are there significant shifts in tone? If so, where and to what purpose?

5. How apparent, and how important to the work, is the personality of the author?

Thesis Does the author state a thesis directly? If so, what is it? (If the thesis is not stated directly, see B.)

B. Connecting Textual Features to Figure Out the Work's Thesis

1. If the work belongs to a distinct genre (kind), in what ways does it conform to and depart from the conventions of the genre?

2. How does the title relate to the work as a whole?

3. What is the relationship between structure and evidence/detail? Is one part of the evaluation or analysis supplied with more evidence or detail than another, for example?

4. How do elements of style (diction, figurative language and allusion, sentence structure) relate to structure and evidence/detail? Does the style seem appropriate to the purpose of the work?

5. What is your interpretation of the author's thesis, based on your analysis of the work and your sense of how its elements are related?

6. Is there a difference between your interpretation of the thesis and the thesis stated in the work? If so, what accounts for this difference?

Questions to Ask in Analyzing Fiction

A. Identifying Textual Features

Subject, Subgenre, Context

1. What is the novel, novella, or short story about?

2. Does this work belong to a particular subgenre (kind) of fiction or fictional tradition (e.g., romance, Gothic novel, science fiction)? What are the main characteristics of this subgenre?

3. Is knowledge of the intended audience and/or the social, historical, or cultural situation in which the work was produced relevant to understanding the work?

Setting The place, time, and social environment within which the action takes place.

1. What are the most important locations in the work? Are they interior locations (inside houses, prisons, caves) or exterior ones? How extensively are they described?

2. During what historical period is the work set? What period of time does it encompass?

3. Does the work create a particular social environment through the portrayal of manners, customs, and moral values?

Characterization Techniques used in portraying the characters.

1. Is the main character a hero(ine), a villain, or an anti-hero (a character presented as decidedly unheroic)? Are the characters round (with complex or contradictory aspects) or flat (type characters, stereotypes). Is there a broad or narrow range of characters?

2. What physical, psychological, and moral traits are associated with particular characters, and how are these traits revealed? Through dialogue? Through description of physical appearance or mental process? Through distinctive behaviour? Through the perceptions or comments of other characters? In some other way?

3. Do these traits change in the course of the novel or short story? If so, how and to what purpose?

4. What do the characters think about each other? Are there significant differences in characters' conceptions of each other?

Narrative Structure The selection and arrangement of events ("plot").

1. Does the narrative structure follow the conventions of a particular subgenre (e.g., the three tasks of many fairy tales)?

2. How does the narrative use spatial and chronological principles of structure? For example:

    a. Are events presented in chronological order? If not, in what order are they presented? Are flashbacks used?

    b. To what extent are events presented as a series of dramatic scenes? To what extent are events summarized (e.g., "Five years had passed, five hard years in which the cow had died, the barn had burned, and Jane had married Tom.")?

    c. What is the principle by which events are linked? Cause-and-effect (e.g., the consequences of wife-selling in Thomas Hardy's *The Mayor of Casterbridge*)? The development of the main character (e.g., Alice Munro's *Lives of Girls and Women*)? A physical, mental, or spiritual quest (e.g., *The Lord of the Rings*)? A seemingly random association?

    d. Is the work divided into parts? Do these parts correspond to stages in the development of the action?

    e. Does the action lead towards a climax or turning point? Is there a resolution of conflicts or a revelation? If there is no climax and resolution, how does the action develop?

    f. Why does the work end as it does?

3. Do typographic devices (e.g., chapter headings) indicate structure?

Diction The general level of usage (formal, informal, colloquial) within the narrative, as well as the speech styles and word choices of particular characters.

1. Is the general level of usage in the narrative that of formal, educated speech; informal, everyday speech; the colloquial speech associated with a particular dialect or subculture; or a mixture of these levels?

2. What is the general level of usage of specific characters? Are there characters who shift among these levels of usage? If so, in what situations? Why?

3. Do any characters use a distinctive vocabulary (e.g., the Jungian psychoanalyst in Robertson Davies' *The Manticore*)?

Figurative Language and Allusions Images are figures of speech and, more generally, descriptions of sensations; symbols are objects, actions, gestures, or patterns of images used to express a more abstract idea; allusions are references to literary, historical, mythological and religious figures, events, places or ideas.

1. Are there figures of speech (metaphors, similes, personification) employed in the narrative or by the characters that seem significant because of repetition or placement (e.g., Hagar's statement that she "turned to stone" the night her son John died in Margaret Laurence's *The Stone Angel*)?

2. Are there descriptions of sensations (e.g., heat, cold, light, dark, colours, smells, sounds) that seem significant because of repetition or placement (e.g., engulfing vegetation in Ken Kesey's *Sometimes a Great Notion*).

3. Are there any objects, actions, gestures, or images that have or take on a symbolic meaning? Are there any conventional symbols (as a bishop's mitre symbolizes religious power)? Are there any universal symbols (as still water symbolizes the unknown in Janet Frame's story "The Reservoir")? Are there any contextual symbols (as the rocking horse symbolizes relentless ambition in D. H. Lawrence's story "The Rocking-Horse Winner")?

4. Do images and symbols combine to form significant patterns of meaning in the novel or story (e.g., food and eating in Margaret Atwood's novel *The Edible Woman*)?

5. Are there allusions (e.g., references to Noah in Timothy Findley's *Not Wanted on the Voyage*)?

Sentence Structure Sentence length and type.

1. What are the characteristic features of the sentences of the narrator and/or main characters? Are the sentences long or short, simple or complex? Is there a pronounced use of parallelism or of other rhetorical devices?

2. Are there significant exceptions to or changes in characteristic sentence structure? If so, where? What is their purpose?

Tone Attitude to subject and audience.

1. How would you describe the tone of the novel, novella, or short story? Serious? Playful? Ironic? Detached?

2. Is there a difference in tone between the narrator's attitude towards the story and the narrator's attitude towards the reader (e.g., Jane Austen presents the dilemmas of her main characters seriously and sympathetically, but the narrative voice also invites readers to maintain some degree of ironic detachment)?

3. Does the tone change at any point? If so, where and to what purpose?

Point of View Vantage point from which the action is presented.

1. What is the point of view from which the story is told? First person ("I"); third-person limited (restricted to one character's thoughts and feelings) or omniscient (moving in and out of characters' minds at will); "camera eye" (objective narration)?

2. Is the narrator also a major or minor character in the action? Is his or her part in the action likely to affect his or her reliability as narrator?

3. Does the novel or short story draw your attention to the process of narration by addressing the reader directly, by discussing the difficulty of telling the story, or by other means?

B. Connecting Textual Features to Figure Out a Theme in the Work

1. If the novel or story belongs to a particular genre (kind) of fiction, in what ways does it conform to and depart from the conventions of the genre?

2. How does the title relate to the work as a whole?

3. How does the narrative structure of the novel or story help to reveal character?

4. How does setting contribute to characterization and narrative structure? Are particular events or particular characters associated with particular places (e.g., in Emily Brontë's *Wuthering Heights*, Wuthering Heights is associated with Heathcliff and the Earnshaws, while Thrushcross Grange is associated with the Lintons)?

5. How do the elements of style (diction, figurative language and allusions, and sentence structure) help to portray action, setting, and character?

6. How do action, setting, characterization, style, point of view, and tone combine to convey a theme?

7. What is this theme?

Questions to Ask in Analyzing Poetry

A. Identifying Textual Features

Subject, Subgenre, Context

1. What is this poem about?

2. Does this poem belong to a distinct subgenre (kind) of poetry or poetic tradition (e.g., lyric, elegy, ballad, dramatic monologue)? What are the main characteristics of this subgenre?

3. Is knowledge of audience and/or social, historical, or cultural situation relevant to understanding the work?

Setting The place, time, and social environment within which the development of the poem takes place.

1. What are the most important locations in the poem?

2. Is the poem set during a specific historical period? What period of time does the poem itself encompass?

3. Is a particular social environment portrayed or suggested?

Characterization The techniques used in portraying details of speaker or characters.

1. Does the poem present various characters, only a speaker, or both speaker and characters?

2. Is the speaker distinctly different from the poet (as in dramatic monologues)? Or does the speaker appear to speak for the poet? What are the important perceptions, observations, or judgments associated with the speaker?

3. What physical, psychological, and moral traits are associated with the character(s) of the poem? How are they portrayed? Do these traits change in the course of the poem?

4. Do we, as readers, see characters differently from the way they are perceived by the speaker or by other characters?

Poetic Structure The selection and arrangement of events, ideas, sensations and feelings, as well as the arrangement of lines.

1. Does the poetic structure follow the conventions of a particular subgenre (e.g., Petrarchan sonnet)?

2. How does the poem use the principles of spatial and chronogical or logical structure? For example:

   a. What is the organizing principle of the poem? A sequence of events? A train of thought? The movement of sensations or feelings? A mixture of these?

   b. Why does the poem begin and end as it does? What are the main stages in its development? Is there a turning point?

3. Do typographic devices indicate structure (e.g., by marking off stanzas)?

Diction The general level of usage, as well as particular word choices, in the poem.

1. Is the general level of usage in the poem that of formal, educated speech; informal, everyday speech; the colloquial speech associated with a particular dialect or subculture; or a mixture of these levels?

2. Can you identify any distinctive word choices in the poem (e.g., use of archaisms, deliberate alteration of expressions normal in prose)?

Figurative Language and Allusions Images are figures of speech and, more generally, descriptions of sensations; symbols are objects, actions, gestures, or patterns of images used to express a more abstract idea; allusions are references to literary, historical, mythological, or religious figures, events, places or ideas.

1. Are there any figures of speech (e.g., metaphors, similes, personification) that seem significant because of repetition or placement (e.g., Burns' "My Luv's like a red, red rose")?

2. Are there descriptions of sensations (sight, hearing, touch, smell, taste, body movement) that seem significant because of repetition or placement (e.g., references to sleep in Frost's "Stopping by Woods on a Snowy Evening")?

3. Do images in the poem group into significant patterns (e.g., controlling metaphor or metaphysical conceit, as, for example, the compasses in John Donne's "A Valediction: Forbidding Mourning")?

4. Are there any objects, actions, gestures, or images that have or take on a symbolic meaning? Are there any conventional symbols (as the moon symbolizes the feminine in Sylvia Plath's "The Moon and the Yew Tree")? Are there any universal symbols (as spring represents a time of rebirth in Shelley's "Ode to the West Wind")? Are there any contextual symbols (as a loaded gun is a symbol of life in Emily Dickinson's "My Life had stood—a Loaded Gun")?

5. Are the symbols in the poem part of a larger symbolic pattern in the poet's work as a whole (e.g., roses in Blake's poems, gyres in Yeats's poems)?

6. Are there any allusions in the poem (e.g., to the Icarus story in Auden's "Musée des Beaux Arts")?

Prosody The use of sound and rhythm in poetry.

1. What is the rhythm of individual lines in the poem? Do they have a regular metre (e.g., iambic, trochaic)? Or no regular metre (e.g., free verse, prose poems)?

2. Is the line length regular (e.g., tetrameter, pentameter) or irregular (free verse)? Does the poem combine metre and line length in a special form (e.g., blank verse—unrhymed iambic pentameter)?

3. Do lines correspond to units of meaning? How are pauses used (e.g., end-stopping, caesura)?

4. Does the poem use rhyme? If so, is it regular end rhyme or a special form of rhyme (e.g., internal rhyme, slant rhyme, eye rhyme)?

5. Does the poem use sound in other ways (e.g., alliteration, assonance, consonance, onomatopoeia)?

Tone Attitude to self, subject, and/or audience.

1. How would you describe the tone of the poem? Melancholy? Playful? Sarcastic? Conversational?

2. Does the tone change at any point in the poem? If so, where, how, and to what purpose?

3. Is the tone of the poem determined by the attitudes to subject and audience of the poet speaking, or by those of a speaker distinct from the poet? If the attitudes are those of a distinct speaker, are there indications of the poet's attitudes as well?

Point of View The vantage point from which the development of the poem is presented.

1. From which point of view is the poem presented? First person? Third-person limited? Omniscient? Camera eye?

2. Is the speaker of the poem closely involved in the events, ideas, sensations, or feelings developed in the poem? Is the speaker's account to be trusted?

B. Connecting Textual Features to Figure Out a Theme in the Work

1. If the poem belongs to a particular genre (kind), in what ways does it conform to and depart from the conventions of the genre?

2. How does the title relate to the work as a whole?

3. How is the structure of the poem linked to characterization and setting?

4. How do elements of style (diction, figurative language and allusions, and prosody) contribute to structure, characterization, and setting?

5. How do poetic structure, setting, characterization, diction, images and symbols, prosody, and tone combine to convey a theme of the poem?

6. What is this theme?

Questions to Ask in Analyzing Drama

A. Identifying Textual Features

Subject, Subgenre, Context

1. What is this play about?

2. Does this play belong to a particular subgenre (kind) of drama (e.g., comedy, tragedy)? What are the main characteristics of this subgenre?

3. Is knowledge of audience and/or social, historical, or cultural situation relevant to the understanding of the play?

Setting The place, time, and social environment within which the action takes place.

1. In what particular locations(s) is the play set (e.g., park, city apartment, classroom)? Is a larger geographical location indicated (e.g., a particular city, region, country)?

2. Is the play set during a specific historical period? What period of time does the play itself encompass?

3. Is a particular social environment conveyed through the portrayal of manners, customs, and moral values?

4. How is the setting created? Through characters' comments (e.g., "Here we are in Rome")? Through stage directions? Through costumes, lighting, make-up, music, props?

5. Does the kind of stage on which the play is represented (Renaissance, proscenium arch, thrust, theatre-in-the-round) contribute to the setting?

Characterization Techniques for portraying characters.

1. Which are the major and which are the minor characters? Is there a distinct protagonist (hero or heroine) and antagonist (villain)? Are there one or more characters who serve as foils for another character by exaggerating his/her qualities? Are there any type characters (confidante, revenger)? Are there any stock (stereotyped) characters (nosy neighbour, faithful servant, tyrannical boss)?

2. What physical, psychological, and moral traits are associated with particular characters, and how are these traits revealed? Through what the character says, or what is said about the character, in dialogue, monologue, soliloquy, or asides? Through the character's (or actor's) actions or gestures? Through physical appearance (including costuming and make-up)?

3. Do these traits change in the course of the play? If so, where, how, and to what purpose?

4. What do the characters think about each other? Are there significant differences in characters' conceptions of each other? Are there significant differences between the characters' conceptions and the audience's (e.g., to Othello, Iago is "honest Iago"; to the audience, Iago is a villain)?

Dramatic Structure The selection and arrangement of events ("action").

1. Does the dramatic structure follow the conventions of a particular subgenre (e.g., revenge tragedy, romantic comedy)?

2. How does the play use the principles of spatial and chronological structure? For example:

   a. Does the action begin with the gradual unfolding of the plot (as *King Lear* begins with Lear's testing of his daughters), or does it begin after the occurrence of some significant event revealed early in the play (as *Hamlet* begins after the murder of Hamlet's father)?

   b. Does the action lead towards a climax (rising action) and a resolution of conflicts (falling action)? If not, how does the action develop?

   c. Why does the play end as it does?

3. Do typographic devices indicate structure? For example, if the play is divided into acts (and scenes), what is the principle that governs these divisions?

Diction The general level of usage (formal, informal, colloquial) within the play as a whole, as well as the speech styles and word choices of particular characters.

1. Is the general level of usage of a particular character that of formal, educated speech; informal, everyday speech; the colloquial speech of a particular dialect or subculture; or a mixture of these levels? What is the general level of the play as a whole?

2. Are there characters who shift among these levels of usage? If so, in what situations? Why?

3. Do any characters use a distinctive vocabulary (e.g., the vocabulary of salesmanship in *Death of a Salesman*)?

Figurative Language and Allusions Images are figures of speech and, more generally, descriptions of sensations; symbols are objects, actions, gestures, or patterns of images used to express a more abstract idea; allusions are references to literary, historical, mythological, or religious figures, events, places, or ideas.

1. Are there any figures of speech (metaphors, similes, personification) that seem significant because of repetition or placement (e.g., metaphors of disease in *Hamlet*)?

2. Are there descriptions of sensations (sight, hearing, touch, smell, taste, body movement) that seem significant because of repetition or placement (e.g., images of sight and blindness in *King Lear*)?

3. Are there any objects, actions, gestures, or images that have or take on a symbolic meaning? Are there any conventional symbols (as a flag symbolizes patriotism, or a certain posture symbolizes despair)? Are there any universal symbols (light, dark, water, fire, etc.)? Are there any contextual symbols (as the action of washing clothes becomes symbolic in Marsha Norman's *Third and Oak: The Laundromat*)?

4. Do images and symbols combine to form significant patterns of meaning in the play?

5. Do costumes, lighting, make-up, sets, music, or props have any symbolic value?

6. Are there allusions in the play (as in the title of Edward Albee's *Who's Afraid of Virginia Woolf?*)? Is there a pattern to these allusions?

Pacing The rhythm of dialogue and action.

1. Does the rhythm of language in the play have a specific form (e.g., blank verse), or can it be described more impressionistically (e.g., deliberate, philosophical, light, staccato, fast-paced)?

2. Are there distinctive features of sentence structure in characters' speech? Does a particular character speak in monosyllables or in long, complex sentences? Is there a pronounced use of parallelism or other rhetorical devices?

3. What is the pace of the action? Is it fast-paced or slow-paced? Does it proceed with deliberation or with unexpected turns and twists?

Tone Attitude to subject and/or audience.

1. How would you describe the tone of the play as a whole? Of particular acts? Of particular scenes? Serious? Romantic? Nostalgic? Ironic?

2. Are there significant shifts in tone? If so, where and why?

3. For performances: How do elements under the director's control (acting, sets, make-up, sound, music, lighting) contribute to the tone?

B. Connecting Textual Features to Figure Out a Theme in the Work

1. If the play belongs to a distinct subgenre (kind), in what ways does it conform to and depart from the conventions of this subgenre?
2. How does the title relate to the work as a whole?
3. How does the dramatic action reveal character?
4. How does setting affect plot and characterization?
5. Are particular images or symbols associated with particular events, places, characters? If so, what is the purpose of this association?
6. How do diction and pacing help to create tone?
7. How do setting, characterization, structure, style, and tone help to convey theme?
8. What is this theme?

Questions to Ask in Analyzing Films and TV*

A. Identifying Textual Features

Subject, Subgenre, Context

1. What is this film or program about?
2. Does it belong to a particular subgenre (kind) of film (e.g., *film noir*) or television production (e.g., soap opera)? What are the main characteristics of this subgenre?
3. Is knowledge of audience and/or social, historical, or cultural situation relevant to understanding the film or program? Is a knowledge of specific conditions of production relevant?

Setting The place, time, and social environment within which the action takes place.

1. What are the important locations in this film or program? Are they interior, exterior, or both?
2. During what historical period is the film or program set?
3. What picture do you get of the society in which the action takes place? What features of the setting convey the society's manners,

---

*To analyze documentaries, newscasts, and similar programs, use Special Categories for Analyzing Nonfiction in conjunction with the questions on shooting and editing techniques given here.

customs, and moral values (e.g., expensive houses, cars, and clothes might suggest a society that values material possessions)?

4. What special techniques (lighting, music, shot length, angle, etc.) are used to portray setting? What do these techniques convey?

Characterization Techniques for portraying characters.

1. What physical, psychological, or moral traits are associated with particular characters, and how are these traits revealed? Through what the character says, or what is said about the character? Through the character's (and actor's) actions and gestures? Through physical appearance (including costuming and make-up)?

2. Do these traits change in the development of the action? If so, where, how, and to what purpose?

3. Are there significant differences in characters' conceptions of each other? Are there significant differences between the characters' conceptions and the audience's?

Structure The selection and arrangement of events ("action").

1. Does the structure follow the conventions of a particular sub-genre (e.g., the climactic shoot-out in the Western)?

2. How does the film or program use the principles of spatial or chronological structure?

3. Do events lead to a climax (turning point) and resolution of conflicts? If so, where does the climax occur and how are conflicts resolved? If not, what happens?

4. Why does the film or television program end as it does? What is conveyed by the closing scene, closing shots, closing titles?

Shooting Techniques Ways of photographing with a motion picture or television camera.

1. Is there a distinctive use of camera placement (close-up, medium shot, long shot) or camera movement (panning, tracking, craning, zoom shots) in the film or program? If so, what is its purpose (e.g., close-up = intensity; long shot = detachment)?

2. Is there a distinctive use of camera angle (e.g., high angle, low angle, oblique angle, tilt shots) in the film or program? If so, what is its purpose?

3. Is there a distinctive use of composition (e.g., symmetry, asymmetry) in the shots? If so, what is its purpose?

4. Is there a distinctive use of camera speeds (e.g., slow motion, time lapse, speed-up) or lenses (wide angle, telephoto)? If so, what is its purpose?

5. Is there a distinctive use of colour, texture (e.g., graining), or lighting (high key, low key)? If so, what is the purpose?

Images, Symbols, Allusions Images are figures of speech and, more generally, descriptions of sensations; symbols are objects, actions, gestures, or patterns of images used to express a more abstract idea; allusions are references to literary, historical, mythological, or religious figures, events, places, or ideas.

1. Are there images that seem important because of repetition or placement (e.g., the hand imagery in *The Color Purple* that conveys many of the film's main issues: silencing, isolation, connection, reconciliation)?

2. Are there objects, actions, gestures, or images in the film or program that have or take on a symbolic meaning (e.g., the feather in *The Joy Luck Club* that symbolizes the hopes and good intentions that bind generations of mothers and daughters)?

3. Do images and symbols combine to form significant patterns of meaning in the film or program (e.g., fishing as a symbol of art, self-discipline, brotherhood, and redemption in *A River Runs Through It*)?

4. Are there allusions in the film or program? Are they established verbally or visually? Do they form a pattern?

Editing Techniques Methods governing the sequence and combination of individual shots.

1. Does the film or program make any distinctive use of cuts (cross cuts, jump cuts, flash cuts) and fades (fade-out, fade-in, dissolves) within scenes? If so, to what purpose?

2. How are episodes put together to convey the passage of time (cuts, fades, dissolves)? Are there flashbacks or other special techniques used in between-scenes editing?

3. How are sound effects, including music, used?

Tone The director's attitude to subject and/or audience, as conveyed by the film or program.

1. How would you describe the tone of the film or program as a whole? Menacing? Comic? Romantic? Nostalgic? Are there shifts in tone? If so, where and why?

2. What techniques (e.g., shooting, editing, music, lighting) are used to help establish the tone of the film or program?

B. Connecting Textual Features to Figure Out a Theme or Thesis in the Work

1. If the film or program belongs to a distinct subgenre, in what ways does it conform to and depart from the conventions of the subgenre?

2. How does the title relate to the work as a whole?

3. How does the structure of the film or program contribute to characterization?

4. How does setting affect plot and characterization? For example, are particular places associated with certain characters or significant events?

5. Are particular images or symbols associated with particular events, places, characters? If so, what does this association convey?

6. How are shooting or editing techniques used to convey action, setting, character?

7. How are action, setting, and characterization linked to the tone?

8. How do the elements of the film or program combine to convey a theme or thesis?

9. What is the theme or thesis?

7

Annotated Survey of Reference Sources[*]

This brief survey provides background material for your reading and writing, especially for textual analysis. Use this survey as a starting place to explore the resources of your own library.

Finding Explanations of Literary and Rhetorical Terms and Literary Theory

Although their coverage varies, most dictionaries of literary and rhetorical terms will include, in alphabetical order, brief discussions of items such as these: (1) the major periods of literary history, such as the Renaissance, and literary movements or groups, such as Imagists; (2) literary genres, from broad forms, such as drama, to specific forms, such as the revenge tragedy, dream allegory, and comedy of intrigue; (3) terms commonly used in literary and rhetorical criticism, such as point of view, irony, metaphysical conceit; (4) historical events, philosophical terms, and similar material seen as especially relevant to the study of literature. Works that explain terms from cultural criticism and literary theory will help you understand what is meant by feminist criticism and postmodernist theory, for example.

Abrams, M. H. *A Glossary of Literary Terms*. 6th ed. Fort Worth: Harcourt, 1993.

Childers, Joseph, and Gary Hentzi. *The Columbia Dictionary of Modern Literary and Cultural Criticism*. New York: Columbia UP, 1995.

Cuddon, J. A. *Penguin Dictionary of Literary Terms and Literary Theory*. 3rd ed. London: Penguin, 1992.

*Compiled by Kevin Crandlemire; revised by Len Falkenstein

Groden, Michael, and Martin Kreisworth. *The Johns Hopkins Guide to Literary Criticism and Theory*. Baltimore: Johns Hopkins UP, 1994.

Lanham, Richard. *A Handlist of Rhetorical Terms*. 2nd ed. Berkeley: U of California P, 1991.

Raman, Selden, Peter Widdowson, and Peter Brooker. *A Reader's Guide to Contemporary Literary Theory*. 4th ed. New York: Prentice Hall, 1997.

Finding Information on Authors, Literary History, Genres

General Guides to Literature in English

Evans, Denise, and Mary L. Onorato, eds. *Nineteenth-Century Literary Criticism*. Detroit: Gale. This series of annual volumes, first published in 1981, collects excerpts from the year's work in nineteenth-century criticism.

Hawkins-Dady, Mark. *Reader's Guide to Literature in English*. Chicago: Fitzroy, 1996.

Narms, Brigham, and Deborah Stanley, eds. *Contemporary Literary Criticism*. Detroit: Gale. This series of annual volumes, begun in 1973, collects excerpts from the year's work in criticism of contemporary writing.

Ousby, Ian, ed. *The Cambridge Guide to Literature in English*. 2nd ed. New York: Cambridge UP, 1993.

Parker, Peter. *A Reader's Guide to Twentieth-Century Writers*. New York: Oxford UP, 1996.

Stringer, Jenny. *The Oxford Companion to Twentieth-Century Literature in English*. New York: Oxford UP, 1996.

Specialized Guides to Literature

Literature by Women

Blain, Virginia, Isobel Grundy, and Patricia Clements, eds. *The Feminist Companion to Women's Literature in English*. New Haven: Yale UP, 1990.

Buck, Claire, ed. *The Bloomsbury Guide to Women's Literature*. London: Bloomsbury, 1992.

Shattock, Joanne. *The Oxford Guide to British Women Writers*. New York: Oxford UP, 1993.

National Literature

Benson, Eugene, and L. W. Conolly. *Encyclopedia of Post-Colonial Literatures in English*. New York: Routledge, 1994.

Bercovitch, Sacvan. *The Cambridge History of American Literature.* Cambridge: Cambridge UP, 1994.

Drabble, Margaret, ed. *The Oxford Companion to English Literature.* Rev. ed. Oxford: Oxford UP, 1995.

Howatson, M. C., ed. *The Oxford Companion to Classical Literature.* 2nd ed. Oxford: Oxford UP, 1989.

Toye, William, ed. *The Oxford Companion to Canadian Literature.* Toronto: Oxford UP, 1983.

Welch, Robert. *The Oxford Companion to Irish Literature.* Oxford: Clarendon, 1996.

Wilde, William H., et al. *The Oxford Companion to Australian Literature.* Melbourne: Oxford UP, 1985.

Zell, Hans M. *A Reader's Guide to African Literature.* New York: Africana, 1983.

Children's Literature

Carpenter, Humphrey, and Mari Prichard. *The Oxford Companion to Children's Literature.* New York: Oxford UP, 1984.

Drama

Though coverage will vary, most theatre handbooks will offer, in alphabetical order, information on topics such as these: (1) forms of theatre, such as Noh, puppet theatre, masque, and Kathakali; (2) important figures, including playwrights, characters, actors, directors, producers, patrons, and theatre owners; (3) technical terminology like *rake, grave trap,* and *cellar*; (4) famous theatres, such as the Strand, Imperial, and Phoenix; (5) histories of the theatre in various countries and the theatres and companies of those countries; and (6) the plays themselves.

Benson, Eugene, and L. W. Conolly, eds. *The Oxford Companion to Canadian Theatre.* Toronto: Oxford UP, 1990.

Berney, K. A. *Contemporary American Dramatists.* London: St. James, 1994.

————. *Contemporary British Dramatists.* London: St. James, 1994.

————. *Contemporary Women Dramatists.* London: St. James, 1994.

Bordman, Gerald Martin, ed. *The Oxford Companion to American Theatre.* New York: Oxford UP, 1984.

Hawkins-Dady, Mark. *The International Dictionary of Theatre.* Chicago: St. James, 1992.

Vince, Ronald W., ed. *A Companion to the Medieval Theatre.* New York: Greenwood, 1989.

Film

Dictionaries of film will cover a wide range of topics, including discussions of (1) principal figures, such as actors, directors, critics, producers, and writers; (2) film genres, such as abstract film, *film noir*, and gangster film; (3) film techniques and processes like deep focus, diffusion, and VistaVision; (4) analytic terms used in film criticism (e.g., *mise-en-scène*); (5) organizations, such as DEFA, SFTA, and the British Film Institute; and other aspects of film production, manufacture, and distribution.

Bordwell, David, and Kristin Thompson. *Film Art: An Introduction*. 3rd ed. New York: McGraw, 1990.

Kuhn, Annette, and Susannah Radstone. *The Women's Companion to International Film*. Berkeley: U of California P, 1994.

Penney, Edmund F. *The Facts on File Dictionary of Film and Broadcasting*. New York: Facts on File, 1991.

Thomas, Nicholas. *International Dictionary of Films and Filmmakers*. 2nd ed. Chicago: St. James, 1990.

Poetry

Most handbooks of poetry will discuss (1) technical devices, such as rhyme and rhythm; (2) forms, such as the sonnet and haiku; (3) philosophies or schools, such as Imagist poetry and concrete poetry; and (4) the history and tradition of poetry.

Hamilton, Ian. *The Oxford Companion to Twentieth-Century Poetry in English*. New York: Oxford UP, 1994.

Packard, William. *The Poet's Dictionary: A Handbook of Prosody and Poetic Devices*. New York: Harper, 1989. Apt, clever, and effective examples of techniques, forms, and principles.

Preminger, Alex. *The Princeton Handbook of Poetic Terms*. Princeton: Princeton UP, 1986.

Short Stories

Haerens, Margaret, and Drew Kalasky, eds. *Short Story Criticism*. Detroit: Gale. A series of annual volumes, first published in 1988, containing criticism on selected short stories.

Walker, Warren S. *Twentieth Century Short Story Explication*. Hamden, CN: Shoe String, 1993.

Biographical Dictionaries and Bibliographies

Most biographical dictionaries contain not only information about authors' lives but also bibliographies of their work and bibliographies of works written about them.

Brown, Susan Widrich. *Contemporary Novelists*. 6th ed. New York: St. James, 1996.

Cambridge Dictionary of American Biography. Cambridge: Cambridge UP, 1995.

Dictionary of Literary Biography. Detroit: Gale. A multivolume series covering various literary periods.

Kirkpatrick, D. L., ed. *Contemporary Poets*. 4th ed. New York: St. Martin's, 1985.

Magnusson, Magnus, ed. *The Cambridge Biographical Dictionary*. Cambridge: Cambridge UP, 1990. Over 19,000 entries ranging from the classical to the current, from Socrates to Madonna. This is not a literary reference work; its range fills in the gaps left by works more closely focused on literature.

Rooney, Terry M., and Jennifer Gariepy, eds. *Contemporary Authors*. Detroit: Gale. This series of annual volumes, first published in 1967, collects short pieces of literary biography on selected writers.

Sutherland, John. *The Stanford Companion to Victorian Fiction*. Stanford: Stanford UP, 1989.

Todd, Janet, ed. *A Dictionary of British and American Writers: 1660–1800*. London: Methuen, 1987.

Vinson, James, ed. *St. James Reference Guide to English Literature*. 8 vols. Chicago: St. James, 1985.

Identifying Allusions: Mythical, Religious, Symbolic, and Other References

Allusions are references to well-known figures, places, events or sayings, often from mythology, religion, or literature. Often allusions work by describing a figure, event, or place in terms of a counterpart from the past. The decline of common knowledge of the Bible, of classical mythology, and of some standard texts like Shakespeare's means that the modern reader is likely to miss many allusions. These dictionaries and guides are thus an invaluable resource.

Allusions—General

Lass, Abraham. *Dictionary of Allusions*. London: Sphere, 1989. Short but invaluable guide that includes not only figures and events from mythology, literature, and the Bible but also well-known sayings, like "Inherit the wind."

Mythology, Religion, and Folklore

Dictionaries and encyclopaedias of mythology, religion, and folklore will normally contain, in alphabetical order, discussions of (1) principal figures, both historical and mythical, including their origins, attributes, feats, symbologies, and relationships to the cultures with which they are associated; (2) important events, such as the biblical flood; (3) significant artifacts, such as the Golden Fleece of Greek mythology or the Ark of the Covenant of the Old Testament; (4) cities, temples, rivers, mountains, and other important places; (5) significant philosophical principles, religious doctrines, superstitions, songs, and other aspects of a particular mythology or religion. Most works are copiously illustrated and many include maps and genealogies.

Achtemeier, Paul J., ed. *Harper's Bible Dictionary*. San Francisco: Harper, 1985.

Brunvald, Jan Harold. *American Folklore: An Encyclopedia*. New York: Garland, 1996.

Bulfinch, Thomas. *Complete Mythology*. London: Spring, 1989.

Gray, Louis Herbert, ed. *Mythology of All Races*. 13 vols. 1916. New York: Cooper, 1964.

Hammond, N. G. L., and H. H. Scullard. *The Oxford Classical Dictionary*. 3rd ed. London: Oxford UP, 1996.

Hinnells, John R., ed. *A New Dictionary of Religions*. Oxford: Penguin, 1995. Includes entries on African, Amerindian, Arctic, and other religions as well as the major world religions.

Jeffrey, David L., ed. *A Dictionary of Biblical Tradition in English Literature*. Grand Rapids, MI: Eerdmans, 1992.

Jones, Alison. *Larousse Dictionary of World Folklore*. Edinburgh: Larousse, 1995.

Larrington, Carolyne. *The Feminist Companion to Mythology*. London: Pandora, 1992.

MacGregor, Geddes. *Dictionary of Religion and Philosophy*. New York: Paragon, 1989. Focuses principally on the Judaeo-Christian tradition and Western philosophical thought, but includes material on the major Eastern religions and philosophies.

Malher, George A., and Larry A. Nichols. *Dictionary of Cults, Sects, Religions and the Occult*. Grand Rapids: Zonderfan, 1996.

Metford, J. C. J. *Dictionary of Christian Lore and Legend*. London: Thames, 1986. A brief guide to Christian tradition in art, music, and literature.

Opie, Iona, and Moira Tatem, eds. *A Dictionary of Superstitions*. New York: Oxford UP, 1989.

Dictionaries of Symbols

Many things have traditional as well as personal symbolic significance: objects, whether natural or manufactured; properties, such as colour and taste; processes, such as journey and growth; and abstracts, such as dreams and emotions. A dictionary of symbols explains both the more common symbolic meaning of a word and the less obvious meaning that an individual writer or culture may attach to it.

Chevalier, Jean. *A Dictionary of Symbols*. Oxford: Blackwell, 1994.

Cirlot, Juan Eduardo. *A Dictionary of Symbols*, trans. Jack Sage. 2nd ed. New York: Barnes, 1993.

Seigneuret, Jean-Charles, ed. *Dictionary of Literary Themes and Motifs*. 2 vols. New York: Greenwood, 1988.

Dictionaries of Quotations

Dictionaries of quotations are designed to help you discover the source of a familiar quotation and its significance in its original context.

Andrews, Robert. *Columbia Dictionary of Quotations*. New York: Columbia UP, 1993.

Bartlett, John G. *Familiar Quotations*. 15th ed. Boston: Little, 1980.

Colombo, John Robert. *The Dictionary of Canadian Quotations*. Toronto: Stoddart, 1991.

Maggio, Rosalie. *The Beacon Book of Quotations by Women*. Boston: Beacon, 1992.

The Oxford Dictionary of Quotations. 4th ed. Oxford: Oxford UP, 1992.

Simpson, John. *The Concise Oxford Dictionary of Proverbs*. New York: Oxford UP, 1992.

Dictionaries of Names

Dictionaries of names are generally arranged alphabetically and include the symbolic meanings of names, their origins, and their historical and/or literary significance.

Davis, J. Madison, and A. Daniel Frankforter. *The Shakespeare Name Dictionary*. New York: Garland, 1995.

Goring, Rosemary. *The Larousse Dictionary of Literary Characters*. Edinburgh: Larousse, 1993.

Hanks, Patricia, and Flavia Hodges. *A Dictionary of First Names*. Oxford: Oxford UP, 1990. Includes East Indian and Arabic names.

———. *A Dictionary of Surnames*. Oxford: Oxford UP, 1988. Contains principally surnames of the British Isles and Europe.

Rintoul, M. C. *A Dictionary of Real People and Places in Fiction*. London: Routledge, 1993.

Room, Adrian. *Brewer's Dictionary of Names*. New York: Cassell, 1992.

Checking Word Meanings and Usage

Dictionaries of Specialized Terms

The specialized diction of art, music, theatre, medicine, law, and other fields is necessary for essays on these topics; this diction is also, of course, found throughout literature.

The Book of Jargon. Don Ethan Miller. New York: Macmillan, 1981. Divided into sections and subsections, such as Business–Advertising. Within these subsections the book is organized alphabetically and is quite comprehensive.

Dictionary of Afro-American Slavery. Eds. Randall M. Miller and John D. Smith. Greenwood, 1988.

Dictionary of Anthropology. Ed. Charlotte Seymour-Smith. New York: Macmillan, 1987.

Dictionary of Ecology and Environmental Science. Ed. Henry W. Art. New York: Holt, 1995.

Dictionary of Economics. Frank Livesey. UK: Pitman, 1993.

Dictionary of Medieval Knighthood and Chivalry: Concepts and Terms. Bradford B. Broughton. New York: Greenwood, 1986.

A Dictionary of Military and Technological Abbreviations and Acronyms. Bernard Pretz. London: Routledge, 1983.

Dictionary of New Information Technology: A Guide for Industry, Business, Education and the Home. A. J. Meadows. London: Chapman, 1987.

Dictionary of Philosophy and Religion. William L. Reese. Atlantic Highlands, NJ: Humanities, 1996.

Dictionary of Psychology. 2nd rev. ed. J. P. Chaplin. New York: Dell, 1985.

The New Grove Dictionary of Music and Musicians. Ed. Stanley Sadie. 20 vols. London: Macmillan, 1980. The most comprehensive music reference work.

The New Harvard Dictionary of Music. Don Michael Randel. Cambridge, MA: Belknap-Harvard UP, 1986. Broad scope, including non-Western music, popular music, and musical instruments of all cultures.

The Penguin Dictionary of Science. E. B. Uvarov, et al. 7th ed. New York: Penguin, 1993.

The Random House Dictionary of Art and Artists. David Piper. New York: Random, 1988.

Dictionaries of Catch Phrases, Idioms, and Slang

Dictionaries of catch phrases, clichés, idioms, and slang contain terms that may not find entry into even the best unabridged dictionaries.

Aylo, John. *The Oxford Dictionary of Modern Slang*. New York: Oxford, 1992.

Brandreth, Gyles. *Everyman's Modern Phrase and Fable*. London: Dent, 1990. Traces origins and explains British, Australian, and American usage.

Evans, Ivor H., ed. *Brewer's Dictionary of Phrase and Fable*. 14th ed. New York: Harper, 1989.

Le Mot Juste: A Dictionary of Classical & Foreign Words & Phrases. New York: Random, 1991.

Major, Clarence. *Juba to Jive: A Dictionary of African-American Slang*. New York: Penguin, 1994.

Partridge, Eric. *A Dictionary of Catch Phrases: British and American from the Sixteenth Century to the Present Day*. London: Routledge, 1985.

————. *A Dictionary of the Underworld*. Routledge, 1986. The vocabularies of the criminal and the itinerant.

Random House Historical Dictionary of African-American Slang. New York: Penguin, 1994.

Rubinstein, Frankie. *A Dictionary of Shakespeare's Sexual Puns and Their Significance*. London: Macmillan, 1989.

Schur, Norman W. *British English, A to Zed*. New York: Facts on File, 1987. Focuses on British usages that differ from American English, and gives American equivalents of English idioms, colloquialisms, and slang.

Dictionaries: Unabridged, Historical, and Etymological

An unabridged dictionary attempts to present a complete description of modern language usage. A historical dictionary traces the changing forms and meanings of a word through time. An etymological dictionary usually traces only the origins of a word.

Allen, R. E., ed. *The Concise Oxford Dictionary*. New York: Oxford UP, 1990. An abridged version of the *Oxford English Dictionary* (below), it is nonetheless a very useful historical dictionary.

Avis, Walter S., et al. *Gage Canadian Dictionary*. Revised and expanded ed. Toronto: Gage, 1997.

Canadian Dictionary of the English Language. Toronto: Nelson, 1997.

Eagleson, Robert D. *A Shakespeare Glossary*. 3rd ed. Oxford: Oxford UP, 1986. Defines and illustrates words in Shakespeare that have changed in usage or disappeared.

Johnson, Samuel. *A Dictionary of the English Language*. 2 vols. 1755. Facsimile edition, New York: AMS, 1967. Often amusing and biased, this is a useful tool for students of eighteenth-century English literature.

Simpson, J. A., and Edmund S. C. Weiner. *Oxford English Dictionary*. 2nd ed. in 20 vols. Oxford: Oxford UP, 1989. The most complete historical and etymological dictionary with over 2,400,000 quotations.

Thesauruses

Thesauruses are usually simple compilations of synonyms of everyday words. Unfortunately for the person who relies on a thesaurus, there are no exact synonyms in the English language. Any word has nuances and shades of meaning that make it distinct from any other word, and to use a word without knowing those nuances is liable to undermine the effectiveness of your work. Have a dictionary at hand when you use a thesaurus.

Chapman, Robert L. *Roget's International Thesaurus*. 5th ed. New York: Harper, 1992.

Maggio, Rosalie. *The Nonsexist Word Finder: A Dictionary of Gender-Free Usage*. Boston: Beacon, 1989. Discusses and offers alternatives not only for words and phrases that are clearly sexist, but for words that may seem to have sexist connotations. Useful guide to appropriate and inappropriate usage.

8

Glossary of
Rhetorical Terms

Analyze To divide something into parts in order to understand both the parts and the whole. This can be done by systems analysis (where the object is divided into its interconnected parts), process analysis (where the object is divided into stages of development), and causal analysis (where the object is divided into the reasons that brought it into being, or into its consequences). The main purpose of analysis is to explain something, such as a concept, a text, an event, or a set of data, by examining its parts in detail. *See also* Content analysis; Textual analysis; Textual analysis, general categories for; Textual analysis, special categories for.

Causal analysis *See* Analyze

Compare To show the similarities and differences between two things, or among more than two things, in order to reveal the qualities of each more clearly.

Comparison, basis of The common element in terms of which

two or more things are compared. Topics that can be put in the form "Compare X and Y in terms of Z" specify the basis of comparison, Z. The basis of comparison tells you which features of the things you are comparing are relevant and thus gives you a focus for gathering information and writing your essay.

Comparison, methods of organizing The block method consists of organizing your middle paragraphs* so that you finish everything you have to say about one of the things you are comparing before taking up another. The point-by-point method consists of organizing your middle paragraphs so that in each paragraph or series of paragraphs you discuss only one aspect of each of the things you are comparing.

Conclusion The concluding paragraph in your essay provides the chance for both you and your reader to step back from the

---

*Asterisks indicate terms defined elsewhere in the glossary.

essay and survey the development of your thesis.* The conclusion should restate the thesis, tie together the points developed in the middle paragraphs,* and mention the wider implications of the discussion, if any.

Content analysis The analysis of behaviour, data, written works, and other sources of information without regard to the form in which the information is communicated.

Context The social, historical, and/or cultural situation in which a text is written or produced.

Deductive and inductive structure These terms provide the most common way of making a distinction between essays that begin with the thesis (deductive structure) and essays that lead up to a thesis at or towards the end of the essay (inductive structure).

Development, methods of The uses of evidence and detail to give substance to a point.

Diction A writer's level of word usage (formal, informal, colloquial) and particular word choices. An aspect of style* that also contributes to tone.*

Discuss An ambiguous term frequently used in essay topics. It does not mean "summarize the relevant information." Check the essay topic carefully to determine whether you are expected to analyze,* compare,* or evaluate* a body of information. "Discuss the significance of X in Y" means to analyze the relationship between X and Y; "discuss X

and Y" means to compare X and Y; "discuss the validity of X" means to evaluate X.

Evaluate To determine the strengths or weaknesses of something—a plan, a performance, a work of art, or a theory, for example. Content evaluation usually asks you to evaluate an idea, position, argument, or viewpoint. Textual evaluation usually asks you to determine how effective the presentation of a theme* or thesis* is.

Evaluation, standard of A set of criteria based on accumulated judgments of things of the same kind that you can use as a standard against which to measure the material you are evaluating. The most common standards of evaluation are aesthetic (how effective is the relationship between form and content in the work?), logical (how convincing is the reasoning?), practical (will it work and is it useful?), and ethical (is it morally right or wrong?).

Evidence The factual information, examples, and references to and quotations from authorities that you use to support your thesis.

Genre and subgenre We use the term *genre* to refer to the broad kinds of text (e.g., novel, play, film). We use *subgenre* to refer to more specific types within the form (e.g., Gothic novel, Greek tragedy, *film noir*).

Inductive structure *See* Deductive structure

Introduction The introductory paragraph prepares your reader both intellectually and emotionally for the essay to follow. It establishes the context by defining necessary terms, giving historical background, and so forth, and indicates the structure of the essay by mentioning, in order, the main points you plan to cover. The introduction usually ends with your thesis.*

Middle paragraphs Paragraphs between the introduction and conclusion that explain and illustrate subpoints of the thesis.* The purpose of each paragraph is defined by a topic sentence* that links the paragraph to the thesis. Middle paragraphs usually contain both explanations of the point made in the topic sentence and specific details illustrating that point. Transitional words and phrases show how points, explanations, and details are related.

Middle paragraphs, order of There are four common ways of organizing a sequence of middle paragraphs.

1. Chronological order: The arrangement of material according to units of time. The simplest chronological order starts with events furthest away in time and ends with events closest in time.

2. Spatial order: The arrangement of material according to locations in space. Spatial order may move from near to far, top to bottom, right to left, etc.

3. Logical order: The arrangement of material according to a chain of reasoning. The order in which material is presented is determined by the need to establish one point so that it will serve as the basis for the next.

4. Order of ascending interest: The arrangement of material to lead up to the most important or most interesting point. An order of ascending interest may also accommodate a chronological, spatial, or logical order. *See also* Comparison, Methods of organizing.

Persona The mask or second self created by the author, especially in poetry and in ironic essays where the stated thesis and the implied thesis are completely different. In "A Modest Proposal," for example, Swift creates a persona who argues that eating the poor is the best way to solve the problems created by the poor. Swift's real thesis is that his readers need to see the Irish poor as human beings and find a humane solution to their problems.

Primary source Any first-hand source of information, such as the literary work you are analyzing, a performance you have seen, your own observations and experience, the raw data from a scientific experiment, or the historical documents on which historians base their interpretations of events.

Process analysis *See* Analyze

Research paper An extended analysis, comparison, or evaluation essay that includes information from secondary sources* as well as from primary sources.* A research paper is not merely a summary of other writers' ideas; it is an essay in which you develop your own opinion on your subject and use your research material as part of your evidence to support that opinion.

Secondary source Material that provides information about, or criticism and analysis of, a primary source. A historian, for example, may write a book (secondary source) interpreting the meaning of historical documents (primary sources). An anthropologist may collect data (primary sources) about various cultures and write an article comparing those cultures (secondary source). A literary critic may write a review (secondary source) of a new novel (primary source). In secondary sources, material is selected and presented to support a particular point of view.

Structure The selection and ordering of parts in a written work or performance. *See also* Middle paragraphs, order of.

Style The distinctive way of writing that belongs to a particular writer. For analytic purposes, it is helpful to see style as consisting of a writer's use of diction,* image and symbol, figurative language and allusions, and sentence structure.

Subgenre *See* Genre and subgenre

Subject The text, issue, theory, proposal, and so on, that a writer writes about. If your essay topic is "Assess the role of the peasants in the French Revolution," the subject of your essay is the role of the peasants in the French Revolution.

Systems analysis *See* Analyze

Textual analysis The analysis of written works or performances (such as plays, television programs, and films) with attention both to what is being said and to how the work or performance is presented. Your purpose in analyzing a text is to determine the relation between the work's form (its manner of presentation) and its content.

Textual analysis, general categories for The parts into which you can divide the text you are analyzing if you are not familiar with the special categories appropriate to that particular kind of text (e.g., play, film, poem). The general categories of textual analysis are subject,* structure,* development,* tone,* and theme* or thesis.*

Textual analysis, special categories for The categories commonly used in literary criticism and related fields to analyze written works and performances.

Theme The main statement made about a subject in fiction, drama, poetry, film, and imaginative literature generally. A theme is usually implied, whereas a thesis* is usually stated directly.

Thesis The main statement made about a subject in nonfiction. In your essay, the thesis will consist of an opinion with one or more reasons to support it. The purpose of the essay is to develop and confirm the thesis. Like the hypothesis in a scientific experiment, the thesis is the statement or assertion you are proving.

Tone The attitude a writer takes to a subject and to a reader, the equivalent of "tone of voice" in conversation. The tone of a work can be described as serious or light, witty or ponderous, condescending or apologetic, and in many other similar ways. In your own essays, tone can be thought of as a product of diction* and pronouns of address.

Topic sentence The sentence in a middle paragraph,* usually at the beginning, that states the main idea of the paragraph and shows how the material in the paragraph supports the thesis* of the whole essay. Topic sentences are thus the bridge between the generalization you make in your thesis and the specific details you give in your middle paragraphs. An "umbrella" topic sentence covers points made in more than one paragraph.

Index

Novels
structure in, 46
Number, amount, 211
Numbers, 257
when to use numerals, 257
when to spell out, 257
exercises on, 259-260
"The Nurses" *See* Driedger, Sharon
Objective narration, 49
Omniscient narration, 48
Opinion *See also* Thesis
as part of thesis, 4, 57-58
checking against topic, 58-59
sample topic, 59-61
in comparison thesis, 101-102
in research thesis, 157-158, 160;
sample topic (*Hamlet*), 163-165
in evaluative thesis, 129-130
forming, from details in material, 58
sample topics, 59-60
missing, in thesis statements, 74
supporting, in thesis statement, 59
sample topic, 59, 61
exercises on, 10
Order
of ascending interest, 46, 66-67
defined, 510
in evaluation essays, 131,
132-133
in sample film analysis, 7-8
chronological, defined, 510
logical, defined, 510
of paragraphs, problems in, 77
in research papers, 158-159
signalling, in thesis, 75
spatial, defined, 510
in "Special English," 51, 79
exercise on, 138
Organization *See also* Structure
of evaluation essays, 131
exercises on, 71, 111 (comparison
essays, 309, 326, 330, 338, 354,
361, 407, 410, 424, 443)
methods of, in analysis essays, 66-67

methods of, in comparison essays,
102-103
block method, 102
point-by-point method, 103
sample topic (two historical
accounts), 106
of research papers, 158-159
sample topic (*Hamlet*), 165-166
of texts
Orwell, George, "Shooting an
Elephant," 367-373
exercises on, 95, 206, 373-374
Outlines
draft, in comparison essays, 102
draft, sample, 65, 69-70
formal, for research papers, 158-159
sample, 159, 165-166 (*Hamlet*)
revision, 64, 73
for evaluation essay (Amiel), 132
for research papers, 159
sample revision outline
(Raphael), 79
exercise on, 95
uses of, in drafting, 64
using computers for, 467
exercises on, 71, 338, 354
Pacing
in drama, 493
Paragraph sequence
checking, in evaluation essays,
132-133
checking sequence and transitions
in essays, 77
Parallelism, 189-190
faulty, 190
exercises on, 190-191, 196-197
in coordinate constructions, 191-192
in lists, 248
uses of, 200
Parentheses, 250-251
for bibliographical information, 250
for explanatory material, 250
punctuation with, 251
exercises on, 251, 254-255